The Bloomsbury Companion to Pragmatism

Bloomsbury Companions

The *Bloomsbury Companions* series is a major series of single volume companions to key research fields in the humanities aimed at postgraduate students, scholars, and libraries. Each companion offers a comprehensive reference resource giving an overview of key topics, research areas, new directions and a manageable guide to beginning or developing research in the field. A distinctive feature of the series is that each companion provides practical guidance on advanced study and research in the field, including research methods and subject-specific resources.

Titles currently available in the series:

Aesthetics, edited by Anna Christina Ribeiro
Analytic Philosophy, edited by Barry Dainton and Howard Robinson
Aristotle, edited by Claudia Baracchi
Continental Philosophy, edited by John Mullarkey and Beth Lord
Epistemology, edited by Andrew Cullison
Ethics, edited by Christian Miller
Existentialism, edited by Jack Reynolds, Felicity Joseph and Ashley Woodward
Hegel, edited by Allegra de Laurentiis and Jeffrey Edwards
Heidegger, edited by Francois Raffoul and Eric Sean Nelson
Hobbes, edited by S.A. Lloyd
Hume, edited by Alan Bailey and Dan O'Brien
Kant, edited by Gary Banham, Dennis Schulting and Nigel Hems
Leibniz, edited by Brendan Look
Locke, edited by S.-J. Savonious-Wroth, Paul Schuurman and Jonathan Walmsley
Metaphysics, edited by Neil A. Manson and Robert W. Barnard
Philosophy of Language, edited by Manuel García-Carpintero and Max Kölbel
Philosophy of Mind, edited by James Garvey
Philosophy of Science, edited by Steven French and Juha Saatsi
Plato, edited by Gerald A. Press
Socrates, edited by John Bussanich and Nicholas D. Smith
Spinoza, edited by Wiep van Bunge

The Bloomsbury Companion to Pragmatism

Edited by Sami Pihlström

Bloomsbury Academic
An imprint of Bloomsbury Publishing Plc

B L O O M S B U R Y
LONDON • NEW DELHI • NEW YORK • SYDNEY

Bloomsbury Academic
An imprint of Bloomsbury Publishing Plc

50 Bedford Square   1385 Broadway
London   New York
WC1B 3DP   NY 10018
UK   USA

www.bloomsbury.com

BLOOMSBURY and the Diana logo are trademarks of Bloomsbury Publishing Plc

First published in paperback 2015

First published as *The Continuum Companion to Pragmatism* 2011

© Sami Pihlström and Contributors, 2011, 2015

Sami Pihlström has asserted his right under the Copyright, Designs and Patents Act, 1988, to be identified as Editor of this work.

All rights reserved. No part of this publication may be reproduced or transmitted in any form or by any means, electronic or mechanical, including photocopying, recording, or any information storage or retrieval system, without prior permission in writing from the publishers.

No responsibility for loss caused to any individual or organization acting on or refraining from action as a result of the material in this publication can be accepted by Bloomsbury or the author.

British Library Cataloguing-in-Publication Data
A catalogue record for this book is available from the British Library.

ISBN: PB: 978-1-4742-3573-0
ePDF: 978-1-4742-3576-1
ePub: 978-1-4742-3575-4

Library of Congress Cataloging-in-Publication Data
A catalog record for this book is available from the Library of Congress.

Typeset by Deanta Global Publishing Services, Chennai, India
Printed and bound in Great Britain

To the memory of Michael Eldridge

Contents

Acknowledgments	ix
Contributors	xi
How to Use This book	xiv

Part 1   Researching Pragmatism

1	Introduction *Sami Pihlström*	3
2	Research Methods and Problems *Sami Pihlström*	37
3	A History of Pragmatism *James Campbell*	64

Part 2   Current Research and Issues

4	Epistemology, Logic, and Inquiry *John Capps*	81
5	Metaphysics *Sami Pihlström*	95
6	Science and Technology *Larry Hickman*	108
7	Aesthetics *Armen T. Marsoobian*	122
8	Ethics *Michael Eldridge*	138
9	Social Theory *Erkki Kilpinen*	154
10	Politics *Shane J. Ralston*	169
11	Education *Barbara J. Thayer-Bacon*	188
12	Economics *Paul B. Thompson*	203
13	Race *Shannon Sullivan*	215
14	Religion *Ulf Zackariasson*	228
15	New Directions *Sami Pihlström*	238

Part 3 Resources

16 Chronology *Michael Eldridge* 257

17 Glossary *Michael Eldridge and Sami Pihlström* 265

18 Research Resources *Sami Pihlström* 284

19 Pragmatism: A Select Bibliography, 1940–2010 *John R. Shook* 287

Index 337

Acknowledgments

It was Michael Eldridge (University of North Carolina, Charlotte) who initially planned this entire book project and recruited most of the authors. As it turned out that he was, because of various other commitments, unable to take full responsibility for working on the *Companion*, I "inherited" the project from him. I am deeply grateful for his excellent start with the book, for his support at various stages during the preparation of this volume, and for his work on the chronology and glossary chapters, in particular.

When taking the project over from him, I of course could not realize that it would, shockingly, turn into an "inheritance" in a quite literal sense. Mike died suddenly in September 2010, having worked on the book materials just the night before. I dedicate this book to the memory of Mike Eldridge.

John R. Shook, Bill Myers, and especially Mike's widow Sue Eldridge helped me crucially with getting access to the files that Mike had left behind. John Shook also contributed the extensive bibliography. I am deeply grateful to these wonderful people.

Let me also extend my warmest thanks to all the contributors, without whom, obviously, this book would never have come about. Furthermore, I should like to thank my editors at Bloomsbury—Sarah Campbell who originally asked me to continue Mike Eldridge's project, and Tom Crick, both of whom have been very patient with extending deadlines—as well as Kirsi Reyes, research assistant at the Helsinki Collegium for Advanced Studies, for very important editorial help in the final stages of completing the manuscript.

In addition to the philosophers whose essays have been included in this volume, there are dozens of pragmatism scholars and other philosophers who have over the years crucially helped me to appreciate the various aspects—and problems—of the pragmatist tradition and of its applications. It would be impossible to thank them all individually. I only want to mention the following: Douglas Anderson, Mats Bergman, Richard Bernstein, Margareta Bertilsson, Howard Callaway, Vincent Colapietro, David Dilworth, Judith Green, Susan Haack, Leila Haaparanta, the late Peter H. Hare, Eberhard Herrmann, David Hildebrand, Nathan Houser, Ivo A. Ibri, Hans Joas, Lauri Järvilehto, Jonathan

Knowles, Heikki Kannisto, Heikki J. Koskinen, Heikki A. Kovalainen, Alexander Kremer, David Lamberth, Joseph Margolis, Hugh McDonald, Torjus Midtgarden, Cheryl Misak, Don Morse, Ilkka Niiniluoto, Jon Olafsson, Ahti-Veikko Pietarinen, Wayne Proudfoot, Bjørn Ramberg, Henrik Rydenfelt, John Ryder, Charlene Seigfried, Robert Sinclair, Chris Skowronski, Ari Sutinen, Emil Visnovsky, Cornelis De Waal, Kathleen Wallace, and Kenneth R. Westphal. (I apologize in advance: it is most likely that I simply forgot to mention someone who absolutely ought to have been mentioned!)

For our readers I wish exciting moments of critical pragmatist inquiry and enriching pragmatist perspectives on a wide variety of academic—but not merely academic—topics.

No substantial changes have been made to this paperback edition of the *Companion*. I would like to thank Bloomsbury Academic and Colleen Coalter in particular for suggesting that a new paperback edition could be published. For the minor changes that have been made, please see the section, "How to Use This Book".

Helsinki, January 2015
Sami Pihlström

Contributors

James Campbell is a Distinguished University Professor at the University of Toledo, a former Fulbright Scholar, and a former President of the Society for the Advancement of American Philosophy. He has authored several books on the history of American philosophy.

John Capps is an Associate Dean at the Rochester Institute of Technology. He publishes articles in epistemology and philosophy of science and is the coeditor of *James and Dewey on Belief and Experience* (2004).

Michael Eldridge was, until his death in 2010, a Lecturer in philosophy at the University of North Carolina at Charlotte, Secretary of the Society for the Advancement of American Philosophy, Treasurer (and cofounder) of the International Pragmatism Society, and former Fulbright Scholar. He is the author of *Transforming Experience: John Dewey's Cultural Instrumentalism* (1998).

Larry Hickman is the Director of the Center for Dewey Studies at Southern Illinois University at Carbondale, Past President of several academic associations, and author of numerous books in pragmatism. His book, *John Dewey's Pragmatic Technology* (1990), initiated the pragmatic approach to the philosophy of technology. He is much in demand as a speaker at academic meetings both in the United States and internationally.

Erkki Kilpinen studied sociology, philosophy, and semiotics at the University of Helsinki, where he served as a Professor, and as a Senior Lecturer. He currently works as an Adjunct Professor of sociology at the same institution. He has published internationally in those fields and in the methodology of the social sciences. He is the author of *The Enormous Fly-wheel of Society. Pragmatism's Habitual Conception of Action and Social Theory* (2000).

Armen T. Marsoobian is the Chair of the Department of Philosophy at Southern Connecticut State University and the editor of *Metaphilosophy*. He has coedited several volumes, including the *Blackwell Guide to American Philosophy*. Currently he is working on a manuscript on aesthetic meaning and opera.

Sami Pihlström is Director of the Helsinki Collegium for Advanced Studies at the University of Helsinki, Finland, and Professor of Philosophy of Religion at the University of Helsinki. He is the author of several books in metaphysics, ethics, philosophy of religion, and related topics, the latest of which are *Pragmatist Metaphysics* (2009), *Transcendental Guilt* (2011), *Pragmatic Pluralism and the Problem of God* (2013), and *Taking Evil Seriously* (2014). He is a cofounder of the Nordic Pragmatist Network and the Book Review Editor of *Transactions of the Charles S. Peirce Society*.

Shane J. Ralston is Assistant Professor of Philosophy at the Hazleton campus of Penn State University. His research interests include American pragmatism (especially John Dewey), social-political philosophy (especially deliberative democracy), ethics (normative and applied), environmental philosophy (especially Aldo Leopold), philosophy of education, philosophy of law, public administration theory, and philosophy of public policy. He is currently the Book Review Editor of *Education and Culture*.

John R. Shook is Vice President and Senior Research Fellow at the Center for Inquiry Transnational and Research Associate in Philosophy at the University of Buffalo since 2006. He has authored and edited more than a dozen books, including, with Joseph Margolis, the *Blackwell Companion to Pragmatism* and he is a coeditor of three philosophy journals, including *Contemporary Pragmatism*. He is the creator of and cybrarian for The Pragmatist Cybrary (www.pragmatism.org/).

Shannon Sullivan is Head of the Philosophy Department and Professor of Philosophy, Women's Studies, and African and African American Studies at Penn State University. She is author of *Living Across and Through Skins: Transactional Bodies, Pragmatism and Feminism* (2001) and *Revealing Whiteness: The Unconscious Habits of Racial Privilege* (2006).

Barbara J. Thayer-Bacon teaches undergraduate and graduate courses on philosophy and history of education, social philosophy, and cultural diversity. An active member of numerous professional organizations, she is Past President of the Ohio Valley Philosophy of Education Society and Philosophical Studies in Education and the Research on Women and Education. She is the author of several books, the most recent of which is *Beyond Liberal Democracy in Schools: The Power of Pluralism* (2008).

Paul B. Thompson occupies the W.K. Kellogg Chair in Agricultural, Food, and Community Ethics. He is the author of *The Spirit of the Soil: Agriculture and Environmental Ethics; The Ethics of Aid and Trade; Food Biotechnology in Ethical Perspective* and coeditor of *The Agrarian Roots of Pragmatism*. He has served on many national and international committees on agricultural biotechnology and contributed to the National Research Council report The Environmental Effects of Transgenic Plants. He is a Past President of the Agriculture, Food, and Human Values Society and the Society for Philosophy and Technology, and is Secretary of the International Society for Environmental Ethics.

Ulf Zackariasson is a Senior Lecturer at the Department of Theology, University of Uppsala, Sweden, and is the author of *Forces by Which We Live: Religion and Religious Experience from the Perspective of a Pragmatic Philosophical Anthropology* (2002).

How to Use This Book

This volume is intended for both students with no substantial background knowledge about pragmatism and more advanced readers, including pragmatism specialists, who want to get an up-to-date view of the state of the art in pragmatism scholarship in various special fields of philosophy and interdisciplinary inquiry. It offers, I hope, its readers a picture of the enormous richness of pragmatist thought in contemporary philosophy and surrounding disciplines in the humanities and the social sciences.

The introduction following this brief preface begins the discussion of the pressing issue of definition—the question of what exactly pragmatism is—and seeks to draw the readers' attention to the vitality of the various pragmatic approaches being employed in a variety of disciplines. A brief historical survey of some of the main stages in the development of pragmatism will also be provided. Furthermore, I have found it important to include in my editorial materials remarks on the international scope of current activity in pragmatism scholarship. While never entirely confined to the United States, historically pragmatism has been understood to be, primarily if not exclusively, an American philosophical movement, as is indicated by the oft-used expression, "American pragmatism." It must be emphasized that pragmatism is today seriously studied and further developed all over the world. In the editorial chapters, attention is also given to current research on some of the major figures of pragmatism, though more detailed discussions can be found in the individual contributions. However, there are in this volume no separate articles on even the most central classical or recent pragmatists. The main orientation of the book is, clearly, thematic rather than person-centered.

The glossary (Chapter 17) with selected key terms and figures was jointly composed by Michael Eldridge and myself; Eldridge also prepared some other very important material for the book, including the chronology (Chapter 16). The chapter on research methods and problems (Chapter 2) deepens the discussion of the introduction by taking up some of the main research issues dealt with in contemporary pragmatism scholarship and applications of pragmatism. That chapter can be read as a series of case studies of how pragmatist approaches challenge standard assumptions in metaphysics, the philosophy of mind, the philosophy of value, and the philosophy of religion.

Between the initial editorial chapters ("Introduction," "Research Methods and Problems") and the final ones ("New Directions," "Chronology," "Glossary," "Research Resources," and "Bibliography," the last of which is compiled by John R. Shook), the reader will find the bulk of this volume: twelve newly commissioned essays (Chapters 3 to 14) by leading experts in the field, exploring current research and issues in various areas of pragmatism scholarship. No book can cover the full range of pragmatist approaches in different fields of inquiry, but these articles included in the present volume do cover many of the central areas of philosophy that pragmatists have, early and late, been preoccupied with.

I have found it a clear policy, hopefully helpful to readers, to organize the essays so that after James Campbell's historical survey, the articles on issues in what may be called "theoretical philosophy" are placed first. These articles deal with pragmatist views on logic, epistemology, inquiry, science and technology, as well as metaphysics. They are followed by articles on "practical philosophy," focusing on ethics, aesthetics, and social theory, and eventually by those on somewhat more specialized topics, such as politics, education, economics, race issues, and religion. However, these divisions are merely organizational, not substantial. Pragmatists usually reject, with good reason, such standard philosophical dichotomies—especially the one between theoretical and practical philosophy, as well as the one between "pure" and "applied" philosophical inquiries. (Pragmatist views on interdisciplinary inquiry, including philosophical interdisciplinarity, will be briefly revisited in the chapter on "new directions," Chapter 15.)

It is important to point out that no attempt has been made to harmonize the views of the 12 very different contributors, representing different areas and specializations of pragmatism scholarship. Also, my own introductory materials offer a particular—and hence inevitably somewhat biased—perspective on pragmatism, informed by my own interpretations of the classical and recent pragmatists as well as my own philosophical approach and interests. This, I believe, is unavoidable, especially in pragmatism, and I have not attempted to hide my own philosophical and interpretive preferences, such as my "Kantian" understanding of pragmatism, which is not shared by all or even most contributors to this volume. As thinkers and inquirers, we are continuously working on our problems and scholarly materials, instead of ever being able to provide a fully neutral overview. Yet, my own perspective, as presented in the sections of the book that I have contributed myself, is intended to remain as open as possible to other perspectives, including non-pragmatist ones (hence I often emphasize the links between pragmatism and other philosophical orientations, such as analytic philosophy or transcendental philosophy); in any event, it should be clear that any statement by the editor or any of the authors of this book is put forward in an open spirit of fallibilism inviting critical comments.

This paperback edition (2015) is substantially identical to the first edition (2011). Only a few minor typographical corrections have been made; in addition, the order of the chapters has been slightly amended. Hopefully, the structure of the book is now clearer. The bibliography contains references to books on pragmatism published up to 2011. Obviously, as research progresses, new works are being published continuously. In our digital world, there is hardly any point in updating comprehensive printed bibliographies, as several web resources are available (see also Chapter 18 of this book, "Research Resources"). One online resource for pragmatism research is the Pragmatism Cybrary (www.pragmatism.org). Information on new books on pragmatism can also be found by browsing the book reviews sections of major pragmatism journals, such as *Transactions of the Charles S. Peirce Society*, *Contemporary Pragmatism*, *European Journal of Pragmatism and American Philosophy*, and *Pragmatism Today*.

Part One

Researching Pragmatism

1

Introduction

Sami Pihlström

If there is a leading idea running through this introductory chapter and the other editorial materials, it is the following. Pragmatism—and its key method, the so-called pragmatic method—offers us not just a theoretical perspective on science and inquiry, but more generally ways of being in the world, of knowing the reality we inhabit, of being in touch with and categorizing what goes on around us. It is *not* a single way of knowing, or a single categorial framework, but a meta-framework for explicating and assessing the different systems we employ for categorizing reality.

This will become especially clear below when we discuss the pragmatic method in the chapter "Research Methods and Problems"; I will interpret that method as an ethically loaded, yet metaphysically relevant, method of "knowing reality" pluralistically and non-reductively, considering all the perspectives and standpoints that might be significant for the matter at issue—letting different voices be heard. First, however, we will start by asking whether there is a definition of pragmatism. This brief discussion of the very meaning of pragmatism will then be followed by historical and "geographical" discussions of the different phases and traditions of pragmatism—most of which will, obviously, be more substantially commented on in the individual chapters.[1]

What is pragmatism?

I find it important to note—and I believe the essays collected in this volume make it clear—that there is no *essence* of pragmatism, no key doctrine or thesis that all pragmatists accept.[2] Rather, there are important, even vital, *tensions* in the pragmatist tradition, different pragmatists defending very different, often conflicting views (cf. the chapter "Research Methods and Problems," for more detailed examples). Historically, it is often a crucial question whether to identify a particular thinker as a pragmatist or not: there are "core" pragmatists (e.g., Peirce, James, Dewey, Mead, Addams . . .), and there are philosophers with pragmatist tendencies and inclinations somewhat farther away from the core group (e.g., Kant, Wittgenstein, Carnap, Quine, Sellars, Brandom . . .). In many cases it is difficult to determine whether a given thinker should be classified as a pragmatist.

The fact that it is often an open issue whether a particular philosopher is a pragmatist or not is a sign of the vitality of the pragmatist tradition: pragmatism is not a closed affair but a truly living philosophical orientation, and historical interpretations of certain philosophers as pragmatists (or as non-pragmatists) contribute to the continuous shaping and restructuring of the tradition, thus keeping it alive by retelling its "narrative."[3] This is still very vague, however. No clear criteria for being a pragmatist have been given here.

One major characteristic of pragmatist thought is that pragmatists turn their attention to human practices and habits. Philosophical views and concepts are examined in such practical, experiential terms. However, this is not to say that practice is "prior to" theory; rather, no sharp dichotomy between theory and practice is presupposed in the first place. Even the most theoretical scientific or philosophical matters are examined in the light of their potential connections with human practical action.

We will see below that it is problematic, to say the least, to include some particular thinkers—say, someone like W. V. Quine—in the pragmatist tradition. (To a lesser extent, this is the case with Richard Rorty as well, who has been claimed by several historically oriented pragmatism scholars to seriously distort pragmatist classics.) The reception of Quine's and Rorty's thought has, however, to a great extent shaped the way we look at the pragmatist tradition today, because it is a tradition we inevitably view from a perspective partly defined by the neo-pragmatist ideas of Putnam and Rorty, which would probably be very different had there been no Quinean influence in their background. One may, then, as well include Quine in the pragmatist tradition, just as one should include Rorty, whom a number of influential scholars also (with good reason) see as betraying some of the central commitments of that tradition, for example, the very conception of philosophy as inquiry that Peirce, the founder of pragmatism, insisted on. In any case, neither Quine nor Rorty should be excluded from the pragmatists' camp for the wrong reasons. One wrong reason would be the assumption that there is a single true essence of pragmatism that could be appealed to in classifying individual thinkers to those "in" and those "out."

Thus, there is no sense in responding with a simple "yes" or "no" to the question of whether Quine, Rorty, or someone else "really" is a pragmatist. The pragmatist tradition, like any philosophical tradition, is dynamically evolving, living, and changing, not fixed once and for all; therefore, placing a thinker like Quine or Rorty in that tradition, or in a place within the tradition having somewhat problematic relations to other thinkers included in it, always transforms the tradition, keeping it alive by keeping alive the ongoing critical discussion of what our (pragmatic?) criteria for calling someone a pragmatist actually are. If it were totally clear who is and is not a pragmatist, pragmatism would hardly be the truly interesting philosophical framework it nowadays still—or once again—is.

Nor can we say that any of the pragmatists we will preliminarily examine in this introduction has finally settled any of the philosophical problems they have been preoccupied with. Pragmatism, indeed, lives from its genuine philosophical problems. Its depth lies precisely in its *not* having provided any final, ultimate theory about anything. Pragmatists are not unified in the sense of accepting any common doctrine, let alone unquestioned dogma taken for granted. They are, rather, unified in the extremely open-ended and vague sense of having to face certain philosophical problems in their distinctive ways. I believe we should agree with Robert Talisse and Scott Aikin when they write: "The resistance of pragmatism to precise definition is a mark of its vitality, an indication that it is a *living philosophy* rather than a historical relic. This means that questions concerning its principal contentions, major themes, and central arguments are still *open questions*, questions that pragmatists are still working through. Pragmatism, whatever it is, is still working itself out, still trying to figure out what it is." (Talisse and Aikin, 2008, p. 3, original emphases.) The present book shares their antiessentialism (though not all of their detailed views).

Both the following historical excursion to major pragmatists and their controversies and the examination of pragmatist methodology in selected areas of inquiry in the chapter on research methods and problems should be read in this spirit of open-endedness. This introduction will not tell you the final truth about the essence of pragmatism, because there is no such final truth to be told.

Some main stages in the history of pragmatism

No philosophical or scientific movement can be understood without knowing something about its development.[4] We may summarize the main stages of the development of pragmatism in the United States and elsewhere as follows: (1) the beginnings, or the prehistory of pragmatism (R. W. Emerson and the other American transcendentalists), the Metaphysical Club, and other early developments (1860–1870s); (2) the discussions, mainly by Charles S. Peirce, William James, and F. C. S. Schiller, on what pragmatism is (1880s–1910s), coinciding with the flourishing period of (Jamesian) pragmatism in the early 1900s and its critical dialogue with Hegelian idealism (represented by Josiah Royce, among others) and other influential currents of thought; (3) the social and political turn of pragmatism in John Dewey and G. H. Mead, in particular (1910s–1940s); (4) the relations between pragmatism and logical empiricism, or early analytic philosophy (Rudolf Carnap, W. V. Quine, Nelson Goodman, Morton White, Wilfrid Sellars), and the simultaneous decades of eclipse of classical pragmatism (1950s–1970s); (5) the rise of neo-pragmatism in Richard Rorty's and Hilary Putnam's works (1980s–1990s), with interesting connections to (post-)analytic philosophers like John McDowell and Robert B. Brandom; (6) the widening international scope of contemporary pragmatism scholarship (2000s).

We may, before studying these stages in turn, begin with a preliminary question regarding the *integrity* of pragmatism. Arguably, one can adopt at least four different, though perhaps overlapping, attitudes to what is labeled "the pragmatist tradition" (cf. also Pihlström, 2003, 2008a). First, some scholars have claimed that only Peirce's own method, which he later famously re-baptized as "pragmaticism," is a piece of solid philosophy and that all subsequent formulations of pragmatism were, and continue to be, distortions or misunderstandings of Peirce's original views. This, however, is a one-sided and dogmatic view. In serious pragmatism scholarship, there is no denying the fact that James and Dewey, too, produced original philosophical systems, even though they were indebted to Peirce in many ways and probably did to some extent misunderstand or misapply some of Peirce's ideas. Secondly, several philosophers have insisted on the primacy of Peirce's version of pragmatism while admitting that there are interesting non-Peircean developments to be found within the tradition. In contrast to the first group of scholars, for whom there is only one true pragmatism, these philosophers maintain that there are "two pragmatisms": Peirce's original *realist* views have gradually been transformed, via James's, Dewey's and others' works, to something totally different, namely, Rorty's *anti-realist* and *relativist* neo-pragmatism.[5] The "two pragmatisms" picture also assumes a dichotomy between Peircean pragmatism, on the one hand, and all later, inferior pragmatist systems, on the other. Thirdly, one may insist on the *continuity* of certain pragmatist themes in all the classics of the movement, especially Peirce, James, and Dewey (as well as Royce, Schiller, Mead, and Lewis), such as experience, purposiveness, human interests, continuity, creativity, growth, habits, dynamic action, non-reductive naturalism, and so on.[6] Those adopting this approach usually insist, however, that neo-pragmatists like Rorty almost entirely distort original pragmatism. This third group nevertheless finds more unity in the pragmatist tradition than the first two.

Finally, there is the fourth attitude, adopted by the present author and informing this volume—though of course not necessarily all of its individual contributions by different authors. The one maintaining this attitude is prepared to admit that even Rorty's neo-pragmatism is part of the extremely heterogeneous tradition we call pragmatism (cf. Pihlström, 1996, 1998, 2003, 2008b, 2009a). There are both unity and enormous differences among the pragmatists—within this one and the same dynamically developing tradition whose amorphousness is a sign of its philosophical strength and vitality rather than of distortion or corruption. It is compatible with this attitude, emphasizing both the unity and the differences-in-unity of the pragmatist tradition, to attack, say, Rorty's (mis) readings of the classical pragmatists. Moreover, this fourth position acknowledges that pragmatism—as well as, possibly, any other philosophical tradition—is to a great extent constituted by the open question regarding who is to be classified as a pragmatist, and on which criteria. Thus, it may be advisable to leave the exact status of pragmatism open, to look and see what kinds of different philosophies and philosophers (as well as nonphilosophers) are discussed under the rubric "pragmatism," and to try to develop philosophical reasons for considering or for refusing to consider some particular line of thought a form of pragmatism. The nature of pragmatism will therefore be continuously open to debate.

The viability of these suggestions cannot be demonstrated in this introduction, or even this entire volume. The sheer number of different perspectives offered by this Companion demonstrates, however, that the boundaries of the pragmatist tradition will be kept open in what follows.

The prehistory of pragmatism

Ralph Waldo Emerson's naturalism, perspectivism, and general antidogmatism are important precursors of pragmatism. Emerson is usually described as a "transcendentalist," and pragmatism should, therefore, be understood as continuing some of the threads of American transcendentalism. (The same idea is sometimes expressed by saying that Emerson and other transcendentalists like Henry David Thoreau were "proto-pragmatists.")[7]

It was, however, only in the Metaphysical Club of the 1870s that pragmatism, properly speaking, was initiated. Charles Peirce played a crucial role in this development, but so did William James and especially the more "positivistically" oriented participant of the Club's meetings, Chauncey Wright. All these thinkers took seriously the emerging Darwinian paradigm—to the extent that pragmatism might be described as a philosophical synthesis of Darwin and Kant. As Kant had argued a century earlier, we structure the reality that is the object of our inquiry and experience. However—and here comes the Darwinian perspective—the way this structuring takes place is constantly open to change instead of being fixed and predetermined. Our world-structuring is a habitual process instead of being mentalistically reducible to a set of fixed categories of the human mind. In this emerging synthesis—which is still emerging, two centuries after Kant's great works and a century and a half after Darwin's—the transcendentalists, especially Emerson and Thoreau, played an important role, even though pragmatism itself was developed by Peirce and James.

The Kantian background of pragmatism ought to be taken seriously, perhaps more seriously than many pragmatism scholars are willing to. After all, everything American has some connection, more or less remote, to something European. While pragmatism as a philosophical movement of course originated in the United States, it is, I believe, useful to examine some of its basic ideas in relation not only to British empiricism—another piece of pragmatism's prehistory, given that James (1907, ch. 2) mentioned the classical British empiricists as precursors of the pragmatic methods—but also to its Kantian roots. Such examination may start from the observation that pragmatism is, among other things, an attempt to understand scientific (and nonscientific) rationality as a part of our human, inevitably ethically problematic existence. It adopts an agent's perspective on our experience, thinking, and reason-use, reminding us that it is only through our practice-laden being-in-the-world (if such a phrase, made famous by Martin Heidegger, is allowed here) that we may fully appreciate our cognitive and rational capacities. Thought—or language, or the mind—is not a mirror of nature, as Rorty put it in the late 1970s, but arises out of our worldly engagements with our natural surroundings, being constantly in the service of human interests and needs.

This practical starting point not only makes pragmatism a most significant framework for contemporary discussions of rationality, knowledge, morality, and value, but also reconnects it with Kant's critical project of understanding humanity's relation to the world through the distinction (albeit not a pernicious dualism or dichotomy) between the perspectives of natural science and moral reasoning. Thus, the problem of how our scientific and ethical (or religious) perspectives on the world ought to be reconciled is, in an important way, both a Kantian problem and a pragmatist one. It was Kant who arranged our human experience of the world in terms of his three *Critiques*, attempting to answer the questions of what I can know, what I ought to do, and what I may hope—neatly summarized in his philosophical–anthropological question, "What is man?" Famously, Kant maintained that we must limit the scope of knowledge in order to make room for faith. In a manner strikingly similar to the later pragmatists, he wished to make sense of both scientific experience, which is the basis of reliable, empirically testable theories of nature, and moral experience, which leads to ethically motivated actions (or at least ought to do so). Kant showed us how to make sense of our empirical cognitions of an objective world without giving up the objectivity (or at least rationally binding intersubjectivity) of ethical value judgments. Very much like Kant, pragmatists have insisted, and must insist, on viewing human beings in a double light, both as natural elements of the natural world and as free and autonomous agents—with agency arising from that very same nature.

If any even remotely Kantian position is labeled *idealistic*, in the transcendental or critical sense familiar from Kant's First Critique, we should admit that there is a crucial idealistic element in pragmatism, too. This, however, is not to deny that there may be, and have been, *realistic* features in pragmatism as well. Insofar as pragmatists are, usually, *naturalists*, they are also realists about the laws and processes of the natural world; yet, this realism is maintained and developed within a more fundamental transcendental idealism (though most pragmatists would prefer to avoid such a Kantian expression) emphasizing the dependence of any categorization of the natural world on human constructive activities.

Even though many of the pragmatists' central problems seem to be Kantian ones, in a sense to be specified below, there is reason to suspect that this fact has too often been forgotten in contemporary readings of pragmatism and interpretations of its history. While it is correct to note that pragmatists have been critical of the reason versus nature (or, analogously, morality vs. science) distinctions that the Kantian transcendental system operates with, and while it is certainly important to bear in mind especially James's and Dewey's heavy criticisms of Kant and aprioristic philosophical methodology more generally, it is equally important to perceive that the pragmatists are asking the same kind of critical questions about the conditions for the possibility of human experience of objective reality that Kant was concerned with—both scientific and moral experience. Unlike Kant, who found those transcendental conditions in the fixed structures of the human mind, the pragmatists—in their quite different ways—have, however, located them in historically changing human practices, which nevertheless have provided us with contexts within which it (only) is possible for us to experience an objectively organized world.

The rise of pragmatism: Peirce and James on the pragmatic method

The birth of the pragmatist tradition is largely the result of the intellectual work of two persons. Charles Sanders Peirce (1839–1914) was a logician, scientist, and philosopher—one of the most original thinkers of not just American intellectual history but of the history of philosophy in general. William James (1842–1910) was a psychologist and philosopher, a distinguished Harvard professor, in contrast to Peirce, who never received any proper academic acknowledgment during his life. Peirce and James were friends, and James even helped Peirce financially, when the latter was in trouble. Both their friendship and their ways of developing pragmatism were, however, continuously in tension.

There is a sense in which James was without doubt the first "real" pragmatist: the published version of his address at the University of California, "Philosophical Conceptions and Practical Results" (1898), was the first place where the term "pragmatism" was used in print, and James was the first publicly known pragmatist. The pragmatist movement was largely developed by James. However, he referred to Peirce's earlier unpublished usage of the term and acknowledged Peirce as the one who formulated a pragmatist doctrine in the discussions of the Metaphysical Club. Thus, there is clearly also a sense in which Peirce should be regarded as the true father of pragmatism, by James's own admission.

Peirce started to call his own view "pragmaticism" after having perceived how the notion of pragmatism had been used after his original coinage of the term.[8] The key passage from his 1905 *Monist* paper, "What Pragmatism Is," is this:

> After awaiting in vain, for a good many years, some particularly opportune conjuncture of circumstances that might serve to recommend his notions of the ethics of terminology, the writer has now, at last, dragged them in over head and shoulders, on an occasion when he has no specific proposal to offer nor any feeling but satisfaction at the course usage run without any canons or resolutions of a

congress. His word "pragmatism" has gained general recognition in a generalized sense that seems to argue power of growth and vitality. The famed psychologist, James, first took it up, seeing that his "radical empiricism" substantially answered to the writer's definition of pragmatism, albeit with a certain difference in the point of view. Next, the admirably clear and brilliant thinker, Mr. Ferdinand C. S. Schiller . . . lit . . . upon the same designation "pragmatism," which in its original sense was in generic agreement with his own doctrine, for which he has since found the more appropriate specification "humanism," while he still retains "pragmatism" in a somewhat wider sense. So far all went happily. But at present, the word begins to be met with occasionally in the literary journals, where it gets abused in the merciless way that words have to expect when they fall into literary clutches. Sometimes the manners of the British have effloresced in scolding at the word as ill-chosen—ill-chosen, that is, to express some meaning that it was rather designed to exclude. So then, the writer, finding his bantling "pragmatism" so promoted, feels that it is time to kiss his child good-by and relinquish it to its higher destiny; while to serve the precise purpose of expressing the original definition, he begs to announce the birth of the word "pragmaticism," which is ugly enough to be safe from kidnappers. (CP 5.414 / EP 2:334–335)[9]

Contrary to what is often believed, Peirce did *not* exactly claim James or Schiller to have "kidnapped" his "pragmatism." Instead, the use of the notion "in the literary journals" caused his anger; he did not want to replace "pragmatism" as such with "pragmaticism," but apparently intended his new coinage to mark a specific subdivision of pragmatism.[10] This is not to say that Peirce would have agreed with James's and Schiller's ways of developing pragmatism. But it may show us that there *is* such a thing as the pragmatist tradition, originated by Peirce and James, continued by Dewey, Schiller, Mead, and their followers. There is no need to insist that pragmatism has nothing to do with Peirce's own pragmaticism. Aggressively orthodox Peirceans have not seriously thought about the remarkable integrity we do find among the pragmatists, despite their sometimes profound disagreements.

Peirce characterized truth and reality in terms of the indefinitely long run "final opinion" of the scientific community. A statement is true if it could stand against all conceivable objections and criticism; it is true if it would be believed as part of the imagined final opinion of the community of researchers diligently pursuing truth. James, on the other hand, individualized this view into a pragmatic conception of truth as the satisfactoriness of a belief. Whereas the scientific community need not even be human for Peirce—it just has to pursue truth by means the a scientific method—what ultimately matters for James is the life and experiences of individual human beings.[11]

However, things are not so simple. It has been suggested, plausibly, that the basic difference between Peirce and James in their partly conflicting characterizations of pragmatism was that the former wanted to develop a strictly logical method that would help us understand the meaning of scientific concepts in terms of their practical experiential "results,"[12] whereas the latter was interested in a wider application of this method in human concerns (see Hookway, 1997, 2000). This difference in the two philosophers' "philosophical temperaments"—to use James's term (see James, 1907, ch. 1)—and in their overall philosophical projects is reflected in a number of more detailed differences regarding realism, truth, and other matters. The differences between these founding fathers of pragmatism should not, however, conceal their deep similarities. In particular, it is a grave mistake to interpret James's pragmatism as a mere misunderstanding or misapplication of Peirce's; James was an independent and insightful thinker.

In Peirce's view, James's (1897) famous "will to believe" argument, assuming that "the end of man is action," pushes the pragmatic method "to such extremes as must tend to give us pause" (CP 5.3, 1902). James's pragmatism is "extreme," implying that "Doing is the ultimate purpose of life" (CP 8.115, c. 1900). Earlier, Peirce had remarked that faith, though "highly necessary in affairs," is "ruinous in practice" if it means that "you are not going to be alert for indications that the moment has come to change your tactics" (CP 8.251, 1897; see also CP 6.485, 1908). Later, commenting on James's *A Pluralistic Universe* (1909a), Peirce was even more critical: "I thought your *Will to Believe* was a very exaggerated utterance, such as injures a serious man very much, but to say what you now do is far more suicidal.... [P]hilosophy is either a science or is balderdash [...]." (Perry, 1935, II: p. 438; Peirce's letter to James, March 9, 1909).

Contrary to James and Schiller, Peirce insisted that pragmatism is not a *Weltanschauung*, let alone a nonscientific and speculative one, but primarily, or even merely, a philosophical method, "a method of reflexion having for its purpose to render ideas clear" (CP 5.13n1, c. 1902). In a letter to the Italian pragmatist Mario Calderoni, Peirce, having made the distinction between pragmatism (among whose representatives he mentioned Schiller, James, Dewey, and Royce) and the narrower pragmaticism, reminded his recipient that pragmaticism is "not a system of philosophy" but "only a method of thinking" (CP 8.205–206, c. 1905). Peirce reflected on the relation between his old and more recent conception of pragmatism in an important letter to James on March 13, 1897 (cf. also CP 8.255–256, 1902):

That everything is to be tested by its practical results was the great text of my early papers; so, as far as I get your general aim in so much of the book [*The Will to Believe*] as I have looked at, I am quite with you in the main. In my later papers, I have seen more thoroughly than I used to do that it is not mere action as brute exercise of strength that is the purpose of all, but say generalization, such action as tends toward regularization, and the actualization of the thought which without action remains unthought. (CP 8.250)

These sentences may be taken to contain the difference between James's and Peirce's pragmatisms in a nutshell (at least when seen from Peirce's perspective). While James should not be interpreted as having favored mere "brute exercise of strength," it is more accurate to say that he considered action or "doing" to be the main purpose of human life. This action-oriented view of philosophy is something that Peirce, more impressed by self-reflective habits and regularized action, especially in science, than by individual actions, could never accept. "[T]he end of thought," he says, "is action only in so far as the end of action is another thought" (CP 8.272, 1902).

These differences between the two great early pragmatists' views on what pragmatism is ought to be kept in mind, should someone hastily remark that according to pragmatism thought is only for the purpose of action. This may to some extent be true about James and Schiller but not at all about Peirce. The latter even condemned, in the opening of his Cambridge Conferences Lectures (1898), "with the whole strength of conviction the Hellenic tendency to mingle Philosophy and Practice," and remarked that in philosophy, "the investigator who does not stand aloof from all intent to make practical applications, will not only obstruct the advance of the pure science, but what is infinitely worse, he will endanger his own moral integrity and that of his readers" (Peirce, 1992, p. 107). He maintains that "pure science has nothing at all to do with *action*," that nothing is "vital" for science, since its accepted propositions are mere "opinions," that "pure theoretical knowledge, or science, has nothing directly to say concerning practical matters, and nothing even applicable at all to vital crises," which can only be resolved by sentiment and instinct, and, finally, that we cannot serve "the two masters, *theory* and *practice*" (ibid., pp. 112–113; cf. CP 1.642). It must be admitted, however, that a simple theory/practice distinction is too crude to have been Peirce's considered view. We should pay attention to the context in which Peirce's 1898 claims were made: Peirce protested against James's suggestion that he should give lectures about "vitally important topics" rather than technical logical or mathematical questions.[13] This context is crucial, if we wish to understand Peirce's and James's complex relation, and the complexities of the early development of pragmatism more generally.

The Deweyan reconstruction of pragmatism and other developments

John Dewey (1859–1952) is usually considered the third great classical pragmatist. His thought extends from traditional philosophical issues of knowledge and inquiry to morality, politics, and education. Among the old pragmatists, Dewey was the one most intensively focusing on social, political, and educational topics—in comparison with the scientifically minded Peirce and the more psychologically and religiously inclined James.

In his essay "The Pragmatism of Peirce," Dewey (1923) briefly compares James and Peirce, noting their standard differences, such as James's focus on individuality and Peirce's emphasis on the social. Peirce, Dewey informs us, emphasized "the method of procedure" more than James did (ibid., p. 307). In another paper discussing Peirce and James, Dewey (1922) points out that James, being a "humanist" rather than a logician, both expanded the pragmatic method by applying it to the theory of truth and restricted it by emphasizing particular instead of general consequences.

There are certain issues in which Peirce and Dewey are closer to each other than either of them is to James—in particular, the social orientation of their pragmatism and their interest in the advancement of scientific knowledge. However, regarding the crucial issue of *realism* (to which we will return elsewhere in this book), Dewey is closer to James than to Peirce. Neither James nor Dewey could accept the relatively strong realism that was perhaps the most original and controversial element of Peirce's pragmatism. Nor did they accept Peirce's purely logical and nonpsychological interpretation of pragmatism. As in James, Peirce found in Dewey the unfortunate tendency to psychologize what he had presented as logical and normative principles of scientific inference. On June 9, 1904, he wrote to Dewey: "You propose to substitute for the Normative Science which in my judgment is the greatest need of our age a 'Natural History' Kant vs. Dewey: of thought or of experience. . . . I do not think anything like a natural history can answer the terrible need that I see of checking the awful waste of thought, of time, of energy, going on, in consequence of men's not understanding the theory of inference." (CP 8.239.) Since pragmatism was, for Peirce, a maxim of logic, and since logic was a normative science, James and Dewey were from Peirce's perspective guilty of a misleading conflation of logical and (socio)psychological issues in their transformations of pragmatism. Even so, later pragmatists like Dewey and Mead can be seen as developing further not only Jamesian but also Peircean themes, particularly the reflexivity of our habits of action and of habitual rationality.

One of the major differences between Peirce's and Dewey's conceptions of inquiry, and one of the similarities between Dewey's and James's, is related to the concept of *truth*. Dewey, just like James, approved of Peirce's 1878 definition of truth as the "ultimate opinion" to be arrived at through inquiry; yet he conceived of the tasks of inquiry more pluralistically than Peirce, remaining closer to James. Still, Peirce's community-driven conception of inquiry was undeniably a crucial background of what Dewey (1929) labeled "instrumentalism"; even within a pluralistic conception of what our inquiries aim at one may retain the Peircean view that there is one definite answer to be arrived at regarding any particular question, provided that inquiry could be carried out long enough.

Dewey was also the most *naturalistically* inclined among the early pragmatists in the sense of maintaining that the natural world—with its immense riches and varieties—is all there is.[14] There is nothing outside this all-encompassing nature. But nature may be much more than is dreamt of by scientific materialists and reductionists. Dewey's naturalism was never a crude form of materialism; in particular, Dewey understood "human nature" in an inherently teleological manner. Just as in Peirce and James, human purposive action is a cornerstone of his pragmatic naturalism.

Dewey urges that classical philosophical dualisms, such as mind and body, experience and nature, knowledge and action, science and technology, facts and values, or theory and practice, should be abandoned. Our human world is a mixture of these. In particular, the "experimentalist" attitude in inquiry rejects the traditional assumption, prevalent since Plato, that theoretical knowledge and practical action are fundamentally distinct. As soon as we abandon the "quest for certainty" characterizing this tradition, we realize that knowledge *is* action and theory *is* practice. While nature, for Dewey, is everything, there is no privileged standpoint from which the fundamental metaphysical structure of nature "in itself" could be determined. Deweyan naturalism is thoroughly non-reductive. No scientific (or any other) discipline stands in an "absolute" position in describing and explaining reality. The Deweyan pragmatist, appealing to what is natural to human life, insists that such scientifically problematic things as values, freedom, purposiveness, and other culturally "emergent" features distinguishing us from mere animals belong to our "human nature." They do not lie beyond the natural world. On the contrary, our concept of nature must be modified in order to accommodate the undeniable fact that we naturally engage in normative evaluation of our actions.[15] It is through our participation in cultural practices, in value-laden forms of life, that we become fully human. This enculturation, however, is a completely natural development. Hence, Deweyan naturalism is compatible with a "culturalist" conception of humanity, maintaining that human life as we know it takes place in a "normative order" constructed and reconstructed within cultural practices.

From Dewey's perspective, the reductive or eliminative naturalists who seek to reduce, say, values to mere facts, to something nonnormative and allegedly more fundamental (or, more radically, seek to eliminate them from the scientific worldview), are not good naturalists. Pragmatic naturalism takes seriously what belongs to the (humanly) natural world. It is a central element of human nature that we are normatively concerned creatures, beings habitually engaging in a continuous evaluation of our actions and practices. Our habits and actions are guided by values, goals, and ideals. Indeed, full-blown naturalism is pragmatic naturalism. It does not deny values or normativity, because they are crucial to our self-understanding as agents. While naturalism, as a general philosophical orientation, has often been criticized because of its tendency to lose normativity, this criticism does not apply to the non-reductive naturalism of the Deweyan stripe, which is, in a way, more thoroughly naturalistic than its reductive rivals. By embedding his non-reductive naturalism in pragmatism, Dewey was able to accommodate values, as pragmatism starts from an action-centered, purposive picture of humanity, refusing to call such a picture into question on the grounds of an allegedly more fundamental scientific image of reality. Even natural science, the chief inspiration of reductive naturalism, is possible only within valuationally structured human life, as a goal-directed practice. As soon as we realize that the pragmatic, experimental way of thinking typical of science is by no means restricted to scientific inquiry, we may extend it to nonscientific inquiries, including ethical, social, and even religious "inquiries." These, too, may reveal natural features of human practices.

Although Dewey argues against Cartesian epistemology (and, generally, against the Western tradition of philosophy beginning with Plato's theory of eternal, immutable Forms as the objects of knowledge), it is not entirely implausible to suggest that his naturalistic pragmatism is in its own peculiar way Kantian: he inquires, from within our natural practices, into what constitutes those practices, regarding reflexive normative evaluation as a (naturalized) condition for the possibility of certain humanly important phenomena, including science. Similarly, the construction of the empirical world in and through our (scientific and other) practices of categorization is a Kantian theme in Peirce's and James's pragmatisms (cf. Pihlström, 2003, 2008a, 2009a). It is against the background of non-reductive pragmatic naturalism and a deeply Kantian conception of philosophy as an investigation of constitutive conditions for the possibility of certain given actualities of human experience that Dewey's remarks on not only scientific inquiry but also aesthetic and political issues, as well as religious qualities in experience, must be understood. Dewey's naturalism is broad, inclusive, and tolerant enough to accommodate humanly natural experiences of and valuational perspectives on reality that can be characterized as moral, aesthetic, or even religious.

A number of other historically influential pragmatists can only be mentioned here, rather than substantially discussed (see the other chapters in this volume for more details). Among the initial pragmatists, Josiah Royce (1855–1916) was an important critic of James and developed a mixture of pragmatism and Hegelian idealism ("absolute pragmatism") that was closer to Peirce's views than were most other classical formulations of pragmatism. George Herbert Mead (1863–1931), who is sometimes too narrowly discussed merely as a social theorist rather than a philosopher, was perhaps the one closest to Peirce among the early figures of the tradition, especially because of his interest in semiotics, the theory of signs, which Peirce to a great extent developed. Mead's emergent naturalism, however, also brings him very close to Dewey. C. I. Lewis (1883–1964), who has been described as the last classical pragmatist (Murphey, 2005), was also closer to Peirce than to James or Dewey. Lewis's "conceptualistic pragmatism," developed in *Mind and the World-Order* (1929), might be seen as lying somewhere between Peirce's and Royce's views. His pragmatic theory of the a priori as conventional and legislative can be seen as a background of the Quinean attack on traditional dichotomies between the a priori and the a posteriori and the analytic and the synthetic (see the section "Pragmatism and logical empiricism: The Quinean turn" below).

The British philosopher F. C. S. Schiller (1864–1937), who later moved to the United States, was probably the most radically subjectivistically oriented among the classics of pragmatism, who both influenced and was influenced by James. While James (1907, 1909b) was often enthusiastic about Schiller's pragmatic "humanism," Peirce did not approve of Schiller's manner of transforming pragmatistic ideas any more than James's: "[. . .] I, by no means, follow

Mr. Schiller's brilliant and seductive humanistic logic, according to which it is proper to take account of the whole personal situation in logical inquiries." His reason for dismissing Schiller resembles his critiques of James and Dewey: "[. . .] I hold it to be [a] very evil and harmful procedure to introduce into scientific investigation an unfounded hypothesis, without any definite prospect of its hastening our discovery of the truth. Now such a hypothesis Mr. Schiller's rule seems to me, with my present lights, to be.' (CP 5.489, c. 1906; cf. also 5.494, c. 1906.) Schiller was, according to Peirce, irresponsibly unclear about what he meant by "the *real*" (CP 5.533, c. 1905; cf. also CP 8.319, undated), as well as about his definition (influenced by James) of truth as something that is "satisfactory" (CP 5.552. 1906). Schiller's humanism, in particular, remained unclear in Peirce's eyes:

> [Schiller] apparently does not wish to have phenomena torn to pieces; or at any rate not if that introduces any falsity; and he does not wish us to devote any attention to the effects of conditions that do not occur, or at any rate not to substitute the solution of such a problem for the true problems of nature. For my part, I think such talk shows great ignorance of the conditions of science. Then again, as I understand it, this Humanism is to be a philosophy not purely intellectual because every department of man's nature must be voiced in it. For my part, I beg to be excused from having any dealings with such a philosophy. I wish philosophy to be a strict science, passionless and severely fair. (CP 5.537, c. 1905)

To ignore the conditions of science was, for Peirce, to ignore the central teachings of his own version of pragmati(ci)sm. On the other hand, we may see in Schiller a clear expression of the Kantian thread in pragmatism: the world is "humanistically" constructed by us in the course of human experience and purposive action; for us, independently of practice-embedded categorization, there is no world *an sich* at all—or, more strongly, the very idea of such an absolute reality is pragmatically (humanly) meaningless gibberish.

Unfortunately, neither James nor Schiller was particularly responsive to the critique Peirce launched against them. Today, however, the essentially pluralist and antiscientistic pragmatism these "humanists" defended must be seen in the context of a pragmatist tradition increasingly, though not completely, drawn toward Peircean scientific realism and Deweyan naturalism. One milestone in the development of this tradition was the integration of pragmatism and logical empiricism in the mid-1900s, particularly in W. V. Quine's work. Quine may be seen as the culmination of the naturalistic development of pragmatism:

philosophy and natural science, instead of being clearly separable, are fundamentally continuous with each other, parts of one and the same project.

Pragmatism and logical empiricism: The Quinean turn

W. V. Quine (1908–2000) has often been claimed to have made a "pragmatic turn" in twentieth-century philosophy of science dominated in the 1950s by the legacy of logical positivism. His own position regarding pragmatism is, however, clear: he never viewed himself as a pragmatist, and it is not even clear to him what it would take to be one (Quine, 1985, p. 415). As Joseph Margolis (2004, p. 44) notes, pragmatism was a "patchwork" from the start. Quine occasionally remarked that his own thought is based on an "international" form of empiricism instead of American pragmatism, and accordingly, that he sees himself primarily as an empiricist. Quine's preference of "empiricism" over "pragmatism" becomes apparent when he recalls his participation in a meeting on pragmatism at the University of South Carolina in 1975:

> I had been identified with pragmatism, but it was not clear to me what it took to be a pragmatist. In my paper I examined the card-carrying pragmatists on each of a succession of tenets to which I subscribed as an empiricist. . . . An article by [Ernest Gellner] about me under the title "The last pragmatist" dominated a 1975 issue of the *Times Literary Supplement,* so he was on the program at South Carolina. He had misunderstood my position, and in the public discussion I undertook to clarify matters. (Quine, 1985, p. 415)

Quine's paper at the meeting was titled "The Pragmatist's Place in Empiricism," and parts of it were incorporated into his "Five Milestones of Empiricism" (Quine, 1981, pp. 67–72), in which he reviews historical points where empiricism in his view has taken a turn for the better. The final fifth milestone is the naturalist rejection of the goal of a first philosophy prior to natural science. Accordingly, it seems that if we are looking for a label of a philosophical school that could adequately be stuck on Quine, the correct one would have to read "empiricism."[16] At the same time, Quine's naturalism is an heir to Dewey's, who similarly abandoned "first philosophy."

Still, though Quine remains an empiricist, he is also widely known as one of the tradition's severe critics. In the beginning of the 1951 article, "Two Dogmas of Empiricism"—his most influential single contribution to twentieth-century philosophy—Quine (1980, p. 20) exclaims that one effect of abandoning the empiricist dogmas of analyticity and reductionism is a shift toward pragmatism.

Of course, Quine was not alone in launching this critique. Another thinker connected with the pragmatist tradition, Morton White—an unduly neglected figure in both pragmatism and analytic philosophy—equally firmly rejected the analytic/synthetic dualism already before the publication of Quine's famous article (see White, 1950, 1956, 1986, 2002).[17]

At the end of "Two Dogmas," Quine (1980, p. 46) appears to renew his endorsement by espousing "a more thorough pragmatism" than the one exhibited by his teachers Rudolf Carnap and C. I. Lewis.[18] These fragments of Quine's most influential article would indeed seem to suggest that he gives up empiricism and its dogmas, affiliating himself with pragmatism instead. Quine (1991, p. 272) does recognize the unanticipated consequences of these passages, and points out the way in which his use of "pragmatism" is limited to the context of his disagreement with Carnap, to "the contrast supposed by Carnap and C. I. Lewis between the factual and the pragmatic":

> "In repudiating such a boundary," I wrote, "I espouse a more thorough pragmatism." This passage had unforeseen consequences. I suspect it is responsible for my being widely classified as a pragmatist. I don't object, except that I am not clear on what it takes to qualify as a pragmatist. I was merely taking the word from Carnap and handing it back: in whatever sense the framework of science is pragmatic, so is the rest of science.[19]

Did the "endorsements of pragmatism" one finds in both "Two Dogmas" and "On What There Is" curiously vanish from Quine's later work, as Hookway (1988, p. 50) claims? This shift of emphasis is related to Quine's increasing tendency to describe himself as a (robust) realist. The straightforwardly realistic starting point of Quine's naturalized empiricism is clearly visible in the opening pages of *Word and Object,* where Quine (1960, p. 1) "begins with ordinary things" and "starts in the middle." In fact, Quine's whole epistemological picture is committed to and already presupposes a metaphysical scenario, where we are physical objects, not only sitting in a physical world, but more importantly, also being stimulated by and interacting with other physical objects in various ways. This is how our sensory surfaces and linguistic machineries get their cognitive input, and also how we begin to gradually climb "from stimulus to science" (cf. Quine, 1995). However, even in the early works, the use of the term "pragmatic" (and related terms) is subordinated to empiricism—and thereby to a treatment not of individual pragmatic purposes or interests but of scientific objectivity. Accordingly, the talk about "pragmatic standards" refers "to an appeal to the pursuit of efficient predictive control over experience which serves as the 'duty' of science. Here Quine's empiricism intervenes to assign a meaning to the 'pragmatic' which puts into question the claim that the presence of pragmatic considerations in scientific growth is in tension with a realist construal of science." (Hookway, 1988, p. 53) One might, thus, view Quine's "pragmatism" as a descendant of Peirce's objective, realistic pragmatism, according to which the relevant kind of pragmatic results or conceivable practical consequences that our concepts and conceptions ought to have are scientific, empirical ones—in contrast to James's and his followers' pluralistic, less science-oriented conception of the "practical consequences" of beliefs.

Morton White's position can here be usefully compared to Quine's. Both begin from the rejection of the analytic/synthetic distinction and from the holistic idea that our sentences or beliefs "face the tribunal of experience" not individually but in "corporate bodies." However, while philosophy of science is Quine's main concern (famously, for him, "philosophy enough"), White (2002, pp. x–xi, 66) argues that the kind of holistic, empirical approach Quine taught us to appreciate ought to be extended to the philosophy of culture, which examines not only science but also religion, history, art, law, and morality. Science is not the only cultural institution requiring pragmatically holistic philosophical investigation. Quine's exclusive focus on the philosophy of science is a remnant from logical positivism (ibid., p. 3). In particular, the view that ethics—more specifically, ethical statements or sentences—ought to be included in the "web" we are holistically evaluating on the basis of new experience (i.e., feelings of moral obligation in the case of ethics) has been White's key antireductionist addition to Quinean holism for decades (ibid., pp. 3, 6, 76, 124–125, ch. 10). Observation sentences and normative ethical sentences cannot be sharply separated, according to White (ibid., pp. 154–155, 160–163). *Pace* Quine, ethics can, then, also be "anchored to experience," fallibly and holistically, just as, say, Quinean naturalized epistemology is designed to be (ibid., pp. 160–162).[20]

Several (neo)pragmatists and scholars of classical pragmatism have challenged the widespread account of Quine as a pragmatist—with good reason, given Quine's own doubts about his place in the pragmatist tradition. Indeed, as Susan Haack (2004, p. 27) points out, "it is hard to take Quine's reference to pragmatism [in "Two Dogmas"] as seriously historically intended, given that he includes Carnap, surely by any standards more positivist than pragmatist." Even so, Quine's place in the pragmatist tradition is intriguing and deserves detailed commentary (cf. Koskinen and Pihlström, 2006). It is undeniable that

Quine influenced the next generation of major (neo)pragmatist philosophers, including in particular Putnam, Rorty, and Brandom. Whether that influence was positive or negative can only be determined against the background of a careful study of neo-pragmatism.

Neo-pragmatism

For Richard Rorty (1931–2007), Quine—along with James, Dewey, Heidegger, Wittgenstein, Sellars, Kuhn, and Davidson, among others—is a philosophical hero, because he launched a devastating attack on logical empiricism, particularly Carnap, and thus helped in opening the gates for something like the neo-pragmatism Rorty himself favors.[21] However, he never drew the correct conclusions from his promising pragmatism, because he remained stuck to the scientistic tradition of analytic philosophy. In short, Quine did a great service to the post-analytic philosophy of the late twentieth century by destroying the version of traditional "first philosophy" that the logical empiricists attempted to develop, viz., the conception of philosophical inquiry as a logical or conceptual analysis of determinate meanings or conceptual contents. When we have got rid of the analytic/synthetic distinction, there is no hope for such a unified philosophical methodology any longer. According to Rorty, the pragmatist is finally liberated from the dream of having a unified philosophical methodology at all.[22]

Here lies, in his view, Quine's error as well. It is, Rorty maintains, misguided to view philosophy in the kind of close relation to the natural sciences that Quine finds ideal. Quine still attempted to preserve something like scientific realism (though his realist credentials have been disputed, too), while the proper path for a pragmatist is, according to Rorty, not realism but something quite different—something more relativistic, if not straightforwardly antirealistic. Science, for Rortyan pragmatists, is only one of our indefinitely many possible human ways of "coping" with reality. There is no need, except for scientistic prejudice, to believe science to be in touch with the world as it ultimately is, or to believe science to be capable of (in Quine's terms) "limning the true and ultimate structure of reality" (Quine, 1960, p. 221). Science has no more privileged perspective on such a nature of reality than, say, poetry. No human practice or "vocabulary" enjoys such a privileged perspective. Thus, while taking up important critical points against traditional philosophical and meta-philosophical conceptions of knowledge, its alleged foundations, meaning, and the philosophical method, Quine remains, at bottom, a logical empiricist privileging the "vocabulary" of natural science, thereby downplaying the value of other vocabularies.

This is how Rorty formulated his criticism in *Philosophy and the Mirror of Nature*, the book that perhaps more than any other single work contributed to the rise of neo-pragmatism as a philosophical movement (even though Rorty was not yet particularly explicit about his commitment to the pragmatist tradition in that volume):

> Quine, after arguing that there is no line between science and philosophy, tends to assume that he has thereby shown that science can replace philosophy. But it is not clear what task he is asking science to perform. Nor is it clear why natural science, rather than the arts, or politics, or religion, should take over the area left vacant. (Rorty, 1979, p. 171)[23]

Still, Quine's and Wilfrid Sellars's (1963) attack on "privileged representations" and epistemological foundationalism did, according to Rorty, pave the way for a truly pragmatist (or, in the terms he preferred in *Mirror*, "epistemologically behaviorist") approach, according to which "nothing counts as justification unless by reference to what we already accept," and we cannot get "outside our beliefs and our language so as to find some test other than coherence" (ibid., p. 178). Therefore, these classical figures of (late) analytic philosophy play a crucial role in the Rortyan narrative of the emergence of neo-pragmatism; there would be no neo-pragmatism without their central developments of analytic philosophy.

Pragmatism scholars generally agree that Rorty's radically relativist or (to use his own terms) "ethnocentrist" and anti-representationalist version of pragmatism,[24] including his interpretation of the classical pragmatists (especially Dewey), is deeply problematic. Nevertheless, as there can be—for a pragmatist, at least—no essentialist, a priori reasons for excluding Rorty's unorthodox version of pragmatism from the pragmatist tradition, his criticisms of Quine should be taken seriously by anyone examining Quine's place in the pragmatist tradition. Given Rorty's self-consciously historicist way of writing the history of pragmatism as a philosophical movement gradually getting rid of the foundationalist and scientistic commitments of traditional epistemology, Quine's so-called pragmatism can, at best, occupy a transitional stage in this movement.[25]

There are contemporary pragmatists (most prominently, Susan Haack and Nicholas Rescher) whose views can be regarded as "Peircean" and thus strongly opposed to Rorty's version of neo-pragmatism, but despite the growing industry of Peirce scholarship, it may be argued that the most original thinkers to be classified as pragmatists today have been more clearly influenced by James and Dewey than by Peirce (e.g., Putnam, Rorty, and others); in addition, there are interesting contemporary pragmatists who are not following any of the classical pragmatists in any clear sense, such as Robert Brandom. Obviously, Putnam, like Rorty, sees James and Dewey as the two great pragmatists he wishes to follow in his own work, although he often rhetorically mentions all the three original pragmatists as precursors of his position. Rorty, in turn, clearly misuses Peircean and Jamesian ideas, for example, by straightforwardly regarding the pragmatist tradition as based on what he calls "anti-representationalism." It is of course odd, to say the least, to claim that the father of semiotics, Peirce, was the father of an anti-representationalist way of thinking. Yet, even Rorty maintains something from the Peircean account of truth: in his insistence on the "cautionary" use of "true" (see, e.g., Rorty, 1998), he notes that we use the notion of truth partly in order to remind ourselves of our fallibility as inquirers. We may always be mistaken, and since (as Putnam, Rorty and many others have persuasively argued) we cannot directly compare our beliefs and theories to an unconceptualized, practice-, perspective- and discourse-independent reality, or to the world as it is in itself, there is no higher authority than "our future selves" to determine whether we have been mistaken or not. The rejection of the cognizability of any Kantian-like *Ding an sich* thus seems to lead to historicism and relativism—or, in Rorty's words, ethnocentrism.

The difference between Peirce's and Rorty's pragmatisms is clear, however, when the Peircean inquirer points out that our fallible beliefs should address an *unlimited* community of inquirers. Rorty has no use for such a notion, as he insists on the limited and contextual nature of all human projects, including all inquiries. Here Rorty is much closer to James and Dewey than Peirce (or Quine).

Hilary Putnam (1926–), presumably, stands somewhere in between. He has for decades attacked Rorty's relativism and argued for a more strongly objective—but *not* "metaphysically realist"—picture of truth and objectivity than the one Rorty endorses (see Putnam, 1994, 1999; Pihlström, 1996, 1998, 2009a). Putnam's contributions to the pragmatist tradition and to historical pragmatism scholarship are closely related to his attempt to avoid both metaphysical realism and radical relativism. His "internal" or pragmatic realism says, like James's and Dewey's pragmatism, that there is no "ready-made world" (Putnam, 1981, 1990): whatever there is must always already have been conceptualized from human standpoints, which again are embedded in our purposive action. Truth itself is not just static correspondence between linguistic items and worldly facts but a normative, epistemic notion tied to our practices of inquiry (which extend beyond science to ethics and politics). This is not only a pragmatist but a deeply Kantian view: the world, insofar as it can be a world for us, is constituted by us, by our inquiries and practices within which we conceptualize anything that may be an object for us. One of the natural outcomes of this approach is that there is no strict dichotomy to be drawn between fact and value. Whatever may be a fact for us can be such only within a value-laden context of human purposes (Putnam, 1990, 2002, 2004; see Pihlström, 2005; and cf. my own chapter, "Metaphysics," below).

Putnam's, Haack's, and other neo-pragmatists' highly pertinent critiques of Rorty's more radical form of neo-pragmatism are among the most important recent twists in the pragmatist tradition. But to acknowledge this is to acknowledge Rorty's place in that tradition. Had Peirce's original views—or James's, for that matter—never been misapplied, had Putnam's and other neo-pragmatists' relatively healthy ideas concerning truth and reality never been carried into the Rortyan antirealist and ethnocentrist extremes, the pragmatist tradition might be much poorer than it presently is—although, of course, we cannot know for sure. Furthermore, it is not clear that Haack (for instance) has any good reply against those critiques of metaphysical realism that have been launched from a pragmatist perspective, for example, Putnam's or Margolis's, rather than Rorty's. The tradition is, thus, constituted by several open questions that may require both rigorous philosophical inquiry and, to use a more Rortyan term, "conversation."

Contemporary pragmatism scholarship

Despite its American origins, the pragmatist tradition is today flourishing in many parts of the globe. Research networks and centers of pragmatism scholarship have been established in different geographical areas. Contemporary pragmatism is not only geographically but also thematically diverse. The traditional issues of realism, truth, inquiry, and meaning (to name but a few of the most central philosophical problems pragmatists have been preoccupied with) are still extremely interesting, but increasingly pragmatists have turned to problems in ethics, aesthetics, and political and cultural philosophy. Also, "meta-philosophical" questions concerning the very nature of philosophy—questions to some extent already encountered above—are on the agenda of pragmatist thinkers and historians of pragmatism.

As this entire volume is devoted to contemporary pragmatism scholarship, it would be quite impossible to offer even a summarizing overview in this subsection. I will, rather, let the individual entries speak for themselves. However, it is important to realize that contemporary pragmatism scholarship is crucially affected by the ways the narrative of pragmatism is told, for example, whether one emphasizes Peirce as the true father of pragmatism or whether one is interested in the heterogeneity of pragmatism (as we have been above). The history of pragmatism, briefly examined in this section, is thus constantly present in contemporary work on pragmatism. What kind of pragmatist one is depends, often crucially, on how one sees the development of pragmatism.

The "Geography" of pragmatism

Pragmatism's European analogies

"Geographical" divisions of philosophy are often misleading—at least if one thinks about the dichotomy between Anglo–American "analytic" and "Continental" philosophy in the twentieth century—but in special contexts it is interesting to consider how certain philosophical traditions have spread geographically. The American tradition of pragmatism became hotly debated in Europe early in the twentieth century, with James as its leading figure and Schiller as its main European (British) representative. There was a special variant of "Italian pragmatism," for instance, with tensions between the Jamesian (and Schillerian) pragmatists like Giovanni Papini, on the one side, and those more influenced by Peirce, like Mario Calderoni, on the other. (See, e.g., Golino, 1955; Gullace, 1962; Zanoni, 1979; Colella, 2005.)

When comparing pragmatism to its European analogies, one must keep in mind not just the Kantian background emphasized earlier but also later (post-Kantian) developments that bear interesting resemblances to pragmatism, such as late-Wittgensteinian philosophy of language. Indeed, the relative neglect of the Kantian roots of pragmatism may also have led to the relative infrequency of philosophical and historical studies on the relations between pragmatism and another very important European movement within the (broadly conceived) "transcendental tradition," namely, *phenomenology*. Again, there are crucial differences between pragmatism and at least Edmund Husserl's phenomenology, especially the ideals of philosophical purity and "presuppositionlessness" inherent in the phenomenological method, which aims to start philosophizing from the very beginning, bracketing all commitments of the "natural attitude," including even the commitment to the existence of the natural world. This is far too Cartesian for the pragmatists' naturalistic taste. Nevertheless, there are also fundamental similarities, including the central role played by the concept of experience (or "primary experience," "pure experience," as in Dewey and James), the active (for pragmatists practice-embedded and habitual) role of the subject in experience, as well as the interplay of realism and idealism, just as in Kant himself. The concept of "lifeworld" familiar from Husserl's late work, *The Crisis of European Sciences and Transcendental Phenomenology* (1936), is obviously analogous to the pragmatic notion of practice. Some pragmatism scholars have noticed these similarities, and of course Peirce's own special brand of phenomenology, "phaneroscopy," has been studied by Peirce specialists. Even so, more systematic and historical work on the integrating features of pragmatism and phenomenology is needed.

The same applies to scholarly work on the relations between pragmatism and Wittgensteinian philosophy, another philosophical movement that originated in Europe in the twentieth century, which can also be seen as transcendental, or neo-Kantian, in crucial respects. In fact, I would be willing to go as far as to claim that Wittgenstein stands at the intersection of the traditions of pragmatism and Kantian transcendental philosophy, in such a way that those two traditions meet in Wittgenstein's later thought—especially *On Certainty*, the posthumously (1969) published late work, whose basic approach has been described as a form of pragmatism by some, though certainly not all, scholars—thereby significantly shaping also the post-Wittgensteinian developments in "post-analytic" neo-pragmatism, including Rorty's and Putnam's thought. Again, this is obviously one way in which European philosophical traditions have influenced the development of American pragmatism and neo-pragmatism. Unfortunately, most Wittgenstein scholars seem to be unwilling to even talk about pragmatism in connection with Wittgenstein—with some notable exceptions, including the pioneering work on the relations between Wittgenstein and James by Russell B. Goodman (2002).

I would be willing to admit that the later Wittgenstein is *both* a pragmatist—after all, his language-games are practical ways of being in the world, based upon practices or "forms of life"—*and* a Kantian transcendental thinker engaged with the question of how meaning is possible—indeed, those language-games and hence, ultimately, forms of life set limits and conditions, albeit reinterpretable and mutable ones, for what can be meaningful for us. Thus, Wittgenstein gives us a key example of the way in which pragmatism and transcendental philosophy can be fruitfully combined. Including Wittgenstein, with some reservations, in the pragmatist tradition would significantly widen, both geographically and philosophically, the scope of pragmatism scholarship and the influence of pragmatism in contemporary philosophy.

"Nordic pragmatism": An example of the international reception of pragmatism

Italian pragmatism was so strong that even James himself devoted a brief essay to it (James, 1906). Nothing like that happened in, say, the Nordic context. However, even Scandinavian philosophers were influenced by the emergence of the pragmatist movement. Thus, we can speak not only about the Italian but also about the Scandinavian reception of early pragmatism. The early flourishing of the pragmatist tradition was a truly international phenomenon, with pragmatist thinkers and groups in Europe—especially Italy and France and to some extent in Germany and Austria (with Wilhelm Jerusalem, the translator of James's *Pragmatism*, as one of the foremost pragmatists writing in German), but even the relatively remote Scandinavia, where pragmatism has obviously never been a mainstream tradition.

A couple of examples may serve us here. Perhaps the most important Swedish thinker directly influenced by pragmatism, particularly James's, was Vitalis Norström (1856–1916), whose main influence was Kantianism, though. Norström was in his time a well-known Swedish philosopher actively engaged in cultural debates.[26] In particular, Norström's 1899 essay, "Hvad är sanningen?" (What Is Truth?), comes close to Jamesian ideas on truth, rejecting the view that truth—in science or elsewhere—would just be a representation of reality. The scientific picture of the world is not a "photography of reality" ("verklighetsfotografi") (cit. Lagerlund, 2003, p. 147), but an instrument for serving our cultural interests. Henrik Lagerlund observes that Norström, by relativizing and pragmaticing the notion of truth, attempts to make room for a spiritual dimension in reality (ibid., p. 148), which is pretty much what James himself attempted as well.

The most important Finnish thinker influenced by pragmatism, especially James's, was Eino Kaila (1890–1958). After his early enthusiasm about James's pragmatism and the "will to believe" doctrine (see Kaila, 1912), Kaila's logical empiricist thought matured, but a version of pragmatism can still be found—or at least reconstructed—in his views on the "practical testability" of metaphysical, religious, and other *weltanschaulich* ideas. In his logical empiricist philosophy of science, Kaila defended a "principle of testability" according to which any meaningful statement about reality must be constructed in such a way that a set of empirical statements—its "real content"—can be derived from it. Metaphysical statements fail to meet this requirement, just as Carnap and other logical empiricists had argued. However, Kaila was a thinker tormented by diverging intellectual interests, and he also wanted to make room for metaphysical ideas. He suggested that metaphysical and religious concepts may be "practically tested," even though their real content is minimal and they are not empirically testable in the way scientific theories are. In his psychological work on personality, *Persoonallisuus* ([Personality], 1934, p. 365), Kaila describes religions as "spiritual insurance companies" defending us against the threats of life, especially our fear of death.

Kaila's conception of the pragmatic value of religious ideas and ideals may be fruitfully compared to Dewey's account of religion, as formulated in *A Common Faith* (1934). For both, it is vitally important to distinguish between religious qualities of experience (religiosity), on the one hand, and the actual historical religions, on the other. Religions, with their supernaturalist dogmas, may not serve but may actually hinder the realization of religious values in experience. For Kaila, "deep-mental" life is the most important goal of human existence, and it can to some extent be actualized in a religious context, though science and art are also among the key practices within which deep-mentality is possible. Kaila's defense of deep-mentality resembles Dewey's defense of a nondogmatic, nonsupernaturalist (fully naturalized) account of the religious dimensions of experience. Religiosity is, according to Kaila, the "deep-mental" core of religions; mental life, in turn, can be said to be deep-mental when the "depth dimension" of an emotion reaches its maximum, that is, when its object, some value, is regarded as "sacred" (Kaila, 1934, pp. 364–365; cf. p. 239).

In his later dialogical work on "deep-mental life," *Syvähenkinen elämä* (1943), Kaila again argues that even though the "real content" of religious and metaphysical views is very small, such *Weltanschauungen* may be practically significant. What he calls practical testability has nothing to do with the real content of beliefs or statements but their results in one's practical action and way of life. Religion and metaphysics are practically testable *qua* motives for action; they may be accepted insofar as their practical results are defensible (Kaila, 1986, pp. 188–189). Religions must be rejected as systems of (supernatural) beliefs, just as Dewey rejected them, but as "systems of action" they may be acceptable. This "practical truth," Kaila says, is however to be distinguished from "truth in the proper theoretical sense" (ibid., p. 189). Kaila explicitly mentions James as a background figure for these views (ibid., pp. 8, 202); also, his wartime diary entries in 1941–1943 demonstrate that he was thinking about James while working on his book. What is more, Kaila's less scientific, more "romantic" and metaphysical voice in the dialogues of the book—the voice that eventually "loses" the intellectual battle to the more scientific (logical-empiricist) "voice," though—speculates that theoretical and practical testability might ultimately collapse into one another (ibid., p. 192), which is clearly something that Jamesian pragmatists might easily subscribe to.

These examples demonstrate that pragmatism has not been an exclusively American phenomenon. To be sure, most central pragmatists and pragmatism scholars have been American, and still are, but today there is growing interest in pragmatism all over the world. Centers of pragmatism scholarship and international research networks have been established in both Southern and Northern Europe, for instance, and many other parts of the world.[27]

Methods and problems

The key *methods* of pragmatism (e.g., the pragmatic maxim) will be more substantially discussed in the chapter "Research Methods and Problems." Here, only a preliminary account can be given. Similarly, the key *problems* of contemporary pragmatism scholarship, and the areas of philosophy in which pragmatism is particularly relevant, can only be briefly commented on; a more substantial discussion will follow in "Research Methods and Problems."

The close entanglement of *historical* and *systematic* issues in pragmatism and pragmatism scholarship must be particularly emphasized. This entanglement can be highlighted by means of a concrete example. As we have seen in the brief discussions of Putnam and Rorty above, neo-pragmatism largely emerged as a response to certain contemporary problems regarding *realism* and its alternatives (in the philosophy of science and elsewhere, in a "postpositivist" situation); moreover, this rise of neo-pragmatism also stimulated new interest in classical pragmatism (and *its* historical background, including Kant's critical idealism and other precursors of pragmatism). The current research on Peirce, James, Dewey, and the other classics is thus not independent of the development of systematic philosophical discussions (such as the realism debate) during the latter half of the twentieth century.

As an example of a historically relevant set of problems regarding the interpretation of the pragmatist tradition intertwined with the realism issue, we may take a brief look at the problem of identifying a distinctive tradition of pragmatist philosophy of science, especially in relation to the debate over scientific realism, which was one of the key topics of twentieth century philosophy of science. Such a task is challenging, because pragmatism, originating with Peirce's writings on the pragmatic maxim, is a background *both* for contemporary Peircean forms of scientific realism and related dynamic theories of scientific progress *and*, via James and Dewey, for the more relativist and/or constructivist forms of neo-pragmatism (e.g., Rorty's and Putnam's) that have sometimes been seen as abandoning the very ideas of scientific rationality and objectivity. In contrast to realism, these constructivist neo-pragmatists claim that scientific objects, or even reality in general, are not "ready-made" or mind- and theory-independent but constructions based on our various scientific (and other) perspectives and social practices. The continuing debate over scientific realism and truth is, hence, crucial in this tradition—*if*, indeed, such a tradition is usefully identifiable at all. Moreover, the above-mentioned simplified picture of there being two basically different pragmatisms, realistic and relativistic, or objective and subjective, ought to be enriched by a more nuanced historical narrative, wherever possible. Acknowledging the importance of the realism debate, both within pragmatism and generally, is not to maintain that the standard attempts to settle that debate would be acceptable.

In addition to the realism versus relativism (or realism vs. constructivism) controversy, the history of pragmatism in the philosophy of science can also be approached from the perspective of another opposition, viz., the one between scientific realism and instrumentalism. While James clearly maintained an instrumentalist interpretation of scientific theories and Dewey explicitly labeled his view "instrumentalism," though in a sense broader than the one in which the term is used by philosophers of science today, it is also simplistic to identify pragmatism with instrumentalism if the latter is understood as a denial of scientific realism (i.e., as the claim that theories lack truthvalues, being mere instruments for prediction and control of observable phenomena). Karl Popper, for example, characteristically ignored pragmatism, equating it with such anti-realist instrumentalism, as well as with the somewhat vague idea that knowledge or truth per se is not valuable, but only practically "useful" knowledge is worth striving for—and many have followed him in adopting this negative attitude to pragmatism.

Given Popper's status as a towering figure among twentieth-century philosophers of science, and the simultaneous rise of scientific realism,[28] such accusations cannot have failed to affect the credentials of virtually all forms of pragmatism in this field. However, pragmatism and instrumentalism, though distinguishable, do meet in Carnap's (1950) logical empiricism, which was "pragmatist" in the sense of treating the "external questions" about the choice of a linguistic framework as only pragmatically decidable, avoiding "metaphysical" postulations of entities. This pragmatic position, as we have seen, was soon replaced by Quine's "more thorough pragmatism."

The pragmatist developments in the philosophy of science provide an example of the complexities involved in any attempt to write the history of this tradition, a case in which several issues are intertwined. These include the issues of (i) realism versus antirealism (i.e., in their various forms, instrumentalism, relativism, constructivism, idealism, and so on); (ii) logical versus socio-historical and practice-oriented approaches to science in general and to theory-choice and scientific change in particular (as manifested, for instance, in the opposition between traditional scientific realists and their opponents inspired by Thomas Kuhn's constructivism and historicism); and (iii) "hard versus" "soft" naturalism (as epitomized in the conflicting accounts of naturalism we find in Quine and more relaxed naturalists; see, e.g., Rouse, 2002). A reconsideration of pragmatism as an identifiable, albeit somewhat indeterminate and inevitably open, tradition in the philosophy of science may thus deepen our understanding of the historical transformations of these—and many other—issues. There is no reason why the historian of the philosophy of science should treat this (or any other) tradition as fixed and closed; keeping the tradition open for constant reevaluation and redescription is itself a most pragmatic attitude.

Here, it is impossible to engage in these historical issues any further. A fuller account would demonstrate that pragmatist philosophy of science cannot be reduced to any particular position defined in terms of the traditional oppositions between scientific realism and its alternatives (cf. Pihlström, 2008b). However, we again arrive at the conclusion that pragmatist philosophers of science, or pragmatists in general, cannot set the realism issue aside, either, but must live with it. Keeping that problem on one's agenda may also help keep pragmatism alive.

Notes

1   In this introduction (and in Chapter 2 below), I have to some extent drawn from the following previous writings of mine on the history of pragmatism: Pihlström, 2004 (on Peirce and James; reprinted in Pihlström, 2008a, ch. 1), 2008b (on pragmatist philosophy of science), 2009b (on "Nordic pragmatism," as an

example of the "geography" of pragmatism), and 2010 (on Dewey's naturalism); as well as Koskinen and Pihlström, 2006 (on Quine's place in the pragmatist tradition). See also Pihlström, 2009a on pragmatist metaphysics.
2   See, for example, Talisse and Aikin, 2008.
3   As Bernstein (1995) argues, the tradition of pragmatism has been constituted by conflicting narratives and metanarratives told about pragmatism, and this lack of essence makes it a living philosophical tradition.
4   See James Campbell's essay below for a more focused historical survey of the pragmatist tradition.
5   For a strictly Peircean conception of pragmatism, see Turrisi, 1997. For variations of the "two pragmatisms" image, see Apel, 1981; Mounce, 1997; Haack, 1998, 2004; Misak, 2000; Rescher 2000, 2005. Mounce explicitly speaks about a "second pragmatism" originated by James's misunderstandings of Peirce which, especially through Dewey, transformed pragmatism into an extreme form of empiricism (not far away from positivism) and finally led to Rorty's views which conflict with Peirce's in essential points. Rescher (2005), in turn, claims that pragmatism is "at the crossroads": the choice is between Peircean realism and the degradation beginning (in his view) with James.
6   In his extensive study on the relations between pragmatism and American sociology, Erkki Kilpinen—one of the contributors to this volume—persuasively argues that there is "a unified pragmatistic tradition, extending from philosophy to sociology and structured around a common conception of habitual action"—a tradition that can be rationally reconstructed on the basis of Peirce's views but cannot be reduced to Peirce: see Kilpinen, 2000, p. 34, pp. 96–97. See here also Sandra Rosenthal's numerous writings, especially Rosenthal, 1986.
7   For an up-to-date account and an original, balanced view on Emerson's relation to pragmatism, see Kovalainen, 2010.
8   On Peirce's progress from pragmatism to pragmaticism, see, among several useful secondary sources, the detailed discussion in Apel, 1981, ch. 8.
9   Another interesting (and somewhat bitter) passage, written two years earlier, is this: "To speak plainly, a considerable number of philosophers have lately written as they might have written in case they had been reading either what I wrote but were ashamed to confess it, or had been reading something that some reader of mine had read. For they seem quite disposed to adopt my term *pragmatism*. . . . I cannot find any direr fault with the new pragmatists than that they are *lively*. In order to be deep it is requisite to be dull. // On their side, one of the faults that I think they might find with me is that I make pragmatism to be a mere maxim of logic instead of a sublime principle of speculative philosophy." (EP 2:134, 1903.) See also CP 6.482, 6.490, 1908.
10 See Haack, 1998, p. 55; Kilpinen, 2000, p. 35.

11 Peirce's most important writings on truth, reality, and the scientific method can be found in EP1: see especially "The Fixation of Belief" (1877) and "How to Make Our Ideas Clear" (1878). James's classical statement of the pragmatic conception of truth can be found in James, 1907, ch. 6. See also James, 1909b for his responses to his critics.
12 The pragmatic method will be more fully discussed in the chapter "Research Methods and Problems."
13 For Peirce's and James's correspondence related to the planning of these lectures, see Perry, 1935, II, pp. 418–421. Peirce noted on January 4, 1898, that his first lecture would be about "vitally important topics," "showing that where they are 'vital' there is little chance for philosophy in them" (ibid., p. 421).
14 See especially his 1925 work, *Experience and Nature* (2nd ed. 1929).
15 Here I would suggest that the Deweyan naturalist, like John McDowell in his influential and debated book, *Mind and World* (McDowell, 1996), engages in a "rethinking" of the concept of nature. For comparisons between Dewey and McDowell in this regard, see Pihlström, 2003, ch. 4. In addition to McDowell's work, there are important collections of articles critical of reductive naturalism.
16 Putnam classifies Quine primarily as a (neo)positivist, even the "greatest logical positivist" (see Putnam, 1990, ch. 20; 1995, p. 13). On Quine's role in bringing (early) analytic philosophy, or logical empiricism, to the United States, see also Isaac, 2005.
17 White's autobiography (1999) contains interesting personal recollections of his longtime relationship to Quine, including the joint attack on analyticity that Nelson Goodman, Quine, and White himself launched in the late 1940s and early 1950s (see ibid., p. 53, 119, and the appendix, pp. 337–357, consisting of these three philosophers' triangular correspondence in 1947). White's own views—which were as critical about the analytic/synthetic distinction as Quine's—were also influenced by Dewey's "gradualistic writings" (ibid., p. 119). White suggests that Quine's view of the external world as a "posit" (cf. Quine, 1980, p. 44) has a precursor in Royce's *The Religious Aspect of Philosophy* (see White, 1999, pp. 122–123; this was pointed out by White in his letter to Quine on March 7, 1969).
18 In another paper from the same period, "Identity, Ostension and Hypostasis," Quine (1980, p. 79) argues that our standard for the appraisal of "basic changes in conceptual scheme" cannot be a "realistic standard of correspondence to reality" but must be a pragmatic standard. This sounds rather Carnapian (cf. Hookway, 1988, p. 50); it should also be noted that Quine here opposes pragmatism (or pragmatic standards of appraisal) and "realistic" correspondence accounts to each other—a traditional opposition, which is by no means uncontroversial, however. See also Creath's (1990, p. 21) remarks, in his introduction to the Quine-Carnap correspondence, on Quine's and Carnap's positions as two different forms of pragmatism.

19 It should be noted that in this passage, Quine does not directly object to being classified as a pragmatist, but he still insists that he does not know what it takes to be one.

20 This view on the deep integration, or even entanglement, of fact and value has later been developed by Hilary Putnam (e.g., 2002, 2004) and his commentators (see Pihlström, 2005).

21 Rorty (1999, p. 24) classifies Quine (along with Goodman, Putnam, and Davidson) as a "neo-pragmatist," distinguished from the classical pragmatists (Peirce, James, Dewey) by the "linguistic turn." For the place Quine occupies in Rorty's version of the history of pragmatism after the linguistic turn, or in the "pragmatization of analytic philosophy," see Sandbothe, 2004, pp. 69–75.

22 For a solid study of Rorty's philosophical career, especially in relation to analytic philosophy, see Gross, 2007. Other recent studies on Rorty and neo-pragmatism include Voparil, 2006; Grippe, 2007; and Dann, 2010.

23 Rorty's critic might point out here that Rorty simply has not bothered to read Quine carefully enough. Quine does *not* propose a simple replacement of philosophy by science (see Koskinen, 2004). Undoubtedly, Rorty must have in mind certain well-known Quinean formulations, for example, the one in "Epistemology Naturalized" (Quine, 1969) about epistemology falling in its place as a chapter of psychology.

24 For the development and different versions of Rorty's equation of pragmatism with anti-representationalism, see Rorty, 1982, 1991, 1998, 1999, 2007.

25 Another neo-pragmatist critique of Quine's nonstandard "pragmatism" worth mentioning here is Putnam's (see, e.g., his 1994, 1999). This criticism of Quine is, to a degree, similar to Rorty's, as both critics firmly reject Quine's scientism. However, Putnam attacks Quine's view *because* it actually leads, by his lights, to something very much like Rorty's irresponsibly relativist neo-pragmatism. If Quine is right, then Rorty is right, Putnam is trying to tell us. From Putnam's perspective, then, Quine's version of pragmatism or naturalism ought to be rejected pretty much for the same reasons that the responsible pragmatist ought to reject Rorty's neo-pragmatism. The key to this criticism is the claim that both Quinean scientistic naturalism and Rortyan relativism tend to lose the humanly inescapable normativity of semantic and epistemic practices.

26 In his dissertation on pragmatism, Malte Jacobsson (1910, p. 189) also notes that pragmatism in Sweden, "särskilt hos Vitalis Norström" ("especially in Vitalis Norström"), requires a special investigation. Norström's connection with pragmatism is noted in Lagerlund's (2003, pp. 146–148) comprehensive survey of the history of Swedish philosophy.

27 Cf. Chapter 18 for more details about currently active pragmatism scholarship networks, such as the Charles S. Peirce Society, the International Pragmatism

Society, the Central European Pragmatist Forum, the Nordic Pragmatism Network, and so on, as well as relevant websites, such as the Pragmatism Cybrary (www.pragmatism.org).

28 Niiniluoto's (1999) book is one of the best examinations of both historical and systematic issues related to scientific realism.

2

Research Methods and Problems

Sami Pihlström

This chapter deepens the discussion of the "Introduction" by taking a closer look at the methodology of pragmatist inquiry, as well as some central problems that pragmatists are, and have been, preoccupied with. Typically, pragmatists rely on both *historical* and *conceptual* methodology and, while employing philosophical distinctions, reject pernicious dualisms, dichotomies, and essentialisms, including the widespread dualism between historical and purely conceptual or analytic philosophical approaches. This attitude to philosophical methodology, especially the so-called pragmatic method, will here be explained, defended, and illustrated with reference to a number of ongoing disputes within specific areas of philosophy; further material can be found in the contributed essays below. Accordingly, this chapter will offer *one* way of understanding the pragmatic method, as applied to a few central philosophical problems. This is by no means a complete survey of the different uses of the pragmatic method. Unresolved meta-philosophical problems also related to pragmatist methodology, such as the extent to which current pragmatists can successfully be public intellectuals, will be identified and discussed in the "New Directions" chapter, as they bear on the future of pragmatism as a philosophical approach.

The pragmatic method: An overview

First, the *pragmatic method*, especially its different interpretations by Peirce and James, must be substantially discussed and analyzed. A critical elaboration of the relevance of, and some different employments of, this method is the core of this chapter. We will begin with some remarks on the history of the pragmatic method, thus for a moment returning to the historical discussion of the introductory chapter.

In the *The Varieties of Religious Experience*, James (1902, p. 351) speaks about "the principle of Peirce, the principle of pragmatism," referring to "How to Make Our Ideas Clear" (1878) and applying the principle to a discussion of God's metaphysical attributes. The same article by Peirce was already quoted by James in his "The Function of Cognition" in 1884, a paper that later formed the first chapter of *The Meaning of Truth* (James, 1909b).[1] James's reception of Peircean pragmatism culminates in his 1898 address at the University of California in Berkeley, "Philosophical Conceptions and Practical Results." Later, in *Pragmatism*, James reports:

> The term ["pragmatism"] is derived from the same Greek word [πραγμα], meaning action, from which our words "practice" and "practical" come. It was introduced into philosophy by Mr. Charles Peirce in 1878. In an article entitled "How to Make Our Ideas Clear," in the "Popular Science Monthly" for January of that year Mr. Peirce, after pointing out that our beliefs are really rules for action, said that, to develop a thought's meaning, we need only determine what conduct it is fitted to produce: that conduct is for us its sole significance. And the tangible fact at the root of all our thought-distinctions, however subtle, is that there is no one of them so fine as to consist in anything but a possible difference of practice. To attain perfect clearness in our thoughts of an object, then, we need only consider what conceivable effects of a practical kind the object may involve—what sensations we are to expect from it, and what reactions we must prepare. Our conception of these effects, whether immediate or remote, is then for us the whole of our conception of the object, so far as that conception has positive significance at all. // This is the principle of Peirce, the principle of pragmatism. It lay entirely unnoticed by anyone for twenty years, until I, in an address before Professor Howison's philosophical union at the university of California, brought it forward again and made a special application of it to religion. By that date (1898) the times seemed ripe for its reception. . . . To take in the importance of Peirce's principle, one must get accustomed to applying it to concrete cases. (James, 1907, pp. 28–29)

In this passage, James seems to believe, mistakenly, that Peirce had used the term "pragmatism," in his 1878 paper, although he had only used it in unpublished discussions at the Metaphysical Club in the early 1870s, James's own 1898 usage being the first one in print. Peirce's original, oft-quoted text from the 1878 paper reads as follows: "Consider what effects, which might conceivably have practical bearings, we conceive the object of our conception to have. Then, our conception of these effects is the whole of our conception of the object" (CP 5.402/W3:266).[2] When presenting Peirce's principle, James, however, appears to slide from acknowledging Peirce's notions of *possible* differences and *conceivable* effects to the requirement that those differences or effects should really be actualized in our concrete experiences or practices, whether immediately or remotely.

Accordingly, one of the differences between Peirce's and James's formulations of the pragmatic maxim is that James required the practical consequences of our conceptions to be, above all, *particular*. This requirement, based on James's insistence that abstract ideas ought to be put to work among the actual facts of the world we experience, conflicts with Peirce's stronger focus on generality and habits of action, as Peirce (especially in his later thought) consistently emphasized—in contrast to any particular, actualized bearings—the "*conceivably* practical bearings" in which "the entire meaning and significance of any conception" lies (EP2:145, 1903; see also EP2:234–235). The Peircean formulation allows that our conceptions, though always conceptions of "conceivable practical effects," "reach far beyond the practical"; it is only required that we maintain a connection with some possible practical effect when examining the meaning of any given concept(ion) (EP2:235, 1903).

Indeed, Peirce remarked in a letter in December 1904 that James's "Humanism and Truth" (reprinted in James, 1909b) had distorted his views:

> You have a quotation from me which greatly astonishes me. I cannot imagine when or where I can have used that language: "The serious meaning of a concept lies in the concrete difference to some one which its being true will make."[3] Do tell me at once where I so slipped, that I may at once declare it to be a slip. I do not think I have often spoken of the "meaning of a concept" whether "serious" or not. I have said that the concept itself "is" *nothing more* than the concept, not of any concrete difference that *will* be made to someone, but is nothing more than the concept of the *conceivable* practical applications of it. (Perry, 1935, II: pp. 432–433)

There is, however, a sense in which James's pragmatism was more consistently pragmatic than Peirce's. Arguably, James applied pragmatism to itself, treating the pragmatist principle as pragmatically true (cf. Conant, 1997; Pihlström, 1998, 2008a). In contrast to Peirce's continuous struggle with "proving" pragmatism, no logical demonstration of the truth of pragmatism, independently of pragmatism, was needed or even possible for him; the pragmatic efficacy and the truth of pragmatism were pretty much the same thing for James, though not for Peirce. The maxim that ideas ought to be tested practically by experience covers this pragmatist idea itself, the requirement of the practical testability of ideas in terms of possible experience.

This meta-philosophical difference over the status and provability of the pragmatic maxim was a corollary of the opposition between the *logical* and *psychological* orientations of Peirce and James, respectively (cf. "Introduction" above). We may say that for James the evaluation of the philosophical status of generalities or abstract ideas was among the applications of the pragmatic maxim, whereas for Peirce the reality of "generals" was a presupposition that made pragmatism possible. James could have responded to Peirce by saying that any such presupposition must itself, again, be pragmatically assessed. Peirce obviously also maintained that the pragmatic maxim, as he understood it, had pragmatic consequences. James, however, was willing to let such consequences—which for him constituted a more open and inclusive class than the merely scientifically relevant consequences Peirce was interested in—determine the philosophical value of pragmatism in a pragmatic manner, independently of any prior logical demonstration. Peirce's pragmatism was subordinated to logic; according to James, whatever philosophical value logic had was to be explained on more fundamental pragmatic grounds.

The following discussion of the pragmatic method will not be faithful to either Peirce's or James's original pronouncements. It will be argued below that the pragmatic method—if not in its original Peircean employment, then at least in its subsequent Jamesian and Deweyan employments—entails a *pluralistic* (and, hence, *antireductionist*) and *contextualist* approach to philosophical inquiry: *all* the relevant conceivable practical, experiential results of a given philosophical (or scientific) concept or conception ought to be taken into account when examining its pragmatic significance in a certain context. What these relevant practical results are crucially depends on the context we are operating in. Pragmatists are usually happy to admit that philosophical problems cannot be usefully examined in abstraction from the contexts of inquiry (and, more generally, our orientation in the world) they genuinely emerge in for real human beings, as "live" issues rather than artificial puzzles. Our criteria for pragmatic relevance, including human significance, are themselves contextual, dependent on our ongoing practice-embedded reflection on such criteria (and the meta-level criteria for the viability of such criteria, and so on, potentially indefinitely). Insofar as this *contextualist pluralism* (as we may call it) is emphasized as *a* key to the proper employment of the pragmatic method, James's version of pragmatism emerges as a truer heir of Peirce's original maxim than has often been supposed by those who tend to view James's pragmatism as a misunderstanding of Peirce's. However, it would be contrary to the pluralistic spirit of Jamesian pragmatism to raise it to the status of *the* uniquely correct form of pragmatism.

The pragmatic method, then, is a *meta-method*, which may be used to evaluate different philosophical methods (e.g., conceptual analysis, phenomenological reduction, transcendental arguments, or other methods of inquiry philosophers have defended and employed) and their "promised" outcome and/or relevance in different actual contexts of philosophical inquiry.[4] Accordingly, the pragmatic method should *not* be understood as a rival to these other philosophical methods but, rather, as providing a context of inquiry within which their specific efficacy in view of particular philosophical problems can be critically examined. Thus understood, the pragmatic method is much broader than a merely meaning-theoretical principle designed to "make our ideas clear." Making our ideas clear is highly central to the pragmatic method, but it is essential that ideas are made clear by experimentally putting them into practice, by genuinely orientating in the world—in scientific, everyday, artistic, political, religious, and other contexts—in terms of them, and by seeing what happens, prepared to learn from one's mistakes.

The pragmatic contextualism and pluralism emerging from the commitment to the pragmatic method, in the (more Jamesian than Peircean) sense outlined above, will now be highlighted in relation to four selected philosophical problems and research areas. We will examine pragmatism at work in metaphysics, philosophy of mind, philosophy of value, and philosophy of religion. All these topics—and many others—will, of course, be more fully covered in the articles below; this chapter will approach them in a methodological fashion, showing how the pragmatic method functions in these areas of inquiry.

The pragmatic method in metaphysics

As metaphysics is, in the Aristotelian tradition, the "first philosophy," it is natural to start our exploration of the employment of the pragmatic method from metaphysics. But what is pragmatic metaphysics, and can there even be such a thing? Aren't pragmatists suspicious of any first philosophy, including metaphysics?

It may be argued that pragmatists can accommodate metaphysical methods usually employed by, say, analytic philosophers, such as "truthmaking" considerations and the analysis of "ontological commitments."[5] Even more importantly, however, pragmatist metaphysics must make sense of the profound "practice-dependence" or "scheme-dependence" of all of our ontological postulations (whether these are explicated in terms of ontological commitments or truthmakers): there is, for pragmatists, no "ready-made world" absolutely independent of the practice-laden perspectives from which we structure and categorize it. However, the distinction between scheme-dependent and scheme-independent entities may itself be contextualized to different practical contexts of inquiry. Nothing is just scheme-dependent or scheme-independent absolutely, non-contextually, not even the distinction between scheme-dependence (or context-dependence) and scheme-independence (or context-independence) itself.

My own entry in this volume, "Metaphysics" (as well as a recent book, Pihlström, 2009a), makes the case for pragmatist metaphysics generally. Here, I will only discuss one—albeit also extremely general—issue, the *contextuality* of metaphysical (ontological) commitments.

We may start from the observation that, in the central traditions of modern philosophy, including the pragmatist tradition, several thinkers have argued that the existence and/or identity of things (entities, facts, or whatever there is taken to be in the world) is in a way or another relative to, or dependent on, the human mind, linguistic frameworks, conceptual schemes, practices, language-games, forms of life, paradigms, or something similar. Among the historically influential defenders of key variations of this "dependence thesis"—starting already from the pre-history of pragmatism, including figures only marginally involved in pragmatism, and ending up with relatively recent neo-pragmatism—are, for instance, Immanuel Kant (the empirical world is constituted by the transcendental faculties of the mind, that is, the pure forms of intuition and the pure concepts or categories of the understanding), William James (whatever we may call a "thing" depends on our purposes and selective interests), F. C. S. Schiller (we "humanistically" construct the world and all truths about it within our purposive practices), John Dewey (the objects of inquiry are constructed in and through inquiry, instead of existing as "ready-made" prior to inquiry), Rudolf Carnap (ontological questions about whether there are certain kinds of entities can only be settled within linguistic frameworks, "internally," whereas "external" questions concern the pragmatic criteria for choosing one or another linguistic framework), W. V. Quine (ontology is not absolute but relative to a theory, language, or translation scheme), Ludwig Wittgenstein (the "essence" of things lies in "grammar," thus in the language-games we engage in, instead of transcending our language-use and form of life), Hilary Putnam (there is no "ready-made world" but only scheme-internal objects), Nelson Goodman (we "make worlds," or "world versions," by employing our various symbol systems), Thomas S. Kuhn (different scientific paradigms constitute different "worlds"), Richard Rorty (our "vocabularies" constitute the ways the world is for us, and we must "ethnocentrically" start from within the vocabularies we contingently possess), and possibly even Wilfrid Sellars (the best-explaining scientific theories are the "measure" of what there is and what there is not), as well as many others.[6]

In their distinctive ways, these and many other thinkers have suggested that there is no absolute world *an sich* that we could meaningfully conceptualize or cognize; if there is such a world, as Kant held, it is a mere limit of our thought and experience, a problematic *Grenzbegriff*. What there is *for us* is a world we have constructed, and are continuously constructing, relative to our schemes of categorization and inquiry. Pragmatists, however, may follow—or *should* follow—Kant in embracing something like *empirical realism* (and naturalism) within a broader pragmatist position comparable to Kantian *transcendental idealism*. Pragmatists should not simply opt for antirealism or radical constructivism and relativism in ontology but, rather, moderate pragmatic realism compatible with naturalism. The problem is how to combine the scheme-dependence of entities[7] with their pragmatic scheme-independence (at the empirical level) in pragmatist metaphysics. This is, essentially, the pragmatist version of the Kantian problem of maintaining both empirical realism and transcendental idealism—both the empirical independence of things and their "transcendental" dependence on the ways we construct them through our various schemes.[8] For Kant, spatiotemporal objects in the empirical world are really "outside us" and in this sense exist empirically speaking mind- or scheme-independently. Nevertheless, they are transcendentally dependent on us, because the spatiotemporal (and categorial) framework making them possible as objects of experience (appearances) arises from our cognitive faculties (i.e., sensibility and understanding). Replace the latter with human cognitive and conceptualizing *practices*, and you have the pragmatist issue of ontological (in)dependence.[9]

A proposal that might be attractive to pragmatists here is the *contextualization* of the distinction between scheme-dependent and scheme-independent entities.[10] Nothing is *absolutely* scheme-(in)dependent but is dependent or independent only in a given context, or from a specific perspective, rather than from an imagined God's-Eye View. Thus, pragmatists may deny not the scheme-dependence versus scheme-independence *distinction* (understood as contextualizable) but only the corresponding *dichotomy* or dualism (understood as absolute, non-perspectival, uncontextualizable).[11] The former can be maintained by redescribing it through practice-relative contextualization.

However, the contexts or perspectives invoked here are also "entities" that need to be contextualized in order to be identifiable as contexts at all. A context

C is "real," and contextualizes the scheme-(in)dependence of certain entities (*a*, *b*), only within a further context C', and so on (*ad infinitum*). Not even the contextualization—and, hence, the contextual validation—of the distinction between scheme-dependence and scheme-independence is non-contextual or absolute (or absolutely scheme-independent). It is in and through our schemes, which describe the contexts we are able to work within in given situations, that we determine the contexts within which things can be scheme-dependent or scheme-independent. This process of contextualization is indefinitely long, as any reflexive process potentially is. The "situations" we are "in," giving rise to certain contexts of thought and inquiry, can themselves, again, be only contextually identified as such. Moreover, "we" are whatever we are only in certain contexts we find ourselves in.

The contextualization we are trying to articulate here amounts to a kind of pragmatic "naturalization" of Kantian transcendental idealism.[12] It is fully natural for us—given the kind of creatures we (context-embeddedly) are—to live within context-dependent and context-creating forms of life and/or practices that constitute (again contextual) conditions for the possibility of various things we assume to be actual in our lives, such as cognitive experience or meaningful language. These practices contain "relative a priori" conditions that structure our lives. A key observation here is that this pragmatic, naturalized view is "transcendentally idealistic" in the sense of emphasizing the constitutive role played by our natural practices of coping with the world we live in, that is, in the sense of acknowledging the dependence of not just social reality but the natural, worldly objects surrounding us on our specifically human, context-laden ways of representing them from standpoints lying within our practices, within contextually situated points of view embedded in those practices.

The picture of the pragmatic contextuality of whatever there is, and the contextuality of drawing the distinction between what there is scheme-dependently and scheme-independently, is undeniably circular, but hardly viciously circular. Our world-constituting, contextual activity is both constitutive of the world and part of it. It is this circularity inherently present in a pragmatic analysis of world-constitutivity that prevents the above-described naturalized version of transcendental idealism from collapsing into a full-blown metaphysical idealism. The fact that there is such world-constitutive activity at all is a natural fact about us, about "human nature." Like all such facts about us, it is itself contextual, but there is nothing more fundamental than that (endless) contextuality itself that can ground this analysis of our world-constitutive activities.

We also need to consider the meta-philosophical status of our contextuality thesis. It can hardly be regarded as an empirical, factual, and contingent truth about the ways things happen to be in the world. Nor can it be an absolute, non-contextual truth in the sense of supposed metaphysical truths traditionally put forward by philosophers criticized by pragmatists. It would also be hard to believe that it could be a conceptually necessary truth, or necessary in the way in which, say, logical and mathematical truths are necessary (whatever we ultimately mean by the necessity of logic or mathematics—this is not a topic of the present discussion). Pragmatic contextualism should somehow combine (relative) necessity with non-absoluteness and reflexive contextuality. What we have here is only necessity in a context, relativized to a certain use of concepts, a certain practice-laden way of viewing the world. Pragmatic contextualism is a truth—or at least a reasonable philosophical conviction—emerging from a continuous reflection on our life with the concepts we use and the world we live in. If it is "made true" by anything, it is made true by our contextualizing inquiries into the contextuality of ontology, not by anything "ready-made" in the world itself taken to be independent of contexts.

The meta-philosophical status of the contextuality thesis might be compared to the status of such controversial philosophical theses as the Wittgensteinian one about the impossibility of a private language. Just as we may see Wittgenstein (1953) as arguing that, necessarily, language is a public human phenomenon, insofar as there can be any linguistic meaning at all, we may see the pragmatic contextualist as arguing that, necessarily, any entities there can be for us are identified within, and hence exist—as the kind of entities they are—only relative to, one or another context of categorization and inquiry. Like the Wittgensteinian impossibility of a private language (or, say, the impossibility of disembodied agency), the impossibility of non-contextual identification of objects, or of any absolute scheme-independence, is a kind of quasi-transcendental necessity, yet again only a contextual and pragmatic one, itself depending on the kind of beings we are (according to the schemes or contexts that we contingently, revisably, and fallibly employ), thus a necessity only in a relativized and not an absolute sense.

The pragmatic method in the philosophy of mind

One of the things (though "thing" is a misleading word here) in the world a pragmatist metaphysician must theorize about is the mind, or subjectivity.

Is there a specifically pragmatist approach to the mind and consciousness? Pragmatism is only rarely commented on in mainstream literature within analytic philosophy of mind; nor are the pragmatists standard points of reference in phenomenological explorations of subjectivity and consciousness. Pragmatism can, however, appreciate not only the *naturalized* methods of contemporary antidualist (e.g., physicalist) philosophy of mind but also, for example, the *phenomenological* method and, more generally, the methods used in *transcendental* inquiry into the necessary conditions for the possibility of experience, including "transcendental subjectivity." The pragmatist may even appreciate the importance of *panpsychist* metaphysics of subjectivity and experience, while also working on *emergentist*, non-reductive naturalism. For pragmatists, there is no final truth to be told about the essential nature of human subjectivity from an absolute perspective. Thus, pragmatist philosophy of mind and subjectivity offers examples of the tensions that easily result from the pluralist orientation of pragmatism.

A pragmatist approach to subjectivity can be characterized by the following six ideas (which, to be sure, are in tension with each other):

1. Pragmatism may be regarded as an *emergentist* version of non-reductive naturalism: subjectivity arises from nature as a natural development of certain kinds of organisms and their interaction with their natural environment.
2. Subjectivity must, in pragmatism, be understood *dynamically*, that is, in relation to (habits of) action. Therefore, pragmatism is essentially a *philosophical anthropology*, not just a philosophy of mind.
3. Not all pragmatists are emergentists, however; some have been, for instance, *panpsychists*. This is one of the key tensions in pragmatist philosophy of mind.
4. Pragmatic, non-reductive naturalism not only avoids scientific reductions of subjectivity but is even compatible with a *transcendental* (Kantian-like) perspective on subjectivity, if the latter is reconceptualized from a pragmatist standpoint.
5. Pragmatist philosophy of mind and subjectivity cannot be thoroughly non-metaphysical (or "postontological") but must engage with *metaphysical questions* about the way(s) the world is for us.
6. Pragmatist metaphysics, both in general and in its particular applications in the philosophy of mind and subjectivity, must be intimately reconnected with *ethics*.

In this subsection, I will briefly consider these points in turn. My discussion will not constitute a deductive chain of argument. Rather, I will offer a kind of narrative, with one idea more or less naturally leading to another. Thus, I hope to be able to rearticulate some aspects of a plausible pragmatist approach to subjectivity. I will just summarize (and to some extent defend) *a* pragmatist philosophy of subjectivity, and I also try to identify tensions, challenges, and open issues. I am obviously aware of the fact that several pragmatists will immediately deny one or more of my allegedly pragmatist "theses."[13] That, however, is precisely as it should be: as we saw in the "Introduction" pragmatism is not a final set of closed, completed doctrines; it is a living philosophical orientation, and creative pragmatic work on subjectivity can be fruitfully continued if—and perhaps only if—philosophers disagree on how exactly pragmatists should view this exciting phenomenon. By no means am I claiming, then, that the six pragmatist perspectives on subjectivity to be discussed form a coherent whole without internal tensions. The tensions they embody should be a source of genuine pragmatist insights. Pragmatism is inherently pluralistic; its tolerant methodology for examining subjectivity—or any other philosophically interesting phenomenon—need not be seen as a rival to, but may be seen as critically transforming and to some extent accommodating, some other methods.

The pragmatist approach to subjectivity, as I see it, starts from *non-reductive naturalism*. This starting point can be made more precise by employing the concept of *emergence*. Subjectivity is something that "emerges from" the natural world, and is thus itself something fully natural, even though it is possible only in complex systems that are in some sense "more than the sum of their parts." Nature, for pragmatists, is multiply layered, and its "higher" levels, including subjectivity, freedom, culture, and values, cannot be completely reduced—either conceptually, ontologically, or explanatorily—to its "lower" ones. This emergent naturalism is especially clear in Dewey's and Mead's pragmatism.

In *The Quest for Certainty*, Dewey (1929, pp. 214–215) writes: "The intellectual activity of man is not something brought to bear upon nature from without; it is nature realizing its own potentialities in behalf of a fuller and richer issue of events." What gradually emerges out of the originally inanimate world in Dewey's system is life, mind, freedom, culture, and value. For Dewey, such emergent structures and properties are "real features of . . . complex systems which cannot be accounted for in terms that would be adequate if the same constituents were organized in a less complex way" (Tiles, 1988, p. 148). Although Dewey was a naturalist, he rejected metaphysical realists' dream of representing nature as it is in itself from an absolute perspective. For him, any ontological structure of reality is a humanly established structure, itself emerging in the course of human experience and inquiry—and thereby, arguably, a structure to some extent presupposing subjective experiential perspectives, continuously getting "structured" through such perspectives of ours. In this sense his realism about emergent properties—if we may call it that—is thoroughly pragmatic. In the evolutionary flow of experience, both subjectivity and the objects constituted through inquiry and our practice-laden perspectives continuously emerge.

Dewey was not entirely happy with the term "emergence," however. Late in his life, jointly with Arthur Bentley, he argued that the "natural man" who talks, thinks, and knows should not, "even in his latest and most complex activities," be surveyed "as magically 'emergent' into something new and strange" (Dewey and Bentley, 1949, p. 45). While being careful with the word "emergence," Dewey did not reject the idea but only what he saw as its magical overtones. He simply required scientific, experimental research on the emergence of life and mind. Subjectivity cannot be studied purely philosophically, from an armchair, but our philosophical examinations of subjectivity must be empirically anchored, continuous with, not separated from, the advancing sciences.

Among neo-pragmatists, Putnam may be the one whose views come closest to an emergentist philosophy of the mind and subjectivity. He has, after all, been one of the leading critics of reductive accounts of the mind for decades. However, he says that emergence is a "bad metaphor" (Putnam, 1999), especially because its advocates tend to construe the mind as a mysterious entity whose existence calls for a (scientific-like) explanation. We should, rather, view the mind pragmatically as a world-involving set of capacities. Instead of maintaining the largely Cartesian framework within which mentality and subjectivity are mysterious, we should, according to Putnam, dissolve this mystery. From Putnam's point of view, it may seem that emergentist philosophers of mind just keep up the mystery by talking about the somewhat magic leap of emergent novelty. However, if we, in a Deweyan fashion, regard mental properties as naturally emerging, no mysterious emergentist assumptions are needed. The problem need not be thoroughly dissolved, even if both dualistic and reductively scientific approaches to it are abandoned.

Pragmatic subjectivity, in its natural emergence, is crucially connected with human (habits of) *action,* hence with the notion of *agency.* This conviction seems to be shared by those pragmatists who are fruitfully (re)interpretable as emergentists (including Dewey) and those who would rather abandon the entire issue of emergence (including Putnam). The emergence of subjectivity is not the emergence of peculiar immaterial entities, properties, or states (e.g., *qualia* understood as some kind of internal mental objects), but the emergence of certain capacities and habitualities, of ways of "being in the world."

This, along with the pragmatists' general naturalism, is a further step toward a total rejection of Cartesian assumptions that pragmatists have developed since Peirce's anti-Cartesian articles of the 1860s (see EP1: chs. 2–5). The mind is "in the world," not "in the head" of subjects or minded beings; subjectivity is inevitably connected with intersubjectivity, when it is understood in terms of subjects' worldly (including social) actions. Pragmatism, then, can never remain merely a philosophy of mind; rather, it is a much more comprehensive orientation in *philosophical anthropology,* seeking to understand not just the mind (mentality, consciousness, subjectivity) but the entire human being in her/his worldly (including social) surroundings, that is, in James's (1897) words, "the whole man in us" (see also Pihlström, 1998; Franzese, 2008). As such a general philosophical project, pragmatism must not only investigate the nature of the mind and its contents—as analytic philosophy of mind primarily does—but the ways in which "minded" creatures like us live in the world, amidst their different projects and habitualities. After all, the concept of a habit, or habitual action, has been central to the pragmatist tradition since its very start.

This is why the recent analytic debates in the philosophy of mind have only limited relevance to pragmatist explorations of the mind and subjectivity. Nor do phenomenological investigations fare much better in this regard. Phenomenologists usually seek to examine mental and experiential phenomena from an allegedly "presuppositionless" standpoint, focusing on the way the world appears to us in experience and bracketing all naturalistic presuppositions (such as the very existence of a material world). One reason why we need to insist on both the natural emergence and the habitual embeddedness of subjectivity in pragmatism is the need to avoid the remnants of such "first philosophy." Despite some highly interesting developments in phenomenology that seem to bring it in many ways close to pragmatism, the worldly—natural and practical—embeddedness of subjectivity is usually not sufficiently emphasized in phenomenological studies of experience.[14]

Is pragmatist philosophy of action and agency, we may further ask, primarily *individualistic* or *holistic*? This question, though one that might naturally be considered here, is misleading, because pragmatism is both. There is a fruitful tension—one more pragmatist tension giving vitality to the tradition—in pragmatism between individualism and faith in sociality, all the way from Emerson's proto-pragmatist discussions of the individual in a society (e.g., in his *Society and Solitude,* 1870). All the classical pragmatists developed, with different emphases, a view of an-individual-in-a-society (or community), reducing neither to the other, respecting both the integrity of the individual and her/his inevitable social context without which no true individuality is possible. Even James, the most individualistically oriented classical pragmatist, did this.

As H. G. Callaway (2006, p. xiii) suggests, discussing Emerson in his introduction to Emerson's 1870 book, we must "go through" our own individual minds in order to arrive at a "universal truth"; in this sense, "genuine individuality is a necessary condition of our arriving at the truth and of finding our appropriate place in society." Conversely, however, "in developing genuine individuality, we need to orient ourselves to [our] own cultural background" and its commonsense assumptions (ibid., p. xiii). The mutual interplay between individual self-reliance and the cultural background within which it takes place is a precondition for arriving at the (or any) truth.

For a pragmatist philosophical anthropologist, it may sound natural to think of both individual subjectivity and sociality as naturally emergent products of forces that are originally devoid of subjectivity. Our evolutionary history has produced complex organisms, world-directed agents, with genuinely "novel" subjective perspectives irreducible to what is objectively going on in their worldly surroundings. There is, however, an important tension in pragmatism between emergentist and non-emergentist views. It is to some extent a mystery how anything subjective can, or ever could, "emerge" from something in which there is no subjectivity (or mentality, experience, and so on) at all. Some pragmatists (and non-pragmatists) have, therefore, been inclined toward *panpsychism* instead of emergentism; arguably, there are elements of panpsychism in all the major classical pragmatists—Peirce, James, Dewey, and Schiller (cf. Skrbina, 2005). James, in particular, is an interesting figure in this regard. Around the middle of the first decade of the twentieth century, he struggled with both radical empiricism and what he labeled "pluralistic panpsychism" (see Pihlström, 2008a, ch. 7).

A crucial insight in pragmatist philosophy of subjectivity is that a dialogue between emergentist and panpsychist standpoints cannot be based upon prior metaphysically realist presuppositions, according to which there either just is, or is not, emergent subjectivity (e.g., *qualia,* or related "mysterious" entities) "out there" in the world independently of us, conceived "absolutely," or from an imagined "God's-Eye View." Rather, a pragmatic perspective on subjectivity should take seriously the idea that the world, insofar as it is an object of human conceptualizing, theorizing, and understanding (even including its mental, subjective, and perspectival aspects), is to some extent a "human construction," contextually structured and categorized by us into what it is or can ever be for us. Subjectivity, then, is also something that we ourselves (in a Kantian-like way) "impose on" or "contribute to" the world we live in. Panpsychism may, if pragmatically articulated, be connected with, or even based upon, Peirce's *synechism*, the doctrine of continuity, according to which both being as such and specific modes of being, such as mentality, spontaneity, or (presumably) subjectivity, are matters of degree, instead of being sharply separable from their opposites.[15] Nor is there any ontological gap between reality or being, on the one hand, and appearances or phenomena, on the other. Thus, the pragmatic embeddedness of subjectivity in our habits of action might be either emergentistically or synechistically conceptualized. This is to some extent an unresolved tension in pragmatist metaphysics and philosophy of mind. For a pluralistically oriented pragmatist, it would be ideal to get both—emergent novelty *with* continuity—but this may be difficult to achieve.

While the naturalized picture of subjectivity here associated with pragmatism—whether it is, in the end, better understood in terms of emergence (and non-reductive naturalism with a "layered" reality) or in terms of panpsychism (sacrificing some, though not all, central assumptions taken to characterize naturalism)—may seem to be strictly opposed to any form of *transcendental subjectivity*, such as the "transcendental ego" invoked by classical transcendental thinkers like Kant and Husserl, there is an important transcendental strain in pragmatist philosophy of subjectivity (and intersubjectivity). According to James (1907, ch. 7), in particular, "we" organize or structure the reality we are able to experience; this world-structuring "we" plays, we might say, an ontologically constitutive and quasi-transcendental role, although in many significant respects pragmatism departs from Kantian and post-Kantian transcendental philosophy.[16]

There is, in addition to undeniable differences, a lot of common ground between the Kantian transcendental tradition and the pragmatist tradition, to the extent that pragmatism may even be regarded as a relatively late twist in the former tradition. The pragmatist perspective on subjectivity, as outlined above, may be seen as a way of articulating the "paradox of subjectivity"—our problematic role as both world-constituting beings and beings existing in a fully natural world, that is, beings whose subjective experiences, including the world-constituting perspectives themselves, emerge within that world—that the transcendental tradition has always taken seriously (see Carr, 1999). The challenge for pragmatists here is to make naturalism and transcendental inquiry better compatible with each other as philosophical methods. Such a reconciliation might be achieved by arguing that the world-engaging, dynamic, practice-embedded subjectivity pragmatism emphasizes itself "constitutes," or even "constructs," reality (objectivity) in a way analogous to the constitution of reality and its objects in transcendental philosophy.

Just like the phenomenological notion of *Gegenstandskonstitution*, the pragmatist conception of world-structuring through human practices would be thoroughly misunderstood if this conception were taken to be committed to the claim that we humans "construct" or "create" reality in a factual, causal, or empirical sense; clearly, much of reality is independent of us, and we should be pragmatic realists and naturalists about it. However, there is a clearly identifiable (Jamesian–Deweyan) sense in which reality does depend on us. The objects of our thought and inquiry are inevitably the result of selective interests, of what is important for us, of what we find significant in the world in which we must continuously act and orientate. Such selective interests and valuational activities—arising out of our human agency and habits of action—then to a crucial extent determine what the world, for us, is like. This is analogous to the way in which the human cognitive faculty at a transcendental level constructs the empirical world in Kant's First Critique.

The transcendental subjectivity involved must, however, be carefully reconceptualized in terms of natural (presumably, emergently real) practices taking place in the world. There is, admittedly, a circular structure here—indicating, however, reflexivity instead of any vicious circularity or question-begging. Transcendental subjectivity is *not* any kind of other-worldly (transcendent) ghost; it is *our* own subjectivity in the world given to us as an object of cognition, that is, our own subjectivity viewed as the subject of world-constitution rather than simply as one object among others in the (constituted) world. We must, therefore, be able to view ourselves, slightly paradoxically, as both subjects and objects. Pragmatism, as much as Kantian transcendental philosophy, may offer us philosophical resources to defend this double-aspect view of ourselves.

As a follow-up to the proposal not only to (non-reductively) naturalize subjectivity but to "retranscendentalize" pragmatism and pragmatic naturalism, a meta-philosophical point on pragmatist philosophy of subjectivity needs to be raised. It might seem that pragmatism approaches the mind and subjectivity in non-metaphysical and non-ontological terms, purely epistemologically and experientially—or, in contemporary pragmatism inspired by Rorty's anti-representationalism, purely linguistically, examining not the "real" phenomenon of subjectivity at all (whether or not we may usefully say that there "really" is such a phenomenon in the world) but just the vocabularies or discourses (or "language-games") we use to talk about subjectivity. Bjørn Ramberg (2000), in particular, has aptly spoken about "postontological philosophy of mind" in this Rortyan context. This is indeed the perspective taken by several neo-pragmatists of the Rortyan stripe; however, for classical pragmatists, as has been argued by Dewey scholars and James scholars alike, the notion of experience is much more central than the notion of language (see, e.g., Hildebrand, 2003).

It would be overhasty to claim that the neo-pragmatists' insistence on language is just mistaken; on the contrary, pragmatists might do well to reconnect their views with late-Wittgensteinian philosophy of language, for instance. A sharp opposition between experience-oriented classical pragmatism (e.g., Dewey) and language-oriented neo-pragmatism (e.g., Rorty) is also one of the misleading dualisms that may hinder our pragmatist explorations of the dimensions of our subjectivity that are clearly both experiential and linguistically articulable. However, it would also be a mistake to conclude that there is no place for ontology or metaphysics in pragmatism at all (either generally or in the special field of subjectivity research). By examining the ways in which subjectivity is experienced, or linguistically structured (spoken about), by us, pragmatists may examine what subjectivity, for us, *is*—or what its role or place in the natural empirical world transcendentally structured by us (by that very subjectivity) is. They will then examine the philosophical–anthropological phenomenon we categorize as subjectivity from within the perspectives of our lives already colored by that phenomenon.

This will be an ontological inquiry into subjectivity, albeit in a heavily reinterpreted form. It is "metaphysics of subjectivity" in a Kantian shape, examining not the way the world is independently of us but the ways in which we may (have to) take the world to be in terms of our experiential and linguistic practices. As already suggested in the previous section, pragmatists should not give up metaphysics but reinterpret it pragmatically. In the case of subjectivity, what this means is that, once again, we should not be concerned with the subject conceived (or imagined) as a Cartesian-like substantial entity—any knowledge about which Kant already persuasively argued is impossible—but with the ways in which our subjectivity construes, for us, the world we live in as the (always reinterpretable) condition for the possibility of being able to experience any objects "out there."

This leads us to the final observations of this subsection. Some pragmatists have suggested that a successful rehabilitation of metaphysics—in relation to subjectivity or more generally—can eventually only take place in pragmatism if we are prepared to reconnect metaphysics with *ethics* (see also Pihlström, 2009a).

Ultimately, our metaphysical perspectives on subjectivity, when subjected to pragmatic evaluation in terms of the pragmatic method (especially in its Jamesian form), will have to be grounded in ethical considerations. This, I believe, is how we should read James's (1907, ch. 3) reflections on "some metaphysical problems pragmatically considered." It is the ethical significance of various metaphysical conceptions of subjectivity that will determine their pragmatic "cash value."

James does not explicitly discuss subjectivity in this context, but he does examine the issue of free will, for instance, and his approach can be readily applied to the problems we are now considering. Here, the acknowledgment of the *other* subject, another human person and experiential point of view independent of ourselves, is a decisive test case, a criterion for any adequate pragmatist metaphysics of subjectivity (cf. Pihlström, 2008a, ch. 5). This will be a genuinely metaphysical endeavor grounded in ethics. Our pragmatist philosophy of subjectivity cannot first settle the metaphysical question of what subjectivity is, or whether there is any, in order to turn to ethical issues afterward, but must approach this topic ethically from the very start. There is no non-ethical, or morally neutral, way of understanding, at a purely theoretical level, our practical world-embeddedness and the quasi-transcendental world-constitutivity itself reflexively embedded in that embeddedness.

Thus, the special case of subjectivity, pragmatically investigated and rearticulated, enables us to draw a general meta-philosophical moral about the need to reconsider the relations between two central philosophical subdisciplines, ethics and metaphysics. For a pragmatist, it is not the case—either here or elsewhere—that metaphysical issues are to be solved first and ethical ones only thereafter; on the contrary, the two are intimately entangled, because there is no way to examine metaphysically the way the world is absolutely and non-contextually, and any investigation of the world as structured from the perspectives of our selective interests will inevitably be colored by ethical considerations.

The pragmatic method in the philosophy of value

This entanglement of the ethical and the metaphysical aspects of pragmatist investigations of our being-in-the-world takes us to issues in (meta)ethics, or the philosophy of value (axiology) in general. How does pragmatism view the relations between fact and value, and what kind of ethics is possible within pragmatism? A major topic in recent pragmatism, for instance, in Putnam's writings, is the *fact-value entanglement* and the corresponding critique of the traditional dichotomy between facts and values (one of the dichotomies pragmatists are suspicious about). This issue is connected with both pragmatist metaphysics (values are taken to be real, in the pragmatic sense of "real") and pragmatist philosophy of mind (values may be claimed to "emerge from" facts roughly in the way in which mentality, spontaneity, or experience evolutionarily emerge from our natural existence), as well as pragmatist philosophy of action and philosophical anthropology (because values are usually taken to be action-guiding and parts of our human forms of life). In ethics, the pragmatist may, again, start from our natural ethical practices and try to determine, from within them, what kind of pragmatic realism about values (and rejection of the fact-value dichotomy) is necessary for us to be able to engage in those practices in the ways we do.

Fact and value, according to both classical (e.g., James's and Dewey's) and more recent (e.g., Putnam's) pragmatism, are deeply entangled. As James (1902, p. 53) put it, values "form the background for all our facts, the fountain-head of all the possibilities we conceive of." The view of the contextuality of ontological commitments, including the distinction between scheme-dependence and scheme-independence, can be applied to the issue of the relation between fact and value, in order to highlight the contextuality of *their* entanglement. This is an application of the pragmatic method, in the sense here interpreted.

One of Putnam's central arguments for the fact-value entanglement and the related picture of moral objectivity he defends is the one he labels the "companions in the guilt argument" (Putnam, 1990), which also is a kind of "indispensability argument." Putnam points out that objective, action-guiding moral values (i.e., values that are no more subjective than facts) should not—*pace* moral skeptics, radical relativists, and "error theorists" like J. L. Mackie (1977)—be regarded as "queer" objects hard to locate in the natural-scientific picture of the universe. Were values queer, *all* normative notions, including the ones we assume when defending the scientific conception of the world that Mackie and other critics of objective values regard as ontologically superior to ethical, value-laden conceptions, would be equally suspect. We would have no empirical world at all as the object of our (scientific and nonscientific) descriptions, if we did not subscribe to the objectivity of at least some values. In order to have a coherent concept of a fact, Putnam believes, we must invoke values. The ways we discuss factual matters reveal and presuppose our entire system of value commitments;

values are, in this sense, indispensable in our dealings with the world. There is no coherent way to deny the normative, action-guiding role played by the notions of rational acceptability, warrant, justification, and the like, and if such notions are allowed in our scientific conceptual scheme(s), then there is no clear motivation for excluding moral values.[17]

Far from being located in any transcendent realm beyond the natural and social reality familiar to us, values are, according to Putnam's pragmatism, entangled with the ordinary, natural facts we find ourselves immersed in. The pragmatist questions the error theorist's tendency to regard virtually everything nonscientific as "queer." The error theorist's naturalism is reductive (or eliminative), while a truly pragmatic naturalism must be non-reductive, preserving the natural features of our human world, including normativity. There is no reason to see the pragmatist's defense of the objectivity of moral values as non-naturalistic; on the contrary, many pragmatists can be read as arguing that we need to rethink our very idea of naturalism and accommodate distinctively human activities, including valuation, within nature, just as Dewey—the paradigmatic pragmatic naturalist—did. (Cf. also the discussion of Dewey's naturalism in the introductory chapter above.)

Putnam's argument for the entanglement thesis is, then, thoroughly pragmatic. He draws attention to the actualities defining our practices of ethical evaluation and argues that as soon as that practical context is adequately taken into account, as any pragmatist should, there is no room for an artificial philosophical dichotomy between factual and evaluative discourse—nor, consequently, for a reductive, physicalist picture of reality that takes only scientifically established facts seriously and disregards values as "queer." The human world is "messy," he tells us. If there is any distinction at all, it is inevitably fuzzy and contextual. Yet, on the basis of what was said above about the pragmatic contextuality of the scheme-dependence versus scheme-independence distinction, we may argue that fact and value are also distinguishable—but even then only in contexts that specify pragmatic criteria for distinguishing them. Hence, our ways of distinguishing between them, contextually, are themselves value-laden, dependent on valuational schemes. Fact and value, therefore, are not absolutely distinguishable, or distinct from a transcendent perspective (which we lack). Their entanglement, we may say, is a condition for our being able to live amidst the contextually identifiable entities we postulate around us. Our living in a world deeply structured by values is, again, a fact about the kind of lives we lead.

In his last collection of essays, Rorty (2007) suggested that cultural politics should replace systematic philosophical questions of ontology, epistemology, and other areas of traditional philosophy. Most pragmatists would hesitate to endorse such a reductive view of philosophy, but an analogy to the present discussion ought to be acknowledged. Just as Rorty notes that the question of how exactly the relation between ontology and cultural politics ought to be construed is itself a cultural–political question (ibid., p. 5), we may suggest that the question of how exactly the fact-value entanglement and/or distinguishability ought to be settled is itself a question that can only be adequately discussed within a valuational context. The specific ways of drawing this distinction or avoiding it are themselves dependent on our values. It is, therefore, always already a valuational issue whether there are any purely factual issues to be distinguished from valuational ones. Even to claim that there are would be a valuationally relevant move (and we may argue that this *is* a move we should make in certain humanly valuable contexts).

Valuation provides one central context within which things and facts may be real for us—or, better, different valuational schemes provide different contexts for identifying things and their relations to each other—and our employing the pragmatic method in the way suggested here indicates that it is (humanly speaking, contextually) necessary that all facts are value-laden. That is, the Putnamian thesis of the fact-value entanglement is not just a thesis about the ways things contingently are in the world; it is not just a thesis according to which fact and value happen to be entangled in the world we live in. Rather, it is a pragmatist metaphysical thesis about the ways things necessarily are for us. Without a valuational context, there could be no things—no facts—at all for us. This claim, however pragmatic, expresses a conditional necessity: something (valuational schemes) is regarded as a necessary condition for the very possibility of something else we take for granted, such as there being factual things and states of affairs identifiable and reidentifiable by us. Again, this discussion provides an example of the kind of contextualism the pragmatic method entails.

The pragmatic method in the philosophy of religion

In addition to the kind of relatively general metaphysical issues discussed above, pragmatism offers interesting methodological approaches to a number of more specific fields of philosophy. For example, pragmatism may seek to reconcile, pluralistically, a variety of different approaches to the issue of *theism versus atheism* in the currently confusing situation in the philosophy of religion. These include (among others) the following: (1) Kantian "moral faith," defending theism as a "postulate of practical reason"; (2) Jamesian defense of theism as an ethically grounded pragmatic metaphysical "over-belief"; (3) Deweyan naturalized conception of "the religious," understood as a quality of experience, reconciling naturalism with "natural piety"; (4) Wittgensteinian mysticism and quietism;[18] and (5) neo-pragmatism, with its indebtedness to both Kant, the classical pragmatists, and Wittgenstein. Pragmatism as such is neither theistic nor atheistic but offers rich resources for philosophical examinations of these and other issues in the philosophy of religion. Once again, pragmatism ought to be seen as an approach avoiding ultimate commitments to any "God's-Eye View" account of anything, including God. This is thus yet another instance of the pluralistic and contextualistic character of the pragmatic method.

Contemporary philosophy of religion is, indeed, in a confusing state; the different approaches deeply disagree about the very nature and methods of the philosophy of religion. These disagreements do not just arise from the theism versus atheism dispute about the existence of God or from the currently popular science versus religion controversy, to which aggressive atheists like Richard Dawkins and Daniel C. Dennett have actively contributed.[19] *Evidentialism* and *fideism* offer very different views on the justifiability of religious faith and on its relation to science and reason: while evidentialism urges that religious beliefs (like scientific ones) require justification in terms of general, religiously neutral criteria of rationality, fideism draws a sharp distinction between faith and reason, advancing faith in the absence of evidence. In addition to this primarily epistemological debate, a metaphysical and semantic disagreement concerns the nature of religious "reality" and our ability to linguistically refer to it.[20] Realists affirm the existence of a mind-, concept-, language- and discourse-independent world, maintaining that language can, in principle, be used to refer to such a reality and that truth is a matter of correspondence between linguistic items and the (generally) nonlinguistic elements of the world that "make true" our truths. Antirealists, in contrast, understand the nature of religious language—and language in general—in terms of its use within practices or forms of life, rather than any referential (representational) relations. The major traditions in Western (analytic) philosophy of religion have been evidentialist and realist, but in the twentieth-century philosophers inspired by Wittgenstein were increasingly drawn toward fideist and antirealist views (though it is by no means clear that

Wittgenstein's own ideas can be accurately interpreted in these terms). The status of pragmatist philosophy of religion here is ambivalent.

While these debates are concerned with the nature of religious beliefs and statements from the perspective of "theoretical philosophy," there are no less serious disputes in "practical philosophy." The relation between religion and morality, in particular, is highly unclear. Secular moralists sharply disagree with, say, divine command theorists on the ultimate grounds of ethical principles (and on whether any "ultimacy" is possible here). It remains unclear what the place of religious values in "the good life" might be, and how this issue ought to be discussed in a largely secularized yet multicultural society promoting religious tolerance. Rorty's (1999, 2007) proposal to treat religion as a private affair disconnected from public use of reason, related to his suggestion that traditional philosophical issues should be redescribed as issues in "cultural politics" (i.e., issues about whether, and how, to use certain "vocabularies"), also raised controversy in the early 2000s. However, long before Rorty's ethnocentrist neo-pragmatism, classical pragmatists sought to mediate between rival extremes in various areas of philosophy—and the philosophy of religion is no exception. A thoroughgoing discussion of pragmatist philosophy of religion would not only demonstrate that a truly pragmatist approach in the philosophy of religion need not be Rortyan—for Rorty's version of pragmatism threatens to give up normative criteria for adequately evaluating religious, or any, discourse—but also that a healthy understanding of religious thought presupposes a pragmatic, practice-oriented standpoint. In particular, it may be argued that this pragmatist standpoint is inherently pluralistic. There is no single, absolute, overarching perspective from which religious issues ought to be viewed but a plurality of relevant contexts for asking questions about the meaning, personal and social significance, and rational acceptability of religious views.

The problems of realism versus antirealism and evidentialism versus fideism, among others, receive new interpretations as soon as they are seen from a pragmatist perspective, because religiosity is then understood as a phenomenon within human practices with certain inherent aims and goals, responding to specific human needs and interests, serving certain human values. This by no means precludes rational criticism of religious ways of thinking; on the contrary, such criticism itself is served by better understanding the ways in which religion functions in our practices—or, better, *is* a practice. The science versus religion dialogue vitally needs a comprehensive and tolerant account of both scientific and religious practices and their diverging conceptions of rationality and intellectual (as well as ethical) responsibility. Pragmatism promises to advance such understanding. It promises to offer us pluralism and tolerance without succumbing to uncritical relativism, according to which "anything goes." This is important in our both philosophically and more generally culturally confusing situation.

Arguably, then, pragmatist philosophy of religion will be able to solve, or at least significantly moderate, several key tensions in the philosophy of religion, including especially the tensions between realism and antirealism and evidentalism and fideism, thus enabling us to avoid not just dogmatic religious thinking but also very different crude, un-philosophical views in this field (such as the currently popular attacks on religion by thinkers like Dawkins), thereby eventually yielding a more balanced understanding of the nature of religious life and values than the mainstream paradigms in the field are able to. The leading thought of pragmatist philosophy of religion—or the pragmatic method as applied to the case of religion—is, we have seen, that the theism versus atheism issue cannot be adequately settled from a single, privileged perspective but requires a plurality of perspectives, pragmatically balanced and harmonized in terms of their functional workability in the (would-be) believer's overall account of the ethico-metaphysical problem of God as a problem of her/his personal life and moral deliberation.[21] I believe we may plausibly defend the pragmatically pluralist idea that all these perspectives—even including Rortyan neo-pragmatism, albeit critically viewed—are needed and that the philosophy of religion, if pragmatically adequate, must hence be profoundly *antireductionist*. Not only should pragmatists be religiously tolerant, they should also philosophically tolerate many different (though certainly not all) ways of understanding religion philosophically.

Finally, in the context of pragmatist philosophy of religion, in particular, it is vital to observe that pragmatism is *not* simply a philosophy of "usefulness," especially if usefulness is understood narrowly and subjectively. Religious belief *may*—or may not—be "useful" in individuals' lives in this sense, but that is not the kind of usefulness or satisfactoriness the pragmatic method examines. On the contrary, the pragmatic method in the philosophy of religion should be able to accommodate the theological or religious value—and perhaps also the philosophical value—of externally or instrumentally "useless" activities or practices, such as prayer, which, if interpreted instrumentalistically, may not be "genuinely religious" prayer at all.[22] Engaging in such useless or even "passive" activities may, for a religious person, be crucial in a wider and deeper satisfactoriness of life. In this way, apparently useless practices may play a significant pragmatic role. The task of the pragmatist philosopher of religion is to apply the pragmatic method as widely as possible in order to understand the enormous richness of the potential practical effects that religious ideas may have in people's lives.

The same can be said about many philosophical topics the pragmatist may find worth exploring by means of the pragmatic method. In particular, metaphysical inquiries into what there is, including inquiries into issues in the philosophy of mind, are certainly useless in a narrow and immediate sense, but they may be extremely useful in a broader pragmatic sense. Thus, the standard dichotomy between useful and useless human activities—a dichotomy usually naively instrumentalistically construed—is one of the dualisms that the pragmatic method should lead us to avoid.

Notes

1 For the quote, see James, 1909b, p. 31.
2 See also CP 5.422, 1905; 5.438, 1905; 5.468, c. 1906; 6.481, 1908; 8.191, c. 1904. A somewhat more complicated formulation of the maxim is the following one from 1903: "Pragmatism is the principle that every theoretical judgment expressible in a sentence in the indicative mood is a confused form of thought whose only meaning, if it has any, lies in its tendency to enforce a corresponding practical maxim expressible as a conditional sentence with its apodosis in the imperative mood" (EP2:134–135, 1903). On James's interpretation of the maxim, see also Hingst, 2000. Cf. Thayer, 1968, pp. 7–8.
3 As Perry (1935: II, p. 432n11) notes, James does not in fact *quote* this passage. It is, rather, a paraphrase, though an inaccurate one by Peirce's lights.
4 The third section will briefly compare pragmatism with other philosophical methodologies.
5 Cf. Armstrong's (2004) critical discussion of Quine's (1980) view that the key method of ontology is the examination of the ontological commitments a theory makes. Armstrong prefers the method of identifying the truthmakers that are needed for a given truth to be true.
6 See Kant, 1781/1787; James, 1907; Schiller, 2008; Dewey, 1929; Carnap, 1950; Quine, 1969, 1980; Wittgenstein, 1953; Putnam, 1981, 1990; Goodman, 1978, 1984; Kuhn, 1970; Rorty, 1982, 1991; Sellars, 1963. However, we should not forget Donald Davidson's (1984) famous critique of such forms of relativism and the implicated distinction between a conceptual scheme and its allegedly

scheme-neutral content, or other noteworthy criticisms of conceptual and ontological relativism.

7 I am assuming an ontological sense of both dependence and independence here. Roughly, an entity *a* is ontologically dependent on another entity *b*, if *a* cannot exist unless *b* exists, that is, *b*'s existence is required for *a*'s existence. For example, tropes (or modes) are dependent on the particulars they qualify: if there is no such entity as this particular shirt, its particular shade of red cannot exist (be real) either—unless particulars themselves are construed as bundles of tropes. The relevant notion of ontological (in)dependence must be distinguished from causal (in)dependence (and of course logical (in)dependence). A table is causally dependent on its maker's activities, but when made, it is ontologically independent of them (at least according to realist metaphysicians), because it could remain existing even if its maker disappeared from the world. For more detailed discussions of ontological dependence and independence, see Lowe, 1998, 2006.

8 Pragmatists generally avoid the Kantian transcendental vocabulary, but it does illuminate at least some pragmatist positions fairly well. When James and Dewey, or neo-pragmatists like Putnam, tell us that the world is in some sense a human construction, it is better to understand this (quasi-)transcendentally than straightforwardly causally or factually.

9 This very general problem becomes relevant, for example, in the debate between scientific realism and constructivism in the philosophy of science. I suggested in the "Introduction" that the rise of neo-pragmatism, as well as the renewed interest in the study of classical pragmatism, in the last decades of the twentieth century was to some extent a reaction to the realism issue actively discussed in the philosophy of science at that time. How, then, do pragmatists relate to the controversy over scientific realism versus constructivism? This is an important case of the need to occupy the "middle ground" between implausibly extreme positions. The pragmatic method is often a search for such a via media. Again, there are important tensions here, such as realism versus constructivism and realism versus empiricist instrumentalism. The pragmatic method may be used to settle these and other tensions (which is not to say that no tensions remain). See further Pihlström, 2008b.

10 We may simply speak about scheme-(in)dependence, instead of, say, mind-(in) dependence, practice-(in)dependence, language-(in)dependence, or categorization-(in)dependence, just in order to stick to a uniform terminology. Individual thinkers may use different expressions here. Also, we may speak about entities, intending this as an extremely broad ontological category ranging over such subcategories as particulars (individuals), properties (whether universals or tropes), processes, or even states of affairs. Nothing serious regarding the realism issue depends on these terminological choices.

11 On the distinction between a (mere) distinction and a (harmful) dichotomy, see Putnam, 2002.
12 See, for further elaboration, Pihlström, 2003.
13 For a more comprehensive discussion of the kind of pragmatist "theses" listed above, see Pihlström, 2009c (a paper I have partly used in this section).
14 Phenomenologists working with Maurice Merleau-Ponty's notion of (lived) *body* might challenge this, with good reason. See, for example, Heinämaa, 2003.
15 Peirce's key writings on synechism are from the early 1890s, reprinted in EP1 and EP2. Cf. Pihlström, 2009a, ch. 6.
16 A similar "humanist" picture of pragmatism is provided in Schiller's (2008) writings.
17 This argument is developed by Putnam in a series of works (1981, 1990, 1994, 2002, 2004). See also Pihlström, 2005.
18 Cf. both James's (1902) account of religious mysticism and Dewey's (1934) need to maintain the notion of natural piety, both of which are comparable to Wittgensteinian approaches in the philosophy of religion (which, obviously, are beyond the scope of the present discussion).
19 On "new atheism," see Dawkins, 2006 and Dennett, 2007.
20 Think, again as an analogy, of the realism issue in general metaphysics and its special instances in, for example, the philosophy of science. As we have seen above, pragmatism presents itself as a mediator in this dispute (and others).
21 A particularly relevant meta-level topic in pragmatist philosophy of religion is the relation between metaphysical and ethical issues, paralleling the distinction between theory and practice. The key pragmatist idea here is that theory and practice in general, and metaphysics and ethics in particular, are deeply intertwined—both in the philosophy of religion in particular and in philosophy in general. This view is related to Putnam's defense of the fact-value entanglement (see above). Again, pluralism is a key to this debate: there is no overarching, metaphysically correct "absolute" view on the true nature of values and facts; there are different value-laden human perspectives on this question, and others.
22 Distinguishing between genuine religion and pseudo-religion, or superstition, is notoriously difficult; for some pragmatism-inspired remarks on this problem, see Pihlström, 2007.

3

A History of Pragmatism

James Campbell

Pragmatism has often been seen as a practical new philosophy for the New World; and, as a philosophical movement, it was continuous with the rest of the developing American society. Still, it needs to be distinguished from at least two other pragmatic strains. One of these strains is rooted in the simple practicalism of the traditional American lifestyle. In part, this admitted pragmatism reflects a popular anti-intellectualism that sees action as more important than thinking, especially when the latter is speculative or purely ornamental or "useless." In part, this practicalism also reflects the immense felt task of taming the American Frontier, where idleness was suspect. A second pragmatic strain in American society, more or less present in all societies, is the shallow opportunism of self-styled pragmatists in many fields of endeavor, individuals whose single-minded concern with personal victory is condemned by William James as "the exclusive worship of the bitch-Goddess *SUCCESS*" (James, 1992, 11:267). Distinct from these two strains is philosophical pragmatism—the work of James, Charles Sanders Peirce, John Dewey, and others—that developed a theory of meaning and a theory of truth grounded in a broader vision of an adequate human existence.

An initial sketch of this larger pragmatic vision might consider four of its central themes. The first is pragmatism's attempt to understand our *natural place.* Here we find humans as experimenters who are both celebrating our relationship with nature and striving for control of our natural situation. We find as well post-Darwinian explorations of the embodied human organism, and of human consciousness and self-consciousness as the means to understand and direct our lives. A second theme in this pragmatic vision is a series of hypotheses about *experience* in its various forms. If we attend in an unprejudiced manner to the stream of experience as it comes, for example, we will more fully grasp its meaning and be better prepared to resist routinization. Similarly, adopting a critical stance toward experience offers us a means to challenge the tyranny of dogma and to replace it with values developed from the numerous apparent goods. A third theme that is central to pragmatism is *possibility*. This emphasis upon openness includes both fostering means for individuals to make more of their lives in a practical fashion and appreciating the connection between the everyday and the eternal. Further, pragmatism's emphasis upon possibility recognizes that we can use our tentative webs of knowledge, without foundation or finality, to help meliorate our existence. Here, both individuals' ability to create systems of living personal beliefs, compelling and free from the interference of others, and their responsibility to develop the educational and social possibilities by means of which society can present vibrant possibilities to future generations, are important. A fourth theme central to an adequate understanding of pragmatism is *community*, which serves both as a means and a goal. Vibrant community provides the means through which cooperative inquiry tests and directs social practice. Without losing a sense of the importance of individuals, the community of cooperative inquirers helps to direct the intellectual life of society to a recognition and celebration of the enrichments of shared existence. As it moves into the future, the pragmatic community addresses our problems of living—metaphysical and scientific and social—and challenges the purely intellectual solutions to which philosophers too often acquiesce.

A quick survey of the early history of pragmatism would consider such high points as: the Metaphysical Club of Cambridge, Massachusetts, in the early 1870s; a long period of latency that included Peirce's essays in *The Journal of Speculative Philosophy* (Peirce, 1982, 2:161–272) and *Popular Science Monthly* (Peirce, 1982, 3:241–338); James's 1897 volume, *The Will to Believe* (James, 1897), followed by his 1898 address, "Philosophical Conceptions and Practical Results," at the University of California in 1898 (James, 1898); the development of the Chicago School from 1894 through at least the publication of the cooperative volume *Studies in Logical Theory* in 1903 (Dewey et al., 1903) and Dewey's departure in 1904; the publication of James's *Pragmatism* in 1907 (James, 1907), and *The Meaning of Truth* in 1909 (James, 1909); and the appearance of *Creative Intelligence: Essays in the Pragmatic Attitude* in 1917 (Dewey et al., 1917).

In his *Pragmatism*, William James indicates that the term is "derived from the same Greek word πρᾶγμα, meaning action, from which our words 'practice' and 'practical' come" (James, 1907, p. 28). He further notes that "pragmatism" was a term that like "post-structuralism" or "modernism" in our time—was in the air. As he writes, "at present it fairly spots the pages of the philosophic journals"

(James, 1907, p. 29). James lays out a very broad ancestry for what he calls his "new name for some old ways of thinking" (James 1907, p. 1), indicating that, while Peirce was the founder of the modern pragmatic movement, in some form or other pragmatism had been practiced by such seemingly diverse thinkers as Socrates, Aristotle, Locke, Berkeley, Hume, and James Mill (cf. James, 1898, pp. 268–269; 1907, p. 30; Peirce, 1931, 5.11–12). While James's listing may accurately delineate the roots of the pragmatic spirit that he felt existed in the Western philosophical tradition, it fails to explore any possible American roots. Similarly, he underplays the role of Kant, or at least of Kantian ideas. Kant had distinguished sharply between *praktisch* and *pragmatisch,* and Peirce dutifully avoided the former because of its *a priori* associations. In Peirce's own words: "for one who had learned philosophy out of Kant . . . *praktisch* and *pragmatisch* were as far apart as the two poles, the former belonging in a region of thought where no mind of the experimentalist type can ever make sure of solid ground under his feet, the latter expressing relation to some definite human purpose" (Peirce, 1931, 5.412). In spite of Peirce's Kantian terminology, however, more idiomatic uses of the term continued, and efforts to explicate the nature of the relationship between thinking and practical activity became an ongoing task of the proponents of pragmatism. While this might seem to be an unlikely base upon which to build a philosophical movement, pragmatism became a powerful force within philosophical circles and a tremendously popular topic of discussion outside of them.

Peirce

Charles Sanders Peirce (1839–1914) was a mathematical and scientific genius of the first order who, for reasons both personal and social, came late to public recognition from the philosophical and broader intellectual community. Peirce describes his own work at one point as "the attempt of a physicist to make such conjecture as to the constitution of the universe as the methods of science may permit, with the aid of all that has been done by previous philosophers." His goal was not to develop demonstrable truths but rather to advance likely hypotheses that would grow out of science's past efforts and that would be "capable of being verified or refuted by future observers" (Peirce, 1931, 1.7). We are these observers; and, for Peirce, we are at our best when we are engaged in cooperative attempts to overcome our intellectual problems.

Central to Peirce's work is his emphasis upon the importance of cooperative inquiry. Dewey writes that Peirce was "notable among writers on logical theory for his explicit recognition of the necessity of the social factor in the determination of evidence and its probative force." Further, Dewey notes that Peirce "was the first writer on logic to make inquiry and its methods the primary and ultimate source of logical subject-matter" (Dewey, 1938, pp. 484 n.3, 17 n.1). Building upon his assumption of ongoing social inquiry, Peirce continues that truth itself is to be understood as the result of "endless investigation" or study that goes on "forever" (Peirce, 1931, 5.565). And, because Peirce writes that "[t]he opinion which is fated to be ultimately agreed to by all who investigate, is what we mean by the truth" (Peirce, 1931, 5.407), he admonished individual inquirers to maintain an attitude of doubt and openness at each particular point in the cooperative process.

"Do not block the way of inquiry," Peirce writes (Peirce, 1931, 1.135). In our lives as inquirers, we should live by the cautious attitude that he calls "fallibilism," that contains among its tenets the following assumptions: no questions are unanswerable, no answers are absolutely true, no formulations are final, no level of examination is ultimate, and so on. In inquiry, there is always more that can be done; and even a failed experiment is an advance, for all possibilities must be considered. The human weakness against which we must be ever on guard, Peirce reminds us, is our often-demonstrated willingness to settle issues too soon by acquiescing to hasty and inadequate methods for the fixation of belief (cf. Peirce, 1931, 1.13, 5.358). We must thus reject what conforms to personal dogmatism, however simple; resist society's unquestioned traditions, however important to social cohesion; and challenge what seems most "reasonable," however comfortable. Peirce's advice is to turn to the methods of science, including cooperation, testing, verification, and publication.

A correlate of Peirce's call for ongoing cooperative inquiry is his belief that we could develop more precision in our philosophical formulations if we could develop a theory of meaning that offered a more adequate public criterion. The focus of Peirce's efforts here was in clarifying our use of "intellectual concepts" or "of hard words and of abstract concepts" like "hard," "weight," "force," and "reality" (Peirce, 1931, 5.467, 5.464, 5.403–5.410). He writes that "a *conception*, that is, the rational purport of a word or other expression, lies exclusively in its conceivable bearing upon the conduct of life." Consequently, he continues, "since obviously nothing that might not result from experiment can have any direct bearing upon conduct, if one can define accurately all the conceivable experimental phenomena which the affirmation or denial of a concept could imply, one will have therein a complete definition of the concept" (Peirce, 1931, 5.412). The important points in this theory of meaning, in addition to its connection to long-term, group inquiry, are that Peirce is interested in applying it only to certain words or concepts and that he requires a consideration of all effects. The weaknesses that this version of pragmatism displays, from James's point of view, follow directly from Peirce's emphases: it focuses too narrowly on the issues of the natural sciences, mathematics and formal logic, and it emphasizes too strongly the public forum of verification.

James

William James (1842–1910) was a trained, if nonpracticing, physician, more interested in the novel and the unique than Peirce. Thus James preferred to explore more individual aspects of experience. And, while James saw himself as carrying forward Peirce's pragmatism, he formulated it more broadly. James wanted to develop pragmatism into a tool for overcoming apparently insoluble philosophical controversies. "The pragmatic method," he writes, "is primarily a method of settling metaphysical disputes that otherwise might be interminable" (James, 1907, p. 28). Although the initial example that he uses is the homey one of the squirrel on the trunk of the tree, the issues to which he intended to apply this method are matters of larger human and philosophical concern. Among them are the questions of substance and attributes, materialism versus theism, and free will or determinism. "The pragmatic method in such cases is to try to interpret each notion by tracing its respective practical consequences," he continues. "What difference would it practically make to anyone if this notion rather than that notion were true?" (James, 1907, p. 28).

While James's concern with results is continuous with the work of Peirce, this shift is fundamental; and, seen in the light of his personal interests, all of James's modifications to Peirce's approach appear to be deliberate. He writes, for example, that "the principle of pragmatism . . . should be expressed more broadly than Mr. Peirce expresses it" (James, 1898, p. 259). James moves away from Peirce's concern with long-term effects for the group of inquirers and his interest in the full spectrum of effects, as might be appropriate when studying the specifics of a planet's orbit or the etiology of HIV/AIDS. And, perhaps most importantly, James moves beyond Peirce's tightly focused concern with only certain words and ideas to consider the meaning of broad philosophical doctrines. James thus revises what he calls "Peirce's principle" to allow for both broader application and narrower verification. As James writes, for example, "the effective meaning of any philosophic proposition can always be brought down to some particular consequence, in our future practical experience" (James, 1898, p. 259).

In addition, James went still further, bringing into a central position in his pragmatism the topic of truth. For James, pragmatism should have something to say not only about the *meaning* but also about the *meaningfulness,* and ultimately about the truth or falsity, of philosophic positions. Once we are able to move beyond idle philosophical controversies to real ones—that is, controversies about which we can "show some practical difference that must follow from one side or the other's being right" (James, 1907, p. 28)—James believes that we can use the pragmatic method to decide truth and falsity. As he writes, "the whole function of philosophy ought to be to find out what definite difference it will make to you and me, at definite instants of our life, if this world-formula or that world-formula be the one which is true" (James, 1898, p. 260). For example, the conflicting answers to the question of materialism versus theism yield what he calls "opposite outlooks of experience." Materialism, for its part, means "simply the denial that the moral order is eternal, and the cutting off of ultimate hopes," whereas theism means "the affirmation of an eternal moral order and the letting loose of hope" (James, 1898, pp. 263–264). Peirce's emphasis upon what in the long run is fated to be agreed upon by the limitless group of belief-suspending inquirers offers us little help in deciding such questions.

For James, the question of "God or no God?" can be reduced to the more personal question of "promise or no promise?" (James, 1909, p. 6). James, as we might surmise from his emphasis on hope, maintains that a position may be considered to be true as the result of a test different from Peirce's: "Any idea upon which we can ride, so to speak; any idea that will carry us prosperously from any one part of our experience to any other part, linking things satisfactorily, working securely, simplifying, saving labor; is true for just so much, true in so far forth, true *instrumentally*" (James, 1907, p. 34). For James, an idea or a philosophical position is true if it satisfies this test of workability. Using as an example a matter close to James's heart, if the theistic viewpoint provides what he calls "*a value for concrete life*," it will be true, he writes, "*in the sense of being good for so much*" (James, 1907, p. 40).

Because of his enthusiastic public championing of these unorthodox views in *Pragmatism* and elsewhere, James quickly became the center of a firestorm of criticism. Peirce himself thought James's changes were harmful; and he rechristened his own, narrower position "pragmaticism," a name he thought would be "ugly enough to be safe from kidnappers" (Peirce, 1931, 5.414). But James's position, however startling it may initially seem, contains many valuable aspects. One of these is that, because his understanding of human nature grounds the activities of mind in the problems of living, his position connects truth with other human values. As James puts it, "truth is *one species of good*" (James, 1907, p. 42). A second value of James's pragmatism is that, as with Peirce's (cf. Peirce, 1931, 5.427), it is forward-looking rather than backward-looking. Pragmatism exemplifies, James writes, "[t]*he attitude of looking away from first things, principles, 'categories', supposed necessities; and of looking towards last things, fruits, consequences, facts*" (James, 1907, p. 32). For James, this means that truth is a process in which we play a role; and, in cases like marriages or careers, our ongoing contributions can be decisive. While "*for rationalism reality is ready-made and complete from all eternity*," he writes, "*for pragmatism it is still in the making, and awaits part of its complexion from the future*" (James, 1907, p. 123). A third value of James's view is his emphasis on the importance of the practical over the purely intellectual. Rather than being satisfied with terms like "God" or "Reason" as what he calls "solving names," James requires us to "bring out of each word its practical cash-value, set it at work within the stream of [our] experience" (James, 1907, pp. 31–32). Purely intellectual solutions solve nothing but purely intellectual problems; and, for James, "[t]he earth of things, long thrown into shadow by the glories of the upper ether, must resume its rights" (James, 1907, p. 62).

Still, James's position on the nature and possibilities of pragmatism has been seen to contain potentially problematic aspects. Some of them can be quickly cleared away before turning to the central issue of James's understanding of truth. The first is James's claim, unsettling to some, that truth lives in large measure "on a credit system." As a result, most of our lives are spent only loosely engaged with truths like the realities of locations and events whose verification we never bother to perform. "We trade on each other's truth," he writes (James, 1907, p. 100). Except for James's idiosyncratic use of the term "truth" here, this is precisely the point made by Peirce when he writes, "our knowledge is never absolute but always swims, as it were, in a continuum of uncertainty and of indeterminacy" (Peirce, 1931, 1.171). A second side issue is James's belief that truth "*happens* to an idea." Rather than focusing upon abstracted propositions or upon static relationships of unchanging validity, his concern is with inquiry, with the process by means of which a particular belief or idea that *"becomes true, is made true by events"* (James, 1907, p. 97). Third, there is no validity to the charge that James somehow believes that any delusion whatever can be true. *"'Reality' is in general what truths have to take account of,"* he writes (James, 1907, p. 117). "Woe to him whose beliefs play fast and loose with the order which realities follow in his experience: they will lead him nowhere or else make false connexions" (James, 1907, p. 99).

The central difficulty with James's position on truth is the problem that, in Peircean terms, it would allow people to "fix belief" too soon, based upon limited evidence or only individual confirmation. As an example of James's impulsiveness, we can consider the following: "A new opinion counts as 'true' just in proportion as it gratifies the individual's desire to assimilate the novel in his experience to his beliefs in stock" (James, 1907, p. 36). The weakness of James's approach here is that it does not require us to take the time necessary to refine the felt problem sufficiently or to evaluate proposed solutions adequately. It is in such instances of aborted inquiry that, for example, prejudices, however false, manage to "work." On a related theme, even if we recognize the accuracy of the vernacular expression that many ideas may "contain a little truth," we still need not defend such troublesome phrases as James's "true in so far forth," "truest" (James, 1907, pp. 34, 36), or "true for *me*" (James, 1911, p. 113). We need to be more hesitant and skeptical; we need to test our new opinion in different contexts and consult with other inquirers. But, as Peirce writes, all too often "as soon as a firm belief is reached we are entirely satisfied, whether the belief be true or false" (Peirce, 1931, 5.375). James's weakness here is thus not that he would have us call the false "true," but that he would allow us to call the initially workable "true" without sufficient testing.

There are reasons for the emphases in James's pragmatism, just as there are for the differing emphases in Peirce's. Whereas Peirce was interested in advancing scientific methods and practice, the more broadly humanistic James was interested in preventing what he saw as science's potential destruction of vital meanings. As he remarks at one point, his enemy is "the baleful social result, if 'Science' in the shape of abstraction, priggishness, and dessication, should lord it over all" (James, 1992, 10:450). His fear is that the rigors of scientific verification will strangle the beliefs necessary to live. As evidence of the reality of this danger, James cites the maxim of William Kingdon Clifford: "It is wrong always, everywhere, and for anyone, to believe anything upon insufficient evidence" (James, 1897, p. 18). The key issue here is what constitutes sufficiency of evidence, and James's position differs sharply from Clifford's (and Peirce's). As Dewey writes, James "maintained the thesis that the greater part of philosophic problems and especially those which touch on religious fields are of such a nature that they are not susceptible of decisive evidence one way or the other" (Dewey, 1925, p. 10). Thus, James writes that at least in certain contexts, not limited only to the religious, "we have the right to believe at our own risk any hypothesis that is live enough to tempt our will" (James, 1897, p. 32).

While James perhaps thought that *Pragmatism* would bring some clarification to the discussion, in fact the opposite happened; and the growing pragmatic perspective offered no finely honed and unified philosophical position. Although some individuals registered dismay (cf. Lovejoy, 1908), no resolution should have been expected. As Frederick J. E. Woodbridge writes in his review of James's *Pragmatism*, "there is as yet no precise general agreement as to just what pragmatism is." Further, he notes that "those who call themselves pragmatists and those who are called so by others exhibit often such marked differences in their individual thinking that one is not always sure who the genuine pragmatists are." He concludes that any attempt to decide what the movement means has itself to be "tentative and subject to revision" (Woodbridge, 1907, pp. 227–228). In a later piece, Woodbridge notes that discussions of pragmatism had been sidetracked into considerations of the question of truth. The promise of pragmatism of helping to clarify our ideas, he writes, "was speedily put into a position of minor importance" when pragmatism became "a controversy about the nature of truth." Rather than "encouraging analyses of the meaning of terms and ideas in the contexts wherein they occur," this controversy "encouraged a debate about the foundations of belief and the criteria of truth and falsity. How can we determine when our ideas are true, became a more important question than how can we determine what they mean" (Woodbridge, 1921, pp. 541–542).

Dewey and the Chicago School

We can now turn to a consideration of the social pragmatists of the Chicago School, who attempted a combination of the critical and cooperative spirit of Peirce with a focus on the issues of general and direct human concern that interested James. This stream within pragmatism incorporates prior aspects like a metaphysics that emphasizes process and relations, a naturalistic and evolutionary understanding of human existence, and an analysis of intellectual activity as problem-oriented and as benefitting from historically developed methods. But the Chicago School also saw itself as bringing to a natural culmination the earlier themes by offering an emphasis upon the democratic reconstruction of society through an understanding of the role of social institutions.

John Dewey (1859–1952) is historically the most important figure among the social pragmatists, although his tenure at the University of Chicago was the briefest (1894–1904). During his decade at Chicago, and later decades at Columbia University (1905–1939), Dewey's efforts in philosophy demonstrated a seamless connection between the life of the mind and a concern with the moral, aesthetic, educational, and other problems of modern social life. His generally scientific approach to generally moral issues is what Dewey called his "Instrumentalism" (Dewey, 1925, pp. 13–18), his attempt to apply the gains of pragmatism to practical judgments. He writes that the "fundamental idea" throughout the various strands of the pragmatic movement is "that action and opportunity justify themselves only to the degree in which they render life more reasonable and increase its value" (Dewey, 1925, p. 19). Instrumentalism offers a logic of practical activity, and Dewey hoped to use it to foster social reconstruction. By means of this instrumentalism, he also attempts to recast the "truth" question that had entangled James to emphasize inquiry, focusing on "warranted assertion" rather than "belief" or "knowledge" (Dewey, 1938, pp. 14–16). At the same time, however, Dewey emphasizes the broad application of this instrumentalism to the reconstruction of social institutions in order to create more reasonable and valuable lives for all. This is the basis of his efforts in areas as diverse as economic policy and legal practice, educational theorizing and political organization.

George Herbert Mead (1863–1931) came to the University of Chicago in 1894 and taught there until his death. In addition to his classroom efforts, he approached the city as an urban laboratory for his pragmatic endeavors, engaging himself especially in educational and labor issues. In an ongoing series of lectures later published as *Mind, Self, and Society* (Mead, 1934), Mead integrates his philosophical interests with his social work. In particular, he offers us his analysis of the intricacies of the self and its social development. For Mead, to be able to function as an individual member of a community at any given time, it is necessary that the person's self contain both aspects existing in a creative balance: the "me" bringing forth the possible ways of the community, and the "I" evaluating and choosing among them. And, for this balance to continue through time, Mead maintains that it is necessary to have an adequate system of egalitarian institutions.

James Hayden Tufts (1862–1942) taught at the University of Chicago from 1892 to 1930. Like Mead, Tufts also combined extensive social work in educational and labor issues with his classroom duties. Throughout his extensive writings, there is an emphasis upon the fundamental importance of institutions in human life and the ongoing need to modify and adapt them to new situations. A clear example of his understanding of institutional reconstruction can be found in his discussions of law, an institution that serves not only to "protect stability" but also to "adjust to change" (Tufts, 1992, p. 332). In our deliberations to establish and maintain justice in our changing world, he writes, we need to consider "not merely the principles recognized in the seventeenth and eighteenth centuries, but the emerging principles of the twentieth" (Tufts, 1992, p. 152). In Tufts's rejection of the view that current social justice can be found in conformity to past arrangements—even if these arrangements were accepted as just at the time—and elsewhere in his discussions of social reconstruction, we see the application of the evolutionary worldview of social pragmatism to the problems of the contemporary situation.

Recent scholarship (cf. Seigfried, 1996) has broadened our recognition of the reach of the Chicago School to include the workings of such institutions as Hull House, and especially the contributions of its cofounder, Jane Addams (1860–1935). In addition to her engagement with educational and labor issues, Addams worked incessantly with the poor and underprivileged of her Chicago neighborhood (cf. Addams, 1910). As her pragmatic activities continued over time, Addams became more convinced of the necessity for an explicitly feminist approach to social reconstruction, and to international attempts to foster peace (cf. Addams, 1906). Through her efforts, and those of the other social pragmatists, a valuable communal approach to advancing social reconstruction through creative intelligence was created.

Later pragmatism

An important question to consider in closing is that of the later development of the pragmatic movement. The familiar story refers to a sort of "golden age" of American pragmatism that continued through the period we have been considering until perhaps the beginning of the Great Depression in 1929, or the start of World War II in 1939, or the death of Dewey in 1952. This period of pragmatic preeminence was then followed, it is usually thought, by a period of marginalization during which pragmatism was supplanted by more scientific and linguistic approaches to philosophy. Pragmatism is then thought to have recovered more recently, resulting in a contemporary renaissance. Running through this familiar account is the underexplored theme of the professionalization of philosophy in America.

Woodbridge, for example, writes in 1929 that, "[a]s itself a philosophy, [pragmatism] is now more a memory than a force" (Woodbridge, 1929, p. 541). More interesting from the issue of philosophical professionalization is the view of Arthur Edward Murphy, who notes in 1945 that "[t]he great influence of [pragmatism] in allied and related fields has not been matched by an equally general acceptance in philosophy itself." Murphy attributes this weakness of pragmatism within philosophy primarily to "the continuing stubborn concern of most professional philosophers with just those hard and technical problems from which the instrumentalist theory of meaning was supposed to have emancipated their subject." We may not want to follow Murphy when he maintains that these technical problems "are just the issues that men have always had to deal with when they tried to solve their problems *philosophically*," or that "the pragmatists, in their zeal to get on with good works, have bypassed these problems, when their job as philosophers was to solve them" (Murphy, 1945, pp. 51–52); but he is surely correct that professional philosophers have continued to puzzle over these problems. Murphy is similarly correct that within the philosophy profession a concern with what he disparages as "good works" has counted for little; and, as the profession developed, pragmatism—especially social pragmatism—was eclipsed.

As I interpret the history of pragmatism (cf. Campbell, 2006, pp. 277–291), its rise was never as high as the traditional story suggests; and its fall, from a more modest perch, came much earlier. As a movement within the philosophy profession, pragmatism was a powerful contributor to the demise of nineteenth-century American idealism. Unfortunately, once that task was accomplished, pragmatism was itself almost immediately swept from center stage by its more intellectual and profession-friendly cousin, realism. Pragmatism thus functioned as only a modest brake on the rush to philosophical professionalization; and, while it ultimately stirred up a great deal of discussion in the broader press and caused some fundamental changes in other disciplines, there was less ongoing interest in pragmatism within philosophy departments. For pragmatism, however, with its fundamental inclination toward the practical possibilities of creative intelligence, professional success in philosophy remained of secondary importance. The storm that followed James's *Pragmatism* thus represented not the beginning of any "golden age" for pragmatism as a force within the American philosophy profession but rather the pinnacle of its success. The 1910–1920s in the United States were a period in which various versions of philosophical realism struggled among themselves, and against the remnants of idealism and pragmatism, for the soul of the philosophy profession. By the late 1920s this battle was long over, in part because the great organic metaphor that had driven philosophic thinking in America since Emerson had been overcome by the new imagery of mathematical physics.

Where Charles Darwin had once been the patron saint of American philosophers, Albert Einstein and a new set of issues now rose to prominence. The abandonment of the organic metaphor by philosophers was due in part to the fact that this whole line of inquiry appeared to many as exhausted, or worse drifting into behaviorism. It was also due to the fact that newly recognized problems and newly developing tools in the overlapping areas of logic, mathematics, and physics offered fresh and fecund alternatives. Like its subject-matter life, biology was fuzzy and indeterminate; but the new areas of endeavor were, or at least seemed to be, clean and precise.

Within the ranks of American philosophers, pragmatism has maintained a modest existence; and a number of professionally important figures—C. I. Lewis (1883–1964), W. V. O. Quine (1908–2000), Hilary Putnam (b.1926), and others—have continued to present themselves as working within the pragmatic tradition. Their continuities with the earlier pragmatists were often overlooked, in part because their interests, along with the interests of most of the rest of the philosophy profession, had been redirected away from biology, and then narrowed into more professionalized discussions of epistemology and language. Still, a consideration of many of their central themes shows continuity with much of the earlier pragmatic movement. These individuals continued to explore topics like the adjustment of old ideas to new contexts, the rejection of dichotomies like the analytic/synthetic distinction, the rejection of the "given," and the hypothesis that science is self-correcting when it is understood as fallible and continuous with philosophy (cf. Bernstein, 1992, pp. 818–827).

Most recently, there has been an attempted reconstruction of the pragmatic movement by neo-pragmatism at the hands of Richard Rorty (1931–2007) and others. Aiming initially at the core of analytic philosophy, Rorty offered a critique of the profession's attempts to ground knowledge claims and prove indubitable conclusions (cf. Rorty, 1979). In their place, Rorty later suggested the prizing of the ideas of insightful individuals of whatever disciplines and the solidarity of liberal democracy to address central human problems (cf. Rorty, 1999).

Additionally, all throughout the period of pragmatic marginalization, there has been a continuing stream of pragmatists who were never seduced by the lure of professionalized philosophy, and who continued to work within the general biological spirit of the earlier figures. Not all of them were philosophers, but all of them keenly felt the importance of addressing the problems of men and women. Among the pragmatist philosophers who have rejected the profession's focus on the internalizing quest for knowledge as the main task of the discipline are a number of individuals—like John Lachs (b. 1932) and John J. McDermott (b. 1932)—who have continued to ask the fundamental question of what thought is for (cf. Lachs, 1995; McDermott, 2007). These thinkers have remained true to the pragmatic mission of public philosophy, with its implications for education and democracy.

References

Addams, J. (1906), *Newer Ideals of Peace*. New York: Macmillan.
—(1910), *Twenty Years at Hull-House*. New York: Macmillan.
Bernstein, R. J. (1992), "The Resurgence of Pragmatism", *Social Research*, 59, (4), 813–840.
Campbell, J. (2006), *A Thoughtful Profession: The Early Years of the American Philosophical Association*. Chicago: Open Court.
Dewey, J. (1925), "The Development of American Pragmatism," in J. A. Boydston (ed.) 1981–1990, *The Later Works of John Dewey, 1925–1953*. Carbondale: Southern Illinois University Press. Vol.2, pp.3–21.
—(1938), *Logic: The Theory of Inquiry, Later Works*, volume 12, Carbondale: Southern Illinois University Press.
Dewey, J., et al. (1903), *Studies in Logical Theory*. Chicago: University of Chicago Press.
—(1917), *Creative Intelligence: Essays in the Pragmatic Attitude*. New York: Henry Holt.
James, W. (1897), *The Will to Believe and Other Essays in Popular Philosophy*. Cambridge: Harvard University Press, 1979.
—(1898), "Philosophical Conceptions and Practical Results". In James (1907), *Pragmatism: A New Name for Some Old Ways of Thinking*. Cambridge: Harvard University Press, pp. 257–270.
—(1907), *Pragmatism: A New Name for Some Old Ways of Thinking*. Cambridge: Harvard University Press, 1975.
—(1909), *The Meaning of Truth: A Sequel to 'Pragmatism'*. Cambridge: Harvard University Press, 1975.
—(1911), *Some Problems of Philosophy*. Cambridge: Harvard University Press, 1979.

—(1992), *The Correspondence of William James*, twelve volumes. Ed. J. J. McDermott. Charlottesville: University Press of Virginia, 1992-2004.

Lachs, J. (1995), *The Relevance of Philosophy to Life*. Nashville: Vanderbilt University Press.

Lovejoy, A. O. (1908), "The Thirteen Pragmatisms". *The Journal of Philosophy, Psychology, and Scientific Methods*, Part 1, 5/1 (2 January 1908), 5-12; Part 2, 5/2 (16 January 1908), 29-39.

McDermott, J. J. (2007), *The Drama of Possibility: Experience as Philosophy of Culture*. Ed. D. R. Anderson. New York: Fordham University Press.

Mead, G. H. (1934), *Mind, Self, and Society from the Standpoint of a Social Behaviorist*. Ed. C. W. Morris. Chicago: University of Chicago Press.

Murphy, A. E. (1945), "The Situation in Modern Philosophy", in B. Blanshard, et al. (eds), *Philosophy in American Education: Its Tasks and Opportunities*. New York: Harper, pp.43-65.

Peirce, C. S. (1931), *Collected Papers of Charles Sanders Peirce*, eight volumes. Eds. C. Hartshorne, P. Weiss and A. W. Burks. Cambridge: Harvard University Press, 1931-1958.

—(1982), *Writings of Charles S. Peirce: A Chronological Edition*. Eds M. H. Fisch, et al. Bloomington: Indiana UP.

Rorty, R. (1979), *Philosophy and the Mirror of Nature*. Princeton: Princeton University Press.

—(1999), *Philosophy and Social Hope*. London: Penguin.

Seigfried, C. H. (1996), *Pragmatism and Feminism: Reweaving the Social Fabric*. Chicago: University of Chicago Press.

Tufts, J. H. (1992), *Selected Writings of James Hayden Tufts*. Ed. J. Campbell. Carbondale: Southern Illinois University Press.

Woodbridge, F. J. E. (1907), "Pragmatism and Education," *Educational Review*, 34, (3), 227-240.

—(1921), "The Promise of Pragmatism," *The Journal of Philosophy*, 26, (20), 541-552.

Part Two

Current Research and Issues

4

Epistemology, Logic, and Inquiry

John Capps

Pragmatism is, in many ways, a divided house. Despite its founders' attempts to present it as a general philosophical method, applicable to a wide range of topics and areas, and despite the wide-ranging interests of early figures such as Peirce, James, and Dewey, pragmatism since the 1950s has generally diverged into two wings. On the one side is pragmatism as applied to ethics, politics, social theory, law, aesthetics, and other normative topics. On the other side is pragmatism as applied to epistemology, logic, science, linguistics, and other areas usually regarded as more descriptive. This chapter will focus primarily on the latter set of epistemological concerns.

But, first, some caveats. The distinction between normative and descriptive areas is, as any pragmatist knows, deeply fraught.[1] One reason that early pragmatists ranged so widely was that they questioned the underlying fact/value distinction that draws a sharp distinction between, say, epistemology (as the study of what we can know and how) and ethics (as the study of what we ought to do). Thus, while pointing out that pragmatism has these two wings, I am not claiming to find this division natural, necessary, or particularly appealing. The fact of the matter, instead, is that pragmatism in the twentieth century underwent a number of changes as it came into contact with other philosophical movements and, by the end, it had changed significantly from its founders' earlier intentions.

Thus, the standard account of pragmatism in the twentieth century has it falling into a period of obscurity around WWII, existing in truncated form in the epistemological writings of such figures as W. V. O Quine, Wilfrid Sellars, and Nelson Goodman,[2] being revived in the late 1970s through the attention of, among others, Richard Rorty and Hilary Putnam, and finally becoming a more standard, albeit not dominant, part of philosophical discussion ever since. The standard account also notes that pragmatism survived as a primarily epistemological theory in the period between 1950 and 1980, but that since then its importance to ethics, political theory, and aesthetics has come back to the fore.[3]

There are problems with this standard account, as historians of philosophy have pointed out,[4] but it has value as a general way of orienting our discussion: in philosophy, as elsewhere, a compelling story can have benefits out of proportion to its actual truth. In particular, this story is noteworthy for recognizing the importance of pragmatism's epistemological side in helping keep pragmatism alive during the postwar period. It is ironic, then, that this side has been downplayed after about 1980, as pragmatism came to be more fully applied to normative matters.[5]

Epistemology

Epistemology (or the study of knowledge) has traditionally focused on the difference between, on the one hand, believing something that just happens to be true versus, on the other hand, really *knowing* something. This is a familiar but crucial distinction. While lucky guesses and true opinions may be good enough on a multiple choice exam, we value actual knowledge much more: being lucky is one thing, but being a knowledgeable expert is something else and, if given the choice, we will always prefer knowledge over hunches and guesswork. Of course, this raises a set of thorny issues with which epistemologists are well familiar. To name a few: what is knowledge? what is truth? what are the limits of our possible knowledge? and what makes a belief well-supported as opposed to unjustified?

From the beginning epistemology has been at the center of pragmatism: before pragmatists ever focused on politics, education, aesthetics, religion, and other topics, pragmatism was concerned with epistemological issues. If we look at the writings that began the pragmatist movement—C. S. Peirce's articles published in *Popular Science Monthly* (1877–1878)—we find that he defined pragmatism primarily as an epistemological theory and in opposition to other ways of thinking about truth, knowledge, and inquiry.

For example, in "The Fixation of Belief" (1877/1986) Peirce claims, first, that the pursuit of truth begins with "real and living," and not merely theoretical, doubt and, second, that it ends with propositions that are not "absolutely indubitable" but rather "perfectly free from all *actual* doubt" (1877/1986, p. 248, emphasis added). These two claims distinguish Peirce's pragmatic epistemology both from Descartes' epistemology—which begins by supposing that we might all be victims of a deceptive evil demon and ends, as a result, by invoking logically necessary beliefs to put this supposition to rest—as well as from the mainstream epistemology that descends from Descartes. Peirce instead takes inquiry to be a profoundly practical affair grounded in practical realities. His project is not to defeat radical skepticism, arrive at eternal certainties, or argue on the basis of indubitable or incorrigible truths. His project is to examine how inquiry *actually* proceeds and determine how to make our inquiries more reliable. Thus even in this early essay we find several enduring hallmarks of pragmatic epistemology: these include an avoidance of Cartesian epistemology and artificial skeptical puzzles, an interest in how inquiry actually proceeds, and a focus on what is practically—not just theoretically—necessary for inquiry to go forward.

Truth

Peirce's touchstone is what he calls the "scientific method" of pursuing truths, a method he claims is more reliable than others for arriving at beliefs that are stable enough to be used in further inquiries: inquiries that then give us additional stable beliefs that can be used to make further inquiries, and on and on. In his second well-known article from 1877–1878, "How to Make our Ideas Clear" (1878/1986), Peirce gives his famous account of what "truth" pragmatically means. A true belief, he claims, is one "which is fated to be ultimately agreed to by all who investigate" (1878/1986, p. 273). This account of truth follows directly on the heels of Peirce's pragmatic theory of meaning (arguably *the* core commitment of pragmatism) that the meaning of an idea is a function of its practical consequences. Thus, Peirce is claiming that true beliefs have the practical consequence that they are maximally reliable and will withstand indefinite scrutiny—unlike false beliefs, which will fail these tests. To call a belief "true," in other words, is shorthand for claiming that it will withstand this indefinite scrutiny and can be relied on as one attempts to discover additional truths about the world.

Epistemology is likewise central to the work of William James—who, building on Peirce's writings, was the first great popularizer of pragmatism. James' *Pragmatism: A New Name for Some Old Ways of Thinking* (1907/1975) focuses on the idea of truth almost from the outset. Glossary "What Pragmatism Means" even blurs the distinction between the pragmatic theory of meaning and the pragmatic theory of truth: according to James, the "pragmatic method" is to ask "what difference would it practically make to any one if this notion rather than that notion were true?" (1907/1975, p. 28). While he seems here to define the pragmatic method in terms of truth, he then defines truth using the pragmatic method. He writes that:

> Ideas (which themselves are but parts of our experience) become true just in so far as they help us to get into satisfactory relations with other parts of our experience.... Any idea upon which we can ride, so to speak; any idea that will carry us prosperously from any one part of our experience to any other part, linking things satisfactorily, working securely, simplifying, saving labor; is true for just so much, true in so far forth, true *instrumentally*. (1907/1975, p. 34)

James' conception of truth recognizes both its practical value (the word serves a very useful purpose in our vocabulary) and its connection with actual inquiries. Like Peirce, James views true beliefs as those that have proved reliable in the past and promise to remain so into the future. Unlike Peirce, however, James is more easily read as *equating* truth with reliability or usefulness, thus giving rise to both a standard conception of the pragmatic theory of truth and a standard rebuttal. According to the standard conception, the pragmatic theory of truth is simply the equation just mentioned: thus, truth = long-term usefulness.[6] The rebuttal is simple and straightforward: because we can easily imagine beliefs that might be useful but not true, the pragmatic conception of truth is clearly wrong. This rebuttal recognizes that, even if true beliefs are useful (and they often are), not only are many useful beliefs false, but many true beliefs are quite trivial and useless (e.g., knowing the number of times one sneezed last week). If a pragmatic theory of truth equates truth with utility, then it is clearly incorrect.

Contemporary philosophers have attempted to clarify and refine what James and Peirce must have really meant, and thus avoid this obvious rebuttal. So, for example, Harvey Cormier (2001) argues that James is radically shifting the terms of the debate, away from treating truth as an abstract *relation* between our ideas and the world and toward treating truth as an "artifact" that is a result of our attempts to understand the world and make our lives easier:

> If James is right, however, truth is no more independent of our lives than aspirin, pencils, and cookies are. All are artifacts: their being is our doing, so what we do with them is what makes them what they are. (2001, p. 29)

On Cormier's reading James is not guilty of *equating* truth with usefulness but James is instead claiming that true beliefs have their basis in actual attempts to solve problems. Truth is then primarily a function of how we make real-life inquiries, and only secondarily a function of how our beliefs abstractly represent reality. Those who reject a pragmatic theory of truth too quickly are then guilty of prioritizing the latter function over the former, of prioritizing the abstract over the practical.

John Dewey (1941/1991) anticipated Cormier's reading when he argued that true beliefs "correspond" to reality in an "operational sense" of:

> *answering*, as a key answers to the conditions imposed by a lock, or as two correspondents "answer" to each other; or, in general, as a reply is an adequate answer to a question or a criticism—as, in short, a *solution* answers the requirements of a *problem*. (1941/1991, p. 179)

Like James, Dewey argued that truth or "warranted assertibility" is *fundamentally* tied to the results of actual inquiry and any other associations are derivative.

Cheryl Misak (2007) has likewise defended and clarified Peirce's claim, quoted above, that a true belief is one "which is fated to be ultimately agreed to by all who investigate." Rather than use the language of "fate," which is unnecessarily opaque, she writes that:

> What we do when we offer a justification of "*p* is true" is to offer a justification for the claim that *p*. . . . The question of the *truth* of the statement does not involve anything more than investigating the matter in our usual ways. And were we to get a belief that would be forever assertible (a belief which would never lead to disappointment; a belief which would be indefeasible or not defeated were inquiry pursued as far as it could fruitfully go), then we would have a true belief. There would be nothing higher or better we could ask of it. (2007, p. 69)

By arguing that calling a belief true is simply shorthand for calling it indefeasible in the above sense, Misak is aiming to make the notion of truth less abstract, less metaphysical, and more grounded in the everyday results of our inquiries.[7] Significantly, Misak also shows how a pragmatic account of truth shares many of the same motivations as other "deflationary" theories of truth (such as disquotationalist and super-assertibility theories) that attempt to make the concept of truth less substantive, and thus less problematic, than it traditionally has been.

The concept of truth is a fundamental concept in epistemology and also plays a central role in articulating a philosophically pragmatic worldview. Despite various internal differences—as we have seen, pragmatic theories of truth vary in how, exactly, they conceive of the practical value of true beliefs—a pragmatic approach to epistemology recognizes the philosophical and practical importance of the concept of truth. More uniquely, a pragmatic epistemology also argues for understanding the concept of truth through the practical contribution this concept makes in helping us express how reliable our inquiries are.

Knowledge and justification

A pragmatic understanding of the concept of truth has consequences for other areas of epistemology. If the concept of truth is grounded in actual inquiries, and if it functions as a shorthand for beliefs that are indefeasible or maximally reliable, then this has implications for how we should go about searching for, and justifying, true beliefs. We have already seen that Peirce recommended the "scientific method" of discovering and justifying truths, arguing that empirical testing is the best way of arriving at beliefs which are maximally reliable and stable. Likewise, Dewey (1938/1991) argued that inquiry follows a general pattern:

> Inquiry is the controlled or directed transformation of an indeterminate situation into one that is so determinate in its constituent distinctions and relations as to convert the elements of the original situation into a unified whole. (1938/1991, p. 108)

These approaches to inquiry, to the discovery and justification of beliefs, are meant to highlight the importance of *context* in determining when a problem is solved or a belief is well supported. As both Peirce and Dewey argue, a belief is not justified in the abstract or distinct from its role in helping bring a specific inquiry to a close. In other words, beliefs are not *intrinsically* well justified because of the kinds of beliefs they are (perceptual, logical, and so on): rather, beliefs are justified based on contextual features of the relevant situations in which they are held.

To take an example, consider my belief that it will rain tomorrow. First, obviously, this is not a belief I have merely in the abstract, as if I were idly pondering the local meteorology. In fact, my interest in whether it will rain tomorrow arises in response to a specific problem: should I go out and water the vegetable garden this evening? In other words, it matters to me whether it will rain tomorrow because that has consequences for what I do this evening. If it is going to rain tomorrow, then I can stay in; if not, then perhaps I should go outside and water the vegetables. That is a practical issue and it motivates searching for an answer. But is my answer, that it is going to rain tomorrow, so well justified that I can be said to *know* it will rain tomorrow? Again, the answer to that question cannot be answered in the abstract, but only by examining the particular context where I hold that belief. Of course, the grounds of my belief matter. It matters whether my belief is based on my recent check of the radar maps, on my reading the weather forecast last weekend, or on my simply appealing to the old saying that "red in the morning, sailors take warning." Some grounds are better than others. But the stakes also matter. That is, how good my grounds need to be, in order for my belief to be justified, depends on the costs of being wrong. If the vegetables will easily survive another day without water, then it doesn't matter much whether I am right about it raining tonight and the grounds for my belief can be correspondingly weaker. On the other hand, if it is absolutely essential that the vegetables get water over the next day, and if the vegetables in question are rare heirloom tomatoes, then it matters quite a lot whether I am right, and the grounds for my belief need to be better than they would be otherwise.

As this example makes clear, it is not always clear-cut whether a belief is well supported and, consequently, whether one really has knowledge about a particular fact. But this is not surprising if, on pragmatic grounds, these questions cannot be answered except by examining the particular contextual factors that guide inquiries to their conclusions. Just as the concept of truth emerges out of actual inquiries, so too do our concepts of knowledge and justification.

In this regard, a pragmatic approach to these epistemological questions bears a striking resemblance to other recent proposals that, while not explicitly pragmatic, do recognize the role of practical interests in setting the boundaries of what is known. To mention a few, John Hawthorne's (2004) "sensitive moderate invariantism," Jason Stanley's (2005) "interest relative invariantism," and Keith DeRose's (2009) "contextualism" all contain pragmatic elements:

> Whether a particular subject-time-proposition triple is included in the extension of "know" depends not merely upon the kinds of factors traditionally adverted to in accounts of knowledge—whether the subject believes the proposition, whether that proposition is true, whether the subject has good evidence, whether the subject is using a reliable method, and so on—but also upon the kinds of factors that in the contextualist's hands make for ascriber dependence. These factors will thus include (some or all of) the attention, interests, and stakes of that subject at that time . . . I wish to explore this picture—call it "sensitive moderate invariantism." (Hawthorne, 2004, p. 158)

> Bare Interest-Relative Invariantism . . . is simply the claim that whether or not someone knows that *p* may be determined in part by practical facts about the subject's environment. (Stanley, 2005, p. 85)

> We can say that the character of "S knows that p" is roughly, that S has a true belief that p and is in a *good enough* epistemic position with respect to p. . . .But how good is good enough? That is what varies with context. (DeRose, 2009, p. 3)

While there are significant differences between Hawthorne, Stanley, and DeRose, they do agree on one crucial point: that whether one has knowledge depends on practical factors in the specific context that a belief is held. While they come to this conclusion from the direction of analytic, Anglophone epistemology, this is also a fundamentally pragmatic point. Hawthorne even muses, "Shades of pragmatism? I leave pursuit of such analogies to others" (2004, p. 180n).

Logic

When we turn to the subject of logic Peirce again looms large: he arguably played one of the most important roles in nineteenth- and twentieth-century logic, likely surpassing even Frege in his actual historical influence on the development of modern formal logic. But logic, for Peirce, is not just about the formal deductive relationships between particular claims or propositions. Instead, logic is a general science devoted to how we can best reason. Deductive inference is an important part of this science, of course, but so too is inductive inference and what Peirce calls "abduction" or the process of generating hypotheses to explain surprising results. Logic, to use Dewey's formulation, is thus "inquiry into inquiry," the study of the methods that are most likely to solve problems, achieve true beliefs, and foster knowledge.

Characteristically, Dewey broadens Peirce's conception of logic to argue that rules of reasoning emerge in the very process of making inquiries. Dewey thus takes a Darwinian approach to logic, arguing that these rules of reasoning (what Dewey calls "logical forms") develop in response to problematic situations and are accepted just so long as they continue to provide adequate support for bringing new problematic situations to resolution. As a result, logic is "progressive":

> Logic rests upon analysis of the best methods of inquiry (being judged "best" by their results with respect to continued inquiry) that exist at a given time. As the methods of the sciences improve, corresponding changes take place in logic . . .

When in the future methods of inquiry are further changed, logical theory will also change. (1938/1991, pp. 21, 22)

As a result, logic depends on the natural and social environments where problems arise and are solved. If these environments were different, then we would expect our logic—that is, our best methods of making inquiries—to be different as well.[8]

Because logic, on this pragmatic approach, is a product of a natural and social environment, and not just the a priori workings of human reason, it is both *naturalistic* and *pragmatically mediated*. Some contemporary philosophers have likewise embraced and further developed these features. Penelope Maddy, for one, has argued that the validity of logic is contingent both on how the world and our brains are structured and that, as a result:

> It is in some senses a priori and in other senses a posteriori; it is empirical, in the sense that it could be overturned on empirical grounds, but some extra theorizing beyond observation and experiment would be needed to help us see how it could go wrong; and finally, there seems little to recommend the view that it is analytic. (2007, p. 281)

Maddy proposes a philosophical approach that, like pragmatism, is opposed to Cartesian "first philosophy": her "Second Philosopher" "simply begins from commonsense perception and proceeds from there to systematic observation, active experimentation, theory formation and testing, working all the while to assess, correct, and improve her methods as she goes" (2007, p. 2). While Maddy doesn't cite Peirce or Dewey directly, the parallels with their approaches are obvious.[9]

More explicitly, Robert Brandom (2008) has argued for an "analytic pragmatism" that supplements the focus, within much Anglophone philosophy, on analyzing one way of talking—our everyday way of talking about science or ethics, for example—into another, more precise, more philosophical, or more fundamental way of talking. Historically, this analysis (which might involve reducing or translating one way of talking into another) was pursued as a purely semantic project, focusing on the meanings of terms as they appeared in our different vocabularies, and then using logic to specify the exact relationships between these. Brandom argues, following Wittgenstein, Dewey, and Quine, that the meaning of a term cannot be understood separately from how it is used (hence the slogan "meaning is use"):

> The thought underlying the pragmatist line of thought is that what makes some bit of vocabulary mean what it does is how it is used. What we could call

> *semantic* pragmatism is the view that the only explanation there could be for how a given *meaning* gets associated with a vocabulary is to be found in the *use* of that vocabulary: the practices by which that meaning is conferred or the abilities whose exercise constitutes deploying a vocabulary with that meaning. (2008, p. 9)

Brandom thus argues that logic's traditional emphasis on semantic relationships needs to be supplemented by a recognition of how these relationships are "pragmatically mediated": we must, he claims, "look at what one must be able to *do* in order to *say* various things" (2008, p. 54) and thereby "reveal a pragmatic structure that turns out already to have been implicit in the semantic project all along" (2008, p, 55).

Final thoughts

As these and earlier examples make clear, there is an important sense in which pragmatism has become woven into contemporary analytic epistemology. For example, Richard Bernstein has recently observed that:

> Philosophers, starting from the most diverse orientations, and without being directly influenced by the classical pragmatists, have been articulating insights and developing theses that are not only congenial with a pragmatic orientation but also *refine* its philosophical import. (2010, p. 15)

Looking at the contemporary scene in epistemology, we see that pragmatic approaches play a prominent, albeit sometimes uncredited, role in debates over truth, knowledge, and justification, as well as in debates about logic and inquiry more generally. For our purposes it isn't terribly important whether, over time, pragmatic philosophy has become more analytic, whether analytic philosophy has become more pragmatic, or whether previously overlooked similarities are becoming more apparent. Rather, it is important to appreciate that there is greater affinity between the pragmatic and analytic traditions than the standard historical account, described at the outset, recognizes. These affinities help us recognize the convergence of the analytic and pragmatic traditions, rather than seeing them as rivals.[10]

As noted earlier, the founders of pragmatism did not embrace a sharp fact/ value distinction. The same is true for contemporary pragmatic approaches to epistemology. While a pragmatic epistemology recognizes important *contextual* differences between normative and descriptive claims, it does not recognize *intrinsic* differences. As a result, a pragmatic approach toward truth, justification, or knowledge does not limit itself to only factual claims. From a pragmatic standpoint, it does not matter whether the claim is about ethics, politics, science, or philosophy: in each case its truth depends on its long-range reliability, its justification is a function of contextual factors, and knowledge is achievable as the result of careful inquiry. There are no intrinsic limits to inquiry, or what can be inquired into, and no intrinsic limit to the topics where logic, pragmatically understood, can be applied.

In other words, this means that pragmatic epistemology is opposed to the common belief that some topics, particularly ones concerned with value judgments, cannot be discussed or settled rationally. For example, many people believe that certain claims are intrinsically off-limits to rational debate. These claims, they believe, are ultimately matters of taste or tradition, and just as there is no arguing about taste, so there is no arguing about religion, politics, morality, and aesthetics, for example. In contrast, a pragmatic epistemology recognizes contextual differences in how we discuss these various claims but does not take these contextual differences to mark an intrinsic difference in how we discuss "facts" and "values" that would, then, justify treating values as beyond debate. Again, just as there are contextual differences in how we discuss history as opposed to science—for example, history and science depend on different types and standards of evidence—so there are contextual differences in how we discuss history and politics. Whatever those contextual differences, they do not lead to the conclusion that rational discussion is impossible in one field or the other. And the same is true, according to the pragmatist, more generally with facts and values.[11]

A pragmatic epistemology is opposed to a sharp fact/value distinction for two reasons. The first is theoretical: as we have just seen, it is difficult to draw a principled distinction between the two categories. The second reason is more practical: if epistemological concepts like truth, justification, and inquiry cannot be applied to certain topics—if, in other words, certain topics are beyond the grasp of rational deliberation—then this has negative effects we would do well to avoid. Values shape our lives, our aspirations, and our expectations of ourselves and others. As social animals, we share these values with others and, as a result, there are obvious benefits in making these values explicit, in examining their basis, in finding their limits, and in testing them against alternatives. If we do not engage in this kind of reflection, if we do not or cannot rationally discuss our values, our standards of right and wrong, and our standards of good and bad, then our lives as social, communal creatures are thereby impoverished and perhaps even, in the long run, jeopardized.

In closing it is worth recalling Peirce's admonition that "Do not block the way of inquiry" should "be inscribed upon every wall of the city of philosophy" (1898/1998, p. 48). As we have seen, pragmatic epistemology—both classic and contemporary—lives by this motto. In its understanding of such concepts as truth, justification, and knowledge, and in its understanding of logic and inquiry, a pragmatic epistemology encourages keeping the way of inquiry open, regardless of the topic. This feature of a pragmatic epistemology is, to blur the fact/value distinction one last time, a compelling reason in its support: and while this may be only a pragmatic reason, it is not, for all that, one to take less seriously.

Notes

1 See Putnam (2002) for one line of argument against the fact/value distinction.
2 Quine is a particularly interesting case: his "Two Dogmas of Empiricism" famously ends with a call for "a more thorough pragmatism" (1953, p. 46) and his "Epistemology Naturalized" (1969) draws on pragmatist themes (particularly by emphasizing the continuity between philosophy and science). Naturalism continues to be a theme in pragmatic epistemology, though not always in the way Quine imagined. For a comparison of how Dewey and Quine attempted to naturalize epistemology, see Capps (1996).
3 See Bernstein (1992) for one telling of this standard account. Bernstein notes that this story of pragmatism's recent past is an "oversimplification" but "is still the dominant understanding of how philosophy developed in America" (1992, p. 817).
4 See, for example, Gross (2008).
5 One additional caveat: there is an obvious risk in speaking of "pragmatic epistemology" as if this is one thing, universally agreed upon by pragmatists and epistemologists. Obviously that is not the case, so the story I tell here will necessarily be selective, highlighting some of the more influential and promising lines of scholarship. One glaring absence is the work of Richard Rorty who, perhaps more than any other philosopher, helped bring pragmatism back into mainstream discussion. But Rorty's approach was often polemical (e.g., when he writes that "for the pragmatist, by contrast, 'knowledge' is, like 'truth,' *simply a compliment* paid to beliefs we think so well justified that, for the moment, further justification is not needed" 1991, p. 24, emphasis added) or even nihilistic (when he writes that pragmatists "do not require either a metaphysics or an

epistemology" 1991, p. 22). For these reasons I will not discuss Rorty to the extent that his prominence would otherwise warrant.
6   Schmitt (1995, p.78) is one example where a pragmatic theory of truth is defined in this way.
7   Misak also discusses these themes in her (2000), where she focuses on moral and political deliberation in particular and in her (2004) where she provides deep textual support for her reading of Peirce.
8   For further discussion of Dewey's theory of logic see Burke (1994).
9   See also Maddy's (1997) where she writes that "it is the success of those [mathematical] methods, not their platonistic inspiration, that justifies their adoption" (1997, p. 193) as well as her (2002) where she writes, "on the proposed view, logical truth is contingent on various features of the world" (2002, p.76).
10 See Boersema (2009) for another example (the concept of reference in the philosophy of language) where pragmatic and analytic approaches have converged.
11 See Misak (2000) for an extended argument against artificially walling off certain topics from rational deliberation. Timmons (1999) and Thomas (2006) also discuss the contextual constraints on moral deliberation.

References

Bernstein, R. (1992), "The Resurgence of Pragmatism," *Social Research*, 59, (4), 813–840.
—(2010), *The Pragmatic Turn*. Cambridge: Polity.
Boersema, D. (2009), *Pragmatism and Reference*. Cambridge, MA: MIT Press
Brandom, R. (2008), *Between Saying and Doing*. Oxford: Oxford University Press.
Burke, T. (1994), *Dewey's New Logic: A Reply to Russell*. Chicago: University of Chicago Press.
Capps, J. (1996), "Dewey, Quine, and Pragmatic Naturalized Epistemology," *Transactions of the Charles S. Peirce Society*, 32, (4), 634–667.
Cormier, H. (2001), *The Truth is What Works*. Lanham, MD: Rowman & Littlefield.
DeRose, K. (2009), *The Case for Contextualism*. Oxford: Oxford University Press.
Dewey, J. (1938), *Logic: The Theory of Inquiry*, in J. A. Boydston (ed.), *John Dewey: The Later Works*, vol. 12. Carbondale, IL: Southern Illinois University Press, 1938.
—(1948), "Propositions, Warranted Assertibility, and Truth" (1991), in J. A. Boydston (ed.), *John Dewey: The Later Works*, vol. 14. Carbondale, IL: Southern Illinois University Press, pp. 168–188.
Gross, N. (2008), *Richard Rorty: The Making of an American Philosophy*. Chicago: University of Chicago Press.
Hawthorne, J. (2004), *Knowledge and Lotteries*. Oxford: Oxford University Press.
James, W. (1907), *Pragmatism: A New Way for Some Old Ways of Thinking*. Cambridge, MA: Harvard University Press, 1975.

Maddy, P. (1997), *Naturalism in Mathematics*. Oxford: Oxford University Press.
—(2002), "A Naturalistic Look at Logic," *Proceedings and Addresses of the APA*, 76, (2), 61–90.
—(2007), *Second Philosophy: A Naturalistic Method*. Oxford: Oxford University Press.
Misak, C. (2000), *Truth, Politics, Morality: Pragmatism and Deliberation*. New York: Routledge.
—(2004), *Truth and the End of Inquiry*. Oxford: Oxford University Press.
—(2007). "Pragmatism and Deflationism," in C. Misak (ed.), *The New Pragmatists*. Oxford: Oxford University Press, pp. 68–90.
Peirce, C. S. (1877), "The Fixation of Belief" (1986), in C. J. W. Kloesel (ed.), *The Writings of C. S. Peirce*, vol. 3. Bloomington, IN: Indiana University Press, pp. 242–257.
—(1878), "How to Make Our Ideas Clear" (1986), in C. J. W. Kloesel (ed.), *The Writings of C. S. Peirce*, vol. 3. Bloomington, IN: Indiana University Press, pp. 257–276.
—(1898), "The First Rule of Logic" (1998), in The Peirce Edition Project (ed.), *The Essential Peirce*, vol. 2. Bloomington, IN: Indiana University Press, pp. 42–56.
Putnam, H. (2002), The *Collapse of the Fact/Value Dichotomy and Other Essays*. Cambridge, MA: Harvard University Press.
Quine, W. V. O. (1953), "Two Dogmas of Empiricism," in W. V. O. Quine, *From a Logical Point of View*. Cambridge, MA: Harvard University Press.
—(1969), "Epistemology Naturalized," in W. V. O. Quine, *Ontological Relativity and Other Essays*. New York: Columbia University Press.
Rorty, R. (1991), "Solidarity or Objectivity?" in R. Rorty, *Objectivity, Relativism, and Truth*. Cambridge: Cambridge University Press.
Schmitt, F. (1995), *Truth: A Primer*. Boulder, CO: Westview Press.
Stanley, J. (2005), *Knowledge and Practical Interests*. Oxford: Oxford University Press.
Thomas, A. (2006), *Value and Context: The Nature of Moral and Political Knowledge*. Oxford: Oxford University Press.
Timmons, M. (1999), *Morality Without Foundations: A Defense of Ethical Contextualism*. Oxford: Oxford University Press.

5

Metaphysics

Sami Pihlström

Pragmatist philosophers, both classical and more recent, have made significant contributions to metaphysics, even though the pragmatist tradition has also played an important role in the ongoing criticism of the very idea of metaphysics that started out in early modern philosophy with David Hume and Immanuel Kant,[1] continuing with figures such as Friedrich Nietzsche, and culminating with the strongly antimetaphysical orientation of the logical positivism of the Vienna Circle in the early twentieth century and the deconstructionist and postmodernist orientations of late-twentieth-century Continental philosophy. While the classical pragmatists were to some extent involved in the campaign against traditional metaphysics that also inspired logical empiricism, arguing against Hegelian idealists, for instance, neo-pragmatists like Richard Rorty were in the late twentieth and early twenty-first centuries active in the more recent postmodernist turn against not only metaphysics but also epistemology and other areas of systematic philosophy.

Contemporary pragmatists are not at all in agreement about how the relation of pragmatism to metaphysics should be understood; nor are these disagreements limited to the controversies over Rorty's radical neo-pragmatism but they extend to deeply conflicting interpretations of classical pragmatists', especially William James's and John Dewey's, legacy in this regard (see, e.g., Seigfried, 2001, 2004; Myers, 2004). Some contemporary pragmatists go as far as advancing "metaphysical quietism" (Macarthur, 2008).

This chapter will explain why, despite the pragmatists' worries about many forms of traditional metaphysics, the pragmatist tradition should *not* be seen as completely hostile to metaphysics as such. First, I will state the pragmatist (and neo-pragmatist) case against metaphysics understood as a study of the ultimate nature of Being, or of the fundamental structure of the world as it is in itself.

Secondly, I will survey some key pragmatist (and neo-pragmatist) ideas in central fields of metaphysical inquiry, distinguishing between ontology or "general metaphysics" (*metaphysica generalis*) and "special metaphysics" (*metaphysica specialis*). Thirdly, I will formulate a pragmatist conception of metaphysics, firmly rooted in the Kantian tradition, that makes sense of the apparently dubious double role of pragmatism as a philosophical approach engaging *both* in the critique of metaphysics *and* in metaphysical inquiry itself, albeit in a reinterpreted form. Fourthly, by way of conclusion, I will add brief comments on the relations between metaphysics, on the one side, and epistemology and ethics, on the other.

These issues are not just historically interesting but are among the most significant contemporary philosophical questions, not only because pragmatism is a widely discussed and controversial approach in philosophy today but also because metaphysics has made a strong comeback especially in analytic philosophy. Pragmatists should reflect on how pragmatism can, and should, be employed in the critical evaluation of that comeback.[2]

Pragmatist criticisms of metaphysical realism

Pragmatists have, especially since James and Dewey, often attacked the very idea of metaphysics as a pursuit of the ultimate truth about Being *qua* Being. It is, however, helpful to understand this criticism *not* as a criticism of metaphysics as such but as a criticism of what Hilary Putnam (1981, 1990) called *metaphysical realism*. By this label, Putnam understood, roughly, the view that (i) there is a way the world is absolutely, that is, there is a definite class of objects and properties that exist mind- and discourse-independently;[3] (ii) the world can, in principle, be truly and completely described by means of a single true theory, from a "God's-Eye View," yielding an "absolute conception of reality"; and (iii) truth is to be understood as a non-epistemic relation of correspondence between propositions, sentences, statements (or whatever the ultimate truth-bearers are) and the nonlinguistic items of the world itself that they are about (see, e.g., Putnam, 1981, pp. 49–50).[4]

Only if a metaphysically realistic conception of the world, viewed "absolutely" from a God's-Eye View, were available to us would we be in the position to practice metaphysics in the sense suggested by metaphysical realists. Putnam, and most neo-pragmatists following him, regard the very idea of such an absolute perspective as a fundamental misunderstanding of our human condition. We are fallible and limited creatures viewing our worldly surroundings inevitably from perspectives located within our human practices. There is no way for us to climb out of this situation. James's and Dewey's—and to some extent Peirce's—antimetaphysical pronouncements can be understood against this background. What they and other pragmatists primarily criticize is the traditional philosophical goal of describing the world as it is in itself, at a fundamental level, from an imagined absolute viewpoint—a "view from nowhere," as it were. Since such an "intellectualist" goal, as James called it, seems to be humanly impossible, little remains from the project of metaphysics, as it has been traditionally understood.[5]

For example, James heavily criticized old-fashioned metaphysical concepts and problems, such as the notion of substance and the debates it has launched. In the third lecture of *Pragmatism* (1907), he provides a devastating critique of the traditional metaphysicians' way of examining such problems on the basis of the assumption that the world is final and fixed ("readymade," as Putnam would later put it). Instead, when seeking to understand the core pragmatic meaning of substance, freedom, or God, the pragmatist metaphysician turns toward the future and asks what kind of potential practical experiences would result if a "world-formula" employing such notions were true—or were held to be true (James, we must note, is characteristically unclear here). Later on in the same volume, James (ibid., ch. 7) elaborates on what would today be called *constructivist* metaphysics, arguing that we can regard something as a "thing" only on the basis of its serving certain human purposes and interests. We can classify and categorize the world and its objects in a number of different ways based on the different practical purposes arising out of our human needs; there is no interest- and purpose-neutral absolute description of reality.

Dewey, in turn, sought to combine scientific constructivism and realism in his naturalist and experimentalist account of the objects of inquiry (see, e.g., Dewey, 1929). Again, those objects do not exist as "readymade" independently of our inquiry. Rather, they emerge as experimental products of the inquiry. On the other hand, inquiry itself is to be understood as natural organisms', particularly human beings', way of being in touch with their environment, continuously seeking to settle the problematic situations they are faced with in their ongoing experience.[6]

In neo-pragmatism, this Jamesian–Deweyan attack on the basic assumptions of metaphysical realism (especially the supposed "God's-Eye View") has been continued not only in Putnam's campaign against metaphysical realism but also, more radically, in Rorty's critique of the idea of the world in itself. For Rorty, such a realistic world is "a world well lost" (see Rorty, 1982, ch. 1). Nothing in the world, or Nature, determines how we should describe it and speak about it in our vocabularies. Rather, our human ways of speaking evolve freely and independently of any need to accurately represent any nonlinguistic reality—to the extent that it becomes unclear whether we, according to Rorty, can even speak *about* the world at all. This is not to say that there is no linguistic reality, although Rorty (and even Putnam) has occasionally been seen as subscribing to a naïve, more or less literal version of the famous slogan coined by Jacques Derrida, "il n'y a pas de hors-texte" ("there is nothing outside the text"). However, even if there is *something* outside our linguistic practices and vocabularies, that "something" has no structure of its own, and the purpose of developing and using human vocabularies—or what Wittgenstein would have called "language-games"—is not the accurate representation of what exists language-independently but simply the need to cope with the physical and social environment.

The issue of realism within the pragmatist tradition offers ample examples of the pragmatist attempt to find a plausible middle ground position between extreme views that are both highly implausible. The reasonable pragmatist should avoid both metaphysical realism and radical constructivism. In classical pragmatism and neo-pragmatism alike, one may perceive a continuous search for something like *pragmatic realism*, perhaps most plausibly formulated as an empirical, commonsensical (and scientific) realism maintained within a broader pragmatist position, comparable to the Kantian integration of transcendental idealism and empirical realism. Correctly interpreted, even "accurate representation" may (Rortyan radical neo-pragmatism notwithstanding) be a pragmatically acceptable goal of thought and inquiry, within a pragmatic or empirical realism based on a more comprehensive—"transcendental" (cf. below)—understanding of pragmatism.

Pragmatist contributions to metaphysics

Some pragmatists' strong critiques of metaphysical realism should not lead us to overlook the fact that pragmatists have also held metaphysical views. It is probably fair to say that most of the classical pragmatists were *process metaphysicians*, maintaining that the basic structure of reality is not to be described in terms of static objects or states of affairs but as a constantly evolving, processual development. The world, along with our human history, is in a continuous flux (cf. Margolis, 1993), in constant change and transformation. Temporality is, therefore, a fundamental feature of the world we live in, even if *nothing* is "fundamental" in the metaphysical realist's sense.

Precisely because of this ambiguity with "fundamental," pragmatic process metaphysics may, however, be problematic from the point of view of the above-discussed critique of metaphysical realism that is also part and parcel of the pragmatist tradition. Even if there is no fixed metaphysical structure of the world that would remain the same for eternity—even if we reject "eternal" metaphysical structures such as Platonic Forms, or contemporary metaphysicians' truthmakers (cf. Armstrong, 2004)—one may ask whether the world is essentially or "in itself" (and, indeed, eternally) a processual development of change and transformation. Is it any less metaphysically realistic to regard processuality as the fundamental feature of ultimate reality than to regard the world as consisting of certain fundamental entities and/or properties?

In order to further clarify the pragmatist contributions to, and critique of, metaphysics, we should distinguish between *general metaphysics*, or ontology, and *special metaphysics*, consisting of such areas of inquiry as (rational, philosophical) psychology, cosmology, and theology—a threefold classification that can be traced back to Christian Wolff's neo-Leibnizian philosophy and that plays a significant role, for example, in Immanuel Kant's *Critique of Pure Reason* (1781/1787) largely influenced by Wolff. Kant's critical philosophy, pretty much like pragmatism later, is both a critique of metaphysics and in its own way a contribution to metaphysics.

Now, the discussions of process metaphysics primarily belong to philosophical cosmology, hence to special metaphysics rather than general metaphysics. However, an analogous notion of processuality can be defended in philosophical psychology, or the philosophy of mind. Not even the mind is a static entity, or object, in the world; it is, rather, in constant interaction (or better, in Deweyan terms, transaction) with the natural events and processes going on in its surroundings. The mind, for pragmatists, is not "in the head" but "out there" in the world, embedded in our habits of action.[7] Moreover, the idea of processuality can be at work in pragmatist philosophy of religion as well. Not even God is eternally and statically what He (or it) is; the idea of processual development and transformation arguably extends to the divinity, too. God is, perhaps, the world-process itself. This, at least, is the picture of divinity we may draw from

James's (1909) pluralistic reflections and Dewey's (1934) suggestion that we understand God as the "*active* relation between ideal and actual."[8]

We may ask, then, whether anything remains from standard general metaphysics, given that pragmatists tend to reinterpret virtually all issues in special metaphysics in terms of processuality and evolution. In a sense, nothing remains. If metaphysics is understood as the quest for *the* ultimate truth about Being, most pragmatists have regarded such a project as hopeless from the start. Giving up such metaphysics is crucial not only in James's (1907) arguments against rationalism and intellectualism but also in Dewey's (1929) criticism of the "quest for certainty," not to mention Putnam's and Rorty's neo-pragmatist attacks on the very idea of a metaphysical structure of the world *an sich*. On the other hand, if metaphysics is not understood in this metaphysically realistic manner but reconceived as a deeply human attempt to make sense of human existence in a world that continuously needs to be categorized from the perspective of, and in terms of, human practices and habits of action, pragmatists are not antimetaphysical at all. One might even argue that any adequately pragmatist analysis of our "being-in-the-world" (to use Martin Heidegger's famous expression in a non-Heideggerian context) is metaphysical in the sense of taking seriously the questions of both general and special metaphysics. Only the traditional metaphysically realist *answers* to those questions must be abandoned—*not the questions themselves*, nor pragmatist ways of coming to terms with them.

Even the pragmatists' processual metaphysics may, then, be seen as an acceptable metaphysical theory—not as a theory about the world in itself but as a suggestion regarding how *we* should best "structure" the world we find ourselves living in. It is, like any other metaphysical theory that can be pragmatically acceptable, *our* categorization of reality, not a picture accurately reflecting the purpose- and practice-independent nature of reality as such.

This, however, is not to say that there are no strongly realistic pragmatist metaphysicians at all. Some leading pragmatists today, including Nicholas Rescher (2000) and Susan Haack (2005, 2008), have been inspired by Peirce's scientific realism, instead of Jamesian, Deweyan, or Putnamian (let alone Rortyan) criticisms of metaphysical realism. The pragmatist tradition, as already pointed out in the introduction to this volume, thrives in its many tensions, and the one between realism and antirealism is one of them. Another one is, crucially, the tension between metaphysics and antimetaphysics. It cannot be denied that pragmatist currents of thought have often been profoundly anti-metaphysical. Nor can it be denied, however, that pragmatists can be interpreted as engaging in a fundamental rearticulation—or perhaps, in Hegelian terms, an *Aufhebung*—of the metaphysical quest. If so, they do not just reject it but to a large extent still engage in it, though in a very different way than, say, Aristotle, Leibniz, or other classical metaphysicians.

Metaphysics reinterpreted: Kantian pragmatism

Instead of understanding metaphysics as an inquiry into Being *qua* Being, then, the pragmatist may understand it as an inquiry into the fundamental—though historically changing and reinterpretable—features of the *human world*, as it emerges in and through our world-categorizing practices (including the practices of inquiry itself). Pragmatists such as Putnam join, at least implicitly, Kant scholars like Henry E. Allison in insisting (with Kant) that we cannot know, or perhaps even form a coherent conception of, the world as it is in itself, independently of the *conditions* of human cognition and representation (Putnam, 1990, ch. 1, 2004a; Allison, 2004, chs. 1–3). Metaphysics in the form practised by metaphysical realism is therefore impossible, according to these pragmatists and Kantians. Contrary to what is often assumed, however, this Kantian approach does not renounce the possibility of an ontological inquiry into the structure of the (human) world, while it does require us to fundamentally reinterpret that inquiry. There is room for a *critical* conception of metaphysics within a more inclusive understanding of its status and tasks—of metaphysics reconceived as an examination of the basic features of a humanly categorized reality, of the practice-embedded conditions necessary for us to be able to experience an objective, structured world. It is (only) this human world, which for us is the only world there is, that we may hope to be able to metaphysically investigate.

It can even be argued that pragmatism, when developed as an inquiry into the structure of the "human world," ought to be seen as a naturalized form of Kantian transcendental philosophy in a deeply reinterpreted sense (several pragmatists' own reservations notwithstanding), and that both transcendental philosophy and pragmatism (and their combination, "transcendental pragmatism," as one might call it) are metaphysically relevant, that is, not simply critical of metaphysics (though they are that, too). Pragmatism, thus modified, provides us with a perspectival approach to ontology, highly critical of metaphysical realism (and antirealism), yet affirming the seriousness of ontological inquiry into the ways the world must be taken by us to be, from within our practices.

Such an ontologically serious pragmatism should not be reduced to a merely methodological perspective or constraint on inquiry; it is a method of inquiring into the way(s) the world (for us) *is*. The so-called pragmatic method, developed by Peirce and James in somewhat different ways, seeks to determine the true core of metaphysical disputes and theories by examining their conceivable practical results (see, again, the chapter above on "Research Problems and Methods"). According to pragmatist metaphysics, objects—and ontological categories or structures in general—emerge from historically evolving human categorizing practices, just as they may in traditional forms of transcendental philosophy be understood as emerging from, or being constitutively based upon, the conditions of possible experience (Kant), the transcendental structures of consciousness (phenomenology), or language-games embedded in forms of life (Wittgenstein). The classical pragmatists' relations to these more obviously transcendental ways of thinking need more detailed scrutiny than is possible in this chapter (cf. also Pihlström, 2003, 2009).

In any case, if we cannot expect metaphysics to deliver a view of the world in itself, we must carefully consider how exactly we humans contribute to "constituting" the world, to "structuring" it into what it is for us. If pragmatists take seriously the Kantian claim that our very notion of reality is, ineliminably, a function of our ways of constituting reality, extending this view to cover historically transformable categories instead of fixed a priori structures of cognition, in particular our human practices and habits of action—as pragmatists since James and Dewey have suggested—then the crucial question arises as to what extent these world-constituting practices involve not only semantic, conceptual, and epistemic but also moral elements.

With James, in particular, we are led to the relatively radical claim that metaphysics might not be possible at all without a crucial connection to, or entanglement with, ethics. This is to say that we cannot arrive at any understanding of reality as we are able to experience it without paying due attention to the ways in which moral valuations and ethical commitments are constituents of that reality, *qua* humanly experienceable.

Conclusion: Metaphysics, epistemology, and ethics

It has been a characteristic assumption of metaphysically realistic philosophy that a clear distinction ought to be drawn between metaphysics and epistemology. Metaphysics should not be epistemologized, in order to avoid smuggling too strongly "human" features to the investigation of the fundamental (non-human) characteristics of the world *an sich*. However, insofar as the pragmatist perspective on metaphysics—not just as a critique of metaphysics but as a critical transformation of it, as described above—is taken seriously, we may say that this is a distinction without any difference that could be pragmatically cashed out. Metaphysics is inevitably connected with epistemology, or even thoroughly epistemologized, insofar as the pragmatist critical stance toward the very project of describing the world as it is (supposedly) independently of our practice-embedded epistemic standpoints is appreciated. Moreover, metaphysics is, equally inevitably, reconnected with ethics, with our value-laden perspectives on the way the world is for us, insofar as there cannot be (again for us) any ethically neutral stance that would simply reveal a purely factual reality. Our values are always already implicated in any factual description of what goes on in the world around us; yet, the exact relation between fact and value should be made more precise in pragmatist metaphysics (Pihlström, 2010).

Accordingly, if the pragmatist maintains that, when dealing with the world in any manner whatsoever (however theoretical), we are always, at least implicitly, making ethical choices, engaging in moral valuations, formulating our categorizations of reality from perspectives or standpoints always already laden with ethical ideals and assumptions, s/he should also maintain that reality is, for us, inevitably value-laden (cf. Putnam, 2002, 2004; Pihlström, 2005). A general question concerning the relations between metaphysics and ethics arises here, and the distinctness of these fields of inquiry cannot be taken for granted by the pragmatist metaphysician. The issue goes much deeper than the rather uncontroversial idea that different metaphysical positions may have different ethical implications.[9] Our question is whether metaphysics, in the critical sense inherited in pragmatism, might be *grounded* in ethical considerations, or based on ethical premises, rather than vice versa.

In contemporary pragmatism, this topic is approached in terms of the *fact-value entanglement*—again a topic that Putnam has made well known. There are, according to Putnam, no value-independent facts (nor, for that matter, fact-independent values), but facts and values are, for us, deeply entangled. A being with no values would have no facts either, as Putnam (1981) puts it. On the other hand, Putnam arguably goes too far in the antimetaphysical direction, possibly as a result of his original logical empiricist inheritance (as a pupil of Rudolf Carnap and Hans Reichenbach), when he suggests that pragmatists should develop "ethics without ontology" (Putnam, 2004). The upshot of the pragmatist tradition in metaphysics, ranging from the process-ontological reflections of pragmatism and naturalism by Peirce, James, Dewey, and others to the Putnamian critique of the metaphysical realism inherent in contemporary scientific realism and naturalism, is that we need not abandon metaphysics but must reinterpret it in a pragmatic and, hence, inescapably value-laden manner.

The pragmatist hoping to retain metaphysics in a revised and reinterpreted form may easily join Putnam in his defense of the fact-value entanglement, while rejecting his antimetaphysics. Metaphysics itself is a deeply valuational activity. Like the empirical world in general, our metaphysical problems and concepts come to us "screaming with values." It is not just a value-neutral matter whether there are, say, human minds or cultural entities like institutions (or values, for that matter) in the world. Such metaphysical issues are deeply valuational and call for an active interplay of theoretical and practical philosophy.[10]

Indeed, a fundamental reinterpretation of the traditional (also Kantian) distinction between theoretical philosophy, including logic, metaphysics, epistemology, philosophy of science, and other fields, and practical philosophy, including ethics as well as social and political philosophy, ought to be seen as a key pragmatist contribution to twentieth (and twenty-first) century metaphilosophy. A reinterpretation of the notion of metaphysics is a crucial element of this—still ongoing—process of rearticulating the division of labor between such fields of philosophical inquiry.[11]

Notes

1 Obviously, there were critics of metaphysics in antiquity as well, particularly the Sophists, some of whom defended what would now be regarded as radically relativist views denying the objectivity of truth and reality. Historically, it might be interesting to examine more closely the similarities and differences between pragmatism and ancient philosophical schools, but this is not the task of the present essay.

2 This chapter is connected with my monograph on the same topic (Pihlström, 2009), but the chapter is self-standing and does not require familiarity with that volume. Moreover, the pragmatist approach to metaphysics is also discussed in the chapter "Research Problems and Methods" in this volume, in the context of the pragmatic method, which I interpret as an essentially pluralistic and

contextualistic method of philosophical inquiry and whose employment in the service of metaphysics I see as, basically, contextualizing. That discussion, however, remains at a highly general level without going into the details of pragmatist contributions to metaphysics that this chapter briefly attempts to highlight.

3 In a pragmatist context, it would also be natural to speak about "practice-independent" existence here. See again Chapter 2, for further discussion of practice-dependence and contextuality in pragmatist metaphysics.

4 The metaphysically realist correspondence notion of truth could be made even more explicitly realistic by employing the concept of *truthmaking*: the world, or its states of affairs (or whatever ultimately exists), make(s) our truths true. See Armstrong, 2004; for a pragmatist reinterpretation of this concept, see Pihlström, 2009, ch. 1.

5 It may, however, be problematic to formulate the Jamesian and/or Putnamian critique of metaphysical realism in terms of what is possible or impossible for human beings. This formulation may already make problematic metaphysical assumptions. In fact, Putnam's late reflections on the incoherence of metaphysical realism are deeply informed by Wittgensteinian considerations (see Putnam, 1994, 1999), which we here, however, must set aside.

6 See Larry Hickman's contribution in this volume for a discussion of the pragmatist conception of science and technology, as well as John Capp's article for remarks on pragmatist epistemology.

7 In his contribution to this volume, Erkki Kilpinen analyzes the pragmatist conception of action and habituality. For the contemporary relevance of pragmatist process metaphysics, see Rockwell, 2008.

8 See Chapter 14, by Ulf Zackariasson, in this volume for a discussion of pragmatist philosophy of religion.

9 For instance, different metaphysical views on the nature of the mind, or person-hood, have implications on the ethical questions concerning the proper treatment of certain kinds of beings, for example, animals, unborn fetuses, or the permanently mentally ill.

10 See Michael Eldridge's contribution to this volume for an extended discussion of pragmatist ethics. On the relation between fact and value, see also "Research Methods and Problems" above.

11 Portions of this chapter were presented as parts of my talks in the Nordic Pragmatism Conference in Uppsala, Sweden; the 10th Anniversary Conference of the Central European Pragmatist Forum in Bratislava, Slovakia; and the Finnish-Russian Philosophy Conference in Helsinki, Finland (all in June 2010). I am grateful to the audiences of all three meetings for important questions and comments.

References

Allison, H. E. (2004), *Kant's Transcendental Idealism: An Interpretation and Defense—Revised and Enlarged Edition*. New Haven, CT: Yale University Press (1st edn 1983).

Armstrong, D. M. (2004), *Truth and Truthmakers*. Cambridge: Cambridge University Press.

Dewey, J. (1929a), *Experience and Nature* (2nd edn). La Salle, IL: Open Court, 1986 (1st edn 1925).

—(1929b), *The Quest for Certainty: A Study on the Relation between Knowledge and Action*. New York: Putnam's, 1960.

—(1934), *A Common Faith*. New Haven, CT: Yale University Press, 1991.

Haack, S. (2005), "Not Cynicism, but Synechism: Lessons from Classical Pragmatism." *Transactions of the Charles S. Peirce Society*, 41, pp. 239–253.

—(2008), "The Legitimacy of Metaphysics: Kant's Legacy to Peirce, and Peirce's to Philosophy Today." *Philosophical Topics*, 36, pp. 97–110.

James, W. (1907), *Pragmatism: A New Name for Some Old Ways of Thinking*. Eds F. H. Burkhardt, F. Bowers, and I. K. Skrupskelis. Cambridge, MA: Harvard University Press, 1975.

—(1909a), *The Meaning of Truth: A Sequel to Pragmatism*. Eds F. H. Burkhardt, F. Bowers, and I. K. Skrupskelis. Cambridge, MA: Harvard University Press, 1978.

—(1909b), *A Pluralistic Universe*. Eds F. H. Burkhardt, F. Bowers, and I. K. Skrupskelis. Cambridge, MA: Harvard University Press, 1977.

Kant, I. (1781/1787), *Kritik der reinen Vernunft*. Ed. R. Schmidt. Hamburg: Felix Meiner, 1990. (A = 1st edn, 1781; B = 2nd edn, 1787.)

Macarthur, D. (2008), "Pragmatism, Metaphysical Quietism, and the Problem of Normativity." *Philosophical Topics*, 36, pp. 193–209.

Margolis, J. (1993), *The Flux of History and the Flux of Science*. Berkeley: University of California Press.

Myers, W. T. (2004), "Pragmatist Metaphysics: A Defense." *Transactions of the Charles S. Peirce Society*, 40, pp. 39–52.

Peirce, C. S. (1992–1998), *The Essential Peirce: Selected Philosophical Writings*, 2 vols. The Peirce Edition Project. Bloomington: Indiana University Press (Cited as EP volume: page).

Pihlström, S. (2003), *Naturalizing the Transcendental: A Pragmatic View*. Amherst, NY: Prometheus/Humanity Books.

—(2005), *Pragmatic Moral Realism: A Transcendental Defense*. Amsterdam: Rodopi.

—(2009), *Pragmatist Metaphysics: An Essay on the Ethical Grounds of Ontology*. London: Continuum.

—(2010), "Toward a Pragmatically Naturalist Metaphysics of the Fact-Value Entanglement: Emergence or Continuity?" *Journal of Philosophical Research*, 35, pp. 323–352.

Putnam, H. (1981), *Reason, Truth and History*. Cambridge: Cambridge University Press.
—(1987), *The Many Faces of Realism*. La Salle, IL: Open Court.
—(1990), *Realism with a Human Face*. Ed. J. Conant. Cambridge, MA: Harvard University Press.
—(1992), *Renewing Philosophy*. Cambridge, MA: Harvard University Press.
—(1994), *Words and Life*. Ed. James Conant. Cambridge, MA: Harvard University Press.
—(1995), *Pragmatism: An Open Question*. Oxford: Blackwell.
—(1999), *The Threefold Cord: Mind, Body, and World*. New York: Columbia University Press.
—(2002), *The Collapse of the Fact/Value Dichotomy and Other Essays*. Cambridge, MA: Harvard University Press.
—(2004), *Ethics without Ontology*. Cambridge, MA: Harvard University Press.
Rescher, N. (2000), *Realistic Pragmatism: An Introduction to Pragmatic Philosophy*. Albany: SUNY Press.
Rockwell, T. (2008), "Processes and Particles: The Impact of Classical Pragmatism on Contemporary Metaphysics". *Philosophical Topics*, 36, pp. 239–258.
Rorty, R. (1992), *Consequences of Pragmatism*. Brighton: Harvester Press.
—(1998), *Truth and Progress*. Cambridge: Cambridge University Press.
Seigfried, C. H. (2001), "Pragmatist Metaphysics? Why Terminology Matters". *Transactions of the Charles S. Peirce Society*, 37, pp. 13–21.
—(2004), "Ghosts Walking Underground: Dewey's Vanishing Metaphysics". *Transactions of the Charles S. Peirce Society*, 40, pp. 53–81.

6

Science and Technology

Larry Hickman

Each of the three major founding pragmatists, Charles S. Peirce, William James, and John Dewey, was at some time during his career directly engaged with experimental science, broadly conceived. Peirce worked as a surveyor for the US Coast and Geodetic Survey. Geodesy is a branch of the earth sciences that deals with the measurement of the Earth, including its gravitational field. James, who earned a medical degree from Harvard, taught physiology and psychology in addition to philosophy. Dewey, with his colleagues at the University of Chicago, performed experiments related to perception and attention. Late in life he collaborated with Myrtle McGraw on studies of physiological development in twins (Dalton, 2002). All three wrote about the nature of scientific inquiry and the status of scientific theories. Although there is a measure of instrumentalism in the pragmatic maxim that was first stated by Peirce and then adopted by James and Dewey, only Dewey of the three developed a complex philosophical account of tools, techniques, and technology.

Peirce

One of Peirce's lasting contributions to scientific method was his recognition of a third form of logical inference. In addition to deduction (inference from a population to a sample) and induction (inference from a sample to a population) Peirce recognized "abduction" (which he also called hypothesis and retroduction) as a form of probable inference that involves conjecture (e.g., b is known, but a would account for b: let us therefore treat a as a potentially fruitful hypothesis). He regarded the three forms of inference as interdependent, cooperative phases of scientific thought. In a series of essays in the 1870s he claimed the superiority of the methods of the sciences over other methods of fixing belief, such as tenacity, authority, and *a priori* reasoning (Peirce, 1986a, 1986b).

Other relevant features of Peirce's thought include his understanding of scientific truth as the ideal point toward which opinions of research communities converge by a process of evolution, and his commitment to fallibilism, or the idea that scientific judgments are always, at least in principle, open to correction. His version of verificationism held that even the most complex scientific concept must ultimately be related to experienceable phenomena. His version of operationalism is summed up in his pragmatic maxim: "Consider what effects, which might conceivably have practical bearings, we conceive the object of our conception to have. Then, our conception of these effects is the whole of our conception of the object" (Peirce, 1986b, p. 266).

According to Burch (2009), Peirce's view of physical concepts is quite close to that of Albert Einstein, who held "that the whole meaning of a physical concept is determined by an exact method of measuring it." Burch also reports that Peirce's influence continues to be felt in areas of scientific research outside the academy: in business, technology, intelligence organizations, and the military (Burch, 2009).

Peirce's lasting influence on philosophy of science also includes his theory of signs and his system of categories. As a part of his semeiotic, or general theory of signs, he developed an extensive account of the triadic relation that involves a thing (an object), represented by another thing (a representamen), to some third thing (an interpretant). Early in his career, Peirce thought that every interpretant is a sign of something further. Later, however, he admitted what he termed "final, veritable, or ultimate" logical interpretants that are characterized by both conditionality and generality and do not presuppose or require an interpretant in the proper sense (Gentry, 1952, pp. 78–79). Peirce's extensive development of his theory of categories exhibits firstness, sometimes characterized as quality; secondness, sometimes characterized as fact; and thirdness, sometimes characterized as law. Extended discussion of these complex theories is beyond the scope of this entry.

Some commentators have argued that there is in Peirce's work a tension between scientific realism—the idea that scientific objects are "ready made," or mind- and theory-independent—and constructivism—the idea that they are constructions based on various scientific (and other) perspectives. On this view, the tension manifests itself in the difficulty of knowing what comes first:

mind-and research-independent reality, or the process of fixing the final opinion about such matters (Pihlström, 2008).

Other commentators have suggested that Peirce's "realism" was of the Kantian or empirical sort, that is, similar to the "internal realism" of neo-pragmatist Hilary Putnam (Putnam, 1987), which holds that any reality that is outside of empirical or logical inquiry cannot be of concern to the sciences (Burch, 2009). More specifically, Putnam's "internal realism" (which he says he should have called "pragmatic realism") holds that even though the world may be causally independent of the human mind, it is the human mind that structures the world (Putnam, 1987, p. 17).

James

The apparent tension that some have found in the work of Peirce, between a version of scientific realism that treats reality as mind-independent, and a version of idealism that emphasizes the cognitive contributions necessary for the convergence toward truth, was also of concern to James. James's doctrine of radical empiricism, unlike previous atomistic versions of empiricism such as that of John Locke (1632–1704), for example, holds that relations between things, conjunctive as well as disjunctive, are as much matters of direct particular experience as are things themselves.

James distinguished two types of knowledge: knowledge of acquaintance and knowledge that can be expressed in judgments. He argued that the feelings that are associated with the data of experience point to connections with other data, and that it is those connections that provide the basis for their cognitive reconstruction as "knowledge about." James was not always clear about whether or to what extent knowledge by acquaintance is an unambiguous case of knowing. Dewey attempted to clarify this matter in his 1905 essay "The Postulate of Immediate Empiricism" (see below).

It is fair to say that there is something of realism in James's radical empiricism, since he claimed that things and their relations are immediately experienced. But his instrumentalism emphasized the constructive activity of the organism, which he thought continually "remodels" nature. He rejected any notion of direct correspondence between statement, belief, or judgment and external reality. He instead treated scientific theories as instrumental, that is, as "mental modes of *adaptation* to reality" (James, 1975, p. 94), and he functionalized essences as "teleological weapons of the mind." Scientific ideas were said to agree with their realities, but only "as if," and not literally so. "Energy," for example, does not in his view stand for anything objective: it is simply "a way of measuring the surface of phenomena so as to string their changes on a simple formula" (James, 1975, pp. 103–104). His constructivism, however, is hardly casual or undisciplined: it requires that a scientific theory must work, that is, that there must be a "tight fit" between its attempts to mediate between old truths and new experiences, on one side, and that "it must lead to some sensible terminus or other that can be verified exactly," on the other. According to James's genetic account, scientific truth is made in the same sense that health or wealth is made: in the course of experience (James, 1975, p. 104).

Croce (1995) recalls that the nineteenth century was a time during which professional scientists as well as lay people gradually replaced their idea that science produces certainty with the idea that science yields only probable knowledge. James understood this cultural shift and took it into account in his popular writings. He attempted to embrace the new probabilism; at the same time, he remained sensitive to the needs of individuals, especially religious individuals, who longed for confidence and assurance.

Dewey

Whereas Peirce had focused on communities of scientific researchers, James and Dewey wanted to extend scientific methods of thinking to a wider community. Like James, Dewey recognized and sought to overcome the traditional tension between realism and idealism. His 1905 essay "The Postulate of Immediate Empiricism," characterizes knowing as but one mode of experiencing. He postulated that things are what they are experienced to be; as such they are 'cognitive" (in the sense of related to cognition). It is the task of inquiry in the sciences and common sense alike to find out what things are when they are experienced as known things; science demands that experienced things enter the sphere of logical inquiry and thus be cognized (Dewey, 1977).

Dewey's version of empiricism thus holds that we have immediate experiences; but his instrumentalism holds that our experiences do not become knowledge until they are related to other experiences in ways that prove fruitful for what he terms the future control of facts. It is the function of inquiry to determine the connections between experienced things on those occasions when doubt is present. Dewey thus clarified and built on James's distinction between knowledge of acquaintance and knowledge about: he effectively removed simple acquaintance from the domain of knowing, treating such things as experienced but not as objects of knowledge. This difference between what is merely "had" and what is cognitively restructured anticipates Wilfrid Sellars's well-known treatment of "the myth of the given" (Sellars, 1956).

Like Peirce and James, Dewey criticized radical Cartesian doubt on two grounds: first, doubt cannot be universal, and second, it must be felt as real, rather than feigned. All three pragmatists admitted, however, that hypothesis formation and investigation in the sciences sometimes require doubt that does not arise spontaneously, but is provoked by studied attention to the details of unresolved projects and even by speculation. What is crucial, as James argued, is that doubt be felt, and not feigned. Also like Peirce and James, Dewey rejected foundationalism. He wrote of platforms of attainment: "Invention is selection, emphasis, and thus readjustment, on the platform of the attained." (Dewey, 1972b, p. 410) This metaphor anticipates Otto Neurath's famous antifoundationalist remark that philosophy is like rebuilding a ship at sea, plank by plank. It also resonates with anti-foundationalist statements by Daniel Dennett that describe cranes constructing other cranes, and so on.

Dewey and his colleagues at the University of Chicago established a school of functionalism which was eventually incorporated into mainstream psychology. Based principally on his criticism of the reflex arc concept in psychology, it treated ideas as functions of mind, and mind as a function of the biological organism rather than a physiological entity with discernable parts. The seminal text of functionalism was Dewey's 1896 essay "The Reflex Arc Concept in Psychology," in which he argued that stimulus and response are not distinguishable during the process of adjustment, but are instead identifiable as phases of the adjustive process only after the fact. He denied that stimulus is "external" to the organism; it is rather a complex field of sensory and motor actions, influenced by environment, including an organism's interests and expectations. Dewey's functionalism has provided the basis for some contemporary strands of cognitive science, such as dynamic systems theory (Rockwell, 2005).

In his account of the history of science and technology, Dewey distinguished Aristotle's observational or empirical proto-science, which he regarded as principally taxonomic, from the systematic experimental science that began to be developed in seventeenth-century Europe. Unlike the former, experimental science develops and utilizes a rich environment of instrumentation as a part of systematic, controlled experiments with a view to repeatability and verifiability. Dewey's treatment of technical issues of scientific inquiry was most thoroughly developed in his 1938 *Logic: The Theory of Inquiry*, a work that still awaits extensive analysis and commentary. One of the more interesting claims Dewey made during his debate with Bertrand Russell in the 1940s is that propositions are proposals: they are neither true nor false, but valid or invalid, relevant or irrelevant, with respect to judgments which may themselves be true or false. One consequence of this idea is that infinite regress of propositional truth claims is obviated and much of what Dewey termed the "Sisyphean task" of the "epistemological industry" is dissolved.

Scientific conceptions are, for Dewey, instruments. Like other instruments, they are "hand made by [humans] in pursuit of realization of a certain interest—that of convertibility of every object of thought into any and every other" (Dewey, 1984a, p. 109). Like Peirce and James, Dewey rejected what he termed the "spectator theory" of knowledge.

> The business of thought is not to conform to or reproduce the characters already possessed by objects but to judge them as potentialities of what they become through an indicated operation. . . . It is to describe experienceable objects as material upon which certain operations are performed. (Dewey, 1984a, p.110)

Dewey treated scientific laws as neither universal nor particular; they are instead means by which spatial–temporal connections are instituted that introduce continuity where there had been spatial–temporal interruptions and isolations (Dewey, 1981, p. 352).

Dewey's version of verificationism differs in important ways from the version advanced by the logical positivists. Whereas the positivists employed their verification principle (meaningful sentences must be empirically verifiable) to characterize as meaningless debates about metaphysics, religion, and even ethics, Dewey's project was quite different. He preferred the term "confrontation" as an indication of the nature of verification. If there is a question of whether a wall is white or brown, for instance, he thought that confrontation with the actual situation should settle the matter. In more complex cases, confrontation is just one constituent of a larger process. In the case of experimental results that are positive with respect to a hypothesis, confrontation is said to tend toward confirmation. In the case of experimental results that are negative with respect to an hypothesis, confrontation disproves the hypothesis as previously stated, but opens the door to modification of it. It is thus the "function of confrontations as experimentally determined consequences that confers upon them verifying power" (Dewey, 1988, p. 59).

Unlike the logical positivists, Dewey did not think statements about religion or art "meaningless" by definition. He distinguished the sciences, which he characterized as stating meanings, from the arts, which he characterized as expressing meanings. He thought that religious emotion involved "the quickening of ideas and affections by recognition of their inexhaustible signification" (Dewey, 1978, p. 402). His view of metaphysics was more complex. In a letter to a colleague he wrote that philosophers such as Russell and Wittgenstein had attempted a "short cut . . . of linguistic syntax to get rid of a lot of philosophical lumber—it ought to be got rid of but if they would do something more real a lot of it would just drop away" (Dewey, 2008a). On the other hand, as a part of his criticism of the logical positivists for their lack of interest in historical culture, he argued that seen from the viewpoint of cultural anthropology, "the appearance of metaphysics of different sorts is a highly instructive evidential phenomenon" (Dewey, 2008b).

Dewey's naturalism does not entail materialism, and he rejected any type of ontological split between what is material and what is ideal. "Matter" is treated as a conceptual tool that complex organisms employ as they seek to adjust to problematic circumstances. Neither matter nor the ideal has priority within experience; both are treated as tools that are abstracted from experience and that function in a variety of ways. Dewey's naturalism was cosmological in the sense that he rejected what is putatively supernatural or extra-natural. It was methodological in the sense that the methods of the sciences must rely only on what is available within experience of the space–time continuum.

Despite the claims of some of his critics, Dewey also rejected scientism. He rejected the claim that the methods or contents of the sciences are applicable everywhere within human experience. He also rejected the claim that the sciences are value free.

In his introduction to the revised edition of *Experience and Nature*, written in the late 1940s, Dewey discussed three key features of his Pragmatic philosophy of science. First, he rejected the idea that the foundations of science are found in epistemology rather than scientific practice. Epistemologists, he wrote, tend to be "unaware of the absurdity of seeking foundations outside the methods of knowing which have been tested and retested in the course of the very operations of inquiry in which they are put to use" (Dewey, 1981, p. 351). Second, he rejected the idea that there is a "problem of induction" outside of actual scientific practice. He referred to what he viewed as the "painful effort by up-to-date philosophers to find a justification for 'induction' outside and independent of the operations constituting the ongoing continuum of scientific inquiry" (Dewey, 1981, p. 351). Third, he argued that scientific laws should be treated as functional, not ontological: "the view that a law is a recurrent uniformity is often regarded as marking the triumph of positivism over metaphysics when in fact it represents an ontologizing of a distinction of functions, of services performed, in the conduct of inquiry" (Dewey, 1981, p. 352).

Quine

During the middle decades of the twentieth century, Willard Van Orman Quine appeared to many to have marshaled a much scaled down version of pragmatism as a part of his response to logical positivism. In his well-known essay "Two Dogmas of Empiricism" (1951) he argued against the empiricist "dogma" that there is a distinct class of analytic statements the truth of which can be known independent of experience. He also argued against the empiricist "dogma" of reductionism, or the theory that individual sense experiences confirm or disconfirm sentences or hypotheses. His alternative was a type of "web of belief" holism according to which a theory is always underdetermined by observation. Quine embraced the doctrine of fallibilism as well, holding that no sentence or hypothesis is immune from revision (Quine, 1951).

Some of Quine's critics, however, have suggested that his connection to classical pragmatism has been overstated. Hilary Putnam, for example, has argued that Quine went too far in the direction of relativism, thus in effect weakening the claims of the sciences. Putnam mounted a similar criticism of the work of neo-pragmatist Richard Rorty who went even further toward relativism by treating science as a type of literature.

A non-exhaustive list of other twentieth- and twenty-first-century philosophers and historians of science whose work exhibits recognizable strands of pragmatism would include Thomas Kuhn, Larry Laudan, Philip Kitcher, Daniel Dennett, and Steven Shapin.

Technology

Viewed in retrospect, it may seem strange that mid-twentieth-century treatments of the philosophy of science take so little notice of technology. The same is true of much of twentieth-century social and political philosophy. Given Dewey's considerable interest in tools and techniques, both quotidian and scientific, as an aspect of his wider program of instrumentalism, and given the fact that his published work is rich in technical metaphors, it is perhaps even more surprising that an extended treatment of his philosophy of technology did not appear until 1990 (Hickman, 1990).

Although Dewey sometimes wrote as if he simply accepted the common idea that technology is applied science, his view is in fact much more complex. In a 1948 essay, for example, he sketched his view of the relations among science, technology, and aesthetic experience. "Not only is scientific inquiry as it is conducted a highly skilled technology, but the consummatory fulfillments that are characteristic of the esthetic phase of life-experience play a highly important part in attaining the conclusions reached in science" (Dewey, 1989a, p. 98). In 1944 he wrote that he might have avoided misunderstanding if he had used the term "technology" instead of "instrumentalism" with respect to his view of the distinctive quality of science as knowledge (Dewey, 1989b, p. 89).

Unlike some European philosophers who viewed technology as alien to human life and a danger to its future, Dewey sought to naturalize technology in several ways. First, he refused to reify technology, that is, to treat technology as a thing or force. Second, perhaps as a part of his interest in anthropology, he located technology within the evolutionary history of human development. Third, his use of the term "technology" acknowledges its etymology. Technology is inquiry into tools and techniques: it is the logos of techne. Dewey's understanding of technology can be glossed as "the invention, development, and cognitive deployment of tools and other artifacts, brought to bear on raw materials and intermediate stock parts, with a view to the resolution of perceived problems" (Hickman, 2001, p. 12).

Dewey's treatment of technology has its roots in the 1890s. It thus anticipates by several decades the work of Martin Heidegger (1889–1976) who is still nevertheless widely acknowledged as the first philosopher to develop an extended account of technology in his 1927 work *Being and Time*. In *Experience and Nature* (1925) Dewey criticized the tendency of the Athenian Greeks to deprecate the work of the craftsman, subordinating technical production to practical and theoretical pursuits. This is a theme that Heidegger would take up two years later. Unlike Heidegger, however, who after the Second World War abandoned his earlier studies of the phenomenological dimensions of tools and techniques and embraced a view of technology that was both highly romanticized and darkly dystopian, Dewey continued throughout his lifetime to develop his initial insights. In 1930, during the Great Depression, he wrote that

"Technology" signifies all the intelligent techniques by which the energies of nature and man are directed and used in satisfaction of human needs; it cannot be limited to a few outer and comparatively mechanical forms. In the face of its possibilities, the traditional conception of experience is obsolete. (Dewey, 1984b, p. 270)

Dewey's position was also quite different from that of Jacques Ellul (1912–1994), whose books greatly influenced thinking about technology in the years during which the philosophy of technology was beginning to gain status as a distinguishable discipline. Ellul understood technology as a thing or force that is autonomous and that crowds out all possibility of human freedom. As is obvious from the passage just cited, Dewey's view is more positive. Instead of reifying technology as a thing or force, Dewey's instrumentalism is empirical: it calls for analyses of advantages as well as disadvantages of specific tools and techniques in specific cultural settings. Instead of the dystopian scenarios advanced by Ellul and the later Heidegger, Dewey emphasizes human freedom and agency, and especially the intimate connections among technology, democracy, and education.

Dewey's position also stands in sharp contrast to the treatment of technology advanced by the first generation of the Frankfurt School critical theorists Max Horkheimer (1895–1973) and Theodor Adorno (1903–1969). Perhaps because they were deeply affected by the horrors of two wars on the European continent, they tended to identify technology with alienation and domination. Dewey's response to arguments of this sort was to locate technology as inquiry into tools and other artifacts within the story of the evolution of human culture and societies. Whereas the critical theorists treated technology as "other," standing over against and threatening what is human, Dewey recognized technology as a central feature of developments that have allowed human beings to overcome the constraints imposed on them by their natural environment, such as disease, hunger, and isolation. He urged that technical successes should be extended in ways that would promote greater social good.

Dewey's use of the term "instrumentalism" to characterize his position has often been the source of difficulty, especially among European philosophers who have tended to confuse his position with what has been termed "straight line" instrumentalism, or "*Zweckrationalität*," which privileges ends over means. Dewey was careful to point out that if inquiry is to be successful, means and ends must inform one another and be balanced with respect to one another. In his 1929 *Quest for Certainty* Dewey wrote that

> Knowledge is instrumental. But the purport of our whole discussion has been in praise of tools, instrumentalities, means, putting them on a level equal in value to ends and consequences, since without them the latter are merely accidental, sporadic and unstable. To call known objects, in their capacity of being objects of knowledge, means is to appreciate them, not to depreciate them. (Dewey, 1984a, p. 238)

His treatment of instrumentalities also distinguishes Dewey's understanding of science and technology from that of "second generation" critical theorist Jürgen Habermas (1929–). Habermas has drawn a sharp line between the methods of the human sciences, on one side, and the methods of the natural sciences, on the other, in effect creating a split between the techno-sciences, which he thinks have to do with facts, and the communicative and emancipatory activities of the human sciences, which he thinks are uniquely concerned with the development of meaning. Dewey rejected ontological and methodological splits of this type. His general theory of inquiry is designed as a kind of "liaison officer," facilitating communication between various sciences, including the empirical, historical-hermeneutical, and critical sciences that Habermas has kept distinct.

Although philosophical studies of technology continue to include a wide range of approaches such as those that are rooted in the work of Heidegger (Albert Borgmann), Christian theology (Carl Mitcham), feminist studies (Donna Haraway), and the history of science (Peter Galison) among others, it is possible to regard recent developments in the field as trending to some of the ideas that were present in Dewey's work from the 1890s to the 1940s.

Peter-Paul Verbeek, for example, has called for philosophers to abandon many of the elements of what he calls the "classical" period of the philosophy of technology. These elements, which include the alienation thesis, attempt to ground the philosophy of technology transcendentally, reification of technology, and technophobia are easily recognizable as themes that Dewey had rejected. Verbeek singles out the late Heidegger for criticism, arguing that his work tended to be monolithic, abstract, and nostalgic. He turns to the work of Don Ihde for inspiration. Ihde's work, which has admittedly been influenced by Dewey, adds a hermeneutic dimension to an instrumentalist, post-phenomenological approach. For Ihde, like Dewey's instrumentalism, tools and techniques are multivalent. Like Dewey, Ihde regards "instruments as actually constituting the objects studied by the sciences and therefore co-determining the content of scientific knowledge" (Verbeek, 2000, p. 142). Briefly put, both Verbeek and Dewey before him want to avoid studies of technology that attempt to place them in the history of Being. Both make the functionalist argument that studies of technology should focus on what things do.

Since the late 1990s, the work of Andrew Feenberg, who was a student of Herbert Marcus (1898–1979), has also taken a pragmatic turn. He has abandoned essentialism for functionalism, developed a thick constructivism, rejected the notion of technology as ideology, warned against reification of the results of inquiry, and proposed a kind of network theory that blurs the line between artifacts and social relations. Each of these moves is consistent with the core pragmatic treatment of technology advanced by Dewey.

It is also possible to find Dewey's pragmatic technology in the work of Bruno Latour. Latour argues that the social history of science properly attends to "techniques in all of the meanings of the word: one of them being art, another being know-how, a third being 'intellectual techniques' or 'paper techniques,' and of course the most important being the new role given to instruments" (Olsen, *et al.*, 2007, p. 131). Dewey had distinguished each of these aspects of technology. He had argued that the difference between tangible and conceptual artifacts is functional, not ontological, and he had pointed out that our tools, techniques, and artifacts teem with meanings that require evaluation and reconstruction when there is a perceived difficulty.

References

Burch, R. (2009), "Charles Sanders Peirce" *Stanford Encyclopedia of Philosophy*, (online) Available at: <http://plato.stanford.edu/entries/peirce/> (Accessed January 5, 2010).

Croce, P. J. (1995), *Science and Religion in the Era of William James: Eclipse of Certainty, 1820–1880*, vol. 1. Chapel Hill: University of North Carolina Press.

Dalton, T. (2002), *Becoming John Dewey: Dilemmas of a Philosopher and Naturalist*. Bloomington: Indiana University Press.

Dewey, J. (1972a), "The Reflex Arc Concept in Psychology," in J. A. Boydston (ed.), *The Collected Works of John Dewey: The Early Works, 1882–1898*, vol. 5. Carbondale: Southern Illinois University Press, pp. 96–110.

—(1972b), "Review of *Social and Ethical Interpretations in Mental Development*," in J. A. Boydston (ed.), *The Collected Works of John Dewey: The Early Works, 1882–1898*, vol. 5. Carbondale: Southern Illinois University Press, pp. 385–422.

—(1977), "The Postulate of Immediate Empiricism," in J. A. Boydston (ed.), *The Collected Works of John Dewey: The Middle Works, 1899–1924*, vol. 3. Carbondale: Southern Illinois University Press, pp. 158–167.

—(1978), *Ethics*, in J. A. Boydston (ed.), *The Collected Works of John Dewey: The Middle Works, 1899-1924*, vol 5. Carbondale: Southern Illinois University Press.

—(1981), *Experience and Nature*, in J. A. Boydston (ed.), *The Collected Works of John Dewey: The Later Works, 1925-1953*, vol. 1. Carbondale: Southern Illinois University Press.

—(1984a), *The Quest for Certainty*, in J. A. Boydston (ed.), *The Collected Works of John Dewey: The Later Works, 1925-1953*, vol. 4. Carbondale: Southern Illinois University Press.

—(1984b), "What I Believe," in J. A. Boydston (ed.), *The Collected Works of John Dewey: The Early Works, 1925-1953*, vol. 5. Carbondale: Southern Illinois University Press, pp. 267-279.

—(1986), *Logic: The Theory of Inquiry*, in J. A. Boydston (ed.), *The Collected Works of John Dewey: The Later Works, 1925-1953*, vol. 12. Carbondale: Southern Illinois University Press.

—(1988), "Experience, Knowledge and Value: A Rejoinder," in J. A. Boydston (ed.), *The Collected Works of John Dewey: The Later Works, 1925-1953*, vol. 14. Carbondale: Southern Illinois University Press, pp. 3-91.

—(1989a), "A Comment on the Foregoing Criticisms," in J. A. Boydston (ed.), *The Collected Works of John Dewey: The Later Works, 1925-1953*, vol. 15. Carbondale: Southern Illinois University Press, pp. 97-101.

—(1989b), "By Nature and by Art," in J. A. Boydston (ed.), *The Collected Works of John Dewey: The Later Works, 1925-1953*, vol. 15. Carbondale: Southern Illinois University Press, pp. 84-96.

—(2008a), "John Dewey to Corinne Chisholm Frost," 22 July 1939 (09313), in L. A. Hickman (ed.), *The Correspondence of John Dewey*. Charlottesville, VA: Intelex.

—(2008b), "John Dewey to Arthur F. Bentley," 07 April 1939 (08614), in L. A. Hickman (ed.), *The Correspondence of John Dewey*. Charlottesville, VA: Intelex.

Gentry, G. (1952), "Habit and the Logical Interpretant," in P. Wiener and F. Young (eds), *Studies in the Philosophy of Charles Sanders Peirce*. Cambridge: Harvard University Press, pp. 75-90.

Heidegger, M. (1927), *Sein und Zeit*. Halle: M. Niemeyer. Republished as *Being and Time*. Translated by J. Macquarrie and E. Robinson. New York: Harper 1962.

Hickman, L. (1990), *John Dewey's Pragmatic Technology*. Bloomington: Indiana University Press.

—(2001), *Philosophical Tools for Technological Culture: Putting Pragmatism to Work*. Bloomington: Indiana University Press.

James, W. (1975), *Pragmatism*, Ed. F. Burkhard. Cambridge: Harvard University Press.

Olsen, J. and Selinger, E., (eds), (2007), *Philosophy of Technology: 5 Questions*. New York: Automatic Press.

Peirce, C. S. (1986a), "The Fixation of Belief," in C. Klossel (ed.), *The Writings of Charles S. Peirce*, vol. 3. Bloomington: Indiana University Press, pp. 242-257.

—(1986b), "How to Make Our Ideas Clear," in C. Klossel (ed.), *The Writings of Charles S. Peirce*, vol. 3. Bloomington: Indiana University Press, pp. 257–276.

Pihlström, S. (2008), "How (not) to Write the History of Pragmatist Philosophy of Science?". *Perspectives on Science*, 16, (1), 26–69.

Putnam, H. (1987), *The Many Faces of Realism*. LaSalle, IL: Open Court.

Quine, W. V. O. (1951), "Two Dogmas of Empiricism." *The Philosophical Review*, 60, 20–43. (Reprinted in *From a Logical Point of View*, 2nd edn. New York: Harper Torch books, 1961.)

Rockwell, W. (2005), *Neither Brain Nor Ghost: A Nondualist Alternative to the Mind-Brain Identity Theory*. Cambridge: The MIT Press.

Sellars, W. (1956), "Empiricism and the Philosophy of Mind," in H. Feign and M. Scriven (eds), *The Foundations of Science and the Concepts of Psychoanalysis: Minnesota Studies in the Philosophy of Science*, vol. 1. Minneapolis, MN: University of Minnesota Press, pp. 253–329.

Smullyan, A. (1952), "Some Implications of Critical Common-sensism," in P. Wiener and F. Young (eds), *Studies in the Philosophy of Charles Sanders Peirce*. Cambridge: Harvard University Press, pp. 111–120.

Verbeek, P. P. (2000), *What Things Do: Philosophical Reflection on Technology, Agency and Design*. Translated by R. J. Clease. University Park, PA: The Pennsylvania State University Press.

Wiener, P. and Young, F. (eds), (1952), *Studies in the Philosophy of Charles Sanders Peirce*. Cambridge: Harvard University Press.

7
Aesthetics

Armen T. Marsoobian

Art and aesthetic experience are central to the human condition and as such are of prime importance to most pragmatist philosophers, who attempt to make sense of experience. John Dewey stands out among the classic American pragmatists for the critical attention he gave to art and, most importantly, aesthetic experience. Aesthetic experience lies at the core of his understanding of human experience, and it plays a vital role in his meliorism. Contemporary pragmatist aestheticians sympathetic to Dewey's vision of philosophy find much to admire in his writings on art and the role it can play in the betterment of life. After a period of eclipse, his writings on aesthetics have grown in influence within mainstream philosophical aesthetics. Of the other pragmatists from the classic period in American philosophy, Charles Sanders Peirce and William James require brief mention, but neither could be said to have fully developed a theory of aesthetics. Many of the sustaining themes that emerge in all these thinkers, especially in James and Dewey, can first be found in the writings of Ralph Waldo Emerson.

Emerson

While his reflections on art predate much of the pragmatist work of the founding decade of the 1870s, many today argue that Emerson was a proto-pragmatist. He was a Transcendentalist philosopher, essayist, and poet, who took many of his themes from the Romantic tradition and gave them a unique formulation that still reverberates in the American intellectual landscape. He was writing in a milieu in which post-Kantian idealism and talk of mind or soul inhabiting nature dominated aesthetic thought. Emerson's idealism is manifested in his claims about artistic creation. He begins his 1841 essay "Art" with these words: "Because the soul is progressive, it never quite repeats itself, but in every act attempts the production of a new and fairer whole. This appears in works both of the useful and the fine arts." Art, he goes on, does not imitate nature but captures the "expression of nature. . . . Thus in our fine arts, not imitation, but creation is the aim" (Emerson, 1841, p. 209). Art is never naïve mimesis.

Emerson often speaks of the artist as a conduit for a higher intelligence: "The artist's pen and chisel seems to have been held and guided by a gigantic hand to inscribe a line in the history of the human race" (ibid., p. 210). The beauty in nature and the beauty of art derive from the same source in the fount of creativity that runs through both the human and the nonhuman world. Emerson identifies this source by many names, often referring to it as the "Soul," or an "Aboriginal Power," or "Art" with a capital *A*. Art and nature are one: "In happy hours, nature appears to us one with art; art perfected—the work of genius" (ibid., p. 213). If nature is art perfected, then artists in creating works of art are attempting to capture or express something intrinsic to themselves. Artistic creation is the expression of human character: "The artist will find in his work an outlet for his proper character" (ibid., p. 214). For Emersonian idealism there is no contradiction in the claim that art expresses nature while at the same time expressing human character. Works of art are intelligible to us because we see "the deepest and simplest attributes of our nature" manifested in them. Artists do not respond to the history of art and art-making. Emerson may well have been puzzled by the fashionable twentieth-century notion that the subject matter of art is art itself. For him, art was not self-referential; its models were "life, household life, and the sweet and smart of personal relations, of beating hearts, and meeting eyes, of poverty, and necessity, and hope, and fear" (ibid., pp. 213–214).

Emerson saw the role of the arts as central to the project of human self-creation. Art serves a unique educative goal. One does not study art merely for the sake of art appreciation. Art is neither created nor experienced for its own sake. One does not study art in order to learn the new or the unfamiliar. On the contrary, art brings us back to the familiar in new and surprising ways. Emerson writes of his travels in Europe and his encounters with its art as an experience of "the simple and true." The cloistering of fine art in the alien confines of a gallery does not prevent him from experiencing the "familiar and sincere; . . . the old, eternal fact that I had met already in so many forms—unto which I had lived." Art must not "dazzle," must not be "too picturesque" (ibid., pp. 214–215). This claim is consistent with Emerson's highly influential cultural criticism that was later to serve as a model for Friedrich Nietzsche. Art loses touch with its true resources in the human when it becomes too preoccupied with technique and surface brilliance. Art that is produced purely for show or extravagance is an art that has not achieved maturity. Art will remain immature "if it is not practical and moral, if it do[es] not stand in connection with the conscience, if it do[es] not make the poor and uncultivated feel that it addresses them with a voice of lofty cheer" (ibid., p. 215).

Emerson is clearly providing a normative conception of art. He is presenting a diagnosis for the moral ills of humankind while identifying its telltale symptoms in the products of art. A clear symptom of these ills is the perversion of beauty. Emerson contends that when humans are dissatisfied with their moral self-image, "they flee to art, and convey their better sense in an oratorio, a statue, or a picture." As a result the practical and everyday becomes devoid of beauty. By divorcing beauty from the useful and placing it primarily in the domain of fine art, we demean and degrade aesthetic beauty. If pleasure and enjoyment find their only source in aesthetic beauty, then art becomes a form of "escapism" from the everyday: "As soon as beauty is sought not from religion and love, but for pleasure, it degrades the seeker. High beauty is no longer attainable by him in canvas or in stone, in sound, or in lyrical construction; an effeminate prudent, sickly beauty, which is not beauty, is all that can be formed" (ibid., p. 215). The cure for this disease is to live life as art. In transposing aesthetic and literary categories to human individuals, Emerson provides a striking reimagining of human possibilities: "All works of art should not be detached, but extempore performances. A great man is a new statue in every attitude and action. . . . Life may be lyric or epic, as well as a poem or a romance" (ibid., pp. 216–217). Beauty will thus be restored to the commonplace and the practical. "Beauty must come back to the useful arts, and the distinction between the fine and the useful arts be forgotten." Everyday experience would be an enhanced aesthetic experience. The strict distinction between instrumental and aesthetic no longer holds. The artistic instinct in all humans would thus "find beauty and holiness in new and necessary facts, in the field and roadside, in the shop and mill" (ibid., p. 218).

The theme that art is an enhanced experience of the commonplace is one that Dewey takes up almost a hundred years later in *Art as Experience* (1934). Art for art's sake is not to be countenanced. The idea that fine art is divorced from the everyday, and can only be experienced by distancing oneself from practical, utilitarian concerns, is an idea rejected not only by Emerson and Dewey but also by many pragmatically influenced aestheticians.

Peirce and James

Among the founding pragmatists, Charles Sanders Peirce is worthy of mention, not for any extensive or sustained treatment of art on his part, but for the fecundity of his semeiotic theory for future analyses of art. In the visual arts, music, theater, and literary analysis, extensive investigations have been undertaken using Peirce's concepts of sign, object, and interpretant. While Peirce identified a place for aesthetics in his philosophical edifice, he never developed its role to any significant extent. In his division of the sciences into the exact and the normative sciences, aesthetics falls under the normative category: "Philosophy has three grand divisions. The first is phenomenology, which simply contemplates the Universal Phenomenon and discerns its ubiquitous elements, Firstness, Secondness, and Thirdness. . . . The second grand division is Normative Science, which investigates the universal and necessary laws of the relation of Phenomena to *Ends*, that is, perhaps, to Truth, Right, and Beauty. The third grand division is Metaphysics, which endeavors to comprehend the Reality of the Phenomena" (Peirce, 1934). The three normative sciences, Logic, Ethics, and Aesthetics, are associated with the three "Ends" (or types of goodness) of "Truth, Right, and Beauty." How these three normative sciences interact is a complicated and never fully articulated affair. That they do interact is a given, for in its concern with the qualities of feeling, the science of aesthetics would not come to much without Semeiotic, that part of Logic devoted to the analyses of sign function. Much subsequent work has been done in employing Peirce's sign theory to understand how aesthetic meaning is engendered by artworks.

William James placed the aesthetic at the core of his conception of human experience. At the most fundamental level we organize human lived experience in terms of certain recognizable patterns of selective interest. The source of these patterns lies in certain fundamental needs, or what James sometimes refers to as activating depositions. We manipulate the great blooming buzzing confusion of our encounters with the world into particular patterns based upon both aesthetic and practical needs. Both are often present, though one may dominate over the other. The details of the role of selective interest in shaping consciousness and our rational thought processes are laid out in James's *The Principles of Psychology* (1890). Unfortunately, no systematic treatment of the aesthetic is given.[1] James uses a variety of terms to characterize the patterns generated by our aesthetic needs. "Harmony" and "unity" stand out, but he also claims that "clarity," "simplicity," and a "profusion of detail and specificity" mark the patterns created by our aesthetic needs. We will see that Dewey is working from a similar palette when he describes his notion of "*an* experience."

James will use his insights into these motivating interests to explain, criticize, and reform higher-level processes of scientific and philosophic reasoning. For instance, James's criticism of philosophical rationalism's drive toward system-building is traced to this aesthetic need for unity and harmony. On the other hand, the practical interest that is borne out in the positive results of the scientific method can itself go awry if the abundance of detail is ignored in the race toward results. While James's discussions of the arts and artistic processes are not extensive, they play an important role in his critique of rationalist philosophy and his promotion of radical empiricism. We should note that in his early manhood he studied painting and hoped to pursue an artistic career. James's interests in the arts, while submerged, are continually evident. He advocates a strong role for artistic vision in reforming philosophy. Artistic vision, or what he sometimes refers to as "seeing in" or "seeing into," is contrasted to the simple seeing underlying positivist science and the unduly rationalist philosophies based on simple observation. Both scientists and artists engage in analogical thinking when observing the world. Yet scientists are often too quick to jump to abstraction, never returning to the richness of detail that initially marks our interaction with the world. Attention to the aesthetic dimension of thinking, making, and doing is implicit in many of James's observations. For Dewey, the aesthetic dimension of human experience will play an even more prominent role.

Dewey

Dewey began his philosophical investigations of art and the aesthetic relatively late in his career. Though he recognized the importance of the fine arts and crafts for his educational theory, it was not until the mid-1920s that he began any systematic treatment of the arts. His friendship with the art collector and former student Albert C. Barnes helped solidify his interests in the visual arts, especially painting. In 1925 Dewey delivered his Carus Lectures, which appeared that year as *Experience and Nature*. Undoubtedly it would have been a significantly different work if Dewey had not been as absorbed in the fine arts during this especially fecund period in his intellectual development. The whole of his metaphysical analysis of experience is shaped by his insights into aesthetic experience. Dewey's intellectual journey culminated in his 1931 William James

Lectures at Harvard University, which were to serve as the basis of his seminal work *Art as Experience* (1934).

In the penultimate chapter of *Experience and Nature*, "Experience, Nature and Art," Dewey brings together many of the themes of the previous chapters. He is concerned to demonstrate the limitations of the distinctions common to both philosophical and everyday discussions of science and the arts. He contends that beginning with the ancient Greeks there has been a tendency to disparage the practical, so-called menial arts, in contradistinction to the theoretical activities of reason and science. Theoretical activity was contemplation, not practice. This prejudice has been carried over into the present day in a slightly altered form: "Modern thought ... combines exaltation of science with eulogistic appreciation of art, especially of fine and creative art" (Dewey, 1929, p. 355). Unlike the Greeks who saw the commonalities between the fine arts and the practical industrial arts, our modern age emphasizes their differences, resulting in an "esoteric" or "museum" view of fine art. Art and the aesthetic are more and more isolated from everyday activities.

For Dewey the lesson to be learned from the success of modern science is that theory is not akin to the Greek notion of contemplation; rather, theory is infused with practice. Dewey would like us to cut through all the unhelpful distinctions that inhabit our intellectual landscape: "It would then be seen that science is an art, that art is practice, and that the only distinction worth drawing is not between practice and theory, but between those modes of practice that are not intelligent, not inherently and immediately enjoyable, and those which are full of enjoyed meanings" (ibid., p. 358). Dewey places his examination of the fine arts within this broader project. Instead of dualisms Dewey provides a naturalistic account that stresses the continuities between the biological, the psychological, the social, and the intellectual. Art in this most generic sense plays a pivotal role in his naturalistic metaphysics of experience. This is how Dewey summarizes his book's argument:

> Thus the issue involved in experience as art in its pregnant sense and in art as processes and materials of nature continued by direction into achieved and enjoyed meanings, sums up in itself all the issues which have been previously considered. Thought, intelligence, science is the intentional direction of natural events to meanings capable of immediate possession and enjoyment; this direction—which is operative art—is itself a natural event in which nature otherwise partial and incomplete comes fully to itself. ... The doings and sufferings that form experience are, in the degree in which experience is

intelligent or charged with meanings, a union of the precarious, novel, irregular with the settled, assured and uniform—a union which also defines the artistic and the esthetic. For wherever there is art the contingent and ongoing no longer work at cross purposes with the formal and recurrent but commingle in harmony. (Ibid., pp. 358–359)

This commingling in harmony is what Dewey in *Art as Experience* calls "*an* experience." While the theme of *Art as Experience* is more explicitly focused upon fine art and aesthetic experience, this notion of "*an* experience" is fundamental for an understanding of his overall project.

In *Art as Experience*, Dewey provides a far-ranging reconstructive analysis of many issues central to philosophical aesthetics, including the definition of a work of art, the nature of expression, the relation of form and content, and the role of appreciation and criticism. To understand this reconstructive approach and the key role that "*an* experience" plays in it, we must first lay out what this notion of experience is not. Dewey denies that he is employing the term in the manner of the British empiricist tradition. For Dewey traditional empiricism provides a much too subjectivist approach. Experience is not something "had" in the mind but is the interaction of the human organism with its environment, an interaction that has reached a particular level of organization. For Dewey "experience is *of* as well as *in* nature." Eschewing dualistic approaches that place experience as some sort of veil between us and nature, he continues: "It is not experience which is experienced, but nature—stones, plants, animals, diseases, health, temperature, electricity, and so on. Things interacting in certain ways *are* experience; they are what is experienced. Linked in certain other ways with another natural object—the human organism—they are *how* things are experienced as well. Experience thus reaches down into nature; it has depth" (Dewey, 1929, p. 4a). Dewey brings this reconstructed concept of experience to his analyses in *Art as Experience*.

In *Art as Experience*, Dewey suggests that in order to understand the meaning of artistic products we must first take a "detour" through "the ordinary forces and conditions of experience that we do not usually regard as esthetic." His aim of "going back to experience of the common or mill run of things" is "to discover the esthetic quality such experience possesses." For he claims that the "work of art," as distinguished from the "art work or product," is an intensification of the aesthetic quality that lies dormant in much of our "normal" or everyday experience. The artwork, for example, the poem, painting, or song, will issue from the work of art. The appreciation of artworks also works in a similar fashion. The implication is that there is nothing alien, mysterious, or otherworldly about artistic creation. Dewey contends that the "full meaning of ordinary experience is expressed" in our experience of art (see Dewey, 1934, pp. 11–13).

The opening chapters of *Art as Experience* trace the "biological commonplaces" that lie at the root of aesthetic experience, the chief of which Dewey identifies as the continual attempt of the organism to reach an equilibrium between itself and its environment. Humans, along with all "live creatures," are forever trying to establish a balance or harmony with their environments. Dewey often refers to this state of harmony as a "consummation" that is "akin to the esthetic" (ibid., p. 15). Such consummations result in what Dewey calls "*an* experience." Without such equilibrium there is no growth. Whether it is at the more complex level of ordinary experience or that of an aesthetic experience with an artwork, the generic traits of "*an* experience" are key to understanding what may justifiably be called Dewey's notion of life as art. Dewey claims that the traits of completeness, uniqueness, and qualitative unity characterize "*an* experience." The live creature in constant interaction with its environment, in a constant tension of doing and undergoing, has moments of fulfillment. In an often-quoted passage, Dewey writes:

> We have *an* experience when the material experienced runs its course to fulfillment. Then and then only is it integrated within and demarcated in the general stream of experience from other experiences. A piece of work is finished in a way that is satisfactory; a problem receives its solution; a game is played through; a situation, whether that of eating a meal, playing a game of chess, carrying on a conversation, writing a book, or taking part in a political campaign, is so rounded out that its close is a consummation and not a cessation. Such an experience is a whole and carries with it its own individualizing quality and self-sufficiency. It is *an* experience. (Ibid., p. 35)

These examples are of varying temporal duration and character and are not necessarily aesthetic in the sense of a fine art sense of the aesthetic. Yet they are all aesthetic in the generic sense Dewey wishes to employ. All these experiences have an emotional element that he calls their "esthetic quality," a quality that "rounds out an experience into completeness and unity" (ibid., p. 41). When experience fails to achieve such consummations we say that the experience was "anesthetic" or "non-esthetic." The aesthetic and the anaesthetic are on a continuum. For Dewey the aesthetic is a matter of degree, not kind. Every experience has in some rudimentary sense the traits of the aesthetic. The task of social intelligence is to make the aesthetic more available in all our doings and makings.

The above task is also true of the fine and performing arts. The pages of *Art as Experience* are rich with suggestions for enhancing our lives through "*an* experience" with the arts. Dewey also reserves sharp criticism for the theories and attitudes about art that are hindrances to such experiences. He often refers to these as the "esoteric theories of art." Highly subjectivist views of expression as well as excessively formalist approaches to art are criticized.

Dewey's criticism of formalism hinges on the distinction he draws between his notion of aesthetic form and that of significant form advocated by such formalists as Clive Bell and Roger Fry. For such formalists the representational content of an artwork is irrelevant and can be a distraction from the aesthetic emotion and experience the work evokes. Dewey does see a virtue to the formalist's desire for a heightened mindfulness to what is in the work itself rather than being drawn away by questions of "aboutness." He believes that there is a "harmony" and "rhythm" in aesthetic seeing that leads to a unique kind of focused attention. For him the aesthetic form of an artwork opens out into one's wider experience and enriches it in important ways. He contends that the formalist appreciation of significant form rests upon a totally ahistorical notion of experience. For Dewey the having of experience cannot be treated as a discrete here and now event. Such ahistorical discreteness smacks of the empiricist tradition he is attempting to overturn. Aesthetic form is not the "exclusive result of the lines and colors" but "a function of what is in the scene in its interaction with what the beholder brings with him." For Dewey the aesthetic emotion that is stirred by aesthetic form is not divorced from the emotional life of the artist or the audience. He always stresses the continuities in experience: "Some subtle affinity with the current of his own experience as a live creature causes lines and colors to arrange themselves in one pattern and rhythm rather than another" (ibid., pp. 88–89). There is for Dewey no state of pristine seeing. Aesthetic sensibility is a complex affair, involving more than the seeing of lines and colors in terms of their formal relationships within a painting.

For Dewey the need for a more focused and mindful experience with art is a reflection of the need for a more focused and mindful experience with our everyday routines and activities. Dewey's ultimate goal is to bring this "reconstructed" sense of aesthetic sensibility and engagement with artworks to the world of our more mundane activities. The goal is to live life as art, but in the uniquely Deweyan sense of art. Living life as art requires that all our experiences attain aesthetic form to some degree. This may be a herculean project, but it is one that Dewey was unwilling to shirk.

Dewey's challenge to base inquiry upon this reconstructed sense of aesthetic experience was not taken up by philosophical aesthetics in the years that followed. On the contrary, the focus narrowed as a result of the rise of logical positivism and its adoption into the academic life of American universities. The period from the 1940s to the early 1970s is marked by a general disinterest on the part of most Anglo-American philosophers in global approaches to art and aesthetic phenomena. With the rare exceptions of Monroe C. Beardsley, Justus Buchler, and Susanne K. Langer, American philosophers eschewed systematic treatments of the arts. While we can trace significant continuities between these three philosophers and the chief figures in the classic American philosophical tradition, especially Peirce, James, Whitehead, and Dewey, they do not fall comfortably within a chapter whose purview is pragmatist aesthetics. For their part, none of these philosophers made explicit claims to be working in the pragmatist tradition.

Contemporary pragmatist aesthetics

Concomitant with the general revival of pragmatism in the 1980s and 1990s was an increasing emphasis on pragmatist and pluralist themes in the mainstream of philosophical aesthetics. Pragmatist approaches to aesthetics were inherently amenable to incorporating the diverse perspectives of feminism and race into their studies. This has resulted in an array of new areas of study within philosophical aesthetics, including but not limited to environmental aesthetics, feminist aesthetics, aesthetics of everyday objects, and somaesthetics. Three contemporary philosophers whose pragmatic roots cut across the Analytic-Continental divide will briefly be examined by way of conclusion: Arnold Berleant, Joseph Margolis, and Richard Shusterman.

The philosophical roots of Arnold Berleant (1932–) lie both in American pragmatic naturalism, especially the work of Dewey, and in Continental phenomenology. In addition, he is an accomplished musician and composer. His early work *The Aesthetic Field: A Phenomenology of Aesthetic Experience* (1970) appeared at a time when the philosophical mainstream was rather inhospitable to such global treatments of art. Berleant began from the premise that any account of art must begin from a phenomenology of how art actually works in human experience. He in effect suspends the traditional question of first having to conceptually define art. He identifies and describes four distinguishable dimensions or perspectives in aesthetic experience: the art object, the perceiver, the artist, and the performer. Each of these dimensions interacts with and affects all the others. For instance, aesthetic appreciation on the part of the perceiver has creative, objective, and performative aspects. When his next book, *Art and Engagement*, appeared years later (1991), the philosophical climate had markedly changed. New areas of scholarly investigation were opening up in philosophical aesthetics. This new aesthetics was challenging the aesthetic theory that had been codified in the eighteenth century and had held sway for two hundred years. Berleant directly challenges this tradition with his concept of engagement. Aesthetic theory had been built upon "three axioms": "that art consists primarily of objects, that these objects possess a special status, and that they must be regarded in a unique way" (Berleant, 1991, p. 11). The emphasis on the art "object" results in a philosophical obsession with identity and its need to isolate necessary and sufficient aesthetic properties rather than focusing on the nature of aesthetic experience. The "special status" of artworks and the "unique way" of regarding them generate the isolation of art from the ordinary that Dewey had bemoaned and create all sorts of dead-end questions about what is real and what is not when it comes to art and its objects. The dominance of "disinterestedness" as the officially sanctioned mode of access to artworks is the chief target of Berleant's reconstruction of aesthetics as engagement. This reconstruction highlights significant pragmatic features: "Aesthetic engagement . . . displays at least three related characteristics: continuity, perceptual integration, and participation" (ibid., p. 46). Like Dewey, Berleant acknowledges that art is an activity that is continuous with other human pursuits and shares a common origin with other forms of human activity and productive technology. Our encounters with art display a perceptual integration in which there is "an experiential fusion of the senses" that provides a wholeness or integrity to the encounter. Finally, artworks, especially most forms of contemporary art, call for active participation, not disinterested perception. In a very Deweyan turn of phrase, Berleant writes: "Art does not consist of objects but of situations in which experiences occur" (ibid., p. 49).

What marks out Berleant's approach from Dewey's is his detailed analysis of contemporary art and the changes that have taken place in art-making in the course of the past century. He contends that "aesthetic theory must examine artistic practice carefully and consider how best to respond to this alteration and enlargement of the traditional station and experience of the arts" (ibid., p. 20). Practice must drive theory, not the other way around. It is in the practice of artists that Berleant finds inspiration for his aesthetics of engagement:

"Artists have been forcing us to realize that entering the world of art requires active engagement of the total person and not just a subjective cast of mind. Such engagement emphasizes connections and continuities, and it leads ultimately to the aestheticization of the human world. Art thus remains distinctive without being separate" (ibid., p. 26). Much of *Art and Engagement* is taken up with close examinations of how making art and appreciating art exemplify Berleant's concept of engagement. His insightful analyses of landscape painting, architecture as environmental design, literature, music, dance, and cinema demonstrate his sensitivity to artistic practice. In a number of subsequent articles and books, in particular *Aesthetics of the Environment* (1992) and *Living in the Landscape: Toward an Aesthetics of Environment* (1997), Berleant has contributed much to the new field of environmental aesthetics and has carried forward his project of aesthetic engagement.

Joseph Margolis (1924–) has been writing about art since the late 1950s and has produced a number of important theoretical works on aesthetics. Though his graduate work in philosophy was at Columbia University in the late 1940s and early 1950s, his early work in philosophical aesthetics does not bear the mark of Dewey's pragmatic naturalism. From his 1958 article attacking Morris Weitz's Wittgensteinian approach to the concept of art to his writings on art in the early 1970s, his approach was clearly in the mold of the analytical aesthetics of the time. It is with his more mature works on aesthetics that some affinities with pragmatism appear. In a number of recent books Margolis has explicitly taken up a dialogue with the classical pragmatists and their neo-pragmatist descendants, in particular Richard Rorty and Hilary Putnam. The highly nuanced and complex arguments of these critical dialogues cannot be adequately summarized here. *Pragmatism's Advantage* (2010), Margolis's most recent book on the state of contemporary philosophy, makes clear both his preference for a pragmatism that is appropriately historicized and his rejection of what he perceives as the dead-end questions of analytic metaphysical realism as it is practiced today. Given this preference, certain affinities with pragmatism can be identified in his treatment of art. Margolis offers the following definition of art:

> An artwork is a historicized utterance that is physically embodied, culturally emergent, possessing Intentionally qualified properties that are determinable but not determinate in the way mere material properties are said to be. (Margolis, 2009, p. 136)

Margolis is attempting to find a middle ground by rejecting idealist theories of art and reductive materialist alternatives. In this anti-dualist approach typical of many pragmatists, culture penetrates the material world and transforms it in meaningful ways. This continually evolving process precludes the possibility of there being a static fixed essence or nature to artworks or to the human beings who create them. Meaning always emerges through the interpretative practices of the historically located makers and appreciators of art. Aesthetic properties are never merely "given" or "found." They are culturally constructed "Intentionally qualified properties" whose very existence is dependent upon the interpretations of the "second-natured" historically situated human selves who create them. While Margolis makes little or no reference to Dewey or to pragmatism in his writings on art, the Darwinian and Hegelian influences on both men are evident, and for Margolis explicitly acknowledged.

Among the philosophers we are concerned with here, Richard Shusterman (1949–) was the first to explicitly use the term "pragmatist aesthetics" to classify his philosophical perspective on the arts. His 1992 book, *Pragmatist Aesthetics: Living Beauty, Rethinking Art*, is an explication, critique, and extension of Dewey's theory of art. This often translated book has been influential in contributing to the international reach of pragmatism. Shusterman, conversant with both the contemporary scene in traditional analytic aesthetics and the postmodern and hermeneutical perspectives originating in Continental philosophy, employs his Deweyan pragmatist inclinations to address the perceived shortcomings of both analysis and postmodernism. He shares many of the same motivations that propelled Dewey in *Art as Experience*. Like Dewey, he would like to enlarge the domain of aesthetics from the role it has traditionally played in modern philosophy. The Deweyan critique of "the museum view of art" is one that Shusterman fully endorses. Dewey and Shusterman's shared aim in enlarging the domain of aesthetics is closely connected to their goal of enhancing the role of art and its appreciation in our everyday lives. They share the melioristic goal of improved experience.

Shusterman's pragmatist aesthetics has an additional motivation that is not evident in Dewey's project. While the works of both men deal with some of the traditional problems in the philosophy of art, Shusterman argues that the continuing relevance of pragmatist aesthetics is contingent on its ability to address the "live aesthetic issues" of today, many of which arise from our rapidly changing contemporary popular culture. He claims that Dewey had a rather conservative taste in art, extending no further than Postimpressionism in the visual arts and the standard late-nineteenth-century genres of the novel and poetry in the literary arts. While Dewey does engage in aesthetic analysis of what is considered "high art" and non-Western folk art, there is no discussion of the avant-garde or the popular arts of his day. A passing reference to "the movie, jazzed music, and the comic strip" as arts that have "the most vitality for the average person" is all that we find in the pages of *Art as Experience* (Dewey, 1934, p. 5). The remoteness and distancing inherent in the museum view of art results in the masses focusing their "esthetic hunger," that is, "their unconquerable impulse toward experiences enjoyable in themselves," on activities that Dewey labels "cheap" and "vulgar." While Dewey himself makes no explicit value judgment on the popular arts here, Shusterman fears that without a sustained analysis of the popular arts, high art's stereotype of popular art as "the cheap and the vulgar" will not be overcome. Dewey has diagnosed the disease but has not provided enough of the right sort of medicine. Shusterman's medicine is reflected in his active engagement with a variety of popular arts and aesthetic activities. Beginning with his explorations of rap music in *Pragmatist Aesthetics*, his explorations have ranged over country, rock, and techno music, urban aesthetics, and most recently contemporary body disciplines, for which he has coined the term "somaesthetics." Somaesthetics is defined by Shusterman as "the critical study and meliorative cultivation of how we experience and use the living body (or soma) as a sight of sensory appreciation (aesthesis) and creative self-fashioning." Embodying the pragmatist desire to closely tie theory with practice and undermine all mind–body dualisms, he elaborates:

> Somaesthetics is thus a discipline that comprises both theory and practice (the latter clearly implied in its idea of meliorative cultivation). The term "soma" indicates a living, feeling, sentient body rather than a mere physical body that could be devoid of life and sensation, while the "aesthetic" in somaesthetics has the dual role of emphasizing the soma's perceptual role (whose embodied intentionality contradicts the body/mind dichotomy) and its aesthetic uses both in stylizing one's self and in appreciating the aesthetic qualities of other selves and things. (Shusterman, 2008, pp. 1–2)

While his writings on popular arts have appeared in scholarly venues and three subsequent books, Shusterman has not restricted himself to strictly academic venues. Like Dewey, he has used the popular media to reach out to a much wider public.

In trying to move pragmatist aesthetics beyond Dewey, Shusterman sees both a value and a limitation in defining art in terms of a Deweyan kind of aesthetic experience. The limitation lies with what he sees as the definition's lack of explanatory power. He argues that despite extensive discussions of the characteristics of aesthetic experience, Dewey is "committed to the indefinability (and indeed discursive unknowability) of aesthetic experience"

(Shusterman, 2000, p. 56). He believes that Dewey errs in claiming that immediate aesthetic experience is essentially "ineffable" and "mute," for this creates difficulties in using it as the basis for critically explaining, evaluating, and judging art. He is not questioning the fact that "the satisfactions enjoyed in aesthetic experience provide a kind of direct 'on-the-pulse' demonstration of art's value," but this does not get us very far in providing "the social preconditions and practices necessary for proper aesthetic appreciation" (ibid., p. 57; Shusterman, 2002). If art criticism is to provide the social space for an expanded conception of art that incorporates the more popular arts, then "discursive means of consensus formation" are required. Shusterman sees himself as working to create this social space by engaging in critical discourse both within the profession of philosophical aesthetics and with the population at large. He concedes that analytic aesthetics' desire for "a traditional wrapper theory of art which would issue in a formal definition giving art's necessary and sufficient conditions" will never be satisfied by searching the pages of *Art as Experience* (Shusterman, 2000, p. 57). Dewey has reconceived philosophical definition in a pragmatic fashion. Shusterman's insight is that for Dewey "a good definition of art effectively directs us toward more and better experience" (ibid., p. 57). Dewey's definition of art as experience will never serve as a gatekeeper for ruling out or ruling in what counts as art. Shusterman will thus aim to "widen art's borders," not by trying to refashion a definition of art, but by engaging in critical inquiry into popular culture and somaesthetics "in the spirit of piecemeal pragmatist labor" (ibid., p. 59).

Conclusion

The increasing popularity of pragmatism internationally and within the Anglo–American tradition promises to bear fruit in a more pluralistic and artistically engaged discipline of philosophical aesthetics. The thinkers we have examined have all played an important role in nourishing this new direction in the philosophical treatment of the arts.

Note

1 See Seigfried (1990) for an excellent treatment of the aesthetic and practical interests.

References

Berleant, A. (1970), *The Aesthetic Field: A Phenomenology of Aesthetic Experience*. Springfield, IL: Charles C. Thomas.
—(1991), *Art and Engagement*. Philadelphia: Temple University Press.
—(1992), *Aesthetics of the Environment*. Philadelphia: Temple University Press.
—(1997), *Living in the Landscape: Toward an Aesthetics of Environment*. Lawrence, KS: University Press of Kansas.
Dewey, J. (1929), *Experience and Nature*, 2nd edn. New York: Dover, 1958.
—(1934), *Art as Experience*. New York: Minton, Balch.
Emerson, R.W. (1841), "Art," in A. Ferguson, et al., (eds), *The Essays of Ralph Waldo Emerson*. Cambridge, MA: Harvard University Press, 1987.
James, W. (1890), *The Principles of Psychology*. 2 volumes. Cambridge, MA: Harvard University Press, 1983.
Margolis, J. (2009), *On Aesthetics: An Unforgiving Introduction*. Belmont, CA: Wadsworth, Cengage Learning.
—(2010), *Pragmatism's Advantage*, Stanford, CA: Stanford University Press.
Peirce, C. S. (1934), *Collected Papers. Volume 5: Pragmatism and Pragmaticism*. Cambridge, MA: Harvard University Press.
Shusterman, R. (2000), *Pragmatist Aesthetics: Living Beauty, Rethinking Art*, 2nd edn. Lanham: Rowan & Littlefield. 1st edn published 1992.
—(2002), "On Pragmatist Aesthetics," *Fathom Knowledge Network*. (online) Available at: <www.fathom.com/feature/35630/index.html> (Accessed June 17, 2010).
—(2008), *Body Consciousness: A Philosophy of Mindfulness and Somaesthetics*. Cambridge: Cambridge University Press.
Seigfried, C. H. (1990), *William James's Radical Reconstruction of Philosophy*. Albany: State University of New York Press.

8

Ethics

Michael Eldridge

Pragmatism, despite its present prominence and explicit value orientation, is not one of the standard moral theories. Most any list will include utilitarianism, Kantianism, virtue ethics, and perhaps contractualism and feminist ethics. But seldom will one find pragmatism being identified and discussed as an ethics, except possibly in a catchall chapter of "other theories." Yet some of the most prominent philosophers in the twentieth century were pragmatists and contributors to moral theoretical discussions. Moreover, Hugh LaFollette's 2007 book, *The Practice of Ethics*, and the several books by James D. Wallace ably demonstrate that pragmatic ethics has the resources to compete with the standard approaches. In what follows I will fill in some background, discuss pragmatism's potential for ethical discussions and explain its lack of prominence as an ethical theory.

Jennifer Welchman, a contemporary ethicist working within the pragmatic tradition, has ably situated pragmatic ethics in the context of American philosophy (Welchman, 2008, pp. 245–251). I will draw on what she has written, for she provides the background and framework for understanding pragmatic ethics, but I will amplify the parts having to do with William James and John Dewey and discuss figures that she does not, notably Richard Rorty. My departures from her account are due primarily to our differing aims: She is providing a more general account of ethics in American philosophy; I am identifying pragmatic ethics and calling attention to its potential as a moral theory.

Welchman correctly points out that pragmatic ethics is a form of ethical naturalism and that "American ethics have not historically been naturalistic" (2008, p. 245). This is but one of the many points at which pragmatism diverges from the mainstream and helps to explain its lack of prominence.

It is not necessary for our purposes to review the history of ethics in the United States from the seventeenth to the middle part of the nineteenth century, as she has done. Suffice it to say that theological ethics dominated this period. In the nineteenth century less theocentric approaches developed, notably Scottish Common Sense Realism, transcendentalism, and various forms of post-Kantian idealism, as well as the more secular British Hedonistic Utilitarianism. Then Welchman notes, "Pragmatic ethics grew out of dissatisfaction with these approaches" (2008, p. 248), a dissatisfaction that was clearly evident in James, "The Moral Philosopher and the Moral Life" (1891). James opens with the bold statement that "the main purpose of this paper is to show that there is no such thing possible as an ethical philosophy dogmatically made up in advance," adding a sentence or so later, "there can be no final truth in ethics" (ibid., p. 141). Further distinguishing the pragmatic approach from conventional views, he continues in his characteristically arresting prose:

> Whether a God exist, or whether no God exist, in yon blue heaven above us bent, we form at any rate an ethical republic here below. And the first reflection which this leads to is that ethics have as genuine and real a foothold in a universe where the highest consciousness is human, as in a universe where is a God as well. "The religion of humanity" affords a basis for ethics as well as theism does. (Ibid., p. 150)

So we cannot know in advance what is to be done, and a humanistic approach is as viable as a theistic one. Yet ethics has as a "genuine" place in our world, devoid though it may be of a divine presence. This is a significant point that continues to characterize pragmatic ethics. Skeptical of many of the claims of moral philosophers, pragmatists nevertheless contend that one can theorize about morality. Unlike the rational and intuitionist approaches, James, compounding the problem that many have with pragmatism, claims that "ethical science, just like physical science, ... must be ready to revise its conclusions from day to day" (1979, p. 157), for "everywhere the ethical philosopher must wait on facts" (1979, p. 158). Not only is there no timeless moral law or values, ethics is at the mercy of empirical findings.

James was not officially anti-theistic; indeed he was vitally interested in religion and proposed a finite theism. But practically speaking, he was ready to construct an ethics in a world without God; he thus, in effect, rejected the sovereignty of God championed by the Calvinists. His was an ethics that would be experimental—not made up in advance and always open to modification as needs and circumstances changed. He thus set the tone for pragmatic ethics—practically secular, nondogmatic, in some sense scientific, and attuned to human need. Welchman characterizes James' ethics as an "ameliorating consequentialism" rather than a maximizing one, for he thought that the moral philosopher's task was to seek a "richer and more inclusive arrangement of ideals" than the present configuration rather than a simple maximizing of each person's preferences. We are to adjust the given situation to reflect the needs and wants of everyone involved. This is of course not an enduring equilibrium; it will change with time and circumstance.

One could collect up many Jamesian essays on morality and values in order to develop a Jamesian ethics but he did not systematically do so. Indeed there is some question if there could ever be a well-worked out pragmatic ethics given the historicity and meliorism advocated by James and embraced by later pragmatists. There are tendencies, orientations, and values. But no definitive, comprehensive ethics. Certainly no systematic, once-for-all treatise is possible.

It is useful to pause here and contrast James' approach with that of the dominant tradition. Henry Sidgwick published seven editions of his influential *Methods of Ethics* (1874–1907) during the period in which James was writing. Sidgwick's *Methods* was regarded by John Rawls as "the outstanding achievement in modern moral theory." It exemplifies not only that which James was reacting against but the mainstream of philosophy in the twentieth century. Rawls continues, "By 'moral theory' I mean the systematic and comparative study of moral conceptions, starting with those which historically and by current estimation seem to be the most important." Note the theoretical starting point. Sidgwick proceeds by systematically comparing the prominent ideas that philosophers have. More on this later. Once again, quoting Rawls: "Moral philosophy includes moral theory, but takes as its main question justification and how it is to be conceived and resolved; for example, whether it is to be conceived as an epistemological problem (as in rational intuitionism) or as a practical problem (as in Kantian constructivism)." Here is a second contrast with the practice orientation of pragmatism. Rawls calls attention to the justificatory aim of contemporary moral philosophy, whereas pragmatism focuses more on explanation. Now we come to Rawls' main point:

> Sidgwick's *Methods* is the first truly academic work in moral theory, modern in both method and spirit. Treating ethics as a discipline to be studied like any other branch of knowledge, it defines and carries out in exemplary fashion, if not for the first time, some of the comprehensive comparisons that constitute

moral theory. By pulling together the work of previous writers, and through its influence on G. E. Moore and others, this work defined much of the framework of subsequent moral philosophy. Sidgwick's originality lies in his conception and mode of presentation of the subject and in his recognition of the significance of moral theory for moral philosophy. (Rawls, 1980, p. 554f)

Many mark the beginning of contemporary ethical theory with Moore, Sidgwick's student, and this is correct in terms of the substance of ethical debate. But in terms of the nature of moral theory Rawls points to Sidgwick, for he proceeded by systematically comparing the moral conceptions of past and present philosophers. James and later pragmatists, on the other hand, begin with moral practice and seek to illumine and guide it. The difference is between a practical and theoretical starting point.[1]

But to note the contingency of pragmatic ethics and that it is nontheoretical in the strong sense of "theory" is not to say there is no use of theory by pragmatists. There have been theoretical refinements and enlargements—and, of course, practical and theoretical disagreements about how we ought to live and think about our common life. James and later pragmatists are committed to thinking about morality; they just regard it as important to begin and end with actual moral experience. Theory is a means, not an end.

There are two other contrasts between pragmatic ethics and the realist ethics of the early twentieth century that should be made explicit. The challenge facing conventional ethical theory at the end of the turn of the century and well into the twentieth was how to preserve a place for ethics in the face of the Darwinian challenge. A philosophical reliance on science threatened not only the autonomy of ethics but ethics itself. So the intuitionists from Moore forward sought to locate the ethical in a direct apprehension of what is good. Much of twentieth-century ethical theory can be understood as a playing out of Moore's identification (and rejection) of the "naturalistic fallacy" (see Darwall, et al., 1992). Moreover the intuited moral concepts could then be carefully examined. Now moral philosophers had a task—conceptual analysis—that was distinct from the physical and social sciences yet could be carried out "scientifically" or at least technically. The development of technical expertise in conceptual matters enabled philosophers to hold their own in the increasingly professionalized academic world. They could do something that others could not, and their efforts were validated by professional journals and associations.[2]

The early pragmatists swam against this unempirical yet technical tide by embracing evolution and modifying their understanding of morality. The latter was not discontinuous with science; indeed values could be empirically known and investigated. It took several decades for the anti-moral experience and excessively theoretical approach to play itself out, opening the way for renewed interest in pragmatic approaches—or so pragmatists would like to think. More on the pragmatic resurgence below. For now I want to return to the narrative from which I digressed with the discussion of Sidgwick and Moore and the mainstream ethics that ensued, picking up the discussion of the role of theory in pragmatic ethics.

One of the first enhancements in pragmatic theory was that of James' idealist Harvard colleague who attempted to incorporate some pragmatic elements into his idealism. As was noted, James thought morality should be inclusive of people's interests and ideals, but Royce, more so than James, paid careful attention to the communal dimension of the moral life. It is with John Dewey, however, that we get the social dimension without the Roycean absolutism that is antithetical to a robust pragmatism. Dewey had begun his philosophic career as an absolute idealist, but in his thirties he began, as he said, to drift away from this orientation, leaving only a "Hegelian deposit" in his thinking. This deposit was his retention of not only a social orientation but also an appreciation of the role of conflict or diversity in our common life.

A difficult question for traditional–conventional ethics is the one of "Why be moral?" The assumption is that there is a good, right or virtuous way to live and we, left to ourselves, can do none of these by nature. Morality is external and imposed. Hence the question, why would a reasonable person choose to accept this? Dewey proceeds from a different starting point, understanding a moral situation to be one in which we are faced with a choice between competing goods, where goods are understood to be values, needs, interests, desires, claims, and so on. We cannot, it would appear, have both somethings, both of which are attractive, and so we must choose. Of course, it is more complicated than this. The apparent goods may not be valued upon reflection; they may in fact not be incompatible as initially understood; or maybe they can both be had in some satisfactory way if one modifies one's expectations or comes to understand the desired objects better. One thus needs to deliberate and not simply choose.

The social dimension of morality is prominent in two ways: one, we and our perceived goods are the product of our being social selves, and, two, our deliberations about what to do are enhanced by our interactions with others.

Thus, contrary to the traditional liberal assumption, Dewey was impressed with our sociality. Here is what Welchman says:

> In texts such as *Human Nature and Conduct*, Dewey, like Royce, argues our personal identities, including our moral characters, are largely socially constructed. We are born with physiological and psychological traits that are the basic stuff of our development as persons. Development of a functional and well-integrated personality out of the multiple competing drives that constitute raw human nature is an achievement, not a given, that would be quite impossible without the assistance of our social communities. (2008, p. 250)

These largely socially formed identities are not exclusively moral, immoral or amoral but all three to varying degrees. The important point is that however we define "moral" the moral component is not something imposed upon us or at least not exclusively so. It is the result of our development within families and in society. These social influences are neither one-way nor are they all positive or negative. They are a mix.

But what is really distinctive of Dewey as a pragmatist is the realization that habits and their reconstruction are key. Charles Peirce and James both emphasized the role of habits in our lives, and Dewey extended their work. A habit is an ongoing set of activities that achieves some purpose. These habits or practices may be worthwhile or, while satisfying in some respect, ultimately destructive overall.[3] Dewey would have us pay attention to our practices and modify them as needed. An intelligent person or group is continually remaking his, her or its behavior to achieve its desirable ends, that is, the ends that upon reflection and experimentation prove worthy. The ongoing reconstruction involves not only consideration of the ends but a testing of the means to achieve these ends.

Earlier I said that our deliberations are enhanced by our interactions with others. In determining what to do—and thus who we are—we are aided not only by our socially formed inheritance but also by our involvement with others in terms of both encouragement and resistance. We need the alternatives suggested not only by our past practices and imaginations but also our encounters with others in order to make informed choices. We grow through conflict and resolution of these conflicts. Hence the value of democracy with its employment of social intelligence. Better practices come about through experimentation and the creative tension necessary to a healthy collaboration.

Morality then, for Dewey, is not conforming to some rule but the intelligent consideration of alternative courses of action that enable us to better adapt to our circumstances or modify the circumstances to suit our purposes. An ethical life is one of continual intelligent reconstruction.[4]

Many a reader will have noticed that I have said nothing of Charles S. Peirce's contributions to pragmatic ethics. So let me pause and explain why that is. I will then discuss two other neglectable or easily overlooked figures before we get to the next major, widely noticed pragmatist, Richard Rorty. Welchman does not neglect Peirce but it is significant that she does not discuss his ethics. Nor will one readily find discussions of Peirce's ethics in books devoted to Peirce. This is because Peirce never developed an ethics. To be sure, normativity plays a vital role in his thinking and there are many scattered references to ethics in his writings. James Feibleman collected and systematized these in a journal article (1943), but to my knowledge there is not a fully worked out Peircean ethics.

Another neglected philosopher is one who was quite prominent in the middle decades of the twentieth century and who was much influenced by Peirce and Royce, as well as Kant. C. I. Lewis was educated at Harvard and spent most of his academic life there, engaging in a wide variety of philosophical discussions, including logic, epistemology, metaphysics, and ethics. But ethics, as he noted in his autobiography for the *Library of Living Philosophers* volume devoted to him, was "the most important branch of philosophy" (Murphey, 2005, p. 315). Eric Dayton amplifies this remark, "Lewis's ethics, toward which the whole of his mature philosophical work aimed, is a richly developed foundation for a common sense reflective morality, broadly within the American pragmatic naturalistic tradition" (Dayton, 2002, 2005). Yet Lewis was never able to complete a promised foundation of ethics. Murray Murphey thinks that it was because Lewis had developed two categorical imperatives, one of prudence and one of other-regardingness, and "he could not find a [principled] way to reconcile them" (Murphey, 2006, pp. 42, 65).

There is perhaps a lesson for those of us working in pragmatic ethics. No pragmatist, according to Murphey, was more systematic, thorough or precise than Lewis. Moreover, he was exceedingly responsive to the philosophical problems of his time, fully engaging his fellow analytic philosophers from a pragmatic perspective. Yet he could not develop a satisfactory metaethics. I do not know exactly what the lesson is, but Lewis would appear to be a case well worth studying. My hunch is that he tried to serve too many masters—Kant, Peirce, his teachers, Royce and James, his contemporary, Dewey, and the philosophical issues of his day. At the very least, Lewis, despite his brilliance, illustrates the difficulty of being a pragmatist in a hostile philosophical environment.

Not neglected by others but barely noted here is Jürgen Habermas' pragmatically informed discourse ethics. I am tempted by Dmitri Shalin's charge that Habermas has "elevated verbal intellect at the expense of non-cognitive intelligence and thereby truncated the pragmatist notion of experience" (Shalin, 1992, p. 238). But I am inclined to substitute "embodied" for "non-cognitive." I am also bothered by Habermas's quest for transcendental certainty and universal standards. Better informed than I is Mitchell Aboulafia, who co-edited *Habermas and Pragmatism*, an anthology to which Habermas contributed. Aboulafia reports that he "once asked Habermas . . . what was the most difficult aspect of his philosophy to defend. He didn't hesitate to answer: quasi-transcendentalism." Habermas then explained that he maintained his link to transcendentalism because of the Holocaust. Pragmatism's attention to experience, contingency, and contextualism does not provide the bulwark against irrationalism that Habermas admirably resists (Aboulafia, 2002, p. 4f). But Mike Sandbothe suggests that "the *quasi* in Habermas' *quasi-transcendental* already says everything. If one is searching for *quasi-transcendental* foundations, then one knows that one actually needs no philosophical foundation for democracy anymore" (Sandbothe, 2010). But whatever the merits of his quasi-pragmatic ethics Habermas' attention as the premier German thinker and public intellectual of his generation to American pragmatism contributed to the resurgence of interest in what had been a neglected way of thinking at mid-century.

The catalyst, however, for its revival was Richard Rorty, whose provocative manner and insider's understanding of analytic philosophy drew attention to pragmatism once more. He, of course, was not alone in bringing about this renewed interest, but he was the visible, articulate exponent. Often presenting himself as merely putting forward Deweyan ideas, he in fact differed from Dewey in many ways. I will call attention to some similarities and differences.

Like Dewey he was anti-foundationalist and antiessentialist in his approach, but he expressed himself more sharply than did Dewey. The latter was willing to engage in polemical discussions but his manner was more inclusive and irenic. Rorty, despite his shyness, intentionally put forward ideas that surprised, even shocked his contemporaries. Take principles. Dewey sought to reconstruct principles so that they were suggestive guides rather than uncompromising ones. Principles, for Dewey, embody the wisdom of prior experience. But they are to be used as tools; not as unyielding propositions. Rorty, however, titled an essay, "Ethics Without Principles." But when one reads the essay s/he finds more continuity with Dewey than difference, despite the title's implication that one is to do away with principles all together. Indeed, the only occurrence of the word "principle" in the essay is in a quotation from Dewey:

> ... in morals a hankering for certainty, born of timidity and nourished by love of authoritative prestige, has led to the idea that absence of immutably fixed and universally applicable ready-made principles is equivalent to moral chaos. (MW 14.164)

Rorty quotes the latter part with approval (Rorty, 1999, p. 75). Then in "Kant vs. Dewey: The Current Situation of Moral Philosophy," he wrote:

> To say that moral principles have no inherent nature is to say that they have no distinctive source. They emerge from our encounters with our surroundings in the same way that hypotheses about planetary motion, codes of etiquette, epic poems, and all our other patterns of linguistic behavior, emerge. Like these other emergents, they are good insofar as they lead to good consequences, not because they stand in some special relation either to the universe or to the human mind. For Deweyans questions about sources and principles, about *das Ursprungliches* and *ta archaia*, are always a sign that the philosophers are up to their old Platonic tricks. They are trying to shortcut the ongoing calculation of consequences by appealing to something stable and permanent, something whose authority is not subject to empirical test. (Rorty, 2007, p. 192)

It would be hard to find much difference between Dewey and Rorty on the nature and role of principles.

Where one can find a major difference is in Rorty's reliance on sentiment to do the work that, Dewey thinks, requires inquiry as well. Inquiry for Dewey is not just an epistemic activity but is a transformational one in which changes in a situation make it more suitable for the needs of those involved. Dewey would certainly recognize the value of the novelists that Rorty thinks are the ones who move people to act, but he does not eschew argument, peer pressure, and education by a variety of means including literature. And Dewey values science much more than Rorty. I cannot imagine Dewey saying what Rorty said in an interview shortly before he died. They would be in general agreement about the first sentence: "The West has cobbled together, in the course of the last two hundred years, a specifically secularist moral tradition—one that regards the free consensus of the citizens of a democratic society, rather then the Divine Will, as the source of moral imperatives." But I doubt that he would agree with the next one: "This shift in outlook," Rorty continues, "is, I think, the most important advance that the West has yet made" (Postel, 2007). Secularity was regarded by Dewey as an important and, within limits, valuable development, but Dewey would not have ranked it as the most important one.

In general, Rorty is more prone to dichotomize than Dewey—literature or philosophy, public or private, argument or emotion. And, of course, as is well known, Rorty had made the linguistic turn. But both were fervently committed to an expansive democracy despite their difference regarding some of the forms that democracy should take. Dewey, to be sure, would not have been content with Rorty's ethnocentrism, for he thought that democracy was demonstrably better at meeting people's needs and aspirations. In *Experience and Education* he asked why we prefer "democratic social arrangements" over "autocratic and harsh" ones and he answered with this question: "Can we find any reason that does not ultimately come down to the belief that democratic social arrangements promote a better quality of human experience, one which is more widely accessible and enjoyed, than do nondemocratic and antidemocratic forms of social life?" (LW 13.18) No doubt Rorty would have regarded this move as one that begged the question. He would certainly have agreed with Dewey's valuation but he thought that one's preference for "democratic social arrangements" was the product of a historical process. We have been socialized to think the way we do. Dewey could have then reminded Rorty of what we have learned from Darwin about human nature and argued that democracy does a better job of meeting human needs than alternative forms of sociopolitical arrangement. Rorty would not have been impressed with this "metaphysical appeal" to "human needs" even as he counted himself a Darwinian naturalist and passionate democrat.

Finally, Rorty puts more emphasis than Dewey does on the formation of one's moral identity. They agree that we become who we are through what we do, but Dewey thinks there is more to morality than forming one's identity through the use of imagination. In short, Dewey is broader in his concerns and more connected to the philosophical tradition than Rorty.

Even more engaged with conventional philosophy is Sami Pihlström, who offers a quasi-transcendental defense of a pragmatic moral realism. Where Rorty takes delight in challenging the dominant philosophical tradition, Pihlström adds to the mix the Kantian tradition and neo-Wittgensteinianism. Of course Rorty is well versed in these traditions as well, but Pihlström embraces them, not only defending a realism that, as Peter Hare points out, is "often thought to be antagonistic toward pragmatism" (2008, p. 257) but also mounting a transcendental argument. Pihlström provokes pragmatists by reclaiming philosophical traditions thought to be antithetical to pragmatism. Pay attention to this explanation from another work:

> Very briefly, what I wish to suggest is that there are always some socially, culturally, and historically constrained (quasi-) *transcendental conditions* operative in our cognitive life. These conditions—which, if the Kantian terminology sounds hopelessly loaded with German idealism, we might also call *structuring conditions*—are necessary conditions of our being able to cognize an objective reality with a certain intelligible and experienceable structure. That structure is provided by us through our practical action (in a very inclusive sense of "practical") within what Wittgenstein called our "forms of life" and their "natural history." In this way, the combination of naturalism and transcendentalism relies on a more fundamental (though essentially anti-foundationalist) pragmatism, which I adopt as the ultimate premise of my argument. Pragmatism, in short, is the key to the naturalization of transcendental conditions." (Pihlström, 2003, p. 60)

In the preceding paragraph he presents his project as a Rortian one of redescription. But clearly the sensibility is very different from both Rorty and Dewey. Pihlström is making use of the resources of philosophy past and present to solve the "problems of philosophers." Yet he does this without foundations and within practices. It is a pragmatism but one that is comfortable with tradition.

I have jumped ahead a bit in order to show the range of contemporary pragmatist ethics. Now I return to the usual order and call attention to Rorty's frequent sparring partner, Hilary Putnam, whose primary contribution to pragmatic ethical theory is a sustained attempt to call into question the fact-value dichotomy. He is surely within the mainstream of pragmatic thinking in so doing. What is distinctive about his effort is the sophistication with which he problematizes this dichotomy while preserving the distinction between facts and values. In a brief notice of *The Collapse of the Fact-Value Distinction and Other Essays* Rorty observes, "Using a strategy pioneered by Dewey, Putnam shows how his opponents have turned commonsensical distinctions into philosophical dichotomies (fact vs. value, objective vs. subjective, mind vs. matter) and then typically, tried to eliminate one side of the dichotomy in favor of the other" (Rorty, 2004).

Also working within the pragmatic tradition but quietly, for he does not advertise it, is James D. Wallace. Author of *Virtues and Vices* (1978), *Moral Relevance and Moral Conflict* (1988), *Ethical Norms, Particular Cases* (1966), and more recently *Norms and Practices* (2009), Wallace effectively makes use of the work of Dewey and Frederick Will to engage a wide range of thinkers *and* deal with a variety of cases past and present. Occasionally the word "pragmatic" will slip into the text but more often he refers to his position as contextualism. Nevertheless, for one with eyes to see Wallace's work is pragmatic.

The effect of these recent efforts of philosophers of the stature of Rorty and Putnam and the erudition and resourcefulness of Pihlström and Wallace (and others soon to be discussed) is to bring pragmatism into current discussions of ethics. Now I want to end with several brief observations that show the scope of current pragmatic contributions to ethics and some dangers as well as possibilities: Rawls' pragmatic move, Welchman's engagement with analytic philosophy, Seigfried's (and Anderson's) pragmatic feminism, and LaFollette's attention to the practice of ethics.

Welchman's account of ethics for the *American Philosophy* encyclopedia edited by Lachs and Talisse concludes with the influence of pragmatism on ethics in the last 75 years or so. She notes that most of the pragmatists in the generation or so following the founders "did not produce distinct normative theories of right conduct or good character to compete with those produced by rival approaches." Instead they concentrated on "criteria for the evaluation of theoretical principles." This leads her to say: "But Pragmatism's enduring influence can nevertheless be seen in later American ethics, even when these depart substantially from the main line of classic pragmatism" (2008, p. 250). This is the case, as she shows with her discussion of Charles Stevenson's defense of emotivism and John Rawls' "more holistic approach that was in effect, if not name, a revival of pragmatic theorizing." Although Rawls used the term "Kantian constructivism" to refer to his effort and there is much in what he did that would not be considered pragmatic—I am thinking of his use of the idea of the "original position"—his employment of the method of "reflective equilibrium" can be considered, as Welchman observes, "an offshoot of classical American pragmatism," in that "neither the principles we choose . . . nor the beliefs . . . we aim to bring into equilibrium are treated as self-evident or epistemically 'privileged'. All are open to revision" (2008, p. 251).

But it would be misleading to think that pragmatism lives on in ethics only in its influence on those who are not primarily pragmatist in their orientation. Look at Welchman's work. She engages the work of mainstream Anglo-American ethics by employing Deweyan ideas. In the encyclopedia article she describes Dewey as a "satisfying consequentialist," which dismays Gregory Pappas, author of the recent *John Dewey's Ethics: Democracy as Experience*.[5] By this she means that Dewey's ethics is a form of "ameliorating consequentialism," in which "our best strategy, rationally speaking, is to focus upon *satisfying* the demands of and capitalizing upon the opportunities in our current situations"

(Welchman, 2008, p. 250). In her recent presentation, "Welfare and Pragmatic Practical Reasoning," at the American Philosophical Association meeting (December 2009), she developed this interpretation, arguing against maximizing and optimizing consequentialisms and engaging the work of several non-pragmatist ethical theorists. Larry Hickman, in his response, affirmed the need to engage contemporary non-pragmatic theorists, but he, citing Pappas' work, thought she had conceded too much to these theorists. While agreeing with her "general reading of Dewey," he thought "she ha[d] given up too much in an effort to play the old tired game of the consequentialists on their own turf" (Hickman, unpublished comment, p. 5).

Less controversial is Charlene Haddock's efforts to develop a pragmatic feminism. Initially, in a special issue of *Hypatia* that she edited, more fully in *Pragmatism and Feminism: Reweaving the Social Fabric*, and later in other edited works, *Feminist Interpretations of John Dewey (Re-Reading the Canon)* and new editions of Jane Addams' work, she has been showing the connections between pragmatism and feminism, and where necessary, reconstructing pragmatism along feminist lines. Judy Whipps observes, "The work of the women who were in philosophic and activist relationships with these [early pragmatist and male] philosophers, and were original philosophers in their own right, had until recently disappeared. Charlene Haddock Seigfried's work, particularly her 1996 book *Pragmatism and Feminism*, has been central in the effort to bring these invisible women back into the philosophical discussion, as well as to bring feminist perspectives to the field of pragmatism." Both pragmatists and feminists are concerned with practice, reject dualism and value diversity, even as they have differing perspectives on the latter. Nevertheless, "In either embracing the diversity of the other, or in critiquing a system that makes persons into object-others, both feminists and pragmatists critique and actively fight against the unjust hierarchies created by racism, classism, and sexism."

Exploiting both pragmatism and feminism to address issues in economics, gender, race, politics, religion, and epistemology is Elizabeth Anderson. Her recently revised contribution to the *Stanford Encyclopedia of Philosophy* on "Dewey's Moral Philosophy" is a carefully crafted contemporary reading of Dewey that emphasizes the experimental nature of his ethics. The last line of a recent article suggests well her experimental and feminist understanding of Dewey: "We cannot get beyond sexism without experiments in living, and we cannot judge their success without listening to our emotion-laden responses to these experiments" (Anderson, 2005, p. 5).

Finally, while pragmatists may engage other philosophic traditions, ultimately they are concerned with the uses of theory for enhancing our lives. Notable among recent books is Hugh LaFollette's *The Practice of Ethics* (2007). He does not advertise his pragmatic approach, but in the conclusion he reiterates his primary purpose: "to show [the] deep connection" between "normative theory, meta-theory and practical ethics" as "three elements of the practice of ethics." Above all, he "wanted to show that theorizing arises from thinking about practical issues," while never losing the focus on practice. In doing so he introduced pragmatism and made use of its resources, but he did not declare his allegiance until the conclusion, declaring that his practice-focus "is most obvious in my discussion of the doing/allowing distinction, the discussion of freedom and responsibility, and in my explication and defense of a pragmatist approach to ethics" (LaFollette, 2007, p. 295).

These recent efforts are notable, but they are in no way exhaustive of the wide variety of current efforts to understand and advance a pragmatic understanding of ethics, much of it sparked by Rorty's provocative work. But as I have tried to make clear, there is no consensus among pragmatists about the value of Rorty's work, the use of philosophic traditions, including pragmatism, and the engagement of contemporary ethical theory. There is, however, considerable agreement that ethics must be broadly empirical, naturalistic in orientation, and experimental in character, but, above all, attentive to practice whether these practices be those of the community or the profession.*

Editor's note: Michael Eldridge completed this chapter substantially but was never able to check its final version or the proofs before his unexpected death in 2010. Therefore some references and other details may remain slightly incomplete or inaccurate.

Notes

1 The distinction is well made by David Hildebrand (2003).
2 This paragraph owes much to my email exchanges with Welchman, who freely shared some of her work in progress and criticisms of an earlier draft of this chapter. She, of course, is not responsible for the use that I made of our conversations.
3 See the article on social theory by Erkki Kilpinen in this volume.
4 Space does not permit me to discuss the many fine interpretations of Dewey's ethics, but the interested reader would be well advised to consult Fesmire (2003),

Hildebrand, Lekan (2003), Pappas (2008), Rosenbaum (2009), and Welchman (1995 and 2010). Note how recent most of these are; also while they may have "pragmatist" in the title they focus on Dewey.

5   Pappas is critical of all consequentialist interpretations of Dewey's ethics, including Welchman's, although he does not discuss this recent account, published in the same year as his book. See pp. 9 and 11.

References

Abalafia, M. et al., (2002), "Introduction," in *Habermas and Pragmatism*. London and New York: Routledge.

Anderson, E. (2005, 2010), "Dewey's Moral Philosophy," *Stanford Encyclopedia of Philosophy*, (online) Available at: </http://plato.stanford.edu/entries/dewey-moral/> (Accessed May 8, 2010).

—(2006), "Replies to My Critics," Symposia on Gender, *Race Philosophy*, 2, (1), pp. 1–6.

Corcoran, J. et al., (2006), "A Symposium on Murray G. Murphey, *C. I. Lewis: The Last Great Pragmatist*," *Transactions of the Charles S. Peirce Society*, 42, pp. 1–77.

Darwall, S., A. Gibbard, and P. Railton (1992), "Toward *Fin de siècle* Ethics: Some Trends," *Philosophical Review*, 101, pp. 115–189.

Dayton, E. (2002, 2005), "C. I. Lewis (1883–1964)," *Internet Encyclopedia of Philosophy*, (online) Available at: <www.iep.utm.edu/lewisci/> (Accessed May 6, 2010).

Feibleman, J. (1943), "A Systematic Presentation of Peirce's Ethics," *Ethics*, 53, 98–109.

Fesmire, S. (2003), *John Dewey and Moral Imagination: Pragmatism in Ethics*. Bloomington: Indiana University Press.

Hare, P. (2008), "Review of *Pragmatic Moral Realism: A Transcendental Defense*," *Metaphilosophy*, 39, pp. 256–261.

Hildebrand, D. (2003), *Beyond Realism and Antirealism: John Dewey and the Neopragmatists*. Nashville: Vanderbilt University Press.

LaFollette, H. (2007), *The Practice of Ethics*. Oxford: Blackwell Publishing.

Lekan, T. (2003), *Making Morality: Pragmatist Reconstruction in Ethical Theory*. Nashville: Vanderbilt University Press.

Murphey, M. (2005), *C. I. Lewis: The Last Great Pragmatist*. Albany: SUNY Press.

—(2006), "Replies," in "A Symposium on Murray G. Murphey, *C. I. Lewis: The Last Great Pragmatist*," *Transactions of the Charles S. Peirce Society*, 42, pp. 61–77.

Pappas, G. (2008), *John Dewey's Ethics: Democracy as Experience*. Indianapolis: Indiana University Press.

Pihlström, S. (2003), *Naturalizing the Transcendental: A Pragmatic View*. Amherst, NY: Humanity Books.

—(2005), *Pragmatic Moral Realism: A Transcendental Defense*. Amsterdam: Rodopi.

Postel, D. (2007), "Last Words from Richard Rorty," *The Progressive* (June), (online) Available at: <www.progressive.org/mag_postel0607?refresh=1> (Accessed May 9, 2010).
John R. (1980), "Kantian Constructivism in Moral Theory," *The Journal of Philosophy*, 77, pp. 515–572.
Rorty, R. (1999), *Philosophy and Social Hope*. London: Penguin Books.
—(2004), "Review of *The Collapse of the Fact-Value Dichotomy*," *Common Knowledge*, 10, p. 151.
—(2007), *Philosophy as Cultural Politics: Philosophical Papers*, vol. 4. Cambridge: Cambridge University Press.
Rosenbaum, S. (2009), *Pragmatism and the Reflective Life*. Lanham, MD: Lexington Books.
Sandbothe, M. (2010), "Habermas, Pragmatism and the Media: An Interview with Mike Sandbothe", (online) Available at: <www.sandbothe.net/719.html> (Accessed May 2, 2010).
Shalin, D. (1992), "Critical Theory and the Pragmatist Challenge," *American Journal of Sociology*, 98, pp. 237–279.
Welchman, J. (1995), *Dewey's Ethical Thought*. Ithaca: Cornell University Press.
—(2008), "Ethics," in J. Lachs and R. Talisse, (eds), *American Philosophy: An Encyclopedia*. New York and London: Routledge, pp. 245–251.
—(2010), "Dewey's Moral Philosophy," *The Cambridge Companion to Dewey*. Ed. M. Cochran. Cambridge: Cambridge University Press, pp. 166–186.
Whipps, J, (2004), "Pragmatic Feminism," *Stanford Encyclopedia of Philosophy*, (online) Available at: <http://plato.stanford.edu/entries/femapproach-pragmatism/> (Accessed February 13, 2010).

9

Social Theory[1]

Erkki Kilpinen

Social theory needs empirically responsible philosophy

Human beings live in societies. However, human beings do not "just live" in their societies. They have to make their living in them, in other words, do things in society. For theoretical analysis this means that an action-theoretic component always belongs to thought-out social theory. The relation between action and society comes out even more clearly and as more inherent, if we remember that though societies have "structures," they do not have them in the same sense as, say, houses have structures. Societies cannot stand empty; their structures are continuously made and re-made, reproduced in the concrete action of the individuals who populate societies. Accordingly, the relevance of the concept of action for social theory is hard to exaggerate.

Pragmatism's relevance for social theory comes out in its new understanding of action, perhaps even more prominently than in its macro-theoretic understanding of society. Pragmatism has produced at least one thinker who has had a wide purview on society and an excellent understanding about its goings-on, namely John Dewey.[2] His eminence as social theorist is widely recognized and it was grudgingly recognized to some extent even during the time when his appreciation as a systematic philosopher was at its lowest ebb. In this chapter, however, I shall concentrate on the contribution that pragmatism as a whole has made. This is not to belittle Dewey's importance, but in order to remind that the classic pragmatist tradition still contains some untapped resources. Those resources are most related to the theory of action and its position as a foundational supposition in social theory. In explicating them one needs to keep all four classic pragmatists, Charles S. Peirce, William James, John Dewey, and George Herbert Mead simultaneously in focus.

Let me briefly explain why they all are needed. Mead is now and then mentioned in these contexts, but too often from a somewhat naïve viewpoint, as a retrospectively established sociological classic. I treat him instead as a psychologically orienting philosopher of mind and theorist of action. Peirce's presence in social-theoretic discussion may arouse some wonder, as it is widely known that he did not actually dwell on these issues. I maintain, however, that his inclusion is essential, because his interpretation of logic is the rational skeleton in the pragmatist conception of action that I shall introduce. Furthermore, as I have demonstrated elsewhere (Kilpinen, 2010), Peirce has not remained quite aloof from all social disciplines but has had considered opinions about the status of economics as a science, and this is relevant also for general social theory. As for James, his most important contribution to this discussion is his magnum opus *Principles of Psychology* (1890) rather than his explicitly philosophical works. James's *Principles* was a sort of Prolegomenon for other pragmatists, who appropriated but also deepened many of its ideas.

Social theory is a problem field where empirical and normative discourse, social science, and philosophy meet and mix with each other. Social theory must not boil down to mere descriptive sociological theory, but needs to include a notion of desirable society, as a regulative principle, to use Kantian parlance, and this brings in the normative element. On the other hand, social theory nonetheless needs to be sociologically informed. Social hope, to use the late Richard Rorty's (1999) parlance, must not remain mere wishful thinking. To show the mutual, not to say dialectical relation between the philosophical and empirical in social analysis, I quote and paraphrase two eminent social philosophers from the late twentieth century.

"Any comprehensive version of sociology contains social philosophy as a necessary component," Alan Ryan once said (1970, p. 145), meaning by social philosophy moral philosophy. The moral theorist Alasdair Macintyre (1985) added for his part that comprehensive ethical theory always contains (usually implicit) psychological and sociological presuppositions. Their presence in ethical theory was precisely the reason why Macintyre found the modern ethical project dilemmatic. Aristotelian virtue ethics might seem viable at first, or at least preferable to Nietzsche's voluntarism, but one just cannot apply Aristotle without further ado in modern days. In so doing one easily buys also into Aristotelian psychology and sociology, but these are hopelessly dated notions, descriptively taken, today.

In seeking a way out of this dilemma, we had better concentrate on what Macintyre says about psychology rather than sociology. It namely is no exaggeration to say that Aristotelian psychology has thrived up to the late twentieth century in philosophical conceptions of action, particularly in those that build on the notion of "practical syllogism." I think that we should take seriously the warning that Aristotelian ideas have seen their best days of application. This is also the point where classic pragmatism comes in, in that it in its heyday proposed a more comprehensive notion of action, one that is capable of embracing the classic Aristotelian view. The Aristotelian action-concept needs not be discarded altogether, even when following pragmatist presuppositions, but it had better be reserved for its proper use in explicitly normative questions. However, it also needs to be embedded in a wider descriptive framework, and classic pragmatism can provide such a framework.

Pragmatism as a philosophy of action

I asserted that pragmatism's conception of action is radically new. It is new in the sense that this philosophy has radically re-interpreted an old action-theoretic concept and given it a completely new meaning. This is the concept of *habit*.

This prima facie colloquial term is for pragmatism the basic concept for human doings, but not in its garden variety meaning, where it refers to the routine aspect in human behavior. In English-speaking philosophy this has been its received meaning at least since Hume, who meant by it such action that "proceeds from past repetition without any new reasoning or reflection" (1739–40/1985, p. 152). For Hume, habit thus was a derivative from previous individual "actions," but in pragmatism this order of things is reversed. In this philosophy, an individual "action" is defined in terms of some habit, as its exemplification, and this entitles us to conclude that the question is not about a mere change in terminology but about a foundational upheaval where the basic concept and residue change places. Indeed, I once had the audacity to say that pragmatism has performed a "Copernican Revolution" in the conceptualization of action, by changing the focus of analysis from individual "actions" onto "habit" (Kilpinen, 2009b, p. 171f.).

I lack the space to go through all classic pragmatists' usage of the habit-term (some examples are provided in Kilpinen, 2000, 2009a, 2009b). Suffice it to note now that Peirce, the first user of the new meaning, is quite explicit that habit should not be taken as "mere slothful repetition of what has been done," as he once says (NEM 4: 143, c. 1898) in direct contradiction to Hume's original meaning. For Peirce, habit is instead "self-controlled and therefore recognized," by the acting subject, the possessor of the habit (EP 2: 431, 1907).[3] He is also explicit about the relation between habit and individual actions: "I need not repeat that I do not say that it is the single deeds that constitute the habit. It is the single 'ways,' which are conditional propositions, each general,—that constitute the habit" (Peirce CP 5.510, 1905). In brief, pragmatists defend the idea that human action is an ongoing process, out of which one can single out individual deeds, if need be, but the process form is human action's natural form and this is what the habit-term highlights. "Actions are agent-managed processes," maintains a contemporary pragmatist and process philosopher Nicholas Rescher (2000, p. 48) and adds that "for processes, to be is to be exemplified," (2000, p. 25). Rescher thus assumes the same order between action-processes and individual deeds that classic pragmatists maintained before him.

The idea about action as process is as such no oddity in social theory. Anthony Giddens defended a very similar idea in the late twentieth century, by saying that action should be taken as reflexive monitoring of the process of conduct in the day-to-day continuity of social life (1984, pp. 43–44; see also passim and Giddens, 1976). Giddens reached this conclusion independently of pragmatism which gives corroboration to both sides in the comparison. He, however, had some worries about the fate of intentionality and rationality in this kind of action-interpretation, but pragmatism is able to show that such worries are unnecessary.[4]

The next thing to be noted is that though action is for pragmatism a process, it is not a linear process but one with a cyclical structure. This is for the reason that pragmatism all the time takes the possible failure of action into account. Sir Karl Popper made the fallibility of human knowledge a central theme in his philosophy. Pragmatists went one better, by deriving this principle already from the fallibility of action, from its vulnerability to failure. This very idea, however, also suggested them to take action as a self-correcting, cyclically proceeding process. In the words of Mead (1938, p. 79),

> Reflective thinking arises in testing the means which are presented for carrying out some hypothetical way of continuing an action which has been checked. Lying back of curiosity there is always some activity, some action, that is for the time being checked. The problem is always a stoppage of something one is doing by the excitement of some other action. The solution of the problem will be some way of acting that enables one to carry on the activity which has been checked in relation to the new act which has arisen.

This model of fallible but (to an extent) self-corrective, cyclically proceeding action, shared by all classic pragmatists, appears for the first time in what is known as Peirce's doubt/belief model of inquiry. As I have argued elsewhere

(Kilpinen, 2010), Peirce presented it mostly for scientific research, but not exclusively so. He was aware of its action – theoretic relevance also, as he said that "Everybody uses the scientific method about a great many things, and only ceases to use it when he does not know how to apply it" (EP 1: 120, 1877). Furthermore, in pragmatism the term "inquiry" does not refer to scientific or intellectual pursuits only. Pragmatism uses it as a basic epistemic concept, to point attention to the fact that the main problem in matters epistemic concerns acquisition of knowledge rather than its possession, and how to justify already existing beliefs. Pragmatism has strived toward a similar conception of "epistemology without (the concepts of) knowledge and without belief" that Jaakko Hintikka has today founded on a solider logical basis but with the same knowledge interest: "The basic insight is that there is a link between the concept of knowledge and human action," as Hintikka says (2007a, p. 13). This link is in the fact that we need knowledge to guide us in action and we obtain knowledge by conducting inquiries. Inquiry being one kind of action, this means that knowledge is indeed here defined in terms of action— as the age-old philosophical prejudice against pragmatism has been—but in truth without violating in any way its philosophical or practical importance. A further argument in favor of this conception stems from pragmatism's supposition of process ontology, as I have proposed elsewhere (Kilpinen, 2009b).

Pragmatism thus does not take the traditional "mind-first-explanation" of action as the whole story about action, to use a slightly sarcastic expression (borrowed from Dennett, 1995). This is worth notice, because this explanation has gone almost unchallenged elsewhere in social theory. Pragmatism does not discard it altogether, but treats it as a special case, whose correct use is mostly in normative questions. As a descriptive model, it too easily leads to assumptions about universally passive humans, as Dewey once warned with great pathos (1922, esp. p. 118f). It approaches action via the acting subject's mind, and does not pay much attention to its more concrete features. This has consequences also outside mere individual action, in that it easily leads to an idealist conception of society, such where ideology is taken as the cement of society. Ideology has its relevance, in offering articulation and justification to what people do, but these doings rather are the cement of society, not so much ideology per se.

Self and social action

One contribution of pragmatism has often been recognized also in mainstream social theory. It concerns the general understanding of the human self, and its foremost contributor is G. H. Mead.[5] His interpretation of the self is occasionally commented on in social disciplines but seldom with correct conclusions. The reason is that it usually is not noticed that Mead's self- concept is founded on his concept of the "act," not the other way round, as is the case elsewhere in social theory. The term "act," furthermore, is not the same thing as "action" as elsewhere understood, because Mead (1982, p. 108) uses it both about human and animal activities: "Wherever we find living beings, we find acts." As a consequence, Mead's "self"-concept does not refer so much to sociological identity but rather to human cognition. Its most important aspect, I maintain, is not the rather well-known division between "the "I" and "Me," as Mead (1934) called the "phases" of the self, borrowing these particular terms from his predecessor James (1890). His third sub-notion, "the generalized other" namely turns out more basic and important. A division of the human self into two components, as in James's and Mead's I and Me, has been a recurrent phenomenon in Western philosophy, from Plato to the late twentieth century, but "the generalized other" is a more original idea.[6] Not least for the reason that Mead (1934, p. 156) means that "only by taking the attitude of the generalized other toward himself can [an individual] think at all." Cognitive research, particularly autism research, which did not exist at the time of Mead's writing, has since then vindicated this assumption. The prevailing opinion is today that "It is the other, not the self, that must be dealt with and figured out first," as Radu Bogdan (2000, p. 143) puts the matter, and this order of things gets corroboration concomitantly with the advancement of cognitive disciplines (cf. Carruthers, 2009; Gärdenfors, 2009). Autists do not learn to figure out other people, and for this reason cannot figure out even their own behavior and mind, look at them from other people's viewpoint. In brief, they lack the intersubjectivity which we luckier individuals do possess. This pertains also to social theory, in that if normativity is to be taken as universally human, as social theorists often like to take it, then its most probable and natural origin apparently is in the intersubjective constitution of the human mind.

Cognitive disciplines have vindicated also another idea of Mead's. It is the idea that social action, rather than individual action, is the original and basic form of human action. This actually follows from the above supposition about the primacy of the other, but it needs to be made quite explicit for its social-scientific use. Mainstream social theory has usually taken the opposite course, has treated individual action as original, and pondered how a notion of social action might be developed from it. That is a dead end, Mead's followers answer; we can and we should proceed in medias res and treat social action first and as basic. One good reason to treat it as basic is the insight that social intelligence is the original form of human intelligence, not epistemic intelligence, although the latter has received the pride of place in Western philosophy. "Social intelligence" was already Mead's own term, and he asserted it to transcend the domain of individual consciousness (1938, p. 68). In our day Bogdan (1997; 2000) uses the term in just the same sense, and takes this intelligence to be the foundational form of human (and also primate) intelligence. The evolutionary ground for this is that "the point is that the epistemic selection operates in environments already shaped by communal and political forces," as Bogdan (1997, p. 35) asserts. In other words, human beings are smart in the epistemic sense thanks to their first having been smart in the social and political sense. As for human action and the order of things in it, individual action is also real, but its intentionality and rationality have their roots in human sociality, at least according to pragmatism and later cognitive research.

In what sense are 'Rational Fools' foolish?

In neoclassical economics the principle of "rational choice" has a foundational status. It asserts that human individuals in day-to-day life continuously make optimizing choices, and make them by calculating the costs and benefits of different options. This choice procedure is said to be characteristic of rational life in general and economic life in particular, and it is crystallized in the classic depiction, the "economic man," sometimes also called the "rational man." Rational choice is taken to be completely neutral about its object-matter, applicable to any walk of life, so that "if you are consistent, then no matter whether you are a single-minded egoist or a raving altruist or a class conscious militant, you will appear to be maximizing you own utility in this enchanted world of definitions," as Amartaya Sen has illustriously put it (1977, p. 323).

Because neoclassical economics enjoys great authority, this model has spread also elsewhere. In general social theory there have been opinions that it is to be taken as a foundational principle even there, as the "default assumption" of all social theorizing, as Peter Wagner (2000) has called it. Others do not agree, but claim to the contrary that economics is just trying to "colonize" other social disciplines by using this principle as a Trojan horse, as Margaret Archer and Jonathan Tritter (2000) suspect.

An attempt to criticize this well established principle might seem futile, were it not for the fact that the aforementioned Sen (1977), later a Nobel Prize winner in economics, has initiated such criticism. He calls those "rational individuals" provocatively "Rational Fools," on account of their lack of social sensitivity, and maintains that phenomena like sympathy and commitment are so universal that even economics ought to acknowledge their existence in its explanatory models. Sympathy expresses human ability to immerse in other people's feelings, whereas commitment refers to social norms and values. Again Sen offers colorful examples by saying (1977, p. 326) that "If the knowledge of torture of others makes you sick, it is a case of sympathy; if it does not make you feel personally worse off, but you think it is wrong and you are ready to do something to stop it, it is a case of commitment." As economic models usually leave no room for these notions, Sen (1977, p. 336) asserts that "The purely economic man is indeed close to being a social moron."

So far so good, but one also reads all this with a feeling of *déjà vu*. This critique of the economic man is an old hat, in the sense that it has been a recurrent sociological point, ever since the founding of sociology in the work of Weber and Durkheim. This impression is deepened as also Sen (1977, p. 332) maintains that "no society would be viable without some norms and rules of conduct. Such norms and rules are necessary for viability exactly in fields where strictly economic incentives are absent and cannot be created." [7] This is just the classic sociological argument about how the economy and its explanatory model are to be embedded into a wider discourse, sociology, and its treatment of norms and rules. The importance of such embedment has been noted repeatedly throughout sociology's history, by all generations of sociological theorists. And as recurrently has the rejoinder from the economic side been that yes, of course, but all this has to be also rational, and this makes rational choice a sine qua non.

In empirical terms it has been known for some time now that choice based on calculation is not the characteristic operation of the rationally working human mind. Such a choice is a cumbersome, time-consuming operation, but the human mind can operate even lightning-fast, if need be. This is the argument by Antonio Damasio (1995), and since his writing it has been corroborated that those lightning-fast operations take place as pattern-recognitions (Edelman, 2006), as he already assumed. Rational choice thus does not deserve any undue respect in empirical sense. This, however, is not the main sense in which it is used in economics and rationalist thought. Rational choice and the economic man are useful abstractions, the economic argument goes, not so much descriptions. By their means we can explain macro-level happenings in society and draw valid conclusions. If the abstraction works, it is not so crucial from what kind of description it is drawn.

I wouldn't be crucial were it not for the fact that social–scientific knowledge is always also social-political knowledge. It is used for political decisions and these affect the fate of flesh-and-blood individuals, not abstract individuals. Of social scientists, economists get best hearing by policy makers, but whether they are best equipped to explain what human rationality is all about is quite another question.

But what has all this to do with pragmatism? Rational action theory is one of those bodies of thought that very consistently build on the idea that knowledge is something that the acting subject possesses, as we observed above about the traditional interpretation of epistemology. Although this theory usually refers mostly to its mathematical operations, the possessed body of knowledge necessarily plays a role also. The point is that this body of knowledge cannot be just static, if action is to be rational, it must also be replenished, and pure calculative operations don't do that. As we noted above, pragmatism has strived toward such an interpretation of knowledge where its continuous replenishment (inquiry) is the starting point and main idea. This knowledge interest comes out most clearly in Peirce's logical theory, not only in his insistence for a third basic mode of inference, abduction, which today begins to be a well-known idea. It comes out even more dramatically in his insistence for the importance of theorematic deduction, such deductive inference that suggests also new truths, not just corroborates the truthfulness of those beliefs that we have in our possession. This latter database-like conception of the body of knowledge, however, is taken more or less for granted in rational action theory. Peirce's theory of ampliative inference is today being developed further in Jaakko Hintikka's (2007b) logical theory, as I have remarked elsewhere (Kilpinen, 2010). For social theory all this suggests strongly the conclusion that rational action theory apparently is to be taken as an auxiliary book-keeping procedure which may help to keep track about the workings of human rationality, (more accurately: about the results that they yield), but is not their general descriptive model.

Pragmatist social theory applied: William I. Thomas and Florian Znaniecki

Above I have discussed in a most abstract manner some important pragmatist ideas that are of relevance for social theory but so far more or less neglected. Space limitations make their treatment necessarily brief and abstract. However, I do not wish to leave the impression that this abstract mode of analysis is characteristic of pragmatist social thinking. Therefore I close this chapter by discussing one central contribution to down-to-earth social analysis where the imprint of pragmatism is to be seen.

During its efflorescence pragmatism produced in the United States also a notable social-scientific tradition, thanks mostly to the influence of Dewey, who "made the American learned world safe for social sciences," in Richard Rorty (1982, p. 63) once nicely put it. This pragmatist influence is to be seen in what is known as the "Chicago School" in sociology, in the (old) "institutional school" in economics, and in the so-called "behavioralist" movement in the study of politics, although their all relevance cannot be traced to this philosophy. Today these cases are remembered, if at all, as historical curiosities, rather than as classic traditions. I maintain, however, that their pragmatist elements are of more lasting value, and as a piece of evidence I discuss briefly one important contribution to sociology, the multi-volume work The *Polish Peasant in Europe and America* (originally of 1918–20), by William I. Thomas and Florian Znaniecki. A good reason to consider it is that the authors use the term 'social theory' about its contents. In this respect they make a more explicit and therefore better example than some other pragmatist social scientists like Thorstein Veblen (1857–1929), Charles H. Cooley (1864–1929), or Arthur Bentley (1870–1957), who also deserve remembrance and theoretical interest even today.[8]

The Polish Peasant was once regarded as a sociological classic, but today is in danger of sinking into oblivion. However, even when it was appreciated, still after the Second World War, this was usually not from the correct viewpoint. For example, a once influential history of sociology (Madge, 1963) treated it merely as a notable contribution to empirical social research. In truth, Thomas and Znaniecki's contribution is to be taken as just as thoroughly theoretical as empirical. It is a contribution to the sociology of modernization in the very same sense as Émile Durkheim's or Max Weber's chief works are. For example, Durkheim's *Suicide* (1897), another example of Madge's (1963), cannot be reduced to a mere empirical study, that would not make it a sociological classic. Its sociological theory gives it its classic status, and just the same is true of Thomas and Znaniecki's contribution. A further complication in the reputation of that work is that it has gone to history as a study on immigration. It has been taken as an empirical study about how Polish peasants immigrate to the United States and what happens to them there. Those who take the book in this sense apparently have not opened it, because when done so it turns out that some 5/6 of its contents deals with peasant life in Poland. The phenomenon of emigration in Thomas and Znaniecki's treatment is a consequence of deeper social processes, not the main topic in its own right. And those deeper social processes are related most of all to social change and modernization in rural Poland.

Thomas and Znaniecki were abreast with the state of the art in their contemporary sociology in that they explicitly took a stand to the famous methodological advice of Durkheim's that "social facts are always to be explained by other social facts." Thomas and Znaniecki acknowledged this suggestion but did not follow it slavishly, but asserted instead that a social fact is to be explained by combining individual and social facts. By individual facts they meant action-theoretic suppositions about the treated subjects; "attitude" being the technical term that they used about it, whereas "value" referred to the normative structure of society.

A sociologist immediately recognizes in these terms some basic concepts of his or her discipline. Thomas and Znaniecki, however, do not use these terms in quite the same sense as mainstream sociology: for them they are not determinants of action. To make the point in philosophical terms: these authors understand these central concepts in a realist rather than nominalist sense, that is, as something that is actualized in action, but does not exist as an immaterial entity outside it. "We compare different actions with regard to the attitudes manifested in them . . . we compare the values *produced by* different actions," the authors explain their procedure in the "Methodological Note" that introduces the work (1974, p. 24; emphases added). Later on, they add a descriptive example to illustrate this principle, by saying that "An act of social help simply strengthens and *actualizes* the general attitude of benevolent solidarity" (1974, p. 181, emphasis added). The authors' chosen order expresses that they are following the pragmatist theory of action, which begins with concrete action and takes its psychological and ideological factors as particular phases in action, not as its "determinants" from the outside, as is the case in "mind-first" explanation.

However, these authors' case also shows that sound sociology can nevertheless be done also on the basis of this altered order of things. Their concept of attitude refers to the more subjective and individual, the concept of value to the more objective and collective side in social analysis. To the former side as a whole they refer by the technical term "social psychology," to the latter with the term "sociology," and together these discourses constitute what the authors call "social theory." Their position is that both the individual and collectively social dimensions are needed in social theory, even so that "social psychology," referring to the individual level of analysis, is to be taken as a wider phenomenon than "sociology," as Harry Elmer Barnes, Thomas's former student and a historian of sociology once aptly reminded (1948, p. 800). This goes well together with today's knowledge about human cognition and emotion that treats these phenomena as "distributed," as something that transcends an individual consciousness. In other words, Thomas and Znaniecki's conception of sociology does not address any supposed "contradiction" between individual and society, because they do not suppose it to exist. They do not take the human mind as purely individual, as was usual in classical sociological theory elsewhere at that time. This does not prevent them from making sociological observations that match with those by other classics. For example, they discuss Polish peasant relations in terms of "reflective versus. unreflective social solidarity" (Thomas and Znaniecki, 1974, pp. 1173–74) and here a sociologist immediately recognizes a paraphrase but also further development of Durkheim's "mechanical versus. organic solidarity." In Thomas and Znaniecki's conception, the social change taking place in rural Poland leads to increasingly unreflective (we may say: rationalistic at the expense of emotive) social solidarity in so far as social relations orient more toward immediate money incentive and payment, for example. Thomas and Znaniecki's magnum opus corroborates what other sociological classics have presented about modernization, but in some issues advances beyond it, particularly in the treatment of action.

For pragmatism, mere social philosophy, uninformed by empirical social knowledge, is empty. Mere empiricist social science, uninformed by philosophy, is blind.

Notes

1 This chapter was written while I had the privilege of a fellowship at the Swedish Collegium for Advanced Study in Uppsala 2009–2010. I wish to express my deepest gratitude and appreciation to its staff and my co-fellows for the most excellent working conditions and research atmosphere.

2 From the voluminous literature on Dewey and his social theory, I single out a contribution, Larry Hickman's (1998) anthology, because it well keeps what its subtitle promises: introduces Dewey to a postmodern generation. I also wish to point attention to a German anthology edited by Hans Joas (2000). For a very comprehensive overview on contemporary social theory, from a sociological viewpoint and building in part on pragmatist principles, see Joas and Knöbl (2009). An anthology edited by Alan Sica (1998) approaches social theory from a philosophical viewpoint, on non-pragmatist principles.

3 For abbreviations in Peirce quotations, see the list of references. I also give the original writing year, if known.
4 Giddens equates habits with "routines" which means that vestiges of a dualism between habituality and intentionality remain even in his thinking. He does not marry these two as pragmatists do.
5 For detailed explications of Mead see Joas (1985) and Cook (1993).
6 It is not quite original to Mead, in that Peirce has had a similar notion about "man's circle of society as a sort of loosely compacted person, in some respects of higher rank than the person of an individual organism" (CP 5.421, 1905). However, Mead has drawn its psychological conclusions more explicitly and thoroughly.
7 The quotation is Sen's own quotation from a previous author, the Norwegian economist L. Johansen.
8 I have presented chapter-length summaries about Thomas and Znaniecki and Bentley, respectively, in Kilpinen (2000, chs. 5–6). Today there is burgeoning scholarship on Veblen, to a lesser extent also on Cooley.

References

Archer, M. and Tritter, J. Q. (eds), (2000), *Rational Choice Theory: Resisting Colonization*. London and New York: Routledge.
Barnes, H. E. (1948), "William Isaac Thomas: The Fusion of Psychological and Cultural Sociology," in H. E. Barnes (ed.), *An Introduction to the History of Sociology*. Chicago: University of Chicago Press.
Bogdan, R. (1997), *Interpreting Minds: The Evolution of a Practice*. Cambridge, MA; London, England: MIT Press.
—(2000), *Minding Minds: Evolving a Reflexive Mind by Interpreting Others*. Cambridge, MA; London, England: MIT Press.
Carruthers, P. (2009), "How We Know Our Own Minds: The Relationship Between Mindreading and Metacognition," *Behavioral and Brain Sciences*, 32, (2), pp. 121–138.
Cook, G. A. (1993), *George Herbert Mead: The Making of a Social Pragmatist*. Urbana and Chicago: University of Illinois Press.
Damasio, A. (1995), *Descartes' Error: Emotion, Reason and the Human Brain*. London and New York: Picador & Avon Books.
Dennett, D. C. (1995), *Darwin's Dangerous Idea: Evolution and the Meanings of Life*. New York: Simon & Schuster.
Dewey, J. (2002), *Human Nature and Conduct*. Amherst, N.Y.: Prometheus Books, 1922.
Edelman, G. (2006), *Second Nature: Brain Science and Human Knowledge*. New Haven and London: Yale University Press.
Giddens, A. (1976), *New Rules of Sociological Method*. London: Hutchinson.

—(1984), *The Constitution of Society: Outline of the Theory of Structuration*. Cambridge: Polity Press.
Gärdenfors, P. (2009), "The Social Stance and Its Relation to Intersubjectivity," in P. Hedström and B. Wittrock (eds), *Frontiers of Sociology*. Leiden and Boston: Brill, pp. 291–305.
Hickman, L. (ed.), (1998), *Reading Dewey: Interpretations for a Postmodern Generation*. Bloomington and Indianapolis: Indiana University Press.
Hintikka, J. (2007a), "Epistemology without Knowledge and without Belief," in J. Hintikka, *Socratic Epistemology*. Cambridge: Cambridge University Press, pp. 11–37.
—(2007b), "Abduction—Inference, Conjecture, or an Answer to a Question?" in J. Hintikka, *Socratic Epistemology*. Cambridge: Cambridge University Press, pp. 38–60.
Hume, D. (1985), *A Treatise of Human Nature*. Harmondsworth: Penguin, 1739–1740.
James, W. (1950), *The Principles of Psychology*, I–II. New York: Dover, 1890.
Joas, H. (1985), *G. H. Mead: A Contemporary Re-examination of His Thought*. Cambridge: Polity Press, 1980.
—(ed., 2000), *Philosophie der Demokratie. Beiträge zum Werk von John Dewey*. Frankfurt am Main: Suhrkamp.
Joas, H. and Knöbl, W. (2009), *Social Theory: Twenty Introductory Lectures*. Cambridge: Cambridge University Press, 2004.
Kilpinen, E. (2000), *The Enormous Fly-Wheel of Society*. Research Report no. 235, Department of Sociology, University of Helsinki. Helsinki: Hakapaino.
—(2009a), "The Habitual Conception of Action and Social Theory," *Semiotica*, 173, (1/4), pp. 99–128.
—(2009b), "Pragmatism as a Philosophy of Action," in Pihlström, S. and Rydenfelt, H. (eds), *Pragmatist Perspectives*. Helsinki: Societas Philosophica Fennica, vol. 86 in the series, Acta Philosophica Fennica, pp. 163–179.
—(2010), "Problems in Applying Peirce in Social Sciences" in M. Bergman et al. (eds), *Ideas in Action: Proceedings of the 'Applying Peirce' Conference*. Helsinki: Nordic Pragmatism Network, pp. 86–104.
Macintyre, A. (1985), *After Virtue: A Study in Moral Theory*, 2nd edn. London: Duckworth, 1981.
Madge, J. (1963), *The Origins of Scientific Sociology*. London: Tavistock.
Mead, G. H. (1934), *Mind, Self and Society, from the Standpoint of a Social Behaviorist*. Ed. C. W. Morris. Chicago: University of Chicago Press.
—(1938), *The Philosophy of the Act*. Ed. C.W. Morris, et al. Chicago: University of Chicago Press.
—(1982), *The Individual and the Social Self: Unpublished Work of George Herbert Mead*. Ed. D.L. Miller. Chicago and London: University of Chicago Press.
Peirce, C. S. (1931–1958), *Collected Papers of Charles Sanders Peirce*, 8 vols, eds. C. Hartshorne and P. Weiss (vols 1–6) and A. W. Burks (vols 7–8). Cambridge, MA:

Harvard University Press. Cited as CP with volume number and paragraph, not pages.

—(1976), *New Elements of Mathematics, by Charles S. Peirce*. Ed. Carolyn Eisele, 4 vols. (in five tomes). The Hague and Paris: Mouton. Atlantic Highlands, NJ: Humanities Press. Cited as NEM.

—(1992–1998), *The Essential Peirce: Selected Philosophical Writings*. Vol. 1 (1867–1893), eds N. Houser and C. J. W. Kloesel; vol. 2 (1893–1913), ed. Peirce Edition Project. Bloomington and Indianapolis: Indiana University Press. Cited as EP.

Rescher, N. (2000) *Process Philosophy: A Survey of Basic Issues*. Pittsburgh: University of Pittsburgh Press.

Rorty, R. (1982), *Consequences of Pragmatism: Essays 1972–80*. Brighton: Harvester Press.

—(1999), *Philosophy and Social Hope*. London: Penguin.

Ryan, A. (1970), *The Philosophy of the Social Sciences*. London: Macmillan.

Sen, A. (1977), "Rational Fools: A Critique of the Behavioral Foundations of Economic Theory." *Philosophy and Public Affairs*, 6, (4), pp. 317–344.

Sica, A. (ed.), (1998), *What Is Social Theory? The Philosophical Debates*. Oxford: Blackwell.

Thomas, W. I. and Znaniecki, F. (1974), *The Polish Peasant in Europe and America*. Unabridged two-volume edition. New York: Octagon Books. (Originally published in five volumes in 1918–1920).

Wagner, P. (2000), "The Bird in Hand: Rational Choice—the Default Mode of Social Theorizing." in M. Archer and J. Q. Tritter (eds), *Rational Choice Theory: Resisting Colonization*. London and New York: Routledge, pp. 19–35.

10

Politics

Shane J. Ralston

Any treatment of the relationship between pragmatism and politics would be incomplete without considering the multiple areas in which pragmatist thought and political studies intersect. Extensive scholarly work on pragmatism and politics can be found in the broad literature on political science, democratic theory, global political theory, public administration, and public policy. To a lesser extent, scholarship employing a pragmatist approach can be found in other subfields of political studies, including American politics and international relations. Unfortunately, the few works in these subfields tend to appeal to a generic form of pragmatism (e.g., pragmatism as brute instrumentalism or pragmatism as vicious opportunism), not the robust version associated with classic and contemporary philosophical pragmatism.[1] Most works on classic pragmatism and politics draw heavily on John Dewey's political and ethical writings. Pragmatism's two other founders remained relatively silent on the subject; in Robert Talisse's words, "neither [Charles Sanders] Peirce nor [William] James wrote systematically about politics."[2] Neo-pragmatist treatments of politics can be found in the works of the late Richard Rorty, Cornell West, and Richard Posner.[3]

By way of organization, the first section of this chapter chronicles pragmatism's influence on the scientific study of politics through a series of articles authored by political scientists and theorists. The second addresses, more specifically, pragmatism's relation to democratic theory. The third section extends the pragmatist's concern with politics to global political theory. The fourth section examines a wide-ranging debate about pragmatism's capacity to guide public administration theory and practice. The fourth and final section draws attention to pragmatism in the policy sciences, as well as the exciting potential for new scholarship at the nexus between pragmatism and politics.

Political science

Political theory and philosophy are the primary areas in which pragmatism overlaps with political studies. Nevertheless, pragmatism has also piqued the interest of political scientists engaged in both the empirical study of political phenomena and the normative evaluation of the results of those empirical studies. The 1999 issue of the *American Journal of Political Science* contains six essays on pragmatism and politics by political scientists and political theorists, addressing the relationship between experts and citizens in a democracy, the place of institutions in a pragmatist political theory, the possibility of a scientific approach to democratic governance and the relevance of pragmatism to empirical research methods in the social sciences, especially political science.

Debrah Morris's "'How Shall We Read What We Call Reality?'" reveals John Dewey's contribution to a "new science of democracy," particularly an emerging framework for postpositivist inquiry in political science (Morris, 1999, pp.608-628). Dewey has been read in diverse ways, from a freewheeling postmodernist (Rorty) to a straightforward positivist (Bullert).[4] However, Morris contends that Dewey's method of intelligence aligns more closely with three themes in postpositivism: (i) a rejection of nomological-deductive explanation, (ii) the embrace of a more holistic account of scientific method that also applies to problems in ordinary experience and (iii) "a direct link to democratic theory" (Morris, 1999, pp. 610-614). While these themes clearly differentiate Dewey's method from positivism, they also separate it from the approach of postmodernism and some varieties of neo-pragmatism: "The postmodernist appropriation of pragmatism fails to recover Dewey's challenge to social science, the ways in which he radicalizes scientific method in the name of political thought and a revitalized democratic ideal" (Morris, 1999, p. 616). According to Morris, "Dewey's principal aim" is to recruit scientifically modeled inquiry in the service of "democratic statecraft" (Morris, 1999, p. 623). Still, what remains uncertain is whether the pragmatist's new science of democracy implies some clear set of ideological commitments or an ambiguous political valence.

In "Inquiry into Democracy," Jack Knight and James Johnson argue that pragmatist thinking about institutions is an impractical guide for addressing related political problems.[5] While Dewey was concerned with how to harmonize the private or egoistic demands of individuals with the greater public interest, his pragmatist philosophy provided little in the way of practical guidance. Borrowing from rational choice theory, Knight and Johnson show that a more feasible approach—for instance, in determining whether government should provide national defense or trash collection—would be to create an auction or artificial market in public goods, such that "the government will supply the good only if they [citizens] assign a combined value to the public good that exceeds the cost ... [such that] citizens have an incentive to honestly reveal the value they attach to the public good" (Knight and Johnson, 1999, p. 581). Knight and Johnson observe that "pragmatists are an unruly lot: they disagree among themselves about various philosophical and political issues" (Knight and Johnson, 1999, p. 566). Nevertheless, they share three things in common: (i) a commitment to evaluating actions relative to their consequences (or consequentialism), (ii) a belief that the state of human knowledge is never fixed and settled for all time (or fallibilism) and (iii) an optimistic attitude about the prospects for democratic reform and social improvement (or anti-skepticism) (Knight and Johnson, 1999, p. 567). While Knight and Johnson acknowledge the value of pragmatist theories of deliberative democracy, they nonetheless insist that "pragmatists are naïve about institutional matters ... [and that] their preoccupation [with democratic deliberation] is very nearly utopian in the pejorative sense" (Knight and Johnson, 1999, p. 569).[6]

James Farr's "John Dewey and American Political Science" explores the possibility that Dewey's critique of political science has dampened contemporary political scientists' enthusiasm for his intellectual legacy.[7] Although Dewey acknowledged the potential for social inquiry to become experimental, he faulted what passed as political science in his day for being a "recluse," an "idle-spectator" of dynamic changes in political phenomena. (Farr, 1999, p. 524) In Dewey's vision of a new experimental political science, civic education and political reform would liberate human potentialities and empower citizens to criticize state-sponsored organs of propaganda. While the general disregard of Dewey's writings by political scientists was in full swing in the early 1960s, many group theorists, including Arthur F. Bentley, Charles E. Merriam and David B. Truman, regularly credited Dewey, especially his *The Public and Its Problems*, for inspiring their scholarly work. Farr also explores the relationship between Dewey's pragmatism and the development of the policy sciences (see "Public Policy" section below). He concludes the essay with a poignant question for political scientists: "Might Dewey help debates over the discipline's self-understanding in the present and future if we undertake some intelligent probing and critical reassessment of his actual writings and of the discipline's real history?" (Farr, 1999, p. 538).

In "Democracy as Inquiry, Inquiry as Democratic," James Bohman examines the link between science and politics in pragmatist theories of democracy.[8]

While researchers often wish to segregate the two, Bohman sees them as continuous in pragmatist thought. Specifically, in John Dewey's writings on science and democracy, the direction of science is subject to democratic choice, and democratic choice is a matter of cooperative problem solving patterned after scientific inquiry. In at least this respect, Deweyan democracy approximates what contemporary political theorists refer to as deliberative democracy (see "Democratic Theory" section below). For deliberative forums to be effective, though, designers must ensure that citizens have recourse to experts, cognitive work is fairly distributed and citizens are willing to defer to the expertise of others: "[P]ragmatists want to point out that better informed decision making requires some social organization of inquiry, and this in turn demands some sort of division of labor. . . . It implies the need for pervasive mechanisms of trust . . . " (Bohman, 1999, pp. 591–592). Since citizens are rarely equipped to verify the authenticity of expert knowledge, deference can occur when expertise is compromised or expert advice is contrary to the public interest, thereby undermining the trust implicit in the principal-agent relationship. While this dilemma is not peculiar to pragmatist thinking about politics, it is especially salient for pragmatists who recommend that democracies cultivate expert-citizen partnerships. Bohman's proposed solution is to empower citizens to participate in meta-deliberations about the norms that govern their own problem-solving and deliberative activities.

In "Experience as Experiment," Eric MacGilvray classifies contemporary pragmatists into two groups: (i) those who criticize traditional epistemology (or what Dewey derisively called "the epistemology industry") and (ii) those who vindicate democracy.[9] From this premise he argues that Dewey offers a moral conception of politics that bridges the divide between the two groups—what he calls "pragmatism as principled advocacy" (MacGilvray, 1999, pp. 561–562). Pragmatism as principled advocacy features a "pragmatic conception of human intelligence," a scientifically modeled method of inquiry and a melioristic faith in the capacity of humans to improve themselves. Unfortunately, Dewey's vision of democratic progress suffers from what MacGilvray calls a "heady optimism," or naiveté with regard to making "tragic choices" about how to fill "gap[s] not only between individual capacities and social circumstances, but also between the plurality of interests in the populace and the ability of institutions to represent them adequately" (MacGilvray, 1999, pp. 560–561). MacGilvray's criticism that Deweyan democracy cannot accommodate the "plurality of interests in the populace" anticipates a more recent debate over the compatibility of Deweyan democracy and John Rawls's notion of reasonable pluralism.[10]

In "Pragmatic Inquiry and Democratic Politics," Marion Smiley explores three commitments that underlie pragmatist theories of democracy—or what she terms "democratic pragmatism."[11] The first is the pragmatist's conception of democracy as a method of scientifically modeled inquiry. In Smiley's words, "we are a community of inquirers who symbolically interpret the results of inquiry through collective symbols shared within what Dewey calls his 'public' " (Smiley, 1999, p. 631). The second theme is the need for rigorous inquiry to determine those standards that will effectively guide democratic practice and institutions toward shared goals. And the third is the open-ended character of pragmatism, which invites ongoing inquiry into the conditions that will promote more robust citizen engagement in democratic politics. In keeping with Dewey's definition of a public in *The Public and Its Problems*, Smiley insists that "pragmatists . . . ask: 'How can we get individuals to acknowledge the consequences of [their] conjoint activity, consequences that they might prefer to ignore?' " (Smiley, 1999, p. 643). While the rational course of action for the voter might involve ignorance and apathy, citizens who wish to sustain a robust democracy must "acknowledge the consequences of [their] conjoint activity" and become informed and engaged members of the public (e.g., through discussion, voting, and organizing).[12] According to Smiley, democratic pragmatists are uniquely equipped to prescribe ways to inform and engage a democratic citizenry given their strong commitment to expert-citizen partnerships.

Democratic theory

In the past decade, claims that John Dewey was a deliberative democrat or a proto-deliberative democrat have become increasingly common, both in the literature on deliberative democracy and the literature on classic American pragmatism. Among deliberative democrats, John Dryzek acknowledges that "an emphasis on deliberation is not entirely new," and points to "[a]ntecedents" in the ancient Greeks, Edmund Burke, John Stuart Mill, and "in theorists from the early twentieth century such as John Dewey."[13] Likewise, deliberative theorists Amy Gutmann and Dennis Thompson note that "[i]n the writings of John Dewey . . . we finally find unequivocal declarations of the need for political discussion . . . [and] widespread deliberations as part of democracy."[14] Deliberative democrat Jürgen Habermas invokes John Dewey's argument that genuine democratic choice cannot be realized by majority voting alone, but must also be complemented by deliberation—or in Dewey's words, "prior recourse to methods of discussion, consultation and persuasion" (Dewey, 1996, LW 2:365).[15] Jane Mansbridge and John Gastil have taken these Dewey-inspired theories of deliberative democracy a step further, employing them to study the actual phenomenon of deliberation in institutionalized forums and small groups.[16] Still, while the general idea can be traced back to John Dewey, the name "deliberative democracy" has a fairly recent origin. With genealogical precision, James Bohman pinpoints "its recent incarnation" in the work of the political scientist "Joseph Bessette, who [in 1980] coined it to oppose the elitist and 'aristocratic' interpretation of the American Constitution."[17]

Among Dewey scholars, the coronation of Dewey as a nascent deliberative democrat has been comparatively slower. One remarkable conversion was signaled by Dewey biographer Robert Westbrook's admission that Dewey's democratic vision resembles deliberative democracy more than participatory democracy. Writing after the publication of his widely heralded Dewey biography, he confesses:

> ... I think we might say that Dewey was anticipating an ideal that contemporary democratic theorists have dubbed "deliberative democracy." Indeed, I wish this term was in the air when I was writing *John Dewey and American Democracy*, for I think it captures Dewey's procedural ideals better than the term I used, "participatory democracy," since it suggests something of the character of the participation involved in democratic associations.[18]

According to Westbrook, Dewey developed an ideal of intelligent social action that outstripped the ideal of participatory politics. While Westbrook initially views the mass politics and direct action of grassroots groups in the 1960s (for instance, the Students for a Democratic Society) as distinctly Deweyan, he later revises his position. For Dewey, ethical deliberation pertains to moral judgment, choice, and action. In *Human Nature and Conduct*, he defines ethical deliberation as "a dramatic rehearsal (in imagination) of various competing lines of action" (Dewey, 1996, LW 14:132). To deliberate, the moral agent must, first, temporarily disengage the engine of action; then, imagine the possible consequences, good or bad, of "various competing lines of action" (i.e., rehearsing them); and, lastly, decide on the best, or most morally defensible, course of action given the rehearsal of possibilities. Dewey compares ethical deliberation to an imaginative "experiment." Each possible course of action, once worked out, remains tentative and "retrievable":

> It [i.e., deliberation] starts from the blocking of efficient overt action, due to that conflict of prior habit and newly released impulse to which reference has been made. Then each habit, each impulse, involved in the temporary suspense

of overt action takes its turn in being tried out. Deliberation is an experiment in finding out what the various lines of possible action are really like. It is an experiment in making various combinations of selected elements of habits and impulses, to see what the resultant action would be like if it were entered upon. But the trial is in imagination, not in overt fact. The experiment is carried on by tentative rehearsals in thought which do not affect physical acts outside the body. Thought runs ahead and foresees outcomes, and thereby avoids having to await the instruction of actual failure and disaster. An act overtly tried out is irrevocable, its consequences cannot be blotted out. An act tried out in imagination is not final or fatal. It is retrievable. (Dewey, 1996, LW 14:132–133)

While deliberation for Dewey is a way of addressing moral problems, on Westbrook's reading, it additionally constitutes a method for resolving social and political problems: "Dewey's goal [in offering a theory of moral deliberation] is to move toward an account of public deliberation on issues of society-wide concern."[19]

When appreciated as a method for coordinating action through norm-governed discussion, deliberative democracy appears surprisingly similar to Dewey's vision of democracy. In Dewey's *The Public and Its Problems*, democratic methods encompass communication and collaborative inquiry undertaken by citizens within a community and against a rich background of supportive institutions: "To learn to be human is to develop through the give-and-take of communication an effective sense of being an individually distinctive member of a community; one who understands and appreciates its beliefs, desires and methods, and who contributes to a further conversion of organic powers into human resources and values" (Dewey, 1996, LW 2:332). Through the activity of appraisal or evaluation, private preferences, or what Dewey terms "prizings" or "valuings" (i.e., what is subjectively valued or desired), are converted into publicly shared values or "valuations" (i.e., what is objectively valuable or desirable) (Dewey, 1996, LW 13:216–218; LW 4:207). Similarly, deliberative democrats model political deliberation as a communicative process for resolving collective problems which depends on converting individual ends and preferences into shared objectives and values. Political theorist Ian Shapiro claims that "[t]he unifying impulse motivating [deliberation] is that people will modify their perceptions of what society should do in the course of discussing this with others."[20]

A critical mass of Dewey scholars enthusiastically endorses the proposition that Dewey anticipated the deliberative turn in democratic theory. Some locate the source of Dewey's ideas about democratic deliberation in his books and articles on politics, while others see a closer connection to his works on ethics.²¹ Three of the more prominent scholars in this group, Melvin Rogers, Noëlle McAfee, and William Caspary, explicitly tie what they see as Dewey's nascent theory of democratic deliberation to operative concepts in his logical, political, and ethical writings. Rogers detects the connection between Dewey and deliberative democratic theory in his logic of inquiry: "It is Dewey's appeal to inquiry as a method for justifying beliefs that feeds directly into and underwrites [the legitimacy of] democratic deliberation."²² For McAfee, it is not Dewey's logic, but his notion of publicity that emerges in *The Public and Its Problems*. "Dewey's emphasis on publicness" and "public discourse" clarifies "how a given policy would or would not satisfy their [i.e., the discoursing citizens'] own concerns, values, and ends—including the value they place on the welfare of the community itself."²³ Publicness for Dewey resembles the contemporary deliberative democrat's full-blooded sense of public deliberation, that is, discourse intended to transform individual perspectives and goals into shared ideals and public values.

Global political theory

Beyond the subject-matter of democracy, pragmatism has also influenced contemporary trends in global political theory. Many of these recent theoretical treatments of global politics invoke Dewey's concept of a public. In *The Public and Its Problems*, Dewey understands a group impacted, either negatively or positively, by the activities of other groups as a "public," that is, "all those affected by the indirect consequences of [other groups'] transactions" (Dewey, 1996, LW 2:255). While publics will often contain members with conflicting interests, what they have in common are the conditions of their shared situation. Frank Cunningham connects Dewey's notion of a public to political pluralism: "On a Deweyan conception . . . publics are not places of homogenous values, but preconditions for addressing common problems among people who otherwise may have a variety of sometimes diverging values."²⁴ Each is similarly affected by the problematic consequences of others' activities. Once those persons belonging to a public acknowledge their shared situation, the occasion arises for them to engage in collective inquiry leading to collective action. According to Paul Stob, "Dewey's terms speak not of what the public *is* but of what the public can *do*" (Stob, 2005, p. 237).

Dewey's conceptualization of a public in terms of those externalities one set of interacting groups creates for another has also made its way into scholarly work on global justice, global citizenship, and cosmopolitanism. According to Cunningham, "since [Deweyan] democracy is of unlimited scope and thus appropriate whenever the activities of some people affect others in an ongoing way, there are no boundaries, state-determined or otherwise, to it."[25] So, extending the notion of a public to include global publics, though absent in Dewey's original formulation, is nonetheless perfectly Deweyan (or in the spirit of Dewey's original formulation). On Larry Hickman's account, "Pragmatism provides tools for fostering global citizenship by indicating some of the ways in which global publics can be formed."[26] Moreover, Marilyn Fischer claims that "it is futile to theorize about cosmopolitanism [or the view that humans all over the world can exist in peace and harmony] as a goal without also attending to the means for attaining it."[27] One of the crucial means employed by pragmatists is to conceive publics as plural in character, global in scope, and problem-solving in function. Indeed, for Colin Koopman, theorists of global justice should concede the pragmatist's point that competing visions of global connectedness are plural and overlapping, since "our ideals inevitably intersect with those of others such that each ideal comes to define itself by reference to other ideals."[28]

Public administration

Public Administration (hereafter PA) is broadly defined as that area of study addressing the development, institutionalization, and reconstruction of bureaucratic-governmental organizations tasked to implement public policies. While some PA scholars argue that there should be a strict separation between politics and administration, pragmatists see the dualism as untenable and the founding of PA and pragmatism at the start of the twentieth century as more than a mere coincidence.[29]

A lively debate over whether classic pragmatism or neo-pragmatism better informs PA began with an exchange between Patricia Shields and Hugh Miller. In "The Community of Inquiry," Shields observes that the classic pragmatist's notion of a community of inquiry captures a practical (or pragmatic) ideal that most PA practitioners would feel is worthy of aspiring to: "In practice, the community of inquiry is an ideal position to which public administrators should strive (Shields, 2003, p. 511).[30] It is the position from which public administrators can most effectively examine how they approach problems, consider data, and communicate" (Shields, 2003, p. 511). Built into the notion of a community of inquiry are three key concepts: (i) the problematic situation (or the onset of a difficulty within a particular context as "a reason to undertake inquiry"), (ii) scientific attitude (or "a willingness to tackle the problem [or difficulty] using working hypotheses") and (iii) participatory democracy (or that "[t]he democratic community takes into account values/ideals ... as it [collaboratively] considers goals and objectives") (Shields, 2003, pp. 516–525). Besides integrating these three concepts, pragmatists in "the PA workaday world" should face the opportunities and challenges that beset their organization's policy environment with what Shields calls "a sense of critical optimism": "Critical optimism [or meliorism] is the faith or sense that if we put our heads together and act using a scientific attitude to approach a problematic situation, the identified problem has the potential to be resolved" (Shields, 2003, p. 514).

In "Why Old Pragmatism Needs an Upgrade," Hugh Miller criticizes Shields's "community of inquiry" idea for relying too heavily on the foundational claims of classic pragmatism in order to ground administrative practice.[31] Miller recommends a form of pragmatism without a strong faith in scientific method to assist public administrators in appreciating the multiplicity of methods at their disposal: namely, neo-pragmatism (Miller, 2004, p. 245). Richard Rorty's new pragmatism satisfies these requirements, since

> ... the foundational link between language and reality [words and objects] that Dewey relied on has been abandoned in new pragmatism. New pragmatists do not revere experience in the same way Dewey did. The word *experience*, in its attempt to denote a relationship with a presence, is accessible only by isolating its specific meaning in a particular linguistic system. (Miller, 2004, p. 245)

Rorty's neo-pragmatism shares some features in common with classic pragmatism, such as commitments to instrumentalism and value pluralism (Miller, 2004, pp. 244–246). However, most neo-pragmatists believe that meaning emerges through the antifoundational process of language use, conversation, or discourse.[32] Classic pragmatists understand the emergence of meaning differently. On Miller's account, they posit experience as a contextual background (or given) that connects words (language) with objects (reality) (Miller, 2004, p. 245). Since classic pragmatists attempt to describe experience as it is in-itself (its essence), they err, similar to traditional philosophers, by erecting a proxy foundation for true knowledge (viz., experience) and a method to gain privileged access (viz., science). Miller recommends that pragmatist PA scholars upgrade their operative theory from classic pragmatism to neo-pragmatism. Neo-pragmatism would replace the classic pragmatist's single mode of scientifically modeled inquiry with plural discourses and diverse approaches to administering public organizations. This would have "radical implications" for PA practice, such as the widespread adoption of innovative methods for solving public problems and the transformation of "government ... [in]to an art and craft composed of practices and procedures invoked in pragmatic situations" (Miller, 2004, p. 248).

This debate over pragmatism's relevance to PA theory and practice nicely illustrates the kinds of intramural disagreements that occur when classic pragmatists and neo-pragmatists seek to clarify the relationship between pragmatism and politics.[33]

Public policy

The final area in which pragmatism and political studies intersect is public policy—or what is sometimes termed the "policy sciences." James Lester and Joseph Stuart define public policy as "a process or a series or pattern of governmental activities of decisions that are designed to remedy some public problem, either real or imagined."[34] An obvious similarity between the governmental process of policy making and the pragmatist process of inquiry is their similar emphasis on problem solving. In this vein, James Campbell argues that pragmatist policy making should resemble an open-ended course of inquiry and experimentation: "[A]ll policy measures should be envisioned as experiments to be tested in their future consequences. As a consequence of this testing, the program will undergo *ongoing revision*."[35] Before resolving a public problem, though, policy makers must initially agree on what features of the policy environment (or situation) make it problematic—what policy analysts call setting the agenda or framing the issue, and Dewey referred to as the "location and definition" of the problem (Dewey, 1996, MW 6:236). According to Sidney Hook, one of Dewey's more renowned students, pragmatism offers a better way of framing a policy problem, "a kind of methodological sophistication that either sharpens the issues at point in public controversy or discloses the absence of real or genuine issues, thus clarifying the options open for decision."[36]

Besides philosophical pragmatists, public policy scholars have also shed light on the commonalities between policy studies and pragmatism. Indeed, one of the key figures in the founding of the policy sciences, Harold D. Laswell, invoked "the work of Dewey and other American philosophers of pragmatism" as a prime "example of what may be expected [. . . when policy scientists] quickly move to the consideration of social [and political] institutions."[37] Commentators, such as Douglas Torgerson and Frank Fischer, note that the policy sciences did not take the strongly positivist turn that the rest of political science did (via the so-called Behavioralist Revolution) largely because Laswell conceived policy making as a naturalistic and contextualized process—that is, on par with how Dewey conceived experimental inquiry.[38] After reviewing the sundry references to pragmatism made by leading policy scholars, James Farr concludes that "[s]uch [varied] reception, in any case, suggests how diffuse and unspecified was Dewey's influence, even in so 'pragmatic' a field as policy science."[39] So, incidental appeals to pragmatism in policy scholarship do not necessarily signal the presence or influence of philosophical pragmatism. They could signify a more generic sense of the term. Still, a public policy does resemble what Dewey called a "proposal" in that it suggests "some possible solution" to a social or political problem (Dewey, 1996, LW 12:116). According to Frank Fischer, "[p]olicies . . . represent [for Dewey] plans of action selected from alternatives having scientifically observable consequences that provide the basis for valid testing."[40] Although the union of pragmatism and public policy has still not crystallized into a definite research program, scholars of both continue to explore how pragmatism can serve as a theoretical resource for addressing specific policy issues and cases.[41]

Building bridges between political studies and philosophical pragmatism is therefore consistent with Dewey's call for philosophy to deal with "the problems of men" (Dewey, 1996, MW 10:42). As witnessed in the PA dispute between classic pragmatists and neo-pragmatists, intramural disagreements over the relative merits of different approaches will inevitably arise. Generally though, serious investments of effort to demonstrate that pragmatist ideas and political realities are continuous features of human experience should repay students and scholars of politics a significant dividend.

Notes

1 In international relations scholarship, there are exceptions. See Cochran (1996, pp. 29–52). See Kaag (2008, pp. 111–131).
2 Robert B. Talisse, "John Rawls and American Pragmatisms," conference paper presented at "Rawlsian Liberalism in Context," University of Tennessee, February 26–27, 2010, available on SSRN at <http://papers.ssrn.com/sol3/papers.cfm?abstract_id=1611859 (accessed May 29, 2010).

3   See Rorty (1989), West (2004), Posner (2003).
4   See Rorty (1991) and Bullert (1983).
5   See Knight and Johnson (1999, pp. 566–589).
6   For an opposing view, see Ralston (2010a, pp. 65–84).
7   See Farr (1999, pp. 520–541).
8   See Bohman (1999, pp. 590–607).
9   See MacGilvray (1999, pp. 542–565).
10 For Rawls's statement of the idea of reasonable pluralism, see Rawls (1996, p. 10). For the debate, see Talisse (2003, pp. 1–21), Ralston (2008, pp. 629–659), Deen (2009, pp. 131–151), Clanton and Forcehimes (2009, pp. 165–183), and Talisse (2009, pp. 185–189).
11 See Smiley (1999, pp. 629–647). See also the chapter "Democratic pragmatism" in Cunningham (2002, pp. 142–162).
12 On rational ignorance, see Downs (1957).
13 See Dryzek (2000).
14 See Gutmann and Thompson (2004, p. 9).
15 See Habermas (1996, p. 304).
16 See Mansbridge (1980) and Gastil (1993).
17 See Bohman (1988 pp. 400–425, 400) and Bessette (1981, pp. 102–116).
18 See Westbrook (1998, pp. 128–140, 138; 1991).
19 See Caspary (2000, p. 140). For the view that appropriating and reinterpreting Dewey's theory of moral deliberation as a theory of political deliberation is illicit see Ralston (2010b, pp. 23–43).
20 See Shapiro (2002, pp. 235–265, 238).
21 See Colapietro (2006, pp. 21–31), Pappas (2008), Ralston (2005, pp. 17–25), VanderVeen (2007, pp. 243–258).
22 See Rogers (2009b, p. 21; 2009a, pp. 68–89).
23 See McAfee (2004, pp. 139–157, 149).
24 See Cunningham (2008, pp. 201–221, 205).
25 Cunningham (2002, p. 213).
26 See Hickman (2007, p. 42).
27 See Fischer (2007, pp. 151–165, 152). Fischer's alternative to Nussbaum's Kantian account of cosmopolitanism is what she calls an "earthy cosmopolitanism," "a description and conception of world citizenship for human beings who are planted in the mud: fully embodied, loving, hating, sometimes rational, sometimes not, strongly attached to their habits and conventions" (2007, p. 161).
28 Colin Koopman, "Pragmatist Public Pluralism: A New Orientation for Egalitarianism and Cosmopolitanism," unpublished manuscript. Also, see his "Statism, Pluralism and Global Justice," paper presented at the International Social Philosophy conference, University of Portland, July 17, 2008. Both are available

at http://cwkoopman.googlepages.com/cv.html. For non-pragmatist accounts of pluralism in global affairs, the first based on the creation of a transnational public sphere and the second on the cultivation of regional decision making networks, see Bohman (2007) and Gould (2004).
29. For the classic statement of the politics-administration dichotomy, see Wilson (1886, pp. 1–15). In opposition to the dichotomy and in support of pragmatism's influence on PA, see Shields (2008, pp. 205–221); also, Hildebrand (2008, pp. 222–229). In opposition to pragmatism's influence on PA, see Keith F. Snider (2000a, pp. 329–354; 2000c, pp. 123–145).
30. See Shields (2003, pp. 510–538).
31. See Miller (2004, pp. 243–249).
32. See Box (2001, pp. 20–39), Rorty (1989), and Voparil (2006).
33. After the original exchange between Shields and Miller, a host of PA practitioners, PA scholars, and pragmatist philosophers responded over a period of three years. See Stolcis (2004, pp. 362–369), Hickman (2004, pp. 496–499), Webb (2004, pp. 479–495), Snider (2000b, pp. 487–489; 2005, pp. 243–247), Evans (2000, pp. 482–486; 2005, pp. 248–255), Hildebrand (2005, pp. 345–359), Hoch (2006, pp. 389–398), Shields (2004, pp. 351–361; 2005, pp. 504–518), and Miller (2005, pp. 360–374).
34. See Lester and Stewart (2000, p. 4).
35. See Campbell (1995, pp. 207–208).
36. See Hook (1970, pp. 461–470, 467).
37. See Laswell (1951, pp. 3–15, 12).
38. See Torgerson (1985, pp. 241–261, 245–246), Fischer (1980, p. 160).
39. See Farr (1999, p. 537).
40. See Fischer (1980, p. 160).
41. See Weber (2008, pp. 608–613) and Clemons and McBeth (2001).

References

Asen, R. (2003), "The Multiple Mr. Dewey: Multiple Publics and Permeable Borders in John Dewey's Theory of the Public Sphere." *Argumentation and Advocacy*, 39, pp. 174–188.

Bessette, J. (1981), "Deliberative Democracy: The Majority Principle in Republican Government," in R. Goldwin and W. Shambra (eds), *How Democratic is the Constitution?* Washington, D C: American Enterprise Institute, pp. 102–116.

Bohman, J. (1988), "The Coming of Age of Deliberative Democracy." *The Journal of Political Philosophy*, 6, (4), pp. 400–425.

—(1999), "Democracy as Inquiry, Inquiry as Democratic: Pragmatism, Social Science, and the Cognitive Division of Labor." *American Journal of Political Science*, 43, pp. 590–607.

—(2007), *Democracy Across Borders: From Demos to Demoi*. Cambridge, MA: MIT Press.

Box, R. C. (2001), "Pragmatic Discourse and Administrative Legitimacy." *American Review of Public Administration*, 32, 20–39.

Bullert, G. (1983), *The Politics of John Dewey*. Buffalo, NY: Prometheus Books.

Campbell, J. (1995), *Understanding John Dewey*. Chicago and La Salle, IL: Open Court.

Caspary, W. R. (2000), *Dewey on Democracy*. Ithaca and London: Cornell University Press.

Clanton, J. C. and Forcehimes, A. T. (2009), "Can Peircean Epistemic Perfectionists Bid Farewell to Deweyan Democracy." *Contemporary Philosophy*, 6, pp. 165–183.

Clemons, R. S. and McBeth, M. K. (2001), *Public Policy Praxis, Theory and Pragmatism: A Case Approach*. Upper Saddle River, NJ: Prentice Hall.

Cochran, M. (1996), "The Liberal Ironist, Ethics and International Relations Theory." *Millenium*, 25, pp. 29–52.

Colapietro, V. (2006), "Democracy as a Moral Ideal." *The Kettering Review*, 24, pp. 21–31.

Cunningham, F. (2002), *Theories of Democracy: A Critical Introduction*. New York: Routledge.

—(2008), "The Global Public and Its Problems," in D. K. Chaterjee (ed.), *Democracy in a Global World: Human Rights and Political Participation in the 21st Century*. Lanham, MI: Rowman and Littlefield, pp. 201–215.

Deen, P. (2009), "A Call for Inclusion in the Pragmatic Justification of Democracy." *Contemporary Philosophy*, 6, pp. 131–151.

Dewey, J. (1996), *The Collected Works of John Dewey*. Ed. L. A. Hickman. Carbondale: Southern Illinois University Press. (Note: The conventional citation method refers to the Later Works (LW), Middle Works (MW) and Early Works (EW), followed by the volume: page number).

Downs, A. (1957), *An Economic Theory of Democracy*. Boston: Addison Wesley.

Dryzek, J. S. (2000), *Deliberative Democracy and Beyond: Liberals, Critics, Contestations*. Oxford: Oxford University Press.

Evans, K. G. (2000), "Response to Stever and Garrison." *Administration & Society*, 32, pp. 482–486.

—(2005), "Upgrade or a Different Animal Altogether?: Why Pragmatism Better Informs Public Management and New Pragmatism Misses the Point." *Administration & Society*, 37, pp. 248–255.

Farr, J. (1999), "John Dewey and American Political Science." *American Journal of Political Science*, 43, pp. 520–541.

Fischer, F. (1980), *Politics, Values and Public Policy: The Problem of Methodology*. Boulder, CO: Westview Press.

Fischer, M. (2007), "A Pragmatist Cosmopolitan Moment: Reconfiguring Nussbaum's Cosmopolitan Concentric Circles." *Journal of Speculative Philosophy*, 21, pp. 151–165.

Garrison, J. (2000), "Pragmatism and Public Administration," *Administration & Society*, 32, pp. 458–477.

Gastil, J. (1993), *Democracy in Small Groups: Participation, Decision Making, and Communication*. Philadelphia: New Society.

Gould, C. (2004), *Globalizing Democracy and Human Rights*. Cambridge, UK: Cambridge University Press.

Gutmann, A. and Thompson, D. (2004), *Why Deliberative Democracy?* Princeton and Oxford: Princeton University Press.

Habermas, J. (1996), *Between Facts and Norms: Contributions to a Discourse Theory of Law and Democracy*. Translated by W. Rehg. Cambridge, MA: MIT Press.

Hickman, L. (2004), "On Hugh Miller on 'Why Old Pragmatism Needs an Upgrade.'" *Administration & Society*, 36, pp. 496–499.

—(2007), *Pragmatism as Post-Postmodernism: Lessons from John Dewey*. New York: Fordham University Press.

Hildebrand, D. L. (2005), "Pragmatism, Neopragmatism, and Public Administration." *Administration & Society*, 37, pp. 345–359.

—(2008), "Public Administration as Pragmatic, Democratic, and Objective." *Public Administration Review*, 68, pp. 222–229.

Hoch, C. (2006), "What Can Rorty Teach an Old Pragmatist Doing Public Administration or Planning?" *Administration & Society*, 38, pp. 389–398.

Hook, S. (1970) "Philosophy and Public Policy." *The Journal of Philosophy*, 67, pp. 461–470.

Kaag, J. J. (2008), "We are *Who*?: A Pragmatic Reframing of Immigration and National Identity." *The Pluralist*, 3, pp. 111–131.

Knight, J. and Johnson, J. (1999), "Inquiry into Democracy: What Might a Pragmatist Make of Rational Choice Theories?" *American Journal of Political Science*, 43, pp. 566–589.

Koopman, C. (2007), "Pragmatist Public Pluralism: A New Orientation for Egalitarianism and Cosmopolitanism." Unpublished manuscript.

—(2008), "Statism, Pluralism and Global Justice." Paper presented at the International Social Philosophy Conference, University of Portland, July 17, 2008.

Laswell, H. D. (1951), "The Policy Orientation," in D. Lerner and H. D. Laswell (eds), *The Policy Sciences: Recent Developments in Scope and Method*. Stanford, CA: Stanford University Press, pp. 3–15.

Lester, J. and Stewart, J. (2000), *Public Policy*. Belmont, CA: Wadsworth.

Lindblom, C. E. (1958), "Policy Analysis." *American Economic Review*, 48, pp. 298–312.

MacGilvray, E. A. (1999), "Experience as Experiment: Some Consequences of Pragmatism for Democratic Theory," *American Journal of Political Science*, 43, pp. 542–565.

Mansbridge, J. (1980), *Beyond Adversary Democracy*. Chicago and London: University of Chicago Press.

McAfee, N. (2004), "Public Knowledge," *Philosophy and Social Criticism*, 30, (2), pp. 139–157.

Miller, H. T. (2004), "Why Old Pragmatism Needs an Upgrade." *Administration & Society*, 36, pp. 243–249.

—(2005), "Residues of Foundationalism in Classic Pragmatism." *Administration & Society*, 37, pp. 360–374.

Morris, D. (1999), "'How Shall We Read What We Call Reality?': John Dewey's New Science of Democracy." *American Journal of Political Science*, 43, pp. 608–628.

Pappas, G. F. (2008), *John Dewey's Ethics: Democracy as Experience*. Indianapolis: Indiana University Press.

Posner, R. (2003), *Law, Pragmatism and Democracy*. Cambridge, MA: Harvard University Press.

Ralston, S. J. (2005), "Deliberative Democracy as a Matter of Public Spirit: Reconstructing the Dewey-Lippmann Debate," *Contemporary Philosophy*, 25, pp. 17–25.

—(2008), "In Defense of Democracy as a Way of Life: A Reply to Talisse's Pluralist Objection." *Transactions of the Charles S. Peirce Society*, 44, pp. 629–659.

Ralston, S. J. (2010a), "Can Pragmatists be Institutionalists? John Dewey Joins the Non-ideal/Ideal Theory Debate." *Human Studies*, 33, pp. 65–84.

—(2010b), "Dewey's Theory of Moral (and Political) Deliberation Unfiltered." *Education and Culture*, 26, pp. 23–43.

Rawls, J. (1996), *Political Liberalism*. New York: Columbia University Press.

Rogers, M. (2009a), "Democracy, Elites and Power: John Dewey Reconsidered." *Contemporary Political Theory*, 8, (1), pp. 68–89.

—(2009b), *The Undiscovered Dewey*. New York: Columbia University Park.

Rorty, R. (1989), *Contingency, Irony and Solidarity*. Cambridge, UK: Cambridge University Press.

—(1991), *Objectivism, Relativism, and Truth: Philosophical Papers Volume 1*. Cambridge: Cambridge University Press.

Shapiro, I. (2002), "The State of Democratic Theory," in I. Katznelson and H. Milner (eds), *Political Science: The State of the Discipline*. New York: W.W. Norton, pp. 235–265.

Shields, P. M. (1996), "Pragmatism: Exploring Public Administration's Policy Imprint." *Administration & Society*, 28, pp. 390–411.

—(2003), "The Community of Inquiry." *Administration & Society*, 35, 510–538.

—(2004), "Classical Pragmatism: Engaging Practitioner Experience." *Administration & Society*, 36, pp. 351–361.

—(2005), "Classical Pragmatism Does Not Need an Upgrade: Lessons for Public Administration." *Administration & Society*, 37, pp. 504–518.

—(2008), "Rediscovering the Taproot: Is Classical Pragmatism the Route to Renew Public Administration?" *Public Administration Review*, 68, pp. 205–221.
Smiley, M. (1999), "Pragmatic Inquiry and Democratic Politics." *American Journal of Political Science*, 43, pp. 629–647.
Snider, K. (2000a), "Expertise or Experimenting? Pragmatism and American Public Administration, 1920–1950." *Administration & Society*, 32, pp. 329–354.
—(2000b), "Response to Stever and Garrison." *Administration & Society*, 32, pp. 487–489.
—(2000c), "Rethinking Public Administration's Roots in Pragmatism: The Case of Charles A. Beard." *The American Review of Public Administration*, 30, pp. 123–145.
—(2005), "Rortyan Pragmatism: 'Where's the Beef' for Public Administration?" *Administration & Society*, 37, pp. 243–247.
Stever, J. (2000), "The Parallel Universe: Pragmatism and Public Administration." *Administration & Society*, 32, pp. 453–457.
Stob, P. (2005), "Kenneth Burke, John Dewey, and the Pursuit of the Public." *Philosophy and Rhetoric*, 38, pp. 226–247.
Stolcis, G. B. (2004), "A View from the Trenches: Comments on Miller's 'Why Old Pragmatism Needs an Upgrade.'" *Administration & Society*, 36, pp. 362–369.
Talisse, R. B. (2003), "Can Democracy be a Way of Life? Deweyan Democracy and the Problem of Pluralism." *Transactions of the Charles S. Peirce Society*, 39, pp. 1–21.
—(2009), "Reply to Clanton and Forcehimes." *Contemporary Philosophy*, 6, pp. 185–189.
—(2010), "John Rawls and American Pragmatisms," presented at "Rawlsian Liberalism in Context," University of Tennessee, February 26–27, 2010. Available (online) on SSRN at <http://papers.ssrn.com/sol3/papers.cfm?abstract_id=1611859 (Accessed on May 29, 2010).
Torgerson, D. (1985), "Contextual Orientation in Policy Analysis: The Contribution of Harold D. Laswell." *Policy Sciences*, 18, pp. 241–261.
VanderVeen, Z. (2007), "Pragmatism and Democratic Legitimacy." *The Journal of Speculative Philosophy*, 21, pp. 243–258.
Voparil, C. (2006), *Richard Rorty: Politics and Vision*. Lanham, MD: Rowman and Littlefield Publishing.
Webb, J. L. (2004), "Comment on Hugh T. Miller's 'Why Old Pragmatism Needs an Upgrade.'" *Administration & Society*, 36, pp. 479–495.
Weber, E. T. (2008), "Learning from Others: What South Korean Technology Policy Can Teach the US." *Review of Policy Research*, 25, pp. 608–613.
West, C. (2004), *Democracy Matters*. New York: Penguin Press.
Westbrook, R. B. (1991), *John Dewey and American Democracy*. Ithaca: Cornell University Press.
—(1998), "Pragmatism and Democracy: Reconstructing the Logic of John Dewey's Faith," in M. Dickstein (ed.), *The Revival of Pragmatism: New Essays on Social Thought, Law and Culture*. Durham, NC: Duke University Press, pp. 128–140.

—(2005), *Democratic Hope: Pragmatism and the Politics of Truth*. Ithaca and London: Cornell University Press.
Wilson, W. (1886), "The Study of Administration." *Political Science Quarterly*, 2, pp. 1–15.
Zanetti, L. A. and Carr, A. (2000a), "Contemporary Pragmatism in Public Administration: Exploring the Limitations of the 'Third Productive Reply.'" *Administration & Society*, 32, pp. 433–452.
—(2000b), "Response to Stever and Garrison," *Administration & Society*, 32, pp. 478–481.

11

Education

Barbara J. Thayer-Bacon

Introduction

One cannot attend a major educational conference in America today without finding a paper being presented on the pragmatist philosopher John Dewey where his name appears in the title, or where he is used as a key source and appears in the reference section. Dewey's influence is still felt strongly in America's education, even though there have been periods (in America's last 150 years of educational history) where Dewey's philosophy of education has been out of favor. I do not think it is possible to write an essay concerning pragmatism and education that does not directly refer to John Dewey, due to his significant contribution to the topic. None of the other founding pragmatist philosophers devoted their attention to education at the same level as Dewey. One could argue that current work in pragmatism and education is all a footnote to John Dewey's work (Breault and Breault, 2005).

Dewey's educational ideas such as the need for a child-centered curriculum that is based on students' interests, and a holistic approach to education that has an interdisciplinary focus and uses an inquiry approach to learning, encouraging students to learn through direct experiences, became associated with "progressive education" during the first half of the twentieth century (Tanner, 1997). Progressive approaches to education have a history of becoming disfavored in American education when the pendulum swings "back to basics," often out of concern for national security and economic prosperity (Tozer, et al., 2008). The present time serves as an example, with the US's concern for economic competition at a global level resulting in a push to increase standards and require more high stakes testing of students. Even though many argue that Dewey's philosophy of education lost influence during the World War II–post-World War II "back to basics" time frame when Russia launched Sputnik, I argue that once Dewey began contributing to the educational conversation, his influence appears to have never really died out. One can find many references in educational journals to Dewey's ideas continually and consistently represented throughout the past century.

The case is not the same for Dewey within the field of philosophy, where his work is being "rediscovered" due to more recent references to classical pragmatism through the neo-pragmatist work of such philosophers as Rorty (1979, 1982), Habermas (1984, 1987), West (1989), and Seigfried (1996). When I was an undergraduate student majoring in philosophy during the 1970s, Dewey's work was not referenced or taught in any of my courses. I was surprised to return to graduate school majoring in philosophy of education, and discover his strong impact. Why is there such a difference in his impact between the two fields of study? Perhaps it has to do with the split between theory and practice that exists in philosophy which pragmatism sought to heal. Traditional philosophy sits in the more valued world of theory while education sits in the less valued world of practice.

As one of the classical pragmatists, Dewey desired to make philosophy serve the needs of real problems people have, making philosophy relevant, useful, and constructive. Dewey (1960) tells us: "Philosophy recovers itself when it ceases to be a devise for dealing with the problems of philosophers and becomes a method, cultivated by philosophers, for dealing with the problems of men [*sic*]" ("The need for a recovery of philosophy," pp. 66–67). His effort to mend philosophical splits between thinking and doing, theory and practice, and make philosophy applicable to people's everyday lives, caused him to focus on philosophy's civil responsibilities in a democracy, which included a civic responsibility to educate its future citizens. Dewey wrote extensively about education and its important role in democracy throughout his career. In fact, Dewey defined philosophy as education (a form of cultural criticism), and education as growth.

Dewey further developed core pragmatist beliefs such as Peirce's (1958) *fallibilism* (belief in the impossibility of attaining knowledge that is certain) and James's (1975, 1976) *pluralism* (belief in the impossibility of attaining knowledge that is universal), and tried to live by them throughout his life as a philosopher who believed his role was to be a cultural critic, helping to develop ideas to deal with the actual crises of our lives. These pragmatist beliefs positioned him as an organic intellectual who was an active citizen seeking to help: women obtain the right to vote (Dewey was actively involved in the women's suffrage movement), African Americans receive equal treatment (Dewey was one of the founding members of the NAACP), and working class citizens receive better working conditions (Dewey supported Myles Horton's *Highlander Folk Center*). He supported "academic freedom" movements on college campuses and the push for tenure for faculty (he defended prominent scholars' rights, such as Bertrand Russell and Leon Trotsky, even though he disagreed with their positions), and worked to help address problems caused by large numbers of immigrants coming to the United States during the industrial revolution (he was a staunch supporter of Jane Adams' *Hull House*). He sought to reform American schools so that they teach children the skills they need to be able to actively participate in their democratic society by starting a lab school in Chicago.

I would like to use this chapter as an opportunity to explore key pragmatist ideas about education, through the work of John Dewey mainly, but not entirely. I will connect Dewey's work to current neo-pragmatist philosophical work. While philosophy has rediscovered Dewey's contributions to philosophy, this does not mean his work in education receives much attention by philosophers still today (Cahn, 1977). Unfortunately, much of the work philosophers of education have contributed to amending and extending Dewey's ideas are yet to be discovered in the world of philosophy. However, in the world of education in general, and philosophy of education, in particular, Dewey still receives a great deal of attention and it is not a stretch to argue that he is one of the most significant philosophers to contribute to the conversation of education (in America) till today. His influence is felt at an international level (as well).

John Dewey and the Chicago Lab School

When Dewey moved from the University of Michigan (1884–1894) to the University of Chicago (1894–1904) for what is now referred to as the middle years of his career, he began a lab school in 1896 that still exists. This school became known as a place where educators could try out ideas for curriculum and instruction that Dewey and others were writing about. Originally it was called the University Elementary School, but in 1902 its name was changed to the Chicago Lab School. When it began there were 15 students enrolled, including Dewey's own children, and by 1990 it enrolled 1,400 students. The Chicago Lab School became so famous it helped to draw distinguished faculty to work at the University of Chicago, and other universities in the US followed suit in creating lab schools.

Jackson describes the school as a privileged environment in his introduction to Dewey's (1990) rereleased *The School and Society (1900)*, and *The Child and the Curriculum (1902)*. "His was to be a school whose inhabitants—students and teachers alike—were invited to find both personal fulfillment and social well-being in their daily activity, a place where the ultimate test of knowledge was to be its usefulness but where the useful was to include the aesthetic, the contemplative, and what some would call the spiritual aspects of human experience" (p. xxxvi). *The School and Society* and *The Child and the Curriculum* are two series of lectures Dewey gave to the public in Chicago about the Chicago Lab School during its beginning, developing years. He added to the lectures in 1915 for later publications, after he had moved to Teachers College, Columbia University, in New York City (1904–1952, he retired from teaching in 1927). I'd like to focus on *The School and Society*, in particular, the first three chapters, to illustrate classical pragmatism's key contributions to education.

Dewey (1990) starts his lecture, *The School and Society*, by urging the people listening to take the broader, social view. "Here individualism and socialism are at one. Only by being true to the full growth of all the individuals who make it up, can society by any chance be true to itself" (1990, p. 7). Dewey moves to define society: "A society is a number of people held together because they are working along common lines, in a common spirit, and with reference to common aims. The common needs and aims demand a growing interchange of thought and growing unity of sympathetic feeling" (1990, p. 14). He points to changes in society at large, in particular industrialization, which have eliminated household and neighborhood occupations. "(O)ur social life has undergone a thorough and radical change. If our education is to have any meaning for life, it must pass through an equally complete transformation" (1990, p. 28). Already in this beginning we can see that Dewey is striving to bring the individual and others together and show how they interact with each other, and are dependent on each other. We can find the seeds of what I am growing into a theory of transactional relationships (Thayer-Bacon, 2000, 2003, 2008). We also can see how Dewey's philosophy of education has stimulated and supported communitarian ideas such as with Barber (1984) and Green (1999), as he places a strong emphasis on commonality.

Dewey (1990) tells us that the aim of the Chicago Lab School is to connect school to home and the neighborhood, and to connect history, science, and art. They want a school that is like an ideal home, with a family-type atmosphere. In Chapter 1 of *The School and Society*, we come across one of Dewey's often cited lines, "What the best and wisest parent wants for his own child, that must the community want for all of its children" (1990, p. 7). Dewey argues that the school needs to take on the job of teaching tasks and skills that were formerly taught at home: work in metal and wood, weaving, sewing, and cooking for example. In his school these occupations are made centers of school life, "active centers of scientific insight into natural materials and processes," which he illustrates with sewing and weaving (1990, p. 19). He also tells us that the school seeks to encourage a spirit of free communication, an interchange of ideas (1990, p. 16). He describes the school as offering "embryonic communities." Dewey (1990) suggests:

> When the school introduces and trains each child of society into membership within such a little community, saturating him with the spirit of service, and providing him with the instruments of effective self-direction, we shall have the deepest and best guaranty of a larger society which is worthy, lovely, and harmonious. (1990, p. 29)

Dewey offers a significant contribution to democratic theory by connecting the home and school to society, and arguing that it is important to look at what we do in our homes and in our schools, for that is where we teach our children how to be members of democratic societies. Gutmann (1987), Greene (1988), Martin (1992), and Noddings (1992, 2002) have all developed further this idea of home's connection to schools. Notice how Dewey's focus is on harmony, suggesting an emphasis more on commonality than individuality and difference, as well as an emphasis on harmony over conflict and disagreement. Also, notice how his emphasis is on reason, with his desire for free communication and an exchange of ideas. This focus is further developed by Habermas (1984, 1987), and Dewey's emphasis on harmony comes under critique by feminist, postmodern, and critical influenced pragmatists such as Biesta (1994, 1995), Marshall (1995), and myself (2008).

In Chapter 17, Dewey (1990) shows how public schools are designed for listening and for mass education with their uniform curriculum and methods. He looks at the ideal home, and then enlarges that ideal to come up with his description of an ideal school. He reminds us that the aim of the school is to further the growth of the child. He discusses various "instincts" that children have: social, language (interest in conversation), inquiry (interest in finding out things), construction (interest in making things), and artistic expression. Then he gives examples that exist in his school where we can see them bringing together these "instincts." Dewey seeks to create a school where the students learn scientific directed inquiry. "When nature and society can live in the schoolroom, when the forms and tools of learning are subordinated to the substance of experience, then shall there be an opportunity for this identification, and culture shall be the democratic password" (1990, p. 62).

We can find in this chapter the seeds of Dewey's (1965) later emphasis on scientific inquiry, or what he later called "reflective thinking." We can also see Peirce's (1958) influence on Dewey in the idea of scientific directed inquiry with the students treated as a community of inquirers. Lipman (1978) began a Philosophy for Children program in the late 1960s that further develops the idea of treating students even at the elementary level as communities of inquirers. We can also find in this chapter Dewey's underscoring of the importance of learning through experience, as well as his valuing of the arts for learning. More recent scholars such as Greene (1995), Jackson (1998), Garrison (1997), and others (see Garrison, 1995) further develop Dewey's ideas concerning the arts. Garrison (1996) has also addressed Dewey's concerns in regard to learning to listen attentively and generously to each other.

What's interesting to note is that Dewey's discussion of "instincts" again emphasizes children's universality, not their cultural differences. His reference to the "ideal home" also emphasizes universality and commonality, not cultural differences. He does not discuss questions concerning what counts as an "ideal home." Even Dewey's reference to "culture as the democratic password," is not to draw our attention to cultural differences but instead to underscore the role cultures—meaning the arts and language—have in bringing us together. We can see that Dewey evades questions of power and assumes a neutral, objective position that denies his own location within a particular culture, and the fallibility and subjectivity of his own judgments concerning what counts as an ideal home or a cultural experience. These are criticisms that political philosophers Laclau and Mouffe (1985) and Young (2000) would likely bring to bear on his work. In the field of philosophy of education, Margonis (2009) recently critiqued Dewey in regard to his racial positionality, and I have critiqued him as well on these concerns (see Thayer-Bacon, 2008).

Chapter 2 looks at school as an institution in relation to society and to its members—the children. Its focus is on waste in education. Here Dewey (1990) deals with the question of organization. Dewey traces the history of the development of schools, and shows the lack of unity and coherence in schools. He tells us and shows us through a chart that the Chicago Lab School connects to home, business, nature, and the university. He has another chart to show how the school is structured within, with a library in the center of the building, and a shop, textile industries, kitchen, and a dining room around the center. With this school structure, Dewey seeks to connect theory to practice. He shows us with another chart, how within the school there could be a second story to the building with a museum in the center, with art, music, physical and chemical labs, and biological labs around the center. Dewey's hope is for a synthesis of art, science, and industry. He advises his listeners and readers: "Relate the school to life, and all studies are of necessity correlated" (1990, p. 91). He tells us he is not looking for others to imitate what he is doing; he just wants to show that this type of school is feasible.

Here again we find Dewey's very important contribution to democratic theory, through his connecting of schools to home, business, nature, and the university. He makes it clear that there is a link between democracy and education and that how we structure our schools as well as what we do within those schools in terms of what we teach and how we teach matters in trying to establish and sustain a democratic society. His examples of school design are holistic and still relevant today. He brings together in an interdisciplinary way subject areas that schools today still tend to keep separate and artificially divided. He values the arts, including music, fine art, and vocational art, as much as he values science and reading. Dewey certainly succeeded in showing the Chicago Lab School was feasible. It has stood as a model for how schools can be for over a century.

In summation, key educational ideas from John Dewey's work in his Chicago Lab School include:

- individuals are members of families that are embedded within larger communities;
- the needs of communities change, and as they do, so must schools adapt and change to meet the needs of the community;
- schools need to be connected to homes and to the neighborhoods;
- schools need to have a family atmosphere, and serve as embryonic communities;
- the curriculum within schools needs to connect history, science, vocations, and the arts;
- children are naturally interested in being social and using language, inquiring, making things, and expressing themselves artistically; school curriculum and instructional methodologies need to tap into these natural interests.

Classical pragmatism

In this section I move to connect the above educational ideas to classical pragmatism, to understand how Dewey's Lab School represents a pragmatist approach to education. Charles Sanders Peirce (1958) is credited with the key pragmatist idea that we cannot separate our ideas from our experiences for there is an inseparable connection between rational cognition and rational purpose, between thought and action, between thinking and doing. Peirce suggested that we determine how clear our concepts are by running them through a functional test, grounding them to experience. He wanted philosophy to act like science and be open to critique, not taking anything as given, but instead viewing philosophy as a field of study that is in process, relying on criteria to make judgments that are corrigible. Peirce's theory of *fallibilism* describes philosophers as limited, situated knowers in need of each other to help us find ever-elusive truth(s). Peirce defeated the idea that philosophers could claim to know universal Truth, individually, on their own, with certainty. He made the case for the need of a *community of inquirers*, those most educated in the subject of inquiry, to work together and share their knowledge in the hopes of getting clearer in their ideas, and then passing on their knowledge to the next generation of scholars to work on further. Peirce's idea of Truth as an emerging absolute demands of us endless investigation.

Peirce recommended that education should bring about the growth and development of reason. Schools should provide practice in inquiry (deduction and induction) and stimulate students' interests in inquiry for Truth's sake. Education should provide the experiences necessary for active learning. He recommended that students need to learn through their senses (experiential learning), and develop their imaginations (rooted in experience), and schools need to foster these tools, as they are central to all knowing. Schools need to help students learn self-control, as well as good communication, as these skills are needed in order for students to learn to be good scientific inquirers. Schools need to teach us history too, to help us understand our experiences through a memory of the past. Students need to develop good habits of reasoning and conduct (Maccia, 1954, p. 212).

One of James's contributions to pragmatism is his willingness to let go of realism. James (1975) follows Peirce's radical lead of incorporating contingency and revision into a theory of truth, yet he unties his theory of truth from Peirce's assumption that Truths are objectively real. James postulates with Peirce an end of Truth but knows that this is just a belief. For James a belief is true if it yields sensibly satisfactory results in experience when acted upon. James soundly critiques the epistemological/metaphysical split that worried Peirce and himself when they were graduate students at Harvard by critiquing a false metaphysics that separates experience from existence and dissolving the absolutist/relativist distinction with his theories of radical empiricism and pluralism. For James (1976), experience has no inner duplicity; it just is, in its pure *thatness*. Experience is subjective *and* objective, it is private *and* public, it is internal *and* external, it is thought *and* thing. What we do with pure experience, when we categorize and separate it and create lines of order for it, is by way of addition, not subtraction, to pure experience. Experience can serve different functions and may be different kinds. In different contexts, it plays different parts. James (1977) argues in *A Pluralistic Universe*, that the world we experience is more than we can describe.

Along with James's (1950, 1958) concept of *experience*, another key concept of his is *habit*. As a psychologist, James looked at habit in terms of individual habits, how these develop over time and form the basis of learning, how they link the body and the mind, and how they help to economize and coordinate our actions. *Talks to Teachers* is a series of lectures James (1958) gave in the Boston area to teachers in order to explain to them how psychology could help them as teachers. James explained how an understanding of habit could be used by teachers to not only help manage their classrooms, in terms of students' behaviors, and avoid problems such as students' balky wills, but also to help teachers establish positive habits of inquiry for their students. Children learn to ask questions and to pay attention to their doubts because they are taught to do so and have the chance to practice inquiry skills. Like Peirce, James recommended that students need to develop good habits of reasoning and conduct, and teachers in our schools can help students develop these. (See Garrison, *et al.*, 2002 for current discussions on James.)

George Herbert Mead (1934) contributes to pragmatism a social behaviorist theory of meaning. As one of America's early sociologists, Mead argues that we become individual selves with minds out of our social relations with others, thus turning upside down psychology's focus on individuals *qua* individuals as well as classical liberalism's view of the individual as separate and autonomous from society. Mead argues we are first of all social beings who then become individuals. His fundamental approach to understanding human behavior is from the point of view of conduct, particularly conduct as it is observable by others. Again we find a theory that focuses on action as its fundamental datum.

Mead's (1934) theory of self-development is that the self is not there at birth, but develops in the process of social experience and activity by becoming an object to itself. Psychology's essential problem, according to Mead, is explaining self-consciousness: how can the self get outside of itself to become an object to itself? Mead's answer to this problem is that the self becomes an object to itself by taking the attitude of others toward her within the social environment. The language process is essential for the development of the self, for communication provides a form of behavior in which the individual may become an object to herself. Because Mead's theory of self-development is based on social construction, he must address concerns of social determinism. He does this by describing our subjective experiences, our memory and imagination, as being accessible only to the individual, the "I," while the social side of us, the "me," stands for the self I am aware of, the conventional self based on the organized attitudes of others. The "I" is unpredictable and uncertain and exists in the now; it is unknowable. It is the self's action over and against the social situation. The "me" acts like a censor, setting the limits of the self through social control. Together they form a self, which adjusts to others' attitudes and at the same time changes others' attitudes.

Dewey and Mead were good friends and colleagues, working together in Michigan and Chicago, even becoming neighbors in Chicago. They greatly influenced each other, as they both were developing their individual theories during the time they worked together. Like Mead, Dewey holds a social behaviorist view of meaning. Dewey, with Mead, recognizes that individuals start out as members of communities. We saw this above in Dewey's (1990) beginning of *The School and Society*. However, Mead's individual tends to be subsumed by the generalized other; the social "me" disciplines and censors the "I," while Dewey's individual, even in its state of immaturity as a young child, interacts with and changes general society. Dewey (1960, 1966) distinguishes his views from Mead's when he creates a *transactional* model that describes social groups affecting individuals *and* individuals affecting social groups. Dewey's significant pragmatist contribution to democratic theory is based on his recognition of the interactive, interrelational, interdependent qualities of individuals in relation to others (Thayer-Bacon, 2003, 2008). (See Biesta, 1999 for a current discussion of Mead.)

From this very concise description of key classical pragmatist ideas, we can understand their influence on education, as illustrated above in Dewey's *The School and Society*. We find Mead's social behaviorism reflected in Dewey's description of individuals as members of families embedded within larger communities. Schools are children's second communities, after their families, what Dewey describes as embryonic communities, and as such, it makes sense that Dewey would see a need for schools to be connected to homes and to the neighborhoods. Mead's influence is also there in Dewey's description of how, as the needs of communities change, schools must adapt and change to meet the needs of the community.

We discover that Peirce's *fallibilism* and a *community of inquirers* concepts are further developed in Dewey's recommendation that students need to be encouraged to explore actively the world around them, and taught the skills they will need to be good re/searchers (scientists). They need "hands on" concrete experiences, from a curriculum that connects history, science, vocations, and the arts to help them learn through their senses and develop their imaginations. Students need to learn how to work together, be able to collaborate and share what they are learning with each other as a community of inquirers, to help them overcome their own limitations as fallible, situated knowers.

From James we are reminded that *habits* are enforced upon students from the day they are born, by the very fact that children are social beings. Habits are imposed upon children through social custom. Habits constitute the self and mind and serve the regulatory role that the generalized other serves for Mead. Yet habits are acquired and secondary, not native to us as impulses are. In agreement with James, Dewey argues that impulses are what give us flexibility and diversity, and habits are what give our impulses direction and shape. Dewey suggests that children are naturally interested in being social and using language, inquiring, making things, and expressing themselves artistically (James's native impulses). School curriculum and instructional methodologies need to tap into these natural interests and help children develop the habits they need to become good inquirers, which includes habits of self-control and reason.

James also helps us understand that *experience* has an active and a passive element, trying and undergoing. We find this trying and undergoing description of experience in Dewey's educational theory as well. In *Experience and Education*, Dewey (1965) tells us, "every experience enacted and undergone modifies the one who acts and undergoes, while this modification affects, whether we wish it or not, the quality of subsequent experiences" (1965, p. 231). An experience that has educational value is one that encourages further growth by arousing curiosity, strengthening initiative, stimulating desires and purposes for effecting change in the environment. As a pragmatist, Dewey shows us that thinking begins with a situation of experience, then a problem develops within this situation (felt need), that triggers the person to seek a solution (hypothesis) by gathering information and making observations (reasoning/solutions), and testing out the ideas by application (testing hypothesis/ideas). His model for reflective thinking is like the scientific method, and it has greatly influenced more recent debates concerning *critical thinking*. With this summation of key pragmatist ideas and how they are represented in Dewey's Lab School complete, I'd like to conclude by reflecting on current work in education that is influenced by pragmatism.

Current work in pragmatism and education

If one wants to find recent contributions to pragmatism and education of significance, one is more likely to find them among philosophers of education such as those I have cited above, rather than with traditional philosophers. Rorty and Habermas can be credited with helping to reinvigorate interest in pragmatism for philosophers, but Habermas has not written about educational issues, as far as I am aware, and Rorty's (1989) recommendations for education are derived from a disappointing traditional liberal arts model that has more to do with Aristotle's influence on education than pragmatism's influence.

Seigfried (1996) is an exception in that her *Pragmatism and Feminism* has made a significant contribution to recovering the work of women pragmatists such as Lucy Sprague Mitchell, Elsie Ripley Clapp, Ella Flagg Young, Alice Chapman Dewey, and Jane Addams, many of whom were students of James, Mead, and/ or Dewey, in Boston, Chicago, and New York, and all of whom she argues contributed to philosophy through their work in education. Ironically, Seigfried does not name or discuss the continuing work of pragmatist scholars in education, thus perpetuating the problems she so carefully describes for women pragmatists and Dewey. If one's philosophical work is connected to the practical world of education, it is vulnerable to not being taken seriously by other philosophers and disappears in short order. Seigfried is careful to relate Dewey's experimental method in education (learning by doing) to Jane Addams's Hull House, but we find that she does little to trace Dewey's influence into the schools of America where he continues to have a major impact. She also neglects the work of scholars in philosophy of education who contribute significantly to discussions about pragmatism's influence in education.

For many philosophers working in the world of education, pragmatism serves as a touchstone that helps us not lose our way, inspires us, and serves as a source of critique when we find we have gone off track. It makes sense that pragmatism has much to offer philosophers who have chosen to connect philosophical theory to the daily practice of schooling and the very real problems all societies face of how to pass on their knowledge to the next generation (what Martin (2002) refers to as *cultural wealth*). For philosophers who recognize education's importance to the possibility of a democracy someday, pragmatism has much to contribute as well. Pragmatism also contributes to educators' support for the importance of holistic curriculums and child-centered approaches to education. Pragmatism contributes to theories concerning critical thinking, constructivism, imagination, sympathetic understanding, and social intelligence.

I began this chapter with the claim that Dewey's work, and through him pragmatism, has been making a continuing contribution to scholarship in various fields of education for the past 150 years. If I am correct in that observation, then it's easy to understand that my task is impossible in terms of trying to name let alone discuss all the current scholars whose works are contributing to the topic of pragmatism and education. Hopefully, I have offered enough evidence to convince the reader that key pragmatist ideas have made a significant contribution to the field of education and they continue to do so today. In particular, Dewey's ideas still receive much attention in education.

References

Barber, B. (1984), *Strong Democracy*. Berkeley: University of California Press.
Biesta, G. J. J. (1994), 'Education as Practical Intersubjectivity: Towards a Critical-Pragmatic Understanding of Education'. *Educational Theory*, 44, (3), pp. 299–317.
—(1995), 'Pragmatism as a Pedagogy of Communicative Action', in J. Garrison (ed.), *The New Scholarship on John Dewey*. Dordrecht: Kluwer Academic Publishers, pp. 105–122.
—(1999), 'Redefining the Subject, Redefining the Social, Reconsidering Education: George Herbert Mead's Course on Philosophy of Education at the University of Chicago'. *Educational Theory*, 49, (4), pp. 475–492.
Breault, D., and Breault, R. (2005), *Experiencing Dewey: Insights for Today's Classroom*. Indianapolis, IN: Kappa Delta Pi.
Cahn, S. M. (ed.), (1977), *New Studies in the Philosophy of John Dewey*. Hanover, NH: The University Press of New England for the University of Vermont.
Dewey, J. (1960), *On Experience, Nature, and Freedom*. Indianapolis: Bobbs-Merrill Co.

—(1965, [1938]), *Experience and Education*, 2nd edn. New York: Macmillan. Reprinted in Cahn, S. (1970). *The Philosophical Foundations of Education*, pp. 221–261. New York: Harper & Row.
—(1966), *Democracy and Education*, 2nd edn. New York: Free Press, 1916.
—(1990), *The School and Society [1900], and The Child and the Curriculum [1902]*. Chicago: The University of Chicago Press.
Garrison, J. (1995), *The New Scholarship on Dewey*. Dordrecht: Kluwer Academic Publishers.
—(1996), 'A Deweyan Theory of Democratic Listening'. *Educational Theory*, 46, (4), pp. 429–451.
—(1997), *Dewey and Eros*. New York: Teachers College Press.
Garrison, J., Podeschi, R., and Bredo, E. (eds), (2002), *William James and Education*. New York: Teachers College Press.
Green, J. M. (1999), *Deep Democracy*. Lanham: Rowman & Littlefield.
Greene, M. (1988), *The Dialectic of Freedom*. New York: Teachers College Press.
—(1995), *Releasing the Imagination*. San Francisco: Jossey-Bass.
Gutmann, A. (1987), *Democratic Education*. Princeton: Princeton University Press.
Habermas, J. (1984), *The Theory of Communicative Action, Volume 1 and Volume 2*. Translated by T. McCarthy, 1987. Boston, MA: Beacon Press.
Jackson, P. W. (1998), *John Dewey and the Lessons of Art*. New Haven: Yale University Press.
James, W. (1950), *The Principles of Psychology*, vol. 1. New York: Dover, 1890.
—(1958), *Talks to Teachers on Psychology*. New York: W. W. Norton, 1899.
—(1975), *The Meaning of Truth*. Cambridge: Harvard University Press, 1909.
—(1976), *Essays in Radical Empiricism*. Cambridge: Harvard University Press, 1912.
—(1977), *A Pluralistic Universe*. Cambridge: Harvard University Press, 1909.
Laclau, E. and Mouffe, C. (1985), *Hegemony and Socialist Strategy*. Translated by W. Moore & P. Cammack. Great Britain: Thetford Press.
Lipman, M. and Sharp, A. (1978), *Growing Up With Philosophy*. Philadelphia: Temple University.
Maccia, G. (1954), 'The Educational Aims of Charles Peirce'. *Educational Theory*, 4, (3), pp. 206–212.
Margonis, F. (2009), 'John Dewey's Radicalized Visions of the Student and the Classroom Community'. *Educational Theory*, 59, (1), pp. 17–39.
Marshall, J. (1995), 'On What We May Hope: Rorty on Dewey and Foucault', in J. Garrison (ed.), *The New Scholarship on John Dewey*. Dordrecht: Kluwer Academic Publishers, pp. 139–156.
Martin, J. R. (1992), *The Schoolhome*. Cambridge: Harvard University Press.
—(2002), *Cultural Miseducation*. New York: Teachers College Press.
Mead, G. H. (1934), *Mind, Self, and Society: From the Standpoint of a Social Behaviorist*. Ed. C. W. Morris. Chicago: University of Chicago Press.

Noddings, N. (1992), *The Challenge to Care in Schools*. New York: Teachers College Press.
—(2002), *Starting at Home*. Berkeley, CA: University of California Press.
Peirce, C. S. (1958), *Values in a Universe of Chance*. Ed. P. P. Weiner. Garden City: Doubleday.
Rorty, R. (1979), *Philosophy and the Mirror of Nature*. Princeton: Princeton University Press.
—(1982), *Consequences of Pragmatism*. Minneapolis: University of Minnesota Press.
—(1989), *Contingency, Irony, and Solidarity*. Cambridge: Cambridge University Press.
Seigfried, C. H. (1996), *Pragmatism and Feminism*. Chicago: University of Chicago Press.
Tanner, L. (1997), *Dewey's Laboratory School*. New York: Teachers College Press.
Thayer-Bacon, B. (2000), *Transforming Critical Thinking*. New York: Teachers College Press.
—(2003), *Relational '(e)pistemologies'*. New York: Peter Lang.
—(2008), *Beyond Liberal Democracy in Schools*. New York: Teachers College Press.
Tozer, S., Senese, G., and Violas, P. (2008), *School and Society, 6th Edition*. New York: McGraw-Hill.
West, C. (1989), *The American Evasion of Philosophy*. Madison: The University of Wisconsin Press.
Young, I. R. (2000), *Inclusion and Democracy*. Oxford: Oxford University Press.

12

Economics

Paul B. Thompson

The discipline of economics might be linked to pragmatism in many ways. For example, *Dewey, Pragmatism and Economic Methodology* juxtaposes chapters written by well-known scholars of classical pragmatism with a few papers by economists proposing to build a new methodology in economics on Dewey's theory of inquiry (Khalil, 2004). The legal theorist Richard Posner, one of the founding figures in the law and economics movement, has recently issued a flurry of books and articles aligning his approach with philosophical pragmatism (Posner, 1995, 2003). This chapter will build its analysis from pragmatism's long association with the institutional school of economic thought. The views of two economists will be discussed at some length. Karl Polanyi (1886–1964) was a Hungarian born in Vienna. His work has been linked to pragmatism (Samuels, 1995) as well as to such contemporary figures as Joseph Stiglitz (MacKenzie, 2004) and Paul Krugman (Acs, 2002). Second, Daniel Bromley, a leading contemporary resource economist, has explicitly linked his work in economics to the pragmatist tradition in philosophy. It will prove useful to set the scene for this discussion of Polanyi and Bromley with a brief discussion of institutional economics.

Setting the scene

A detailed probe of pragmatism's connection to institutional economics would require substantive discussion of writings by leading institutionalists such as Thorstein Veblen (1857–1929) and John R. Commons (1862–1945). Veblen and Commons were contemporaries of John Dewey, and it is clear that these figures had some familiarity with one another's work. However, there is no obvious connection or mutual influence of the sort that existed between Dewey and William James, George Herbert Mead (1863–1931), Jane Addams (1860–1935), or even Josiah Royce (1855–1916). Excepting James, all of these individuals were born within a span of seven years. Excepting Addams (whose work was as widely read as any) all conducted successful careers at American universities during a time when the social sciences were far less distinct from philosophy than they are today. Nevertheless, it would be misleading to think of Veblen and Commons as part of the pragmatist school.

The putative connection between pragmatism and institutional economics may owe a significant debt to the writings of Clarence E. Ayres (1871–1972). Ayres argued for congruence between the thought of Veblen and Dewey. He defined institutionalism in economics as the view that the economizing mentality was a product of the culture and material practices in which people lived. He put this view in opposition to the assumption that rational calculation and pursuit of self-interest were fixed elements of human nature. Like Larry Hickman today, Ayres argued that Dewey's instrumentalist theory of value would be better understood as a technology—a theory of the way that pursuit of ends-in-view shape and are in turn shaped by the material means available to economic agents at any given time. From Veblen, Ayres derived the idea that rational pursuit, monitoring, and adjustment of ends-in-view were often in conflict with standing practices and social rules (institutions) that had ceased to function in support of progressive problem solving (Ayres, 1951).

Whatever merits Ayres's marriage of Veblen and Dewey might have had, his vision of institutional economics was not well received among academic economists. A 1953 essay on economic method by Milton Friedman (1912–2006) argued that economic theory has no deep connection to psychology, mentality, human nature, or consciously entertained projects of human beings. Instead, economic theory should be understood as a construct to be evaluated solely in terms of its ability to predict and explain economic phenomena: prices, supply and demand relationships, business cycles, inflation, and so on. These phenomena are the product of individuals acting in the aggregate, and constructs such as John Stuart Mill's "economic man"—the self-interested optimizer of expectations—are to be evaluated not in terms of how realistically they describe human psychology, but in terms of whether using them as ideal types yields economic theory and models that meet Friedman's preferred tests (Friedman, 1953).

Friedman called this view "positivism," despite the fact that it contradicts some tenets of positivist philosophy. It is in fact a fairly straightforward example of what contemporary philosophers of science were referring to as "instrumentalism," and is most consistently interpreted in those terms (Boland, 1979). Friedman may well have avoided the term "instrumentalism" because that was how Ayres was describing his own Dewey-inspired view. Although Friedman's paper generated many critics, it now seems clear that the vast majority of academic economists have practiced what he preached. For many of them, Ayres's version of institutional economics came to be associated with the Marxian view that rational pursuit of self-interest was an artifact of capitalist social relations that would, like the state itself, wither away once socialist relations were established (Portis, 1984). Given Friedman's instrumentalism, the truth or falsity of this view of human nature was utterly irrelevant to the goals and methods of economic theory.

Nevertheless, institutional economics grew steadily in influence during the last quarter of the twentieth century. One group of key figures in this were part of the so-called Austrian school, founded by Carl Menger (1840–1921) and subsequently represented by Ludwig von Mises (1881–1973) and Friedrich von Hayek (1899–1992). Like the American institutionalists, the Austrians held that economic behavior was dramatically shaped by established rules and patterns, and that this limited the relevance of mathematical theories being constructed by mainstream economists. The Austrians, however, advocated minimal planning and government intervention on the grounds that more appropriate institutions would emerge spontaneously if economic agents are left to their own devices. Thus Austrian style institutional economics tended to converge with Friedman's own predilection for libertarian politics and policy (Holcombe, 2004).

The other group contributing to the rise of "new institutional economics" included Ronald Coase (b. 1910), Oliver Williamson (b. 1932) and Douglass North (b. 1920). Like other institutionalists, Coase, Williamson, and North emphasize the way that structured rules influence economic behavior. The key concept in their analysis is the transaction cost: costs accompanying any attempt that two or more people might make to cooperate. Such costs can be due to a multitude of factors ranging from lack of trust and lack of information to compliance with regulations and bureaucratic procedures. The new institutionalists argued that these costs were not adequately reflected in neoclassical theories, that organizations (such as both government and private firms) are attempts to manage these costs, and that both informal norms or standing practices and the policies of public and private organizations have a huge influence over the transactions that people actually undertake (North, 1990).

Whatever personal links or mutual influences may have existed between Veblen, Commons, and Ayres, on the one hand, and pragmatists such as Dewey, Addams, or C. S. Peirce (1839–1914), on the other, it is clear that no such links or influences can be claimed for either the Austrian school or new institutional economics. The summary just given, however, provides a basis to recognize commonalities of approach. All of these schools of economic thought oppose a priori theories of economic rationality such as have been derived from Mill's conception of economic man. All of them find contingency in economic behavior that can be traced to habits, standing practices, and formal policies. All of them see economic institutions being shaped by evolutionary change in a manner inspired by the way that Charles Darwin (1809–1882) described the process of speciation. And in each of these commonalities, institutional economics shares elements with the classical pragmatism of Peirce and Dewey (Hodgson, 1998). In examining where the links between pragmatism and economic thought might be headed in the twenty-first century, these commonalities are the touchstones.

Polanyi and pragmatism

On the surface, *The Great Transformation* is a historical study of nineteenth-century European industrialization, told with an emphasis on how critical elements of public policy either frustrated or facilitated the emergence of markets for wage labor, on the one hand, and international trade in industrially produced commodities and raw materials, on the other. This history culminates in the economic crises of the 1930s and the rise of fascism. Polanyi interweaves detailed discussion of the legal elements and economic implications of specific public policies such as the English Speenhamland Law of 1795 and the Poor Law Reform of 1834. Polanyi's analysis of these events is enjoying a resurgence of interest among economists because it is regarded as a powerful and even definitive demonstration of the failings inherent in neoliberal free-market approaches to economic policy. This critique operates at economic, political, and ethical levels.

First, Polanyi exposes the fallacy inherent in allowing prices for labor, natural resources, and credit to be set by market forces. Liberal theories presume that the market price reflects a balance point between supply and demand. Lower prices would result in reduced willingness for suppliers to produce commodities, while higher prices result in reduced willingness for consumers to buy them.

The fallacy consists in the fact that the amount of labor, natural resources, and credit available at any given time is almost wholly unrelated to the costs of producing these goods. The amount of labor available is largely a function of population, and even if people do have children in response to economic incentives, such children do not disappear when the need for labor declines. Although people *develop* natural resources in response to economic demand, their eventual disappearance (and unavailability) has more to do with natural process (think of the incredibly long process of forming fossil fuels, or even the seasonal process of crops maturing once planted) than with current market demand. And even credit has to do with accumulated saving and risk, rather than being produced in response to demand. If market forces are allowed to set prices for labor, for natural resources or for credit, there will be rapid and extreme fluctuations that will, in turn, create unacceptable risks for investment of capital, resulting in extended periods of economic dysfunction.

Second, Polanyi argues that no political system is capable of accommodating the distress and destabilization that such fluctuations bring about. Hence governments do not in fact *allow* market forces to set prices for labor, natural resources, or credit for long. The "free-market ideal" is a pipe dream that ignores the way that those who hold power are, in fact, powerless in the face of widespread discontent and the threat of social upheaval. No powerful agent, whether king or parliament, that depends on social stability and the rule of law (and this includes not only governments but also corporations), will tolerate the chaos that must ensue during the period when markets for labor, natural resources, or credit are attempting to clear. Governing powers cannot wait for supply and demand to equalize, resulting in a stable price.

Finally, Polanyi makes the moral argument that a dysfunctional economy creates such misery and suffering for people that it is ethically wrong for society to persist in policies that allow labor or natural resources to be priced at market clearing levels. He is less concerned about credit prices with respect to the moral argument because it is business interests that are most adversely affected by fluctuations in the cost of credit and because he is confident that business interests are generally capable of looking after themselves. The economic credit crisis of 2007 might suggest that he was wrong in making this exception. Nevertheless, Polanyi is aware that in framing this as a moral argument pertaining to society as a whole, he is appealing to forms of moral agency and significance unrecognized by the political economists he is discussing. He concludes the book by warning that in the absence of democratic political institutions that give political voice to the interests of labor and land equivalent to those of the business community, political responses to economic instability are likely to take irrational, utopian, and repressive forms.

Polanyi is especially clear with respect to the way in which economic relations are embedded in the social world. He argues at length against the view that self-serving optimization in the form of "truck and barter" (these are Smith's words) can be generalized to provide a kind of universal solvent for analyzing the economic dimensions of social relations. The point he wishes to make against both classical and neoclassical theorists is that "the economy" cannot be analyzed as an ontologically distinct domain of human social activity, subject to the universal laws of economic theory. At the same time, neither optimization in general nor self-interested behavior in particular is entirely absent from noncapitalist societies, nor should one expect them to disappear under a noncapitalist set of postindustrial social institutions. Ayres' suggestion that institutionalists were claiming that people would cease to be self-interested upon the cessation of capitalism was one of the reasons that institutional economics went into decline during the third quarter of the twentieth century. Instead Polanyi's point is that this aspect of human behavior cannot be treated in a reductive fashion without inviting error and fallacy.

Embeddedness also accounts for the reason that economists have been able to stray much farther from experimentalism than physicists. The physicist is occasionally able to create experimental conditions that allow for a precise test of theory, but economics, like all the social sciences, cannot. Part of the reason relates to ethics, a point discussed below in connection to Bromley, but other reasons relate to the reflexive nature of the social world. Theoretical conceptualizations of language and of society are part of the world that they purport to represent. They affect the social reality in a dynamic way, and by the time that any theoretical representation of social reality has been specified with rigor sufficient for the kind of experiments that are decisive in physics, the actual social world will have changed and the experiment will no longer be relevant (Putnam, 1978). Contrary to the positivist hopes of Milton Friedman (1953), social sciences, including economics, are never falsifiable in a Popperian sense. Polanyi's treatment of this theme is to point out that the adjustments regarded as "natural" in theories of self-regulating markets create forms of social stress that provoke political responses (including fascism). Polanyi advocates a philosophy of economics that interprets these social and political reactions as a pragmatic (rather than Popperian) test of the theory. To ignore such responses is to ignore the way in which economic relations are but one dimension of a larger social world. The resilience of neoclassical theory, in contrast, relies upon a philosophy of social science that allows its central tenets to be viewed as a universal standard hovering above the social world, unaffected and not even testable by what happens in it.

Bromley and pragmatism

Daniel Bromley's 2006 book *Sufficient Reason: Volitional Pragmatism and the Meaning of Economic Institutions* argues that economic behavior is best understood as being based on a pragmatic theory of action. The philosophical insight that Bromley takes to be at the core of pragmatism is that the action of any individual already presupposes an elaborately interconnected set of background assumptions that constitute the individual's understanding of the world in general and of his or her situation in particular. It is impossible to "get beneath" this understanding through epistemology, as was the hope of modern philosophers, for even philosophers begin their epistemology with an already worked out conceptualization of the world.

John Dewey offered a version of this core insight in his 1896 "Reflex Arc" article. Behavioral scientists can only classify a given pattern of behavior *as* a response to stimuli if they have some prior understanding of how the world works. This prior understanding allows an observer to pick specific pairs of events from the infinite manifold of events that might be considered and see them as correlated. What is more, different observers can interpret a simple correlation in many different ways. Thus, the coherence of science presupposes significantly overlapping interpretive frameworks among observers. Bromley ties this general point in pragmatist epistemology to economics, arguing that preference satisfaction and utility maximization models of human behavior fall victim to the same critique Dewey leveled against stimulus-response psychology. But while pragmatists argue that all human behavior is intelligent in the sense that it presupposes a worked-out interpretation of one's situation, they also argue that much human behavior is habitual, which is to say that it is not particularly reflective or self-aware. It is, in fact, only in response to the *failure* of habits that people normally engage in active consideration of their circumstances and consider a number of alternative possibilities for action. Bromley encourages readers to "Notice that this account is at odds with the decision process envisaged by many economists. In that standard approach, individuals (and groups) start with a clear end (goal) in mind, they gather evidence of the costs and efficiency of alternative means for reaching that end, and they then select the most advantageous means for achieving that predetermined end" (Bromley, 2006, p. 144).

Habits, are, of course, institutions, especially where regularized patterns of behavior are critical to cooperative or collective action, interaction, and transaction. Bromley goes on to argue that contrary to the received view, the actual work of choice occurs in situations where habits fail. Here, choice does not involve maximization of utility or satisfaction of preexisting preferences, but search for new interpretations and understandings that will repair the fabric of the decision maker's interpretation of the world. The proper role for economics consists in abetting this search through insight into the way that alternative institutions do and do not contribute to achieving the ends-in-view that motivate the search for alternative arrangements.

Bromley is, in this respect, focused almost exclusively on legal rules and public policy. His analysis of institutions covers ground familiar to most institutional economists. "Institutions define and specify opportunity sets, or fields of action, for the members of a going concern" (Bromley, 2006, p. 31). He follows John R. Commons in distinguishing three "fundamental realms of human action" (Bromley, 2006, p. 34). *Ethics* involves rules enforced by moral sanction and collective opinion; *Economizing* involves sanctions of profit and loss; while *Jurisprudence* involves state-sponsored coercive sanctions. Bromley then summarizes his framework as follows:

> Any economic system is defined by—parameterized by—collectively ascertained and articulated rules and entitlement regimes that indicate what individuals must or must not do (duty), what individuals can do with the aid of the collective power (right), and what individuals cannot expect the collective power to do in their behalf (no right). The ethical realm constitutes the epistemic grounds (the reasons) for these institutions, the jurisprudential realm provides the articulation and ultimate enforcement of these institutions, and the economizing realm provides the arena in which individuals act in a domain parameterized by these institutions (the rule structure), subject to the prospect of financial gain or loss (Bromley, 2006, p. 35).

Bromley's emphasis on legal institutions follows Wesley Hohfeld's analysis of rights, privileges, power, and liability. These concepts sketch the way that legal rules determine opportunities, especially through the establishment of property relations. Bromley summarizes rights as legal institutions that "allow an individual to compel the coercive power of the state to come to her assistance." Property, in contrast, is "control over a benefit steam . . . that runs into the future." Property rights then bring these notions together and "parameterize the nature and extent of income appropriable from control of income-producing settings and circumstances" (Bromley, 2006, p. 63). Bromley then completes this section of the book by characterizing policy as "nothing but thinking about, weighing, and ultimately choosing among alternative institutional setups that will give rise to alternative imagined and plausible futures" (Bromley, 2006, p. 72). The Hohfeldian analysis allows economists to link alternative setups to imagined and plausible futures using fairly standard approaches to economizing behavior.

Where mainstream economics errs is in its exclusive reliance on the welfare-maximizing conception of human behavior to rank these alternative setups according to the sum of individual preference satisfactions. In place of this, Bromley offers the pragmatist idea that collective decision—"thinking about, weighing and ultimately choosing,"—consists simply of the public process of justifying a given course to "an audience of attentive sapient agents" (Bromley, 2006, p. 28). A more detailed account of this process might have been drawn from the work of Jürgen Habermas, but Habermas appears to be one of the few contemporary pragmatists that Bromley did not read in his preparation for *Sufficient Reason*. Importantly, however, Bromley limits the proposals presented to this attentive audience to *warranted assertions*, that is, to claims or beliefs that have been endorsed by a scientific discipline.

To the extent that warranted assertions have something to do with economizing, it thereby becomes crucial that economics as a discipline has an adequate conception of warranted assertability. Bromley first contrasts three modes of inference: deductive, abductive, and inductive. The first is focused on logical entailment relations while the last involves generalizations, extrapolations, and analogies based on data. Abduction, Bromley argues, is the notion omitted from too many economists' working philosophy of science. It is the process of hypothesis formation that occurs to explain otherwise unexpected or anomalous phenomena. Like the pragmatist conception of action itself, abduction presupposes a set of framing understandings about how the world works. In the case of scientific disciplines, however, these framing assumptions go well beyond commonsense understandings and constitute what Thomas Kuhn has called a paradigm. Paradigmatic understandings shared by practitioners of a discipline determine a set of expectations about how the phenomena in question generally work, but they also establish a set of questions needing further investigation.

Abduction is the process of offering hypotheses that if supported through observation and experiment would render questionable or doubtful circumstances consonant with other aspects of the paradigm, so that otherwise surprising or unexplained phenomena can be seen to follow as a matter of course. Or to put the matter differently, abduction is the process of imagining the circumstance, causal regularity or, in the case of intelligent agents, reason for acting that would explain the otherwise unexplained event. What counts as an explanation, thus, depends largely on the framing assumptions and working knowledge that a community of inquiry—a scientific discipline—brings to the table. For pragmatists, any particular element of this framework is regarded as fallible, but placing one aspect of the framework under scrutiny requires that one utilize other aspects of one's working knowledge to do so. The entire framework may, of course, be faulty, but pragmatist economists see the accumulation of working knowledge—of a scientific paradigm—as an evolutionary process. Its effectiveness as a means to "get by" combines with the community's willingness to continuously revise any and every given element within the framework to provide the basis for warranted assertability.

Bromley expends considerable effort criticizing economists for being insufficiently willing to revise aspects of the dominant paradigm associated with the idea of a welfare-maximizing economic agent. The notion of economic rationality as a process of calculative maximization has, he argues, been elevated to dogma. Rather than considering alternative hypotheses that might better explain economic phenomena, economists have devoted their creative efforts to the innovation of concepts and methods that reconcile observed phenomena with a deductive application of the axioms that specify rational behavior. Preserving the deductive structure of welfare maximization has become the *sine qua non* for economics, a phenomenon that Bromley himself explains in terms of its compatibility with politically conservative applications of neoliberalism. *Sufficient Reason* is, in these pages, a call for economists to be more like other empirical sciences and less like geometry.

But it is also important to see that these sections of the book also lay out the main elements of the pragmatist concept of reasoned action that I have already characterized in describing Bromley's keystone chapter. One potential difficulty that readers will encounter with the book is that its account of scientific methodology is also its characterization of human action and decision making. Thus economists need a better understanding of sufficient reason to better model economizing behavior and especially to understand how their models play their most useful and legitimate policy choice. But economists should also emulate this model of sufficient reason in their disciplinary practice. Bromley is not being unpragmatic in this approach. John Dewey wrote a short book describing *How We Think*, but he also read implicit norms into his view of thinking. When these norms are more fully realized than is often the case, thinking rises to the level of science. Thus Bromley's sufficient reason is both a description of human action that economists should more faithfully model in their theory, but it also implies norms about how economists *should* practice their science.

Conclusion

My aim here has been to provide some remarks that would provide self-avowed pragmatists with a way to think about connections to economic theory that would seem more congenial to their own views than most of what they hear espoused in the name of economics, on the one hand, or from those who, like Richard Posner, seem to have been taken by the neoliberal musings of the Austrian school, on the other. Polanyi never associated his work with philosophical pragmatism, and there is no evidence that he would have been familiar with the writings of classical American philosophers. What is more, his most influential work was originally published in 1944—hardly an auspicious basis for my suggestion that his work provides a linkage to pragmatism. Yet as Nobel Laureate Joseph E. Stiglitz writes in his introduction to the republication of *The Great Transformation*, Polanyi is having a greater influence among academic economists today than ever before. Bromley, in contrast, identifies himself as a pragmatist and notes that in preparing his book he studied not only the classical pragmatists but also neo-pragmatists such as Rorty, Putnam, and Brandom. This is, of course, only the scantiest of beginnings. I hope that others will take the opportunity to explore these possible linkages more thoroughly.

References

Acs, Z. J. (2002), *Innovation and the Growth of Cities*. Northampton, MA: Edward Elgar Publishing.
Ayres, C. E. (1951), "The Co-Ordinates of Institutionalism." *The American Economic Review*, 41, (2), pp. 47–55.

Boland, L. (1979), "A Critique of Friedman's Critics." *Journal of Economic Literature*, June, 503–522.

Bromley, D. (2006), *Sufficient Reason: Volitional Pragmatism and the Meaning of Economic Institutions*. Princeton, NJ: Princeton U. Press.

Friedman, M. (1953), "The Methodology of Positive Economics," in Friedman, M. (1966), *Essays In Positive Economics*. Chicago: Univ. of Chicago Press, pp. 3–16: 30–43.

Holcombe, R. (2004), "Government: Unnecessary but Inevitable." *The Independent Review*, VIII, (3), Winter, pp. 325–342.

Hodgson, G. M. (1998), "The Approach of Institutional Economics." *Journal of Economic Literature*, 36, (1), March, pp. 166–192.

Khalil, E. (ed.), (2004), *Dewey, Pragmatism and Economic Methodology*. New York: Routledge.

MacKenzie, D. W. (2004), "Review of Joseph Stiglitz, *Globalization and Its Discontents.*" *Public Choice*, 120, pp. 234–239.

North, D. C. (1990), *Institutions, Institutional Change and Economic Performance*. Cambridge: Cambridge University Press.

Portis, E. B. (1984), *Reconstructing the Classics: From Plato to Marx*. Chatham, NJ: Chatham House Publishers.

Posner, R. A. (1995), *Overcoming Law*. Cambridge, MA: Harvard University Press.

—(2003), *Law, Pragmatism and Democracy*. Cambridge, MA: Harvard University Press.

Polanyi, K. (1944), *The Great Transformation: The Political and Economic Origins of Our Time*. Forward by J. Stiglitz, New Introduction by F. Block, 2001. Boston: Beacon Press.

Putnam, H. (1978), *Meaning and the Moral Sciences*. International library of philosophy and scientific method. London: Routledge & K. Paul.

Samuels, W. J. (1995), "The Present State of Institutional Economics." *Cambridge Journal of Economics*, 19, pp. 569–590.

13

Race

Shannon Sullivan

The philosophical tradition of American pragmatism does not have a very good track record when it comes to issues of race, racism, and white supremacy. As Cornel West has claimed, "If a Martian were to come down to America and look at the American pragmatist tradition, they would never know that there was slavery, Jim Crow, lynching, discrimination, segregation in the history of America."[1] In the late nineteenth and first half of the twentieth century, W. E. B. Du Bois and Alain Locke explicitly and regularly took up issues of race and racism in their work, but they only recently have been reclaimed as canonical pragmatist philosophers.[2] John Dewey and Josiah Royce each wrote a couple of essays that focus on race, and Jane Addams' work in Hull House dealt with different ethnic groups that did not always or fully count as white at the time, but overall issues related to race are marginalized in their published work.[3] Charles S. Peirce and William James, two other philosophers in the main canon of American pragmatism, never discussed race in any substantial way in their philosophical writings. All and all, American pragmatism has tended to evade race rather than address it. "This is a major indictment," as West explains, since "pragmatism is a tradition that we expect more from . . . [b]ecause it really talks about wrestling with concrete realities in various historical contexts."[4] Race and racism are two of the concrete realities that pragmatism needs to wrestle with more often and more vigorously.

Cornel West's 1989 *The Evasion of American Philosophy* does this by developing the notion of prophetic pragmatism. Working with a Deweyan conception of democracy as a way of life and a DuBoisian analysis of the limits of capitalist democracy in particular, prophetic pragmatism strives for a better future through criticism of present culture that is fueled by sharp awareness of past tragedies.[5] Those tragedies include racism and white supremacy. West's pragmatism is not prophetic in the colloquial sense of foretelling the future, as if a fixed future existed and needed only to be divined. Instead prophets are those who have the courage to speak honestly about the present, bringing "urgent and compassionate critique to bear on the evils of their day."[6] Prophetic pragmatism carries no illusions that those evils can be completely eliminated, but it does insist that they can be ameliorated. Combining the rich tradition of black Christianity with pragmatist strategies for social change, West's philosophy struggles against racism and other evils that plague oppressed peoples throughout the world.

More recently, major publications in American philosophy that have focused on race have engaged in the ongoing debate in philosophy and critical race theory over the reality and usefulness of racial categories.[7] That debate starts from the understanding that there are no fixed racial essences. Racial categories are historical and political products of human activity, not biological or genetic essences that determine the division of human beings into different racial groups. In that sense—which is to say, in the sense that race historically was defined and commonly continues to operate—race does not exist. But does the de-biologizing of race mean that racial categories should be completely discarded? Is there any ongoing usefulness from an antiracist perspective for the concept of race understood as a social construction? While some analytic philosophers such as Kwame Anthony Appiah and Naomi Zack have answered that last question with a resounding "no," pragmatist philosophers have tended to reply with a reconstructivist "yes."[8] As Lucius Outlaw, Eddie S. Glaude, Shannon Sullivan, and Terrance MacMullan have argued, pragmatism can help reconstruct and redefine understandings of race in ways that benefit antiracist theory and practice.[9] From a pragmatist perspective, the racist bathwater in the United States and elsewhere needs to be thrown out, but the baby of race need not and should not be thrown out with it.

Can racial categories provide meaning and life-sustaining order to human existence? Lucius Outlaw answers "yes" to this question and argues that human life would be impoverished if race were eliminated. To make this argument, Outlaw draws an important distinction between *racialism* and *racism*.[10] Racialism is the broader term, encompassing racism. Racialism is defined by the use of racial categories to provide conceptual, social, political and other forms of order to human existence. These forms of order do not necessarily involve oppressive hierarchies. When they do, racialism takes the form of racism. Racism occurs when racial categories are hierarchically valued such that some races are deemed inferior to others and excluded from full participation in society. Throughout much of the past four hundred years, racialism has taken the form of racism, sometimes making it difficult to distinguish between the two. But as Outlaw argues, a distinction between them can and should be made. Racism needs to be challenged whenever and where it occurs, but being opposed to racism shouldn't mean being opposed to the use of racial categories.

According to Outlaw, the use of racial categories enriches human life by providing life-sustaining diversity and plurality to the human species. Outlaw is not claiming that race is the only means by which to do this. Certainly other group attachments, such as those based on gender, religious affiliation, or sexual orientation, can provide meaningful ways of ordering human existence. But race should not be eliminated from this list in an effort to fight racism. Doing so, Outlaw worries, "may well come to have unintended effects that are too much of a kind with racial and ethnic cleansing."[11] Doing so also would reduce the human diversity that is crucial to the flourishing of the species. Here Outlaw combines inspiration from W. E. B Du Bois with an evolutionary-based argument. In his 1897 "The Conservation of Races," Du Bois argues that each race has its own distinctive "message" to give to humanity, a contribution to human development in the form of literature, art, science, religion, and so on. Humanity benefits when each race can fully deliver its message, but "the full, complete Negro message of the whole Negro race has not as yet been given to the world."[12] For the good of humanity, then, race needs to be conserved so that a black message can be shared with others.[13]

Outlaw adds to Du Bois's argument the evolutionary consideration that diversity within a species is beneficial for it. He asks, "if bio-diversity is thought good for other species and for the global ecosystem, why not for the human species and its bio-cultural ecosystems?"[14] There are reasons, Outlaw holds, that human beings aren't all "light khaki" after all these years of reproduction, and those reasons include more than racist aversion to interracial "miscegenation." They include affections and attachments to one's own race that make good evolutionary sense, that are legitimate from an antiracist perspective, and that should be appreciated by a democratic society that prides itself on its pluralism.

Outlaw also draws on Du Bois to argue for the importance of biology in race. Outlaw defends Du Bois against those such as Appiah, who criticizes Du Bois's appeal to "common blood" to explain race and replaces the concept of race with the idea of "communities of meaning."[15] Outlaw argues that Du Bois has a much subtler understanding of the role of "blood" or biology in race than Appiah appreciates. In one of the boldest arguments in his work, Outlaw aligns himself with Du Bois to conclude that race does have a biological basis. This basis does not completely fix or draw absolute lines between different races, but it should not be omitted from our understanding of race in an attempt to avoid the boogeyman of biological determinism. Du Bois's appeal to "common blood" was part of an effort to understand how biology combines with social and cultural factors to produce race. As Outlaw explains, "in complex interactions with environmental, cultural, and social factors and processes [biological factors] provide certain boundary conditions and possibilities that affect raciation in terms of the development of distinctive gene pools" from which different races arise.[16] On their own, biology and physical differences more broadly cannot explain race, but they do play a role in how human beings group themselves, and those groupings have effects on gene pools and human reproductive practices. If we are going to take seriously the fact that humans are embodied beings with embodied identities, then race must be considered a *bio*-cultural group attachment, not merely a community of meaning or some other grouping that omits the biological aspects of humanity.[17]

In his work on pragmatism and race, Eddie Glaude draws primarily on Dewey, rather than Du Bois. But like Outlaw, Glaude believes that pragmatism can help solve vexing problems regarding the use of racial categories. Glaude begins by confronting criticism from those such as Hilary Putnam and Cornel West that Dewey's pragmatism naively underestimates the presence of evil in the world and thus cannot deal adequately with the tragic aspects of human experience. Glaude argues that while it's true that Dewey failed to wrestle with "the tragedy at the heart of American democracy—the problem of racism, . . . it doesn't follow that Dewey lacked a tragic vision."[18] Glaude uses Toni Morrison's novel *Beloved* to draw out a blue note, as he calls it, in Dewey's pragmatism. Reading *Beloved* as a "pragmatic view of the tragic in light of the devastating effects of white supremacy that continue to haunt American democracy," Glaude shows how Dewey's abandonment of the quest for certainty results in a tragic attitude toward human experience. Given that most situations that human beings find themselves in involve competing values, then conflict and loss inevitably are part of human experience on Dewey's view. Not every desire can be satisfied, not every value can be pursued, and there is no guarantee when we choose between conflicting values that we have chosen the one that will produce the most human flourishing. Dewey's insistence on contingency and uncertainty and his refusal to provide reassurance in the form of the absolute means that tragedy is woven throughout his pragmatism even if he does not often highlight that fact by using obvious terms such as "evil," "dread," or "tragic."[19]

Having brought out a shade of blue in Dewey's philosophy, Glaude demonstrates how Dewey can help black America deal with questions of black identity, black history, and black agency. These questions have created problems that plague contemporary black discourse, according to Glaude, and they need pragmatic answers to avoid those problems. For example, black identity too often is thought of archeologically. On an archeological approach, "black identity is concerned with uncovering our true selves and inferring from that discovery what we must do."[20] All sorts of problematic efforts to discover what is "truly" black and who counts as a "real" black person result from this approach. Not only are these efforts contentious and prone to failure, they divert attention away from the choices made and actions taken by black people. Instead of an archeological approach to identity, Glaude argues, black America needs a pragmatic historicist approach, which would view black identity as a consequence of human activity. Black identity doesn't precede and determine the actions and choices engaged in by black people. Instead, the choices made by black people in the face of problematic situations—including racism and white supremacy—help make up the lives and identities of black America.[21]

Just as non-pragmatist understandings of black identity tend to treat it as a fixed, pre-existing entity, non-pragmatist understandings of black history often reify blackness as a single-minded struggle against white supremacy. Glaude argues that black theology in particular has treated black history as something that has "settled the problems of our living in advance of our experience."[22] This treatment oversimplifies both black history and the possibilities for black people's present and future. "There is much more to our living than simply resisting white supremacy," Glaude claims, and black people need an understanding of their history that recognizes this fact. Dewey's pragmatism helps provide that understanding by viewing history as a tool "that helps us by illuminating our present predicaments."[23] Black history is important, but not as a repository of settled answers. Its importance lies in the light it can shed on current situations, including how past history conditions, but does not determine their meaning and consequences.

On Glaude's account, most conceptions of black agency need pragmatizing as well. Just as black history is misunderstood as a constant struggle against white racism, black agency often is "theorized within the terms of subversion and resistance, leaving unexamined the various 'projects, discourses, and desires' that escape these terms."[24] Dewey's pragmatism, in contrast, shows how agency emerges within particular environments and situations. Agents, black or otherwise, don't arrive on the scene fully formed with a predetermined plan for how they are going to act. This view of agency overlooks the work that people do when responding to the complexities of concrete situations, work that often causes them to readjust their goals and that leads them to transform the situation to which they are responding. Glaude argues that especially in the context of African American Christianity's responses to slavery, black America needs a nuanced understanding of black agency and emancipatory politics that pragmatism can help provide.

Glaude's pragmatist rethinking of black identity, black history, and black agency culminates in a striking argument for a "post-soul politics." This term refers to both the black individuals and their particular sensibilities that emerged in the generation after the civil rights movement and the black power era of the late 1960s through the mid-1970s. Glaude argues that black people who came of age in the 1980s are creating a different vision of black politics in which "the sixties [do not] occupy, and I mean this in its military sense, our political imaginations."[25] While Glaude praises the political efforts of past generations of black leaders, he criticizes current black politics for allowing "old strategies and personalities [to] continue to define how we engage in race-based politics."[26] Glaude calls for a post-soul politics that would not use the 1960s as a point of reference for all contemporary black political activity. On Glaude's view, this would be a black politics in a Deweyan shade of blue: a black politics that focuses on future consequences for black people rather than dwelling on a supposedly settled past.

When Lucius Outlaw argues for the value of conserving race, he makes clear that his argument includes whiteness. As he provocatively asks, "how might we work to conserve 'colored' populations and subgroupings (*and white is a color, as well*), races and ethnies, without making it easier for racialism and ethnocentrism to 'go imperial'"?[27] Shannon Sullivan and Terrence MacMullan have taken up this question, using Dewey and Du Bois to explore how racist habits of whiteness might be transformed so that they do not continue to perpetuate white supremacy. Sullivan combines pragmatism with psychoanalytic theory to argue that in a post-Jim Crow era, white habits tend to function unconsciously. Inspired by Du Bois's "realiz[ation] that in the fight against race prejudice, we were not facing simply the rational, conscious determination of white folk to oppress us; we were facing age-long complexes sunk now largely to unconscious habit and irrational urge,"[28] Sullivan examines how white privilege often operates in hidden, subversive ways. In contrast to the conscious and deliberate moves of white supremacy, white privilege often functions through the good intentions of liberal-minded white people. As Sullivan explains, "it is all too easy for white people's good intentions to address racism in responsible, antiracist ways to reenact the very white privilege that they wish to undermine."[29]

One example of this phenomenon can be found in Sullivan's experience of the racial integration of her hometown schools.[30] Unconscious habits of white privilege operated undetected (at least by most white people) through the white officials' good intentions of ending segregation. Black and Latino students were bused to predominantly white schools, resulting in the loss of a relatively safe cultural and educational space in which black students could challenge, or at least avoid white domination. White people and white interests continued to control how the educational spaces of the town were used, and the needs and desires of black and Latino families were disregarded. As Sullivan argues, this privileging of white people and harm to black and Latino people were done in good conscience in an effort to eliminate racism and white privilege.[31]

The fact that habits of white privilege often operate unconsciously means that it won't be easy to change them, at least not directly. Sullivan argues that indirect methods are needed instead, methods that attempt to transform white privileged habits by transforming the political, social, cultural, and other environments that feed into them. And yet even here white privilege can insidiously and invisibly reassert itself. Efforts to change a racist world can be expressions of the white privileged desire for complete control. As Sullivan claims, "well-intentioned attempts to change racist environments can be just another expression of the white privileged habit of unconsciously thinking that and behaving as if all spaces were available for . . . white people to appropriate."[32] This habit is one of ontological expansiveness, as Sullivan calls it. As ontologically expansive, white people tend to consider all spaces—geographical, linguistic, economic, and so on—as fully available and open to them.[33] If a particular space, such as a predominantly black neighborhood, seems closed off or hostile to white people, this is seen as a violation of their basic right to legitimately move in and out of a space whenever they choose to do so. Ontological expansiveness means that even indirect methods to uncover and transform habits of white privilege are likely to reenact the problem they are meant to solve.

Sullivan concludes that the dangers of reinforcing white privilege through attempts to undercut it cannot be avoided. There is no place of purity from which white people can struggle against racism. When asking what white people can do, the best hope is that sometimes they can use white privilege against itself. Witness the example of a white couple in the 1950s who used their white privilege to challenge residential segregation by purchasing a house in an all-white neighborhood for the express purpose of selling it to a black people who could not buy it directly on their own.[34] Other times habits of white privilege can be blocked by the separatist efforts of people of color. The importance of separatism for preserving protected spaces for people of color means that white people need to question multicultural and diversity initiatives that would destroy those spaces. In all these cases there are no guarantees of success, Sullivan argues, but antiracist struggle will benefit if white people attempt to take responsibility for their unconscious habits.

Habits of whiteness also are the focus of Terrance MacMullan's pragmatist work on race, which offers a more encouraging account of the possibilities for the transformation of whiteness. Drawing from Dewey, MacMullan emphasizes the impulses that help form habits and the role that Deweyan inquiry can play in their transformation. Because impulses can take a variety of forms, they are the best means by which habit can be changed. Habits of white domination can be directly addressed through this means because, *contra* Sullivan, white domination is not primarily unconscious. Nor is it deliberately conscious, as it is for white supremacists. As MacMullan explains, "many of our problems regarding race are not rooted in conscious racial hatred, but in unexamined behaviors and impulses that lead people to say and do things that are at odds with the ideals of equality and humanity that almost all people hold."[35] White people generally don't notice how their racial habits clash with their antiracist ideas. Processes of inquiry can help them increase their awareness, and increased awareness gives them the ability to change their habits. According to MacMullan, "whiteness [i]s an interactive phenomenon over which white Americans have a great amount of control, and [thus] ... white Americans have an obligation to identify and uproot habits of whiteness."[36]

When they do this, white people need reconstructed habits of whiteness to affirm in place of the old, deleterious ones. As does Outlaw, MacMullan follows Du Bois in arguing that an antiracist future needs to be built by means of, not in spite of racial categories, and that white people need to figure out what nonracist message or gift they have to give to humanity. Part of white people's gift will be found via a recovery of cultural and ethnic traditions that white people generally have discarded in the name of being white. Whiteness clearly has harmed nonwhite people, but less noticed is the way that whiteness has been detrimental to white people as well. "White people have been encouraged to forget all the other ways that our ancestors thought of themselves: according to clan, family, nation, language, music, vocation, and place," MacMullan observes.[37] Recounting the different Italian, German, and Irish traditions and experiences that make up his ancestral history, MacMullan shows how lost racial gifts can be recovered. Those gifts can provide life-sustaining meaning to white people, as well as help white people build solidarity with people of color who suffer from oppression today. In an example from his own life, MacMullan explains, "when I remember that I am the child of a people [the Irish] who faced prejudice, I realize that the only way I can heal the wound that they suffered is to help heal the wound in front of me, here and now. . . . I therefore learn that I must bite my tongue when the habits of whiteness tempt me to think that I own this country and that [illegal immigrants] are invaders."[38]

MacMullan identifies three main habits of whiteness that need to be dismantled in order for white people to develop their distinctive nonracist gifts to humanity. Those habits are ones of antipathy to the strange, entitlement, and guilt. Identifying the impulses behind each of these habits, MacMullan explains how the impulses can be repatterned into different habits. The habit of antipathy to the strange is fueled by simple antipathy.[39] Simple antipathy is universal and unproblematic. Feelings of antipathy toward things that are dangerous, such as open flames, probably have been crucial to the survival of the human species. The problem with whiteness is that it has taken the basic impulse of antipathy and channeled it toward anyone who is different from white people. According to MacMullan, "we can't help having raw feelings of antipathy; we can and must take control of the form that these feelings take."[40] The form that they should take, on MacMullan's account, is that of habits of antipathy to suffering, or more succinctly the habit of compassion.[41] An aversion to suffering is a habit that uses the impulse of antipathy to work for a better world by reducing, rather than causing, the pain of others.

Likewise the impulse behind white people's habit of entitlement needs to be identified. According to MacMullan, the habit of entitlement is fueled by the impulse of pride in the sense of holding that "*who you are, or the group of which you are a part, is valuable.*"[42] Again, the simple impulse of valuing one's own group isn't problematic. What is problematic is that the impulse has been linked to pride in not being a member of another, oppressed group. This kind of pride "leads white people to think they are entitled to control how, when, and if their group mingles with other groups perceived as different or strange."[43] Here we see how the habit of entitlement is similar to what Sullivan calls the habit of ontological expansiveness and intertwines with the habit of antipathy to what is strange. When white people inquire into their racial habits and discover the habit of entitlement, they should rechannel the impulse of pride into the habit of remembrance. Without forgetting a shameful white past, white people need to search their past for examples that don't involve white domination. In MacMullan's words, "what we need to remember is that every person who is now white has, somewhere in the stretch of history, a history or set of histories that either predate the invention of whiteness or offer the sort of life-sustaining value that whiteness lacks. If we go back far enough or look carefully enough, we can find a culture and a history that is predicated on *particular memories and particular experiences*, and not on the exclusion of others."[44]

Finally, MacMullan examines the white habit of guilt, which has become prominent in the last couple of decades.[45] This habit recognizes the atrocities of whiteness and generates guilt in response to them. As a result, however, guilty-feeling white people tend to engage in cultural plundering of other racial groups' gifts out of an attempt to flee their whiteness or replace it with something nonwhite. Witness blackface minstrelsy, the music and dance moves of Elvis, and other more recent forms of white theft of African American cultural traditions. This habit is fueled by an impulse of emptiness, a lack caused by whiteness that needs to be filled in some other way. According to MacMullan, the better way to handle this impulse is to develop habits of shame. Unlike guilt, shame goes beyond the recognition of wrongdoing to the acceptance of responsibility for it.[46] Habits of shame call for white people to develop their own distinctive gifts to humanity, via habits of remembrance that recover their own cultural traditions, rather than stealing the gifts of others.

American philosophy still has a ways to go before its track record on race and racism is substantially improved. Increasingly, however, the field is paying attention to the concrete realities and historical contexts presented by white domination. Martians landing on earth today might be only dimly aware of slavery and its aftermath by looking at the history of American pragmatism, but there is good reason to hope that the field will provide a different view in the future.

Notes

1. See West (2004, p. 225).
2. See, for example, Du Bois (1970, 1994) and Locke (1925). Taylor (2004a, pp. 99–114) explains why it matters whether Du Bois is considered a pragmatist.
3. See Dewey (1988, 1989); Royce (2009); Addams (2001).
4. See West (1989, "Afterword," pp. 225, 226).
5. See West (1989, pp. 212, 228).
6. See West (1989, p. 233).
7. By major publications, I mean single-authored books. I will focus on four books published in the last decade or so: Outlaw (1996), Glaude (2007), Sullivan (2006),

and MacMullan (2009). See also the two edited collections on pragmatism and race that have been published recently: Lawson and Koch, (eds), (2004), *Pragmatism and the Problem of Race*, and C. Kautzer and E. Mendieta, (eds), (2009). While Scott L. Pratt's (2002) does not focus on race per se, it argues for the importance of Native American thinking to the development of classical American philosophy.

8 See, for example, Appiah (1989); and Zack (1993).
9 Paul C. Taylor (2004b) provides an additional argument to this effect in "Pragmatism and Race," in Lawson and Koch, (eds), *Pragmatism and the Problem of Race*, pp. 162–176.
10 See Outlaw (1996, p. 8).
11 See Outlaw (1996, p. 11).
12 See Du Bois quoted in Outlaw (1996 p. 154).
13 For an objection to Du Bois that argues that black political solidarity should be disentangled from a collective black identity, see Shelby (2005).
14 See Outlaw (1996. p. 13).
15 See Outlaw (1996, p. 152).
16 See Outlaw (1996, p. 170).
17 See Outlaw (1996, p. 17).
18 See Glaude (2007, p. 39).
19 For a critical account of Dewey's pragmatism that examines the relevance of his racial identity to the "blueness" (or lack thereof) of his philosophy, see Taylor (2004c, pp. 227–241).
20 See Glaude (2007, p. 53).
21 Inspired by Kwame Anthony Appiah, Tommie Shelby would agree with Glaude's criticisms of an archeological approach to black identity but disagree with Glaude that identities, even on a pragmatist historicist approach, are relevant to struggles for racial justice. See Shelby (2005) and Glaude's (2007, pp. 55–57) criticism of Shelby.
22 See Glaude (2007, p. 78).
23 See Glaude (2007, p. 86).
24 See Glaude (2007, p. 98).
25 See Glaude (2007, p. 149).
26 See Glaude (2007, p. 149).
27 See Outlaw (1996, p. 21), emphasis added.
28 See Du Bois, W. E. B. (1984, p. 296); quoted in Sullivan (2006, p. 21).
29 See Sullivan (2006, p. 167).
30 See Sullivan (2006, pp. 177–178).
31 For an excellent use of Du Bois to address race and racism in educational settings, see Heldke (2004, pp. 224–238).

32 See Sullivan (2006, p. 13).
33 See Sullivan (2006, p. 10).
34 See Sullivan (2006, pp. 165–166).
35 See MacMullan (2009, p. 3).
36 See MacMullan (2009, p. 5).
37 See MacMullan (2009, p. 141).
38 See MacMullan (2009, p. 215).
39 See MacMullan (2009, p. 172).
40 See MacMullan (2009, p. 175).
41 See MacMullan (2009, p. 206).
42 See MacMullan (2009, p. 177), emphasis in original.
43 See MacMullan (2009, p. 176).
44 See MacMullan (2009, p. 202).
45 See MacMullan (2009, pp. 178–179).
46 See MacMullan (2009, p. 195).

References

Addams, J. (2001), *Democracy and Social Ethics*. Chicago, IL: University of Illinois Press.

Appiah, K. A. (1989), "The Conservation of 'Race,'" *Black American Literature Forum*, 23(1): 37–60.

Dewey, J. (1988), "Racial Prejudice and Friction," in J. A. Boydston (ed.), Volume 13 of *The Middle Works, 1899–1924*. Carbondale, IL: Southern Illinois University Press.

—(1989), "Address to the National Association for the Advancement of Colored People," in J. A. Boydston (ed.), Volume 6 of *The Later Works: 1925–1953*. Carbondale, IL: Southern Illinois University Press.

Du Bois, W. E. B. (1970), "The Conservation of Races," in P. S. Foner (ed.), *W. E. B. Du Bois Speaks: Speeches and Addresses, 1980–1919*. New York: Pathfinder Press.

—(1984), *Dusk of Dawn: An Essay Toward an Autobiography of a Race Concept*. New York: Schocken Books.

—(1994), *The Souls of Black Folk*. New York: Dover Publications.

Glaude, E. (2007), *In a Shade of Blue: Pragmatism and the Politics of Black America*. Chicago: The University of Chicago Press.

Heldke, L. (2004), "A Du Boisian Proposal for Persistently White Colleges", *Journal of Speculative Philosophy*, 18, (3), 224–238.

Kautzer, C. and Mendieta, E. (eds), (2009), *Pragmatism, Nation, and Race: Community in the Age of Empire*. Bloomington, IN: Indiana University Press.

Lawson, B. E. and Koch, D. F. (eds), (2004), *Pragmatism and the Problem of Race*. Bloomington, IN: Indiana University Press.

Locke, A. (ed.), (1925), *The New Negro: An Interpretation*. New York: A. and C. Boni.

MacMullan, T. (2009), *Habits of Whiteness: A Pragmatist Reconstruction*. Bloomington, IN: Indiana University Press.
Outlaw, L. (1996), *On Race and Philosophy*. New York: Routledge.
Pratt, S. L. (2002), *Native Pragmatism: Rethinking the Roots of American Philosophy*. Bloomington, IN: Indiana University Press.
Royce, J. (2009), "Race Questions and Problems," in J. Royce, *Race Questions and Other Essays: Expanded Edition*. Eds S. L. Pratt and S. Sullivan. Bronx, NY: Fordham University Press.
Shelby, T. (2005), *We Who Are Dark: The Philosophical Foundations of Black Solidarity*. Cambridge, MA: Harvard University Press.
Sullivan, S. (2006), *Revealing Whiteness: The Unconscious Habits of Racial Privilege*. Bloomington, IN: Indiana University Press.
Taylor, P. C. (2004a), "What's the Use of Calling Du Bois a Pragmatist?" *Metaphilosophy*, January, 35, (1–2): 99–114.
—(2004b), "Pragmatism and Race," in Lawson and Koch, (eds), *Pragmatism and the Problem of Race*, pp. 162–176.
—(2004c), "Silence and Sympathy: Dewey's Whiteness" in G. Yancy, (ed.), *What White Looks Like: African-American Philosophers on the Whiteness Question*. New York: Routledge, pp. 227–241.
West, C. (1989), *The American Evasion of Philosophy*. Madison, WI: The University of Wisconsin Press, pp. 212, 228.
—(2004), "Afterword: A Conversation with Cornel West and Bill E. Lawson," in B. E. Lawson and D. E. Koch (eds), *Pragmatism and the Problem of Race*. Bloomington, IN: Indiana University Press, p. 225.
Zack, N. (1993), *Race and Mixed Race*. Philadelphia: Temple University Press.

14

Religion

Ulf Zackariasson

Introduction

Pragmatism emerges as a distinct philosophical movement in the decades after the publication of Charles Darwin's *The Origin of Species* in 1859, and much of the classical pragmatists' reflection on religion reflects the crisis religion suffered in a culture where modern science and industry made stunning progress. The pragmatic revival of the last three decades, on the other hand, occurs at a time when public and intellectual interest in religion has been steadily rising. No wonder, then, that religion has received a fair share of pragmatic attention.

There is, however, no pragmatic consensus on whether religious practices are worth retaining, and, if so, in what form. James cites with approval the Italian pragmatist Giovanni Papini's picture of pragmatism as a hotel corridor, from which religious as well as anti-religious chambers can be accessed. The multitude notwithstanding, it is possible to discern some recurring pragmatic themes in much pragmatic reflection on religion:

1. Reflection should start from where we stand, and this requires sensitivity to the current form of religious practices and the way they function in human life;
2. There is nothing unique about religion as a set of human practices: we should expect that they emerge and continue to exist because they have a function in human life;
3. Critical reflection is just as possible and important within religion as in any other human practices.

To religious authorities and believers who teach that your eternal welfare depends on your uncritical submission to some divinely revealed message, the pragmatic approach is not only pointless, but probably heretical. Critics of religion might, on the other hand, detect an apologetic agenda here, and in a way, they are right: many pragmatists are prepared to accept the "good," including religious "goods," present in human experience, provided that such acceptance will not create problems elsewhere—a requirement that may prove rather demanding.

Themes (1)–(3) are not omnipresent in every pragmatist's reasoning on religion. Peirce, for instance, rejected (3) since he was suspicious of all uses of pragmatism in topics "of vital importance" such as ethics and religion. They may also be afforded different relative weight. Put somewhat schematically, we can say that pragmatists want to know what religion is good for, and whether that good can be made more "secure in existence neoclassical" to borrow a phrase from Dewey. In what follows, I concentrate on James' and Dewey's approaches, and draw parallels to some contemporary pragmatists, before I try to relate pragmatic reflection on religion to contemporary Anglo-American philosophy of religion.

James on religion

Typical of James' approach to religion is his focus on religion's role in the life of individuals, rather than on creeds or religious institutions. Religion is primarily a source of existential and moral courage that enable believers to lead richer and more "saintlike" lives. Collectively mediated experiences and religious institutions with their theologies are "secondary outgrowths" on this originally individual impulse.

James' individualistic approach is best exemplified in two of his most important works on religion: the essay "The will to believe" and his Gifford lectures *The Varieties of Religious Experience*. In *Varieties*, James defines religion as "the feelings, acts and experiences of individual men in their solitude, so far as they consider themselves to stand in relation to whatever they may consider the divine" (James, 1902, p. 31). Consistent with this definition, James repeatedly emphasized the role of experience in any religious life. In "The will to believe," James defends a right to let your "passional nature" decide between belief and unbelief in cases where the evidence is inconclusive, provided that both options are *live* (otherwise, the choice is not genuine), that the choice is *forced* (to refrain from choice is in effect to choose unbelief), and *momentous* (the choice is important for us). In situations such as these, it is appropriate and even necessary to let your deepest-felt needs decide what to believe (James, 1897, pp. 2ff, 11).

Note how James connects justification to the individual's perspective: the will (right) to believe only applies to those cases where there is something at stake for you personally, and in these cases, the fact that certain beliefs meet your deepest-felt needs supplies the justification you need to adopt a believing stance (again, in the absence of conclusive evidence).

To many philosophers within mainstream Anglo-American philosophy of religion, even a thus qualified right to believe comes dangerously close to a right to make believe, an all too human shortcut to avoid paying serious attention to the philosophical evidence for and against God's existence. There are a couple of possible Jamesian responses to this objection. First, you may ask whether the probability-based beliefs that arguments for and against God's existence supply us with are the *religious* beliefs we originally set out to discuss. Beliefs in probabilities seem unable to play any religious role in your life, and so, they seem to need fortification from some act of faith, perhaps motivated by a religious experience. Then, you have in fact adopted the "will to believe" doctrine.

Second, James is not defending a right to believe in the omnipotent, omniscient, omnipresent, perfectly good, and immutable God of classical (Christian) theism. This is illustrated by the way he contrasts religious institutions and creeds with the image of God that emerges from reports of religious experiences, and his discussion in *Varieties* of which beliefs, if any, religious experiences justify. Faithful to the approach I sketched above, James supplies the following pragmatic analysis of the difference between real and unreal in a religious setting:

> Yet the unseen region is not merely ideal, for it produces effects in this world. When we commune with it, work is actually done upon our finite personality, for we are turned into new men, and consequences in the way of conduct follow in the natural world upon our regenerative change. But that which produces effects within another reality must be termed a reality itself, so I feel as if we had no philosophic excuse for calling the unseen or mystical world unreal. (James, 1902, p. 516)

To use a simple example: we are quite competent at distinguishing between, say, a real and a fake shovel—we just test them by putting them to use. What James is saying is that we are also quite competent at distinguishing real from illusory gods: a real god is the one that makes a definite difference in *your* life, the god that actually supplies the moral and existential support you sorely need. Since these needs differ, there is nothing strange about disagreements about God, or even about God's existence. Of course, the critic can seek to restore traditional argument-based philosophy of religion by distinguishing between "God in

God-self" and our *conceptions* of God, and claim that James is only interested in the practical question of what *conceptions* of God it would be good for us to adopt, while the question of truth is left over to philosophical investigation.

I do not have enough space to examine James' view of truth in general or religious truth in particular here. However, we can safely say that this is a rather unpragmatic move for two reasons. First, it assumes that we can articulate what it is for a being such as God to be real independently of how judgments about real and illusory gods are made in the practices under discussion. Second, if the point is that the intellectual question of truth is somehow the most important issue here, then you neglect the fact that for many people—those for whom the answer *matters*—the decision has to be made here and now and cannot be postponed indefinitely.

Dewey: Faith in the ideal

While James kept a door open for supernatural agency in religion, Dewey's thoroughgoing naturalism leaves little space for religion in its traditional forms. It is religion's great misfortune, according to Dewey, that it has become so linked to the supernatural that today we can hardly imagine what religion would be without it. Nevertheless, the link needs to be broken, Dewey thinks, for two rather different reasons: supernaturalism repels modern minds, but at the same time, the enduring prestige of religion lends supernatural methods of inquiry an air of legitimacy that creates obstacles for intelligent resolution of shared problems.

In *A Common Faith*, Dewey makes a distinction between *religion* and *the religious*. "Religion" denotes the institutions, creeds, and established rites of different religious traditions as they are historically constituted. These institutions have (at least in a Western context) become tangled up with a metaphysics founded on a spectator theory of knowledge, according to which the process of knowledge acquisition can be likened to that of seeing: the knower is passive, and the object of knowledge remains unaffected throughout the process. The religious version of this metaphysics is the immutable and perfect God of classical theism (Dewey, 1929).

"The religious," on the other hand, is, according to Dewey, inextricably linked to *agency*. It is an aspect of experience present whenever there is some *achievement* in the form of a development toward states of affairs that we consider ideal. Here, we are anything but passive observers: religious experiences typically follow upon intelligently conducted action. Religions that appeal to supernatural sources to solve problems are hence effectively combating the religious impulse they once drew strength from.

Once the link to supernaturalism is broken, what can religion be about? Dewey's suggestion is: the ideal. Our gut reaction to this suggestion—that this denigrates religion—only reveals, Dewey claims, our inability to see the enormous significance ideals have for conduct. In fact, without the ability to entertain ideas about some state of affairs as better than others, intelligent thought and action would be impossible. At the same time, ideals are no more immune to critical reflection than other beliefs we hold. Dewey suggests that we can capture the central role of ideals by giving the name "god" to the total sum of ideals that we acknowledge and that has authority over conduct. He writes: "It is admitted that the objects of religion are ideal in contrast with our present state. What would be lost if it were also admitted that they have authoritative claim upon conduct just because they are ideal?" (Dewey, 1934, p. 41).

If religious institutions were to accept this analysis and reject the outdated spectator theory of knowledge, they may once again become genuinely religious. Such institutions would, Dewey holds, take a more active public role, engaging in the cultivation of sustainable ideals and discussion of which concrete "ends-in-view" to pursue, and would make do without appeals to supernatural sources of knowledge and authority. Here, Dewey has a slightly more positive view of religious institutions than James, for whom religious institutions were stiffened forms of religious life determined to stifle all originality in their adherents' spiritual lives.

Dewey scholars are divided on the question of how wise it was of Dewey to offer religious institutions a role in the intelligent transformation of society. Stephen Rockefeller holds that one important insight here is that radical transformations are simplified by "strong communities" capable of taking action and of upholding a sense of belonging throughout the process. Michael Eldridge, on the other hand, claims that it was a mistake of Dewey to think that the social transformation he advocated could be better affected by going through, rather than around, religious institutions, given their historical ballast and (current) self-understanding (Rockefeller, 2003; Eldridge, 1998).

Religion in contemporary pragmatism

Contemporary pragmatic reflection on religion continues to raise the question of what religion is good for, and also how religion can be related to modern science and a liberal political order. Here, I confine myself to two examples.

In his later works, Richard Rorty describes his view of religion as a mix of anticlericalism and a personal lack of religious "musicality." Rorty suggests that religious faith can be seen as resembling *romantic projects* linked to our "passional nature." Although we sometimes question, for example, someone's choice of spouse, we do not normally think that people are under some general obligation to justify such choices—we simply appeal to their passional nature to explain why they hope against hope that a relation can be mended, or a loved one will recover. Something similar is true, Rorty holds, of religious believers.

Here, Rorty brings together two important distinctions: Wilfrid Sellars' distinction between that which falls within and that which falls outside the "logical space of reasons" and the classical liberal distinction between the public and the private sphere. Rorty argues for an (at least partial) identification of the public sphere and the space of reasons, which means that it is only in public, cooperative projects such as science and politics that we should give and require reasons. The compromise Rorty offers is, he claims, not new; it is one of the "great achievements of the enlightenment": religion retreats from the public sphere, and is, in exchange, granted space in the private sphere beyond public criticism. (Rorty, 1999)

Rorty nowhere claims that this is a discovery about what religion *really* is like. Instead, his suggestion that privatized forms of religion can coexist with both modern science and a liberal political order is a good example of what philosophy might look like once it abandons its foundationalist aspirations and becomes instead a form of "cultural politics" (Rorty, 2007).

Rorty's privatized account of religion highlights a tension running through pragmatic reflection on religion, a tension arising from the fact that while religion's function—what it is good for—is often analyzed in largely individual terms, pragmatists agree that critical reflection is inextricably social. But it is also a pragmatic point that even "private" beliefs, if they are genuine beliefs at all, have consequences for others. Just think of a sexist, a vegetarian, or a teetotaller. If privatization creates a safe haven for beliefs that *ought to* be critically discussed in public, then perhaps Rorty's compromise is not very successful, especially not as a piece of cultural politics.

Eberhard Herrmann, a Swedish philosopher of religion, offers an attempt to overcome the risk that pragmatic focus on the individual makes religion a subjective affair by linking objectivity to our shared existential condition. Human beings are always situated in a reality that offers resistance and constantly threatens to frustrate our purposes. To deal with such resistance in the best possible way(s), humans have developed practices (with different conceptualizations) such as science, which enable us to predict and control the environment better than before.

But, Herrmann argues, reality offers not only physical resistance, but also existential resistance. We are contingent beings that experience love, hatred, grief, joy, birth, flourishing, illness, and death in the course of life, and though science may help us cure illness and postpone death, it cannot afford existential meaning to experiences as the above mentioned. Here, we see the outlines of a Deweyan division of labor between science and religion: for certain purposes, we need science, for others, we need *views of life*—religious and/or nonreligious pictures of what life is like at its best—which provide us with existential "orientation" and help us articulate what it is, existentially, to be human.

Since the human existential condition is shared, views of life are no private fancies. In fact, views of life are discussed all the time, for instance in films, novels, sermons, and so on. Through experience and critical discussion we learn that we cannot simply live as if death were no big deal, or as if lovers can be treated in just any way. Given views of life's orientating function, it is always possible to raise the question whether a certain view of life is *adequate* or not—that is, whether it supplies us with insights about the human existential condition that we can acknowledge and draw on in our transactions with the environment. (Herrmann, 2004)

Pragmatism and contemporary philosophy of religion

Before I close, let us look at how pragmatism relates to contemporary mainstream Anglo-American philosophy of religion. One of the central, albeit disputed, distinctions within contemporary philosophy of religion is that between religious *cognitivism* (religious beliefs are *about* a being that either exists or does not exist, and they are, thus, either true or false), and *noncognitivism* (religious beliefs are not about some religious "object," but should be understood in some other—moral, spiritual—way, where the distinction between true and false does not apply, or only applies in a highly qualified sense). Mainstream philosophy of religion is clearly cognitively oriented, and examines the "evidence"—the arguments of natural theology, religious experience, miracles, the problem of evil, and so on—to see whether theism or atheism is the most reasonable stance.

From a pragmatic viewpoint, the cognitive/noncognitive distinction looks rather problematic. It seems to somewhat arbitrarily link cognitivism almost exclusively to discourse about objects, a rather unpragmatic view. Dewey is arguably a cognitivist about religious beliefs in the sense that ideals are as open to critical reflection as other beliefs, though from a mainstream perspective, his approach is clearly noncognitivist, since it rejects the idea that talk of God is about some "object." The distinction also looks awkward when applied to James, who seems cognitivist enough when he keeps the door open for supernatural agency, but not so cognitivist when he scorns traditional arguments for God's existence and argues for the use of pragmatic criteria in their place.

The really important question from a pragmatic perspective is hence not whether religious beliefs are about some object or not, but rather, as Richard Bernstein puts it, "whether a religious believer (or a nonbeliever) is committed to the type of open critical dialogue that has been central to the pragmatic tradition" (Bernstein, 2003, p. 139). How we *regulate* beliefs is more important than what they are (allegedly) about, and on the former issue, James' and Dewey's positions are actually rather similar.

However, the stress on the pragmatic testing of religion may lead to another charge from the side of philosophy of religion: that pragmatists are not describing religion *as it is*, but saying something about what they think religion *should* be like. In the terms of a common distinction: pragmatists are *revisionists* rather than committed to *describing* religion from the perspective of "ordinary" believers. The underlying idea here is, of course, that cognitively oriented theistic philosophy of religion does justice to the believers' perspective ("ordinary believers *really* believe that God exists"), in a way that revisionists do not.

Although Dewey and Rorty would not object to the revisionist label, it might seem strange that a tradition that prides itself with taking the experiences of flesh-and-blood human beings seriously seemingly comes down squarely on the revisionist side. However, as was the case with the former distinction, I believe that here, too, the important insight underlying the distinction between descriptive and revisionist accounts can be retained, perhaps even better articulated, in a pragmatic framework.

Presumably, the problem with revisionist accounts is not their appeal to values *per se*, since some values are, arguably, *internal* elements of religion. Problems seem to arise where appeal is made to some *external* values, such as Rorty's appeal to civil peace in support of his proposed privatization of religion. However, it is not clear that the internal/external distinction matters much in concrete cases. Let me illustrate with a simple example. For some time now, tennis enthusiasts have discussed whether the rule that it is permitted to serve a second time if your first serve fails, should be dropped. One line of argument is that tennis as a sport has been impoverished by the one-sided focus on serves that the current rules have led to. Another line of argument is that the current set of rules makes tennis less entertaining, which means less public interest and fewer sponsors. Arguably, the first line of argument appeals to values that are relatively more internal to tennis as a practice than those appealed to in the second, but it is not clear that a person moved by both arguments is less committed to tennis than someone who only acknowledges the first kind of argument—on any realistic analysis of "committed." This is because, pragmatists insist, reflective judgments go beyond the confines of any limited range of internal considerations and aim to be "all things considered" judgments—and if you are really committed to tennis, then things like public perception of tennis matters.

What is the upshot of this for religion? Well, if religion (or tennis) were an insulated sphere of life, only internal values would matter. But religion is inevitably tangled up with all spheres of life for the simple reason that religious believers are never "mere" believers: they are also men and women, citizens, family members, friends, relatives, colleagues, employees, and so on. Given this entanglement, the really critical question we need to ask when we seek a platform for critical reflection on religion is not whether this or that value is internal or external to religion *per se*, but whether at least a significant number of religious believers are prepared to acknowledge it as valid and relevant. Since religious believers are as heterogeneous as any other groups, we should not expect that they will all agree here. Accordingly, not all believers will be moved by the same kind of criticism, but this is only a problem if you retain unrealistically high standards for what critical reflection must accomplish to have a point.

The important insight of the internal/external distinction is, I believe, that philosophical reflection on religion must take religion *seriously*. For many people, religion is not an optional lifestyle (though for some it is), something that critical reflection on religion must acknowledge. We need not, however, succumb to the normative self-understanding of those religious authorities which claim that external values are completely irrelevant for genuinely religious believers. Neither should we take for granted—as I pointed out in the section on James—that cognitively oriented mainstream philosophy of religion, committed to examination of evidence for and against God's existence, actually takes religion very seriously.

Summary

A crucial task for pragmatic philosophy of religion is thus to show that taking religion seriously by starting with the way it functions in human life is no obstacle for critical reflection, but rather a precondition of it. Only once we understand how religion functions in human life, can we come to see how a pragmatic critique of religion—aiming to make the "good" of religion more secure in existence by critically discussing the problems that arise within religious practices, and in our attempts to relate these practices to other spheres of life—is important.

Taking religion seriously is, then, from a pragmatic point of view something different than weighing evidence for and against God's existence, or simply succumbing to the normative self-understanding of religious authorities. Despite its special status in many people's lives, religion is much like any other human practice: it is only when it is put to use by humans of flesh and blood that we can detect problems and seek for better approaches. The pragmatic imperative is thus the same here as elsewhere: do not block the path of inquiry!

References

Bernstein, R. (2003), "Pragmatism's Common Faith," in S. Rosenbaum (ed.), *Pragmatism and Religion: Classical Sources and Original Essays*. Urbana: University of Illinois Press, pp. 129–140.

Dewey, J. (1929), *The Quest for Certainty: A Study of the Relation of Knowledge and Action*. New York: Minton Balch.

—(1934), *A Common Faith*. New Haven: Yale University Press.

Eldridge, M. (1998), *Transforming Experience: John Dewey's Cultural Instrumentalism*. Nashville: Vanderbilt University Press.

Herrmann, E. (2004), *Religion, Reality, and a Good Life*. Tübingen: Mohr Siebeck.

James, W. (1897), *The Will to Believe and Other Popular Essays in Philosophy*. New York: Longmans Green.

—(1902), *The Varieties of Religious Experience: A Study in Human Nature*. New York: Modern Library.

Rockefeller, S. (2003), "Faith and Ethics in an Interdependent World," in S. Rosenbaum (ed.), *Pragmatism and Religion: Classical Sources and Original Essays*. Urbana: University of Illinois Press, pp. 303–320.

Rorty, R. (1999), "Religion as Conversation-stopper," in R. Rorty, *Philosophy and Social Hope*. London: Penguin Books, pp. 168–174.

—(2007), *Philosophy as Cultural Politics* (Philosophical Papers vol. 4). Cambridge: Cambridge University Press.

15

New Directions

Sami Pihlström

This chapter, dealing with meta-philosophical issues in pragmatism and comparisons between pragmatism and some other traditions of contemporary philosophy, is above all concerned with the future of pragmatism as a philosophical orientation and framework. Having examined in some detail various special issues arising within pragmatism, both in the individual articles above and in the chapter on research methods and problems (Chapter 2), we will now return to a relatively general level of discussion and again take a look at pragmatism as a whole—as a philosophical approach that, hopefully, has an interesting future, not as an isolated corner in today's philosophical debates but in continuous dialogue with other philosophies.

Having briefly shown in the introductory materials (especially the chapter "Research Methods and Problems") how pragmatism offers a distinctive perspective on different philosophical problem areas, including metaphysics, philosophy of mind, philosophy of value, and philosophy of religion, we should now, in order to understand the potential future developments of pragmatism, take up a number of *meta-philosophical* issues concerning the nature of pragmatist approaches. To be sure, we have already examined meta-philosophical problems, including the status of the pragmatist "contextuality thesis" invoked in Chapter 2. This time the relevant meta-philosophical issues are, however, even more general. Here, again, we will be employing the pragmatic method (at a meta-level), trying to determine what results, in practice, in the contexts of inquiry (and life) we are in, from our pragmatist ways of dealing with the problems just mentioned.

Historical and systematic approaches

Again, it must be emphasized that in adequate pragmatism scholarship in different fields—of which more specialized treatments have been given in the individual contributions—an *entanglement of historical and systematic, argumentative, analytic approaches* is necessary. The historical development of a philosophical problem may be a crucial element of the context within which it may be pragmatically approached. There are no ahistorical—acontextual—philosophical problems or ahistorical ways of solving problems, let alone ahistorical "results" of philosophical inquiry. Pragmatists should be among the first to recognize this historicity and contextuality, while avoiding the relativistic assumptions that we are simply "trapped" within our historical circumstances and can never critically transcend our particular starting point or context.

This entanglement of historical and systematic approaches can be illuminated by an example we are already familiar with—the realism issue. It was the systematic debate over scientific realism, with its more generally epistemological and metaphysical overtones, that led to a new interest in pragmatism as a promising via media, an alternative to both radical relativism or constructivism and strong (metaphysical) realism in the philosophy of science. When Putnam and other neo-pragmatists developed such mediating solutions, the most famous of which was undoubtedly Putnam's (1981) internal realism, they did not yet refer to the classical pragmatists, at least not in any great detail. However, as soon as it was realized that the new mediating positions in the realism debate had a lot of common ground with pragmatism, philosophers' interest turned toward the pragmatist classics, too. Obviously, those classics had been studied independently of the analytic realism debate, but that debate definitely gave a fertilization injection to such scholarship. In addition, as the realism debate inevitably has a Kantian background as well—just think of Kant's famous attempt to reconcile empirical realism with transcendental idealism—it also turns out (largely thanks to Putnam, once again) necessary to take seriously the Kantian aspects of the "mediating" solutions. Realizing this leads us to another observation: it is important to study not just the pragmatist or the Kantian background of current controversies over realism, but also the mutual relations between these two only apparently independent backgrounds. In short, it is necessary to take seriously the Kantian background of pragmatism itself and the role played by the intertwinement of Kantian and pragmatist ideas in the realism debate.

Accordingly, continuing the realism debate in contemporary philosophy requires at least some familiarity with both classical pragmatism and Kant. Thus, pragmatism scholarship and Kant scholarship should not be as separate from each other as they seem to be in the increasingly specializing world of contemporary academic philosophy. More generally, historical pragmatism scholarship is only rarely "merely" historical. From its inception, pragmatism has set out to transform the ways we use and determine the meaning of our concepts. This progressive, forward-looking attitude is also maintained when pragmatists look into the past of their own tradition. The classical figures of pragmatism are studied in order to genuinely learn from them and to put their ideas into work amidst our contemporary concerns—whether in the realism debate or elsewhere. Part of this program of putting old ideas to work may be the attempt to trace out their connections with *other* old (or new) ideas, including Kantian ones.

Constructive and deconstructive approaches

Another meta-philosophical issue regarding pragmatists' ways of approaching the above-mentioned (and other) philosophical problems may be put in terms of a contrast familiar from recent Wittgenstein scholarship: should the pragmatist examine her/his philosophical problems *constructively* and *substantively*, seeking to offer new theoretical (albeit practice-oriented), even metaphysical, insights into them, or rather *therapeutically* or even *deconstructively*, seeking to demonstrate that those problems are not (or need not be) genuine problems for us, or that we can get rid of them by means of pragmatist intellectual "therapy"? Well-known recent interpreters of Wittgenstein, including James Conant, Cora Diamond, and Stephen Mulhall, have preferred the latter way of understanding Wittgenstein's attitude to philosophical problems and philosophizing "without theses," while others (e.g., P.M.S. Hacker, Danièle Moyal-Sharrock) have defended more traditional ways of reading Wittgenstein as a philosopher engaged in (though perhaps not in entirely traditional ways) argumentation and constructive philosophizing, sometimes with pragmatic or even pragmatist insights.[1]

This controversy between two very different conceptions of philosophical methodology and philosophical problems can be seen to be present in pragmatists' disagreements, too, especially in the Putnam versus Rorty debate. A qualified defense of genuine, constructive, substantial philosophical inquiry within pragmatism can, I believe, be offered. Again, the realism issue is an illuminating case. Some (neo-)pragmatists, including Rorty, want to eliminate this entire issue, viewing it as little more than a remnant of the unglorious past of systematic philosophy that we should set aside. More specifically, Rorty argues that the realism issue only arises within representationalism, and as soon as one adopts pragmatic anti-representationalism, giving up the view that there are any representational relations between language and the world, the issue itself disappears (see Rorty, 1991, 1998). In contrast, Putnam's neo-pragmatism takes the problem of realism much more seriously, though also criticizing many standard versions of both realism and antirealism. Throughout his writings on realism and related matters, Putnam (1981, 1990, 1994, 2004) has sought to avoid metaphysical realism as well as radical relativism, but he has never claimed that the problem as a whole should be just deconstructed or eliminated. It is a deep problem we cannot help dealing with, even if (or especially if) we are pragmatists.

Pragmatism, we might say, is constructive and systematic philosophy precisely by being deconstructive and therapeutic in the right place and in the right way, that is, by deconstructing pernicious traditional dichotomies and assumptions, such as the ones between mind and body, facts and values, or even theism and atheism (or religious and secular approaches). Such dichotomies may hinder the free movement of philosophical thought. Insofar as we get rid of them, we may reconstruct the traditional controversies surrounding them and arrive at new insights. Therefore, deconstructive and (re)constructive philosophical work are not opposed to each other in pragmatism but may supplement each other.

Academic and public intellectuals

Can pragmatists be *public intellectuals*? A full discussion of this question—yet another meta-philosophical issue—would require drawing attention to both historical figures (e.g., James) and contemporary ones (e.g., Cornel West in the United States, Jürgen Habermas in Germany, or the late Georg Henrik von Wright in Scandinavia). At the same time, it may be asked whether pragmatism amounts to something like *applied philosophy*, or whether, on the contrary, the distinction between theory and its applications ought to be given up in pragmatism. Arguably, this distinction is of only limited applicability, insofar as we are committed to a pragmatist conception of theory, according to which *any* humanly interesting theory is potentially practically relevant in the first place, all the way from the beginning. Pragmatism might even be "defined"—though keeping in mind the problems with defining it, as discussed in the "Introduction" above—as a philosophical perspective *denying* any sharp theory versus practice dichotomy (see Pihlström, 1996, 2005). Insofar as that dichotomy is assumed in the very notion of applied philosophy, that notion is incompatible with pragmatism and needs deconstruction instead of reconstruction.

Once more, the problem of realism may serve as an example here. Our being-in-the-world is a deep problem concerning us all, hence calling for a Jamesian kind of "popular philosophy" intended to potentially everyone interested in problems in being human, yet it is a problem too deep to be adequately articulated in terms of a crude dichotomy between philosophical theory and its applications. We must be realists of some kind to make sense of the world we live in; however, metaphysical realism is, according to pragmatism (and neo-pragmatists like Putnam), hopeless. We must discuss this issue both accessibly—maintaining its relevance to a wide audience—and profoundly, without sacrificing its truly philosophical aspects. It may be difficult to maintain a balance between popularized approaches and rigorous philosophical argumentation, but pragmatists must continuously try to take both sides into account.

In addition to the problem of realism—the problem ultimately concerning our relation to the world we live in—many other philosophical issues are of potentially broad relevance. Obviously, pragmatist explorations of mind and subjectivity, or metaphysics in general, let alone moral and social values, are highly relevant to people's daily concerns, at least if such explorations can be formulated in a sufficiently accessible manner. Accordingly, one need not be a "public philosopher" or a popularizer in order to be able to discuss philosophical issues of human relevance. Whatever one's scope, whatever one's degree of specialization, a pragmatist way of philosophizing should always already be in touch with the world as experienced by us humans as problematic.

Interdisciplinarity and the "Road of Inquiry"

We have seen how pragmatism can help to overcome several unhelpful dualisms. Sharp dichotomies or boundaries between different academic disciplines may also be among such dualisms. For example, it may be important to take a critical stand to the often too easily invoked dualism between the natural and the human sciences. As we have noted, there is a sense in which all sciences are human sciences, offering human perspectives on the world we live in. Again, the issue of realism is crucial here, because we need to avoid both metaphysical realism—which in its contemporary versions tends to raise natural science, especially physics, to the status of a privileged representation of the world as it is in itself—and relativism, which threatens to stop all normative conversation on the criteria of good inquiry.

Let me examine a hopefully illuminating example, the current situation of the human sciences, a bit more closely.[2] I see basically three challenges we need to take up. First, a major challenge coming *from outside the academia* is the increasing tendency to view universities in general instrumentally as means to certain extra-academic ends. Let us call this the challenge of (naïve) *instrumentalism*. Universities, as well as other institutions of research and higher education, are more and more considered valuable merely, or at least primarily, because they produce useful knowledge—"innovations" that may eventually support the environing society and the economic system—not because of their intrinsic value or the value of truth and knowledge as such. The worry is by no means unique to the human sciences but concerns also the natural sciences: basic research, we increasingly feel, is threatened by the strengthening demand for immediately applicable results.

This first challenge can be met, and should continuously be met, by reminding the political leaders (upon whom at least state research funding depends) and the general public that the very notion of "useful knowledge" ought to be broadened from narrow usefulness in relation to certain specific goals to a much more inclusive notion of usefulness in relation to human life generally. The human sciences are clearly "useful" for us, as they investigate some of the most basic problems in being human. By replacing instrumentalism with a richer pragmatist perspective on research as a human practice, we can maintain both the traditional view of academic autonomy and the idea that scientific research (whether within humanities or generally) is "useful." This, at least, would have been all the classical pragmatists' perspective on the matter. None of them was a narrow instrumentalist in the sense described here. The kind of relevance to human practices that the classical pragmatists were interested in when developing their views on meaning, knowledge, inquiry, and truth was significantly broader than the technocratic relevance familiar from recent political jargon.

In addition, academics and other defenders of basic research have, with good reason, repeatedly reminded the instrumentalistically and technocratically oriented politicians that the most profound innovations and applications can be reached in the long run only if basic research is granted a significant degree of autonomy. Accordingly, it is the notion of useful knowledge itself, rather than traditional academic freedom, that requires pragmatist re-conceptualization and rearticulation. On the other hand, this rethinking also concerns the notion of basic research: we should not deny the "usefulness" of the kind of research whose motivation arises from concerns internal to the academic world.

The technocratic demand for applicable results foreseeable in advance ("where to invest money and resources most effectively") is contrary to the celebration of *contingency, novelty,* and *plurality* characteristic of academic institutions and genuine academic innovativeness. Our human ability to freely create new ideas and put them to work, in a broad sense of "work," is taken seriously by pragmatism, which encourages us to test all of our ideas and theories by future experience and to fallibilistically admit the permanent possibility of error and the resulting need to learn from one's mistakes. This is the spirit of scientific inquiry as conceived by thinkers like Peirce and Dewey. As Richard Bernstein (2005) has shown in his profound small book on the "abuse of evil" in contemporary political and religious discourse, such pragmatic fallibilism has relevance outside the philosophy of science, too.

The second challenge I want to focus on comes *from within the academia* but basically *from outside the human sciences*: one frequently hears natural scientists, physicists among others, claiming that it is up to natural sciences, especially physics, to describe and explain reality at the most fundamental level. Let us call this the challenge of *scientism*. Physics, we are told, offers "full coverage" (to borrow a phrase from Quine). Certainly, I am not claiming that physicists themselves, or the majority of them, would inevitably view physics as the most important science, or more important than the humanities. Rather, this challenge is very strong in contemporary philosophy: for example, philosophy of mind today is strongly physicalistically oriented. On the other hand, several philosophical orientations, including phenomenology and Wittgensteinian approaches, have been sharply critical of such physicalist and scientistic tendencies of reducing human experience and conceptual capacities to something that is ultimately explainable in terms of natural science.

The threat here is an increasing polarization of the academic world—the "two cultures" debate all over again, to some extent paralleling the traditional *Erklären versus Verstehen* (explanation vs. understanding) opposition. For us within the humanities, the challenge is to maintain *both* a healthy respect for the very important work done within the natural sciences *and* an antireductionist perspective on whatever it is that the human sciences are doing. Here it would be impossible to defend in any philosophical detail the view that human experience, subjectivity, language- and concept-use, values, and so on, cannot be either ontologically or explanatorily reduced to entities and processes describable by natural science. Again, I do see hope in the pragmatist attempt to integrate nonreductive naturalism with a deeply culturalist understanding of human beings as irreducibly cultural and social creatures (See the section on pragmatism and the philosophy of mind in Chapter 2 above: "Research Methods and Problems.").

We should, as the classical pragmatists did, actively seek a dialogue between natural-scientific and humanistic orientations, arguing that in an important sense *all* sciences are human sciences, committed to viewing the world from a human perspective. Instead of polarization, dualism, or dichotomies, I would argue for a continuous nonscientistic rethinking of *the unity of science*—clearly not in the logical positivists' (scientistic) sense but in a sense continuously learning from both sides of the supposed dichotomy. All sciences, according to this radically revised picture of the unity of science, are value-laden in the sense that any normatively constrained inquiry presupposes a context of value commitments, and is indeed *possible* only in such a context. An ethical orientation in the world is necessary for anything like scientific inquiry to be so much as possible for us. This insight could even be developed into a Kantian-like transcendental argument. The important point here is that physicalism (or scientism generally) has a "blind spot": it is incapable of understanding itself, or the kind of reasoning resulting in such a position, as an outcome of an ethically—and more generally normatively—oriented scientific inquiry and argumentation.

Finally, the third challenge we must consider is *internal to the human sciences themselves*. What I have in mind is the tendency—closely related to the above-described threat of polarization—of some people within the humanities (including philosophers) to give up all objective or even intersubjective standards of methodological rigor. Let us, lacking a better term, call this the challenge of *relativism*. This familiar issue arises from a legitimate need to protect the autonomy of the human sciences from both technocracy and the scientistic (imperialist) pressures that are felt to come from the side of the natural sciences. The critique of scientism may, however, go too far. Sometimes it goes as far as the claim that there are no normative criteria for good and bad research at all, no methodological norms that could be set up from any meta-perspective over and above whatever it is that individual researchers and groups of scholars are contingently doing. Science, then, would be just one narrative among others, just one way of telling stories about ourselves (in the case of the human sciences) or about the environing world (the natural sciences). Radical philosophers of science like Paul Feyerabend (1975) and controversial neo-pragmatists like Rorty (1982) have been seen as advancing this position, though it is debatable whether their actual views can be interpreted in such a way. At least the classical pragmatists were not guilty of relativism in the sense in which, say, Karl Popper (1994) has called it the "myth of the framework"; instead of relativism, they may be said to have embraced an "engaged pluralism" (see Bernstein, 2005, 2010).

There is no easy way out of the problem framework of relativism; it is something we have to live with. However, *continuous critical methodological self-reflection* is needed as the (only) way of responding to this challenge. Again, I see the pragmatists as offering plenty of resources for such reflection. The kind of dialogue between the human and the natural sciences promoted above can be seen as an important element of this methodological self-reflection. Obviously, a reflective attitude to the methods one uses—contrary to the habit of some scholars of just sticking to the methods one has contingently learned and come to employ—is something that ought to characterize, and thereby integrate, all scientific disciplines; hence, again, I am recommending a new way of maintaining the *unity* of science amidst all the undeniable differences in concrete methods employed.

Maintaining the spirit of pragmatic fallibilism and the resulting acknowledgment of human contingency both in science and elsewhere requires that we give up all "first-philosophical" dreams of grounding our inquiries on an unshakeable foundation. Insofar as we want to achieve that without despair, we might better be pragmatists.

One aspect of the rejection of first philosophy is the acknowledgment of the need for deepening *interdisciplinarity*—not only multidisciplinarity—in our inquiries into the world and ourselves. Pragmatism is, arguably, an inherently interdisciplinary approach in inquiry, because pragmatists oppose all dichotomies and boundaries that may "block the road of inquiry" (quoting Peirce's famous words). Of course, in practice there may be cases in which it is difficult to determine what exactly interdisciplinarity should mean. For example, in interdisciplinary research institutions, there might be at least three alternative "readings" of this requirement, significantly varying in strength. (i) According to the strongest conception of interdisciplinarity, each individual scholar and/or research project might be required to be "internally" interdisciplinary (though possibly there can be degrees in the strength of interdisciplinarity). Thus, no scholar/project should represent a single academic discipline but must represent at least two (or, perhaps preferably, more). (ii) According to a somewhat weaker interpretation, an individual scholar and/or project can represent just one discipline, but they must be open to interdisciplinary relations to other disciplines. There must be "interdisciplinary potential" in a research proposal, even though it need not be internally interdisciplinary. (iii) The weakest interpretation requires only the interdisciplinary research institution as a whole to be truly interdisciplinary. This allows individual scholars and/or projects to be even relatively strictly "disciplinary," but their combination must be such that (perhaps unexpected) interdisciplinary cooperation may grow out of it.

How should the "correct strength" of the interdisciplinarity requirement be determined? There is no immediate answer to the question of how strong interdisciplinarity pragmatism should promote. On the contrary, this is again a contextually pragmatic matter. The pragmatic value of interdisciplinarity should always be relativized to the aims or goals of the particular inquiry (or institution) considered.

An obvious example of philosophical interdisciplinarity is the debate over *naturalism*—a debate to which pragmatists since Dewey have made major contributions. Traditional philosophical inquiry is "pure" in the sense of being strictly conceptual and nonempirical: epistemology is understood as a nonempirical study of knowledge, justification, and related concepts; philosophy of science as a nonempirical study of the scientific method, scientific inference, scientific explanation, and so on. However, naturalism, including pragmatic naturalism, rejects this ideal of purity, arguing that philosophical inquiry should be interdisciplinary in the sense of being more closely connected with empirical inquiry. Philosophical issues, problems, concepts, or theories can, and should, be "naturalized" by reinterpreting them in terms of concepts and theories available in empirical science. (Relevant examples include naturalized epistemology, philosophy of mind informed by neuroscience and cognitive science, as well as human sciences based on evolutionary approaches.)

Now, again, there are stronger and weaker forms of naturalism: (i) *reductive* naturalism maintains that philosophical problems and/or concepts can be reduced to empirical or scientific ones; while (ii) *non-reductive* naturalism is satisfied with the weaker claim that philosophical problems and/or concepts can be illuminated by means of empirical inquiry, but they cannot be reduced to the latter. The pragmatist is typically a non-reductive naturalist (see also "Introduction" above), but in order to keep the road of inquiry open in an interdisciplinary spirit, even this commitment should not be a dogmatic one. In some carefully considered cases even a reductive naturalist approach might be pragmatically welcome; this once again depends on the context of inquiry and the aims and goals that guide it.

Arguably, the philosophical advancement of interdisciplinarity itself needs "discipline." Here we should go back to Kant's *Critique of Pure Reason* (1781/1787), especially its Doctrine of Method, which contains an often neglected chapter on "The Discipline of Pure Reason." Human reason, Kant reminds us, needs discipline to protect it from arriving at misconceptions and methods or approaches leading to illegitimate metaphysical speculation. Any reason-use, however interdisciplinary, needs "discipline" in this sense: critical self-reflection on the purposes, background assumptions, and methodological approaches of the research one engages in. (In Kant, this reflection focuses, e.g., on the differences between philosophy and mathematics.) The pragmatist cannot offer any direct solutions to the problems of how to promote interdisciplinarity and how to interpret this ideal. Pragmatism, however, may encourage philosophers and other scholars to reflect on these issues in the spirit of "Kantian discipline"—by taking seriously the crucial requirement of the self-discipline of human reason, of constant vigilance of one's own reflective capacities and limitations as an inquirer. This critical reflection should be extended to all the individual and social practices of inquiry we engage in. Thus, it is, at least potentially, a deeply interdisciplinary process. In such a critical promotion of interdisciplinarity, pragmatism may then have enormous future potential, at least insofar as it does not completely abandon its Kantian background (cf. "Introduction").

Pragmatism as pluralistic anti-foundationalism

Pragmatic fallibilism, as described above, should lead us to understand pragmatism as a deeply *anti-foundationalist* philosophy. Pragmatism emphasizes contingency and openness to novelty in experience; this emphasis should be seen as a distinctive characteristic of the pragmatic method.

In his important book on the concept of evil[3] and its abuse in contemporary politics and religion, Richard Bernstein (2005) helpfully distinguishes the "mentality" of pragmatic fallibilism from the opposed mentality of absoluteness, of rigid dichotomies, of moral certainty based on a religious (or some other) authority. He notes, for instance, that "we can (and must) learn to live without 'metaphysical comfort,' to live with a realistic sense of unpredictable contingencies—and at the same time to have a passionate commitment to understand, resist, and fight concrete evils and oppose injustices" (ibid., p. 13). It is striking how well this insight applies not just to politics and religion (Bernstein's concern here) but also to science. The scientific analogy to the lack of metaphysical comfort is the hopelessness of any naïve form of scientific realism according to which our theories simply correspond to the way the world mind- and theory-independently is. The relevant kind of unpredictable *contingency* is based on human creativity and (genuine) innovativeness, on the fact that, given the ways in which we differ from each other and are, each one of us, unique persons and unique inquirers, our ideas and thoughts cannot be predicted in advance.

Without such contingency in life and inquiry there would be no inquiry, either in science or in common life, at all. It is hardly implausible to suggest that pragmatism is, perhaps uniquely, capable of integrating living without metaphysical comfort (both in science and in general) with "passionate commitment"—whether to the fighting against evil or to the pursuit of truth.

Note also how Bernstein draws on Hannah Arendt's conception of *plurality*: "[. . .] Arendt gives plurality a distinctive political meaning. Plurality involves individuality, distinction, and equality. There is distinctiveness about each and every individual who brings to a common world a unique perspective. And this plurality is rooted in our *natality*, the capacity to begin, to initiate action spontaneously. . . . Human plurality is the basic condition of action and speech, because they take place *in between* human beings in their singularity and plurality" (ibid., p. 73). Arendt, as is well known, analyzed totalitarianism and the concentration camps as attempts to liquidate such plurality and distinctiveness. On a considerably less dramatic scale, attempts to force scientific inquiry and the creativity it requires into clearly foreseeable structures subordinated to strictly planned innovation and technology policies might be regarded as another, obviously very different, attempt to chain human plurality.

From a pragmatist perspective, there is actually a plurality of pluralisms. For example, one might ask what exactly James's famous pluralism amounts to. It could be argued that pluralism, in *A Pluralistic Universe* (James, 1909b), ultimately amounts to a metaphysical theory according to which there are bits and pieces of "pure experience" pretty much everywhere, and that it is therefore inseparable from James's radical empiricism. James's theory can undoubtedly be read in this way. However, a somewhat different approach may also be proposed: perhaps pluralism, for James, is not primarily a *metaphysical* doctrine but a *meta-philosophical* one, emphasizing the possibility of a plurality of different "correct" metaphysical positions maintained from different practice-embedded perspectives. This latter kind of pluralism emphasizes the plurality of legitimate ways of viewing the world; hence, it might be employed to support the kind of academic freedom and contingency of individual perspectives defended above. Among James's works, this alternative comes closer to the argument of

Pragmatism (as well as the later defense of "conceptual relativity" by Putnam and other neo-pragmatists).

In fact, it is hard to see how James's metaphysical doctrine of pure experience, analog to the view known as "neutral monism," favored at some point by Ernst Mach and Bertrand Russell, among others, could be seriously regarded as "pluralistic." *Could* such a monism really be a form of pluralism? Shouldn't we, rather, maintain the possibility for metaphysical monism(s) only within a pluralism of different metaphysical frameworks? Such frameworks would all be pragmatically accountable within a more inclusive pragmatic pluralism. Analogously, the pluralism relevant to academic freedom does not just encourage the production of a quantitative plurality of scientific contributions—ever new journal articles and research projects—but also the opening up of qualitatively novel ways of exploring and understanding reality.

This, then, is what we may mean by talking about a plurality of pluralisms. There are both metaphysical and (at a meta-level) conceptual, methodological, and meta-philosophical versions of pluralism. But there is also a social and political aspect to James's treatment of pluralism, possibly indebted to R. W. Emerson's version of individualism. We should understand that complete unification is a false ideal and "resist undue centralization and excessive organization"; we should let individual human potentialities "grow from their own resources" (Callaway, 2008, p. xxxi). Integrating such natural growth of human potentialities into our conception of science and research is a major challenge for pragmatists and has obvious consequences for the future of academic freedom.

The challenge of maintaining genuine contingency in human life, scientific life included, is also a key challenge for any such pragmatist inquiries. If Dewey and the other classical pragmatists were correct, this challenge can be met only by supporting *democracy*, not just as a political system—either generally or in science policy—but as a deep, substantive way of life, an ethical ideal requiring internal moral development. Again, we may find Bernstein's remarks appropriate here:

> Those who share a democratic faith that abhors the appeal to rigid ideologies must seek alliances with like-minded individuals throughout the world. There is also a lesson to be learned from Dewey and Arendt. Both teach us how *fragile* democracy really is—how its fate is always uncertain. There are no guarantees that it will persist and flourish. . . . There is a *democratic ethos* that must be kept alive. And this takes constant attention, work, and practice. The creation and sustenance of what Dewey called "creative democracy" is *always* a task before us. (Bernstein, 2005, p. 122.)

Moreover, at a meta-level, the question of how best to keep alive the "democratic ethos" can itself be adequately approached *only in a democratic spirit*, listening to a plurality of voices. There can be no undemocratic way of experimentally testing the "hypothesis" of democracy either in science or in politics.

This reflexive inquiry is endless, if only because the project of *self-applying* pragmatic fallibilism and the pragmatic method is endless. We must be constantly wary of not constructing oversimplified dichotomies—also those between, say, the two "mentalities" of pragmatic fallibilism and the dogmatic search for absolutes either in science or elsewhere. This, in fact, is what I see as slightly problematic in Bernstein's (ibid.) admirable discussion. We should never be certain that our own pragmatically naturalist and fallibilist position is the absolutely correct one but must constantly seek to self-critically examine *its* fundamental presuppositions. Indeed, we cannot be sure it is fallibilistic enough. This is our permanently groundless predicament, our contingency—the kind of contingency the pragmatists never failed to acknowledge.

Let us therefore recall the following words by James, whose active, life-celebrating, melioristic pragmatism was always surrounded not only by the acknowledgment of the reality of evil but also by a full realization of the fragility of our natural human projects, scientific and non-scientific alike:

> Must not something end by supporting itself? Humanism is willing to let finite experience be self-supporting. Somewhere being must immediately breast nonentity. Why may not the advancing front of experience, carrying its immanent satisfactions and dissatisfactions, cut against the black inane as the luminous orb of the moon cuts the caerulean abyss? (James, 1909a, pp. 55–56.)

Pragmatism and other philosophical traditions

I want to conclude this chapter and this entire *Companion* by comparing the pragmatist approach(es) to some of the other philosophical traditions and their methods. Once more, the issue of realism is most relevant in such comparisons. I hope to be able to illuminate my suggestion (made in Chapter 2 above) that the pragmatic method is a meta-method to be used for evaluating different philosophical methods. This dialogue of different traditions will, I suggest, become even more important in the future, and the vitality of a philosophical orientation may to a great extent be measured in terms of its ability to engage in such dialogues. Some non-pragmatist orientations, including very technical analytic philosophy and some esoteric brands of postmodernism (or "Continental philosophy," whatever that means), may not fare too well in this regard.

First, pragmatism clearly shares with *analytic philosophy* the emphasis on argumentative rigor and conceptual clarity (though relatively few pragmatists are willing to phrase their arguments in formal language). What pragmatism does not share with (at least some parts of) analytic philosophy is the occasional narrow-mindedness of the latter. Very often, analytic debates in epistemology, metaphysics, or the philosophy of mind are narrowly focused in the sense that voices from outside one's own tradition—from, say, pragmatism or phenomenology or Wittgenstein studies—are not taken seriously at all. Pragmatism scholarship, in my view, is at its best when it truly communicates with other traditions, including of course analytic philosophy.

Secondly, pragmatism shares with *phenomenology* the attempt to draw attention to (subjective or intersubjective) experience. However, it does not accept some phenomenologists' foundationalist approaches that wish to offer an a priori foundation for the sciences, for instance—nor the related dream of presuppositionlessness, the attempt to start from an absolutely certain standpoint with all "natural" presuppositions, including the existence of a natural world, "bracketed." Pragmatism, as we have seen, can even be "transcendental" without being foundationalist.

Thirdly, I have already indicated how our being-in-the-world—to use Heideggerian terminology—can be seen as a basic problem in pragmatism. This is something that pragmatism shares with *existentialism* and *hermeneutics*. Together with these in many ways rather different philosophical orientations, pragmatism emphasizes our self-understanding, as well as our need to take seriously our mortality and turn toward the future, to the ways in which the experienced world opens to us. In Sartrean jargon, "man is a project," never completed, and this is something that most pragmatists would be happy to subscribe to—without, however, subscribing to the thesis that human existence is absurd. It is precisely by understanding ourselves as incomplete projects that we may revolt against absurdity.

Fourthly, pragmatism—or at least some currents within pragmatism, especially Deweyan ones—are at least as actively political and aiming at social justice as *critical theory* (or the Frankfurt School), despite the latter's key representatives', especially Max Horkheimer's, uncompromising critique of pragmatism as being based on instrumental reason. What pragmatism does not share with critical theory is the latter's deep cultural pessimism. Pragmatism looks toward the future and, for example, to the development of modern technology, more open-mindedly, refusing to allow technological determinism and pessimism to overshadow the positive promises inherent in the development of new methods of thinking and acting in the world.[4]

Fifthly, and finally, pragmatism is (as repeatedly indicated in the editorial materials of this book) reinterpretable as a form of (Kantian-like though clearly not orthodoxly Kantian) *transcendental philosophy*. In particular, pragmatism emphasizes the kind of reflexivity—the self-reflection of human reason and intelligence, as rooted in our practices—that has been a cornerstone of transcendental philosophy since Kant. However, as noted in connection with phenomenology, pragmatism is not at all happy with transcendental philosophers' aim to provide an aprioristic first foundation for philosophy and science. There is, and can be, no first philosophy. The pragmatist attitude is deeply fallibilist. Everything, including the transcendental conditions we may identify as necessary for certain given human actualities, is revisable and reinterpretable in the course of ongoing experience and inquiry.

Most of the philosophical traditions or schools here only very briefly compared to pragmatism are unfortunately somewhat narrow-minded and shortsighted when it comes to seeking and maintaining communicative relations outside one's own approach. The same is, admittedly, true about pragmatism. All too often pragmatists just debate among themselves over what pragmatism actually is or who should (or should not) be called a pragmatist. Such debates do play an important role in keeping pragmatism an open tradition, but they may also to some extent hinder the development of dialogues between pragmatism and other orientations. The pragmatic attitude itself would strongly favor encouraging such dialogue.

In sum, pragmatism—or the pragmatic method in the sense analyzed in the editorial chapters of this book—amounts to a philosophical attempt to understand human being-in-the-world. It is not primarily, let alone exclusively, a philosophical theory about anything more specific than that, although it is highly relevant in a number of theoretical discussions in various areas of philosophy. Pragmatism may not be immediately applicable to philosophical or scientific problems, but then again pragmatists are, or should be, suspicious of the very idea of applying philosophical theory to some practical problem. Good philosophy is always already "applied" simply by being humanly relevant. On the other hand, pragmatism is certainly not independent of the surrounding scientific disciplines. Very often, our philosophical attempts to understand ourselves and the world we live in emerge from the developments of the empirical sciences. In addition to the dialogues between rival philosophical schools, pragmatism should promote interdisciplinary dialogues in science, especially across the supposed gulf between the human and the natural sciences.

Taking all of this into account, I cannot think of a better categorization for pragmatism than the one according to which pragmatism is ultimately a form of *philosophical anthropology*. Like pragmatism itself, this field of philosophical inquiry virtually extends through philosophy as a whole. Metaphysical, epistemological, ethical, and many other issues are crucial in philosophical anthropology. The pragmatist is a philosophical anthropologist in the sense of considering every philosophical issue in terms of human practices and habits—of human culture, generally speaking. Moreover, pragmatism is both naturalistic and culturalistic, as we have seen, though non-reductive in both ways. Thus, pragmatism may in fact be promising in contemporary philosophy also because it may be able to make philosophical anthropology flourish again as a philosophical orientation and program. This is at least one of the potential "new directions" that pragmatists may look forward to.

Notes

1. See the papers collected in Crary and Read, 2000 (with a dissenting voice by Hacker).
2. See also Pihlström, 2011. (This section and the following one are partly based on that article.)
3. On pragmatism and evil, see also Pihlström, 2008a, ch. 4.
4. See especially Larry Hickman's work on Deweyan philosophy of technology here (Hickman, 1991, 2007), including Hickman's contribution to the present volume.

Part Three

Resources

16

Chronology

Michael Eldridge

Pre-history note

Several philosophers influenced the early pragmatists, but a few are worthy of mention here. Charles Sanders Peirce took the term "pragmatic" from Kant. John Dewey, early in his career, was a Hegelian. William James dedicated *Pragmatism* to Mill: "to the memory of John Stuart Mill from whom I first learned the pragmatic openness of mind and whom my fancy likes to picture as our leader were he alive to-day." All of the early pragmatists were well versed in Emerson, but Stanley Cavell has insisted that it is a mistake, despite influences and similarities, to regard Emerson as "the forerunner of pragmatism." Despite affinities to various philosophical predecessors, all pragmatists, however, are anti-Cartesian.

Chronology

1870s: The Metaphysical Club—It is generally acknowledged that philosophical pragmatism's origins are to be found in the loosely organized group of Cambridge, Massachusetts, intellectuals that met in the 1870s. Prominent in the group were Chauncey Wright (1830–1875), Charles Sanders Peirce (1839–1914), and William James (1842–1910). Other active members included Nicholas St. John Green (1830–1876) and Oliver Wendell Holmes, Jr. (1841–1935).

1872: James, who had a medical degree, begins teaching comparative physiology at Harvard.

1874: James establishes the first American psychology laboratory.

1877–1878: Peirce's "The Fixation of Belief" and "How to Make Our Ideas Clear," *Popular Science Monthly*, are two early pragmatist texts, although the term "pragmatism" is not used. Nevertheless the latter article contains the first formulation of the "pragmatic maxim": "Consider what effects, which might conceivably have practical bearings, we conceive the object of our conception to have. Then, our conception of these effects is the whole of our conception of the object."

1880: James is appointed Assistant Professor of Philosophy at Harvard.

1889: Jane Addams (1860–1935) and Ellen Starr Gates (1859–1940) found Hull House in Chicago.

1890: William James, *The Principles of Psychology*, was written at a time when there was no sharp division between psychology and philosophy. Although considered a classic of modern psychology, many of the chapters, notably the ones on habit and the stream of thought, are particularly significant for philosophical pragmatism. But note that Dewey (1859–1952), in a March 15, 1903 (date approximate) letter to James, cites the latter's *Psychology* as "the spiritual progenitor" of *Studies in Logical Theory*.

1894: Dewey moves to the University of Chicago, joining James Tufts (1862–1942), who had previously been at Michigan, and George Herbert Mead (1863–1931), whom Dewey brought with him from Michigan. Tufts had advocated Dewey's appointment.

1897: Publication of James's influential essay, "The Will to Believe," about which Peirce later observed that James had pushed the pragmatic method "to such extremes as to give us pause."

1898: William James, "Philosophical Conceptions and Practical Results," was delivered to the Philosophical Union, University of California, Berkeley. It is the first public use of "pragmatism." James gives credit to Peirce for "the principle of pragmatism" but acknowledges that he is using it more broadly than Peirce intended.

1903: Dewey, *et al.*, *Studies in Logical Theory*, is a collaborative volume that was dedicated to James, who heralded its publication (in an October 29 letter) with these words: "The result is wonderful—a real school and real Thought. Important thought, too!"

1903: Oxford don, F. C. S. Schiller, dedicates his *Humanism* to William James and publicly associates himself with the American pragmatists.

1903: In his American Philosophical Association presidential address Josiah Royce distinguishes the "pure pragmatism" of James, Schiller, and Dewey, which he regards as inadequate, because impractical, from his own absolute pragmatism.

1904: Dewey leaves the University of Chicago and moves to Columbia University, from which he would retire in 1939.

1905: C. S. Peirce coined "pragmaticism" in "What Pragmatism Is": "So then, the writer, finding his bantling 'pragmatism' so promoted ('in the literary journals,' where it gets abused), feels that it is time to kiss his child good-by and relinquish it to its higher destiny; while to serve the precise purpose of expressing the original definition, he begs to announce the birth of the word 'pragmaticism,' which is ugly enough to be safe from kidnappers." James attends the Fifth International Congress of Psychology in April. While there he meets with several Italian pragmatists—Giovanni Papini, Giovanni Vailati, Mario Calderoni, Giovanni Amendola, and others.

1907: James publishes *Pragmatism: A New Name for Some Old Ways of Thinking*.

1908: A. O. Lovejoy publishes the "The Thirteen Pragmatisms" in the *Journal of Philosophy*, which, as the title suggests, is a careful, albeit sarcastic discrimination of the many ways in which philosophers had come to use the term.

1917: Randoph Bourne (1886–1918) published three essays that were critical of Dewey's support of Woodrow Wilson's war policy. Scholars disagree about the pragmatic character of Bourne's critique of Dewey's instrumentalist support of the war. Robert Westbrook argues that Bourne employed Dewey's pragmatism against Dewey. Others find Bourne appealing to absolute values.

1925: Dewey distinguishes his "instrumentalism" from the pragmatisms of Peirce and James in his "The Development of American Pragmatism."

1926: Lewis Mumford, in *The Golden Day*, like Bourne, faulted pragmatism for a lack of vision and thus an inability to be effective in troubled times. With regard to Dewey he claimed that his "faith" was "in the current go of things." Hence pragmatism was an apology for conventionalism.

1927: Dewey's "Pragmatic Acquiescence" defends James, whom he regarded as Mumford's primary target. Dewey rejected Mumford's claims as unfair and mistaken. Pragmatism or instrumentalism possessed the ability to be critical of convention.

1931: Jane Addams awarded the Nobel Peace Prize. First volume of the *Collected Papers of Charles Sanders Peirce* published.

1932: Reinhold Niebuhr, in *Moral Man and Immoral Society*, accuses Dewey of a naïve reliance on education and social intelligence. Only power could confront power. Thus he adds his voice to that of Bourne, Mumford, and later C. Wright Mills, claiming that pragmatism is not sufficiently radical to deal with an intransigent human nature or politics as it is actually practiced.

1935: The John Dewey Society was founded to promote Dewey's commitment to social intelligence in education and culture. Originally called "The Association for the Study of Education in its Social Aspects," the name was changed to the John Dewey Society in early 1936.

1938: In his *Logic: The Theory of Inquiry* Dewey, who did not normally refer to his philosophy as a pragmatist one, but rather an instrumentalist or experimental naturalism, writes: "The word 'Pragmatism' does not, I think, occur in the text. Perhaps the word lends itself to misconception. At all events, so much misunderstanding and relatively futile controversy have gathered about the word that it seemed advisable to avoid its use. But in the proper interpretation of 'pragmatic,' namely the function of consequences as necessary test of the validity of propositions, *provided* these consequences are operationally instituted and are such as to resolve the specific problem evoking the operations, the text that follows is thoroughly pragmatic."

1939: Sidney Hook's *John Dewey: An Intellectual Portrait* is published. Hook (1902–1989) had been Dewey's student and through the 1930s assisted him with many publications. Because of his defense of Dewey he was known as "Dewey's bulldog." At the end of the year conferences were held to celebrate Dewey's eightieth birthday.

1946: The Charles S. Peirce Society was founded.

1951: W. V. O. Quine, "Two Dogmas of Empiricism," is an attack on logical empiricism and a defining document of analytic philosophy, but in it Quine suggests that an abandonment of the empiricist dogmas will mean a "shift toward pragmatism," but one that "espouse[s] a more thorough pragmatism" than that of Rudolf Carnap and C. I. Lewis. (Quine, nevertheless, is ultimately an empiricist.)

1956: An early effort toward rapproachment between the two schools of Anglo-American philosophy, pragmatism and analytic philosophy, was Morton White's *Toward Reunion in Philosophy*.

1961: The Center for Dewey Studies was established at Southern Illinois University—Carbondale.

1965: *The Transactions of the Charles S. Peirce Society*, the premier journal devoted to American philosophy, was founded in 1965.

1967: John J. McDermott contributed to the renaissance of American philosophy (and pragmatism) with his collection, *The Writings of William James*. Subsequently critical, comprehensive editions of Peirce, James, Royce, and Dewey have been or are currently being published.

1967–1970: Three studies were published in Germany by Karl-Otto Apel and Jürgen Habermas within this period: 1) Apel, "Der philosophische Hintergrund der Entstehung des Pragmatismus bei Charles Sanders Peirce," 2) Habermas, *Erkenntnis und Interesse*, and 3) "Peirces Denkweg vom Pragmatismus zum Pragmatizismus." (Hans Joas, "American Pragmatism and German Thought," credits Apel and Habermas with the new approach toward pragmatism in Germany, one that overcame the previous misunderstandings.)

1972: The Society for the Advancement of American Philosophy was founded at the Eastern American Philosophical Association (APA) meeting in Boston that year.

1976: The Peirce Edition established at Indiana University—Purdue University Indianapolis, in order to document the manuscripts of, and produce a chronological edition of, the work of Peirce.

1979: Richard Rorty's praise of Dewey in *Philosophy and the Mirror of Nature*, along with Heidegger and Wittgenstein, signalled a resurgent interest in pragmatism.

1979: Representing non-Ivy Leaguers, Catholic schools, phenomenologists, classic American philosophy, process philosophy, metaphysicians, and those who emphasized undergraduate instruction, the Pluralists organized a challenge to the leadership of the APA's Eastern Division, the largest of the three regional divisions. Rorty was president of the Eastern Division at the time. Pragmatists, along with other non-analytic approaches, benefitted from the resulting changes. John Smith of Yale University, with broad interests in American philosophy, including pragmatism, was elected vice president in 1980 and consequently served as president in 1981.

1981: One can perhaps mark the beginning of the long-running conversation/debate between the two most prominent (neo)pragmatist philosophers of the last part of the twentieth century, Richard Rorty and Hilary Putnam, with the latter's *Reason, Truth and History*, published in this year. But perhaps the views they held in common and the differences between them did not become clear until

Rorty's "Solidarity or Objectivity," which was originally presented as a lecture in 1983 and published in a revised version in 1985. The discussion regarding realism, relativism, scientism, and other matters was to continue for two decades. Note the entry below for 2009.

1982: Rorty's *Consequences of Pragmatism* even more explicitly marked his embrace of pragmatism.

1989: Cornel West's *The American Evasion of Philosophy* is an account of the "emergence, development, decline and resurgence of American pragmatism" (p. 4). But it is also an argument for a conception of philosophy as cultural criticism that focused attention on issues of power, race, and religion in ways that could not be ignored.

1990: Larry Hickman's *John Dewey's Pragmatic Technology* interpreted Dewey as a philosopher of technology, thus effectively translating Dewey's instrumentalism into the language of contemporary philosophy of technology that non-Deweyans could appreciate and engage.

1995: Morris Dickstein organized a major conference on the revival of pragmatism at the City University of New York Graduate School in November. The papers from the conference as well as additional essays were published in 1998 as *The Revival of Pragmatism: New Essays on Social Thought, Law and Culture*. The conference and the book signalled the breadth and acceptance of pragmatism at the end of the twentieth century within academic circles.

1996: Building on previous work by a variety of scholars and philosophers with which she had been associated, as well as her own research, Charlene Haddock Seigfried published *Pragmatism and Feminism*. Not only did it show important commonalities shared by the two movements that had not been generally recognized, it also identified many early female pragmatists whose contributions had not been appreciated, notably Jane Addams.

1997: The Midwest Pragmatist Study Group, organized by Hans Seigfried and Charlene Haddock Seigfried, began meeting at Loyola University of Chicago.

1998: The Center for Pragmatism Studies was founded at the Pontifical Catholic University of São Paulo, Brazil, by Ivo A. Ibri, and the first meeting on pragmatism was held. Two years later these annual meetings became international ones. Also in 2000 the journal *Cognitio* was begun in order to publish work in pragmatism and the contributions to the International Pragmatist Meetings.

1999: The European John Dewey Society was established through the efforts of Giuseppe Spadofora. Also the first Dewey Center outside the United States.

In 2003 the offices of the Foundation were opened in Consenza. In May 2007, at the Università della Calabria (Cosenza) an international conference, John Dewey: Reconstructing Democracy, was held.

2000: The Central European Pragmatist Forum, co-chaired by Emil Visnovsky, Comenius University, Bratislava, and John Ryder, State University of New York, held its first meeting in Stara Lesna, Slovakia, and has met regularly every two years in May or June since. Meetings, limited to 30 participants with no more than half from the United States, have been held in Krakow, Potsdam, Szeged, Brno and, uncharacteristically, Cadiz.

2004: *Contemporary Pragmatism*, an interdisciplinary, international journal, began publication. The Center for the Study of Dewey and American Philosophy, Fudan University, Shanghai. The director of the Center for the Study of Dewey and American Philosophy at the Fudan University, Liu Fang Tong, is directing a project that is to provide Chinese translation of the entire 37 volumes of Dewey's *Collected Works*.

2005: The Center for Dewey Studies at the University of Cologne, through the efforts of Kersten Reich and Stefan Neubert, was established.

2006: Initiated in this year, the Nordic Pragmatism Network aims at bringing scholars together and establishing contacts both inside and outside the Nordic countries. It held its first conference in 2008 in Helsinki with subsequent conferences in Reykjavík (2009) and Uppsala (2010). It has also held workshops and symposia in Helsinki and other Nordic cities. The Atlantic Coast Pragmatism Meeting, organized by Jacob Goodson, met at the University of Virginia in April. In succeeding years it has met at Virginia Tech, UNC-Ashville, University of South Carolina, and UNC-Charlotte.

2007: In April the Center for Dewey Studies at Soka University, Japan, was established. Its director is Koichi Kandachi. The next month the John Dewey Research Center of Hungary opened in Szeged under the direction of Alexander Kramer, University of Szeged. Later in the year the John Dewey Research Center was founded in Krakow under the direction of Krystyna Wilkoszewska, Jagellonian University in Krakow. The American and European Values Conference, held in June in Opole, Poland, was devoted to Peirce's normative thought. Also two conferences in Romania: "Philosophy of Pragmatism: Salient Inquiries," organized by Babes-Bolyai University, Cluj Napoca; "Democracy, Liberalism and the Relevance of Pragmatism/Neopragmatism for the Constituting of Political Ideologies—Interdisciplinary Approaches," organized by Constantin Brancusi University, Targu-Jiu. Back in the United States, the National Endowment for the

Humanities Summer Seminar for College and University Teachers: Pragmatism: A Living Tradition, directed by Russell Goodman, was held at the University of New Mexico, Albuquerque.

2008: After a 2-year hiatus, following the death of founder Hans Seigfried in 2006, the Midwest Pragmatist Study Group was reorganized and has been meeting at Indiana University Purdue University—Indianapolis. Martin Coleman is the contact person.

2009: At a conference in Buffalo celebrating the 150th anniversary of Dewey's birth, Putnam lamented Rorty's passing two years earlier with these words, "I sorely miss the presence here of my great friend and favorite debating partner Richard Rorty."

2010: Organized by Gregory Pappas, Texas A&M, the First International Conference on Pragmatism and the Hispanic/Latino World was held in March in College Station, Texas. The seventh Dewey Center was founded at Bilkent University in Ankara Turkey. The contact persons are Kory Sorrell and David Thornton.

2012: The First European Pragmatism Conference organized jointly by the Italian Pragma group and the Nordic Pragmatism Network in Rome. The European Pragmatism Association established.

17

Glossary

Michael Eldridge and Sami Pihlström

Please note that this is only a very restricted selection of some key terms and figures of pragmatism. The reader is referred to the individual articles as well as to the other editorial chapters ("Introduction," "Research Methods and Problems," "New Directions") of this volume for more substantial characterizations of these and many other concepts and persons central to pragmatism and its history. Names and other words set in **boldface** below refer to other entries in this glossary.

Jane Addams (1860–1935) was one of the "Chicago pragmatists," who not only was influenced by John **Dewey** and George Herbert **Mead**—the best known classical representatives of pragmatism associated with the University of Chicago at the turn of the twentieth century—but also influenced their thinking and thus played a perhaps more original role in the development of pragmatism than has been generally recognized. Addams is most famous for the Hull House, a social innovation intended to ameliorate the situation of the poor, especially women, in Chicago. Thus, Addams was primarily a public philosopher and a social activist, developing pragmatist ideas on democracy, community, and education, closely entangled with her practical work at the Hull House—instead of being a theoretically focused philosopher with major novel theoretical insights into these or other topics.

Anti-representationalism is the name Richard **Rorty** gave for his special version of neo-pragmatism, especially in his writings in the 1990s. The anti-representationalist denies that there are any representational (semantic) relations between language and the world, or between mental states and the world. Anti-representationalism can be seen as a generalization of Rorty's leading idea, put forward in the seminal volume, *Philosophy and the Mirror of Nature* (1979), that neither language nor the mind "mirrors" a language- and mind-independent reality. As such, it is a continuation of William **James**'s and other classical pragmatists' criticisms of the view that **truth** is just a matter of "copying"—accurately representing—reality as such. However, Rorty's anti-representationalism amounts to a radicalization of this pragmatist critique of the correspondence theory of truth. In the end, the Rortyan anti-representationalist maintains that there are only causal or physical—no representational or normative—relations between language and the items of reality language is supposed to be "about." Thus, in a sense, language is not "about" anything at all. It is merely a matter of using different vocabularies to cope with the world, not a matter of getting the world right in any sense. The "representationalist" assumption that language ought to mirror the world, and may succeed or fail in this task, is, according to Rorty, the source of a number of unfortunate philosophical confusions, including the problems of realism and skepticism, which the anti-representationalist pragmatist is willing to leave behind. Less radical pragmatists, including Hilary **Putnam**, have heavily criticized Rorty's anti-representationalism as a view sacrificing linguistic, semantic, and epistemic normativity as hopelessly as any reductive physicalism or eliminativism.

Corridor metaphor. In Lecture II of *Pragmatism*, William **James** refers to a metaphor he took from the Italian pragmatist Giovanni Papini. Pragmatism can, according to Papini and James, be compared to a corridor in a hotel: in one room, there may be an author writing a religious or theological treatise, while in another one somebody else is putting forward an atheistic argument. In a third room someone is working on a scientific problem, and so forth. Pragmatism can be a method that all these very different thinkers find useful. Thus, pragmatism is not a full-blown worldview or metaphysical system; it is above all a method of investigating various problems of philosophy (and problems outside philosophy as well).

John Dewey (1859–1952) was one of the most prominent developers of classical pragmatism. Educated at the University of Vermont and Johns Hopkins University, he taught philosophy at the Universities of Michigan, Minnesota, and Chicago, but his longest tenure was at Columbia University, from which he finally retired in 1939. At a celebration of his work in that year he was honored for "his life-long effort to practicalize intelligence," but Dewey corrected this attempt at praise by observing that his effort had been the reverse—to intelligize practice (Eldridge, 1998, p. 5). In so doing Dewey was true to the pragmatist project of beginning with our lived experience rather than some theory. We find ourselves engaged in habits or ongoing activities and we discern the need to improve them, to make them more intelligent. Thus meliorism, that is, social improvement, was at the heart of Dewey's thinking. He thought philosophy had a role to play in making our lives better by examining and remaking, if necessary, the ideas shaping the way we live. We do so not by considering these ideas in isolation but in the context of our lives.

His collected works are quite extensive, comprising 37 volumes in the critical edition. Although his work was focused on intelligent action or social intelligence, his thought ranged over aesthetics, education, ethics, logic, religion, politics, and arguably metaphysics and epistemology. The latter are controversial, because he was an anti-metaphysician and anti-epistemologist, yet he made contributions to our understanding of what there is and our ways of knowing. What he thought there is was what can be discovered by science; thus he was a naturalist. But he was no reductionist. Knowing for him was not the primary aim, but living well. Yet to live well one should look to experimental science not only for its results but even more importantly to discern how one should conduct one's life. Rather than regarding our cultural heritage as something finished and complete, we are to build on this inheritance by inquiring carefully.

Perhaps his most prominent books are *Democracy and Education* (MW 16, 1916), *Reconstruction in Philosophy* (MW 12, 1920), *Human Nature and Conduct* (MW 14, 1922), *Experience and Nature* (LW 1, 1925), *The Public and Its Problems* (LW 2, 1927), *The Quest for Certainty* (LW 4, 1929), *Ethics* (with James Tufts, LW 7, 1932), *A Common Faith* (LW 9, 1934), *Art as Experience* (LW 10, 1934), and *Logic: The Theory of Inquiry* (LW 12, 1938). However, Sidney Hook, his most prominent student and collaborator during the 1930s, thought *Liberalism and Social Action* (LW 11, 1937) could well be "to the twentieth century what Marx and Engel's Communist Manifesto was to the nineteenth" (Hook, 1939, p. 158).

Esteemed during his later life as America's premier philosopher, his reputation suffered some following his death. His work was regarded as vague by some and lacking in bite by others, either because he made no appeal to fundamental truths or values or because his reformist, educative democratic proposals were insufficient to deal with the problems of the day. But with a renewed interest in practical philosophy later in the twentieth century, there was a resurgence of interest in Dewey's possible contributions. A catalyst for this was the work of Richard **Rorty**.

Experience is one of the most central concepts of pragmatism. Pragmatists are generally empiricists, arguing that knowledge must be anchored in experience and that pure reason is insufficient as the source or ground of our cognitive endeavors. For example, William **James** saw the classical British empiricists—John Locke, George Berkeley, and David Hume—as the true precursors of pragmatism and suggested that the avenue of philosophical progress runs from them "round Kant" (*not* "through Kant") to his own days. (This conception of Kant's role as a background figure of pragmatism is considerably modified, however, in the editorial chapters of this book.) However, the classical pragmatists developed notions of experience that significantly diverged from the earlier empiricists' ideas in at least the following crucial respect. While the old British empiricists had a more or less atomistic and passive conception of experience (later adopted by the twentieth-century logical positivists, among others), the pragmatists' conception of experience was, and is, holistic and dynamic. We do not simply receive individual sense impressions from the external world, but we actively engage in the world through our **habits** of action, thereby continuously transforming the totality of our experience. (It is easy to see here that this account of experience is actually closer to Kant's than, say, Hume's.)

James also developed the notion of "pure experience," referring to the ultimate stuff of which the world is made, beyond the traditional subject versus object dichotomy. He called his theory *radical empiricism* (see James, 1912). John **Dewey** insisted on the central place of experience in philosophy even more strongly than James. Dewey's notion of "primary experience" (explored by Hildebrand, 2003, among others) is a close relative of James's "pure experience." It is debatable to what extent either of these pragmatists developed a metaphysical theory of experience as ultimate reality, though. Typically, their conceptions of experience integrate epistemic and metaphysical aspects—and even ethical and political ones.

Fallibilism is a key pragmatic value and reflects the influence of scientific practice. Any belief is adopted provisionally and is based on the available evidence. Yet with new information and increased understanding, this belief may need to be modified or discarded. Some beliefs are quite settled and not likely to be changed, but in principle any belief is revisable. **Peirce** is credited with extending the notion of possible error that was widely accepted in the natural sciences to other areas of knowledge, and as Elizabeth Cooke notes, this sort of doubt drives inquiry (Cooke, 2006, p. 1). Thus fallibilism might be described as a moderate form of skepticism, one that encourages one to seek answers while being cautious about one's findings. It is not that the fallibilist denies that knowledge is possible; she only realizes that her "knowledge" may turn out not to be warranted upon further investigation—hence, Dewey's doctrine of "warranted assertions." We may have good reason to hold a belief, but we may well find in the future better reasons to reject or modify this belief. Of course, pragmatists are not the first moderately skeptical philosophers, but they are more comfortable with their provisional findings than many. Being possibly wrong is not something they fear, but rather as the situation warrants something that inspires inquiry. One's confidence is not so much in the belief produced as in the self-corrective nature of ongoing inquiry. One will have confidence in a well-established, reliably produced truth, but she will have even greater confidence that should this truth be called into question there are methods that enable one to affirm, reject, or revise it.

God. In principle, a pragmatic approach is compatible with any existing situation, including a society with a belief in God. But the **pragmatic maxim** (the pragmatic method) is potentially a destabilizing force in that it encourages a society to reconstruct itself. The classical pragmatists found themselves in a society that was calling into question traditional understandings of divinity. Because of their commitment to evolution and the scientific method, and for many of them, naturalism, God was problematic. Nevertheless C. S. **Peirce** proposed his "Neglected Argument for the Reality of God" (1908), and William **James** published his (in)famous "The Will to Believe" (1896). Neither are traditional arguments, and James is only contending for the right to believe in the absence of clear-cut evidence one way or the other. Moreover, the sort of deity he proposed in *A Pluralistic Universe* was a "finite god" (1977, p. 60). The fully naturalist John **Dewey**, disappointing some of his followers, was willing to use the term "God" to refer to the "*active* relation between ideal and actual" (LW 9.34). By this he meant those natural and cultural conditions and human efforts where ideals are realized through an interactive process. Furthermore, Richard **Rorty**, while a non-theist and comfortably secular, was not a militant atheist. He did think, however, that pragmatism and theism were incompatible. Thus historically, pragmatists have tended to be pluralistic, leaving room for various notions of divinity, but on the whole they have not inclined toward traditional religion, and the theistic pragmatist has felt the need to justify his or her belief, given the secularizing tendency of a movement committed to the wide use of experimental and empirical methods. But one can well conceive a pragmatist in a different time and place in response to the situation in which s/he finds herself affirming the existence of a divinity. While pragmatism over time may well be corrosive of inherited beliefs, one cannot predict that belief in a deity or deities will be the belief that will be called into question. It depends on what is felt to be problematic at the time. At any rate, given pragmatism's commitment to

fallibilism, the pragmatist will not be a dogmatic theist. Ulf Zachariasson's essay on pragmatism and religion in this volume provides a fuller discussion of some of the issues raised here.

Habit is a key notion in pragmatist thought. According to the classical pragmatists, **Peirce**, **James**, and **Dewey**, in particular, our beliefs are "habits of action." To believe anything is to be engaged in habitual and purposive action in the natural world. Moreover, human action in general should not, according to (most) pragmatists, be understood and examined merely (or even primarily) in terms of individual actions separate from other actions, but in terms of habits. (See Erkki Kilpinen's contribution to this volume for further elaboration.) In addition, one of our most important habits is the meta-level habit of critically reflecting on, revising, and transforming our habits. Thus, our habits are not simply given to us once and for all; we are responsible for continuously self-critically examining whether they enable us to achieve our purposes (which are themselves in view only through the habitual actions we engage in) or not. The notion of habit is thus intimately connected with pragmatic **fallibilism**. We are fallible beings, and a key element of our acknowledging that fallibility is the recognition that in many cases we have to revise our habits of action (including obviously any beliefs we might hold about the world). This is, indeed, what **inquiry** ultimately amounts to in pragmatism: as our habitual actions in some cases may lead to unexpected consequences, we may start to doubt the beliefs (i.e., habits) that led to those actions; it is this doubt that then launches an inquiry into the matter, aiming at new—revised—beliefs and thus to a smooth continuation of the interrupted habitual actions. The revision of habits is thus at the core of the famous "doubt-belief" theory of inquiry that pragmatists, starting from Peirce, developed.

"**Hegelian deposit**" is a term John **Dewey** coined in an autobiographical essay titled "From Absolutism to Experimentalism" (1930) to describe his permanent debt to the philosophy of Hegel. Dewey was vague about the extent of the deposit, which has been a significant topic in scholarship. Although it is well known that he studied the British neo-Hegelian philosophers, less is known about the extent of his direct study of Hegel. Among other issues, the nature of Dewey's debt to Hegel in his mature philosophy is relevant to debates about whether or not he could be said to have a metaphysics, the nature of his organicism and holism, and the type of empiricism he espoused. For decades, the term was most closely examined in biographical studies such as Dykhuizen, *The Life and Mind of John Dewey* (1973); Coughlan, *Young John Dewey* (1973); Westbrook, *John Dewey and American Democracy* (1991); Rockefeller, *John Dewey* (1991); and

Ryan, *John Dewey and the High Tide of American Liberalism* (1995). Recently, the term has come under more direct scrutiny in Shook, *Dewey's Empirical Theory of Knowledge and Reality* (2000) and Good, *A Search for Unity in Diversity* (2006). (See the bibliography at the end of the volume for full references.)

Inquiry, for pragmatists, is usually not limited to scientific inquiry but extends to virtually all areas of life, including art, morality, politics, and even religion. As explained above (see **habit**), inquiry is something that arises in situations in which our habitual actions lead to unexpected surprises and thus to doubt concerning the beliefs that were embedded in our habits. Thus, inquiry arises in what **Dewey** called "problematic situations" or "indeterminate situations," which it seeks to transform into determinate ones. Inquiry leads, then, to what **Peirce** called the "fixation of belief." It does not start from all-encompassing doubt, as the Cartesian conception of inquiry does, but from habits of action (and, hence, beliefs), which lead to doubt only in the case of a surprise.

According to Dewey, in particular, it is very important to extend inquiry from science to other areas. Thus, for instance, ethics or moral philosophy is not beyond rational pragmatic inquiry based on experience. Rather, moral values—as well as, say, aesthetic, political, or religious ones—ought to be inquired into precisely in the same pragmatic, experiential ways in which natural facts are inquired into. Accordingly, the notion of inquiry in pragmatism is closely connected with the notion of **experience**. Inquiry is inevitably experiential—but not at the cost of reason or intelligence. Rather, these play a mutually supporting role: the inquirer actively and creatively uses reason in intelligently resolving the problematic situations that arise in various experiential contexts.

William James (1842–1910) was, in addition to Charles Sanders **Peirce**, a cofounder of pragmatism. As a distinguished Harvard professor, James was one of the leading intellectuals of his time, although his philosophical status is somewhat debated, especially in comparison with Peirce.

James's psychological work (culminating in his *Principles of Psychology*, 1890) played a crucial role in the emergence of scientific psychology. His explorations of the psychological and philosophical dimensions of religious experience (as presented in *The Varieties of Religious Experience*, 1902) have gained recognition across disciplinary boundaries. Trained as a medical scientist, James was an original thinker with an unusually broad scope, ranging from psychology and philosophy to religious studies and even psychical research. In his core pragmatist writings, such as *Pragmatism: A New Name for Some Old Ways of Thinking* (1907) and *The Meaning of Truth* (1909), James defended key ideas of pragmatism, including the pragmatic conception of **truth** and the view that the world—whatever there is—ultimately depends on, or is in some sense constructed by, our practical interests and purposive actions. As his fellow pragmatists Peirce and **Dewey**, he was a thoroughgoing fallibilist.

Although James wrote little directly on ethics, scholars have also increasingly recognized that a central current of his work is ethical. The 1891 essay, "The Moral Philosopher and the Moral Life" (included in James's 1897 volume, *The Will to Believe and Other Essays in Popular Philosophy*), is his only article explicitly dealing with ethics; yet, ethical considerations are built into his pragmatism, especially its leading idea that theories and worldviews should be examined in terms of their practical relevance. If one argues that ethics is the core of James's thought, as some scholars today do, one must recognize that it is found in no single place in his corpus, no book specifically on ethics; it is, rather, to be found everywhere in what he wrote, at least implicitly.

George Herbert Mead (1863–1931) neither completed his Ph.D. nor published books but nevertheless became one of the most influential early pragmatists and continues to be studied today. Hans Joas regards him as "the most important theorist of intersubjectivity between Feuerbach and Habermas" (Joas, 1985, p. 2). While pursuing his doctorate in Germany, **Mead** received an offer to replace James Tufts as John Dewey's assistant at Michigan. He returned to do so, then moved with **Dewey** to the University of Chicago in 1894, where he remained for the rest of his career. Dewey and Mead continued to remain close personally and intellectually even after Dewey moved to Columbia University in 1904. Tufts and Mead were also close, not only professionally: Mead's son married Tufts's daughter.

Mead shared with the other pragmatists the focus on **habits** and the need for reconstruction of our practices as we encounter obstacles or the habits become dysfunctional. His originality lies in his account of how a self becomes a self through communication. The social situation is what is basic for Mead. In this situation an organism communicates initially by gestures but a self is formed through meaningful communication, that is, through symbolic interaction. The latter was Mead's idea but the term was coined by Harold Blumer, who studied with Mead at Chicago. But some, such as Joas, regard symbolic interactionism as having deviated from Mead's thought, having given it an overly subjectivist emphasis (ibid., p. 7).

In addition to his distinctive theory of the social development of mind and self, Mead shared with the other "social pragmatists"—Dewey, Tufts, and Jane

Addams—a high regard for the promise of social science (properly practiced), and involvement in social reform. Among his involvements in social reform was his participation in the activities of Hull House, labor mediation, and the reform-minded City Club. Joas comments, "Mead's multifarious practical involvement in education and politics exercised a very great influence on his theoretical evolution" (ibid., p. 23).

The books authored by Mead were published posthumously and taken from Mead's notes and the notes of his students. Hence careful students of Mead's work, such as Joas (ibid., p. 10) and Gary Cook (1993, p. xvii), pay attention to his published articles and correspondence as well as the books.

The Metaphysical Club met in Cambridge, Massachusetts, in the early 1870s, roughly in 1872. The pragmatist movement has been seen as arising from those meetings. Its cofounders **Peirce** and **James** were usually present at the Club, as well as Oliver Wendell Holmes, Chauncey Wright, John Fiske, and others. The papers Peirce published in the late 1870s, "The Fixation of Belief" (1877) and "How To Make Our Ideas Clear" (1878)—papers that largely came to define the pragmatist conception of **inquiry** and the **pragmatic maxim** or method—emerged out of the Metaphysical Club discussions. The term "pragmatism" was not used in those articles by Peirce but was most likely used in the Metaphysical Club. (The term appeared in print only in James's 1898 essay, "Philosophical Conceptions and Practical Results," with a due recognition of Peirce's key role in the birth of the pragmatist way of thinking.) The book, *The Metaphysical Club*, by Louis Menand (2001), is a historical exploration of the Cambridge Metaphysical Club and its background.

Later "Metaphysical Clubs" have attempted to revive the spirit of the original one. Peirce founded a new Metaphysical Club at Johns Hopkins in 1879 after having accepted a post there. Also contemporary pragmatism scholars may have their own Metaphysical Clubs, such as the one in Helsinki, Finland, established in the late 1990s and still functioning.

Charles S. Peirce (1839–1914), the founder of pragmatism, is generally recognized as the most important and original American philosopher of all times. Peirce was not only a philosopher; he also made very important contributions to a number of academic fields, including logic, mathematics, science, and semiotics. His theory of signs is classical in the history of semiotics, and he was one of the pioneers of modern logic together with Gottlob Frege and Bertrand Russell. However, much of his work remained relatively unknown during his lifetime. He never gained the academic recognition he would have deserved, and while he was the son of a famous Harvard mathematician, Benjamin Peirce, he never occupied a permanent academic position himself. He was one of the key figures of the **Metaphysical Club** associated with Harvard in the 1870s, and later he founded another such Club at Johns Hopkins University, where he held a teaching post (which he had to give up, however).

Peirce's writings from the late 1870s, "The Fixation of Belief" (1877) and "How to Make Our Ideas Clear" (1878), are his most important and widely read contributions to the emergence of pragmatism, although the term "pragmatism" does not explicitly occur in these articles. The former essay develops the pragmatist "doubt-belief" theory of **inquiry**, while the latter introduces the **pragmatic maxim**, a cornerstone of the pragmatic method in philosophy. Later, Peirce was more than slightly dissatisfied with the developments the pragmatist movement took in **James**'s and other more popular pragmatists' writings; in 1905, he coined the word "pragmaticism" to distinguish his own specific brand of pragmatism from some of the others.

In addition to being a pragmatist and a semiotician, Peirce was a deep metaphysical thinker with highly original insights. For instance, his *synechism*, the doctrine of continuity, along with *tychism*, the doctrine of chance, and *agapism*, the doctrine of evolutionary love, constitutes a complex evolutionary theory of speculative metaphysics. In his late thought, Peirce also offered a "neglected argument for the reality of God." One of Peirce's lasting concerns from his very first publications up to the final stages of his career was the development of a theory of *categories*.

Peirce's *Collected Papers* appeared as an eight-volume edition in 1931–1958—a long time after his death—but that edition, though invaluable for generations of Peirce scholars, is in many ways problematic and fragmentary. The more comprehensive chronological edition, *Writings of Charles Sanders Peirce*, has been published by Indiana University Press since 1980. It is now in its eighth volume, and far from completion. A two-volume set of Peirce's most important writings, also based on the efforts of the Peirce Edition Project at Indiana University, was published in 1992–1998 as *The Essential Peirce*.

Peirce's role in the history of pragmatism, and his influence on later pragmatists, is discussed in more detail in the historical survey included in the "Introduction," as well as James Campbell's article on the history of pragmatism in this volume.

The practical starting point (PSP) is taken by many pragmatists as a given. Yet, the "Introduction" to this volume reminds us that there can be "no sharp dichotomy between theory and practice" for the pragmatist. In this sense, we perhaps should *not* think, or read the pragmatists as claiming, that "practice is 'prior to' theory." Pragmatists, with their appeal to experience and focus on situations, often say that one should begin with practice and not with theory. Thus David Hildebrand (2003), who coined the PSP phrase, argued for the priority of the "practical starting point" over the theoretical one. Moreover, in the essay on pragmatic ethics in this volume, Eldridge contrasts Henry Sidgwick's and William **James**' approaches. Sidgwick, whom John Rawls regarded as establishing the model for twentieth-century moral philosophy, saw his task as systematically comparing philosophical ideas about ethics, whereas James and the later pragmatists understood their task as one of reflecting on and improving moral practice, making use of theories as tools. These tools, John **Dewey** insisted, were to be sharpened and refined through their use. Whatever priority practice may have comes neither from a radical separation of practice and theory nor the literal beginning of **inquiry** but the empirical use of practice as a refiner of our theoretical tools and ultimately in its contribution to lived experience. Dewey suggested this test of any philosophy: "Does it end in conclusions which, when they are referred back to ordinary life-experiences and their predicaments, render them more significant, more luminous to us, and make our dealings with them more fruitful?" (LW 1.18). The priority of practice then is neither in temporality nor in ontology but in functionality. Practice is the test of a theory's value for our practices or **habits**, which, after all, are constitutive of our lives.

Pluralism (the one and the many). There is a plurality of different pluralisms at work in the pragmatist tradition. In *Pragmatism* (1907), **James** applies the pragmatic method to the problem of "the one and the many." The pragmatist must, he says, inquire into the multitude of ways in which the world can be taken to be "one" (or "many"). The world is, first, one subject of discourse. There are, secondly, continuities ("hanging together") in the world. There are, thirdly, "lines of influence" of various kinds—including, James's fourth point, causal unity. More importantly, there is, fifthly, "generic unity": things belong to different classes of *genera*, existing "in kinds." James's sixth and seventh dimensions of "oneness" are unity of purpose and aesthetic unity. The eighth and philosophically the most controversial dimension is, finally, the notion of "the one knower"—that is, the Hegelian monistic idealists' Absolute, which James critically examines at length. James argues that the pragmatist prefers the pluralistic and empiricist approach to the monistic and rationalistic postulations celebrating the Absolute—a popular metaphysical postulate in the late nineteenth and early twentieth centuries—whose only pragmatically acceptable cash-value, according to James, is the occasional "moral holiday" it might grant us. The debate with monistic idealists, including particularly the British philosopher F. H. Bradley's, views was one of the most important controversies James engaged in toward the end of his philosophical career.

Both monism and pluralism must, hence, be treated pragmatically: no rationalistic metaphysics dogmatically set up in advance of our piecemeal inquiries into the different ways in which the world can be said to be "one" or "many" can do the job of settling the issue. Applying the pragmatic method, James also arrives at what may be characterized as the ethical superiority of pluralism over monism.

There are a number of different pluralisms at work even in James's own pragmatism. In one important sense, pluralism amounts to a *metaphysical* theory (set against the Absolute), according to which there are, instead of one single "knower" "bits and pieces" of "pure experience" pretty much everywhere; it is therefore inseparable from James's radical empiricism, according to which pure experience is the "neutral stuff" (beyond the subject–object dichotomy) out of which the world is "made." According to pluralism, as characterized in *A Pluralistic Universe* (1909), "the substance of reality may never get totally collected" and "some of it may remain outside of the largest combination of it ever made" (p. 21). Multiplicity is pragmatically preferable to all-inclusiveness—both scientifically and ethically.

However, just as James argues in *Pragmatism* that the world can be "one" or "many" in a variety of different ways, there are other ways of being a pluralist. An alternative to purely metaphysical construals of pluralism is the idea that pluralism, for James, is not primarily a metaphysical doctrine (presupposing radical empiricism) but a *meta-philosophical* one, insisting on the possibility of a plurality of different "correct" metaphysical positions, and thus coming closer to the general argument of *Pragmatism*, as well as the later defense of "internal realism" and "conceptual relativity" (or even explicitly "pragmatic pluralism") by Hilary **Putnam** and other neo-pragmatists. This meta-philosophical pluralism can also be called *meta-metaphysical*, as it is concerned with the very nature and the correct (pragmatic) methodology of ontology or metaphysics, replacing the assumption of there being a single absolute conception of reality (or, as Putnam often puts it, the idea of a "God's-Eye View") by the notion of several acceptable ontologies, each serving different pragmatic purposes.

Pragmatic maxim: "Consider what effects, which might conceivably have practical bearings, we conceive the object of our conception to have. Then our conception of those effects is the whole of our conception of the object." The maxim was first proposed by Charles Sanders **Peirce** in "How to Make Our Ideas Clear" (1878) as a way to understand clearly the meaning of a concept, but William **James** employed it more broadly to distinguish between possible courses of action. If there is no difference in conduct then there is no difference in concept. Thus James could eliminate those abstractions that could not be "cashed out" in conduct. James was clearly interested in the latter; Peirce in the meaning that was understood by the practical effects. For some students of pragmatism, such as Tom Burke (see http://theblog.philosophytalk.org/2007/01/what_is_pragmat.html), the maxim provides a touchstone for identifying pragmatists. One needs to be able to tell a story that links the thinker to the maxim. Thus James is clearly a pragmatist for he employs Peirce's maxim, albeit for his own purposes. Nevertheless, it is with the maxim that he begins. For both Peirce and James our beliefs can be understood because they are rules for action, or habitual ways of thinking. A **habit** of thought (or belief) leads to certain practical effects thus enabling it to be understood (Peirce) or chosen as one's own (James).

Hilary Putnam (1926–) is one of the most important living pragmatist thinkers. Early in his career Putnam taught mathematics at Northwestern University and at Princeton University, and philosophy of science at MIT. In 1976 he became Walter Beverley Pearson Professor of Mathematical Logic at Harvard University; later he was appointed as Cogan University Professor in the Department of Philosophy at Harvard. He retired in June 2000. Harvard, the birthplace of American pragmatism, has thus been his intellectual home for decades. Together with Richard **Rorty** and other "post-analytic" thinkers, Putnam is responsible for the recent renewal of interest in pragmatism among both analytic philosophers and their critics. In addition to Rorty, Putnam has been influenced by many other major late-twentieth-century philosophers, including his Harvard colleagues W. V. **Quine** and Nelson Goodman, with whom he has shared many insights but whose more or less relativistic views he has criticized. While Putnam can be classified as a post-analytic philosopher, he has never abandoned aims and methods characteristic of the analytic tradition, such as argumentative rigor and conceptual clarity.

Putnam has written extensively on virtually any topic deserving philosophical attention. We may roughly divide his significant philosophical activities into three main areas: (1) the philosophy of mind and language; (2) the debate over realism in metaphysics and the philosophy of science; and (3) the meta-philosophical discussion of the nature of philosophy itself, including its ethical relevance in contemporary society. Putnam's views in each of these areas are fundamentally pragmatist, although his philosophical interests are by no means restricted to pragmatism. It must be kept in mind, however, that Putnam is, as his critics have often perceived, a "moving target." He has probably changed his views more often than any other first class philosopher, except perhaps Russell. Yet, his transformations—frequently toward views close to the classical pragmatists'—have not been opportunistic reactions to critics' arguments but results of self-reflective intellectual work, of his having found serious flaws in his own former positions.

W. V. Quine (1908–2000) was perhaps primarily the "last logical positivist" (as **Putnam** once described him; see Putnam, 1990), rather than a pragmatist, but his work played a major role in the reemergence of pragmatism as a significant philosophical orientation during the latter half of the twentieth century. This is largely as a result of his famous proposal in one of his best-known papers, "Two Dogmas of Empiricism" (1951), to advance a "more thorough pragmatism" than his logical positivist predecessor Rudolf Carnap, who had argued for the pragmatic nature of questions concerning the choice of linguistic frameworks within which only we are able to make meaningful ontological statements about the existence of some specific entities. In what he called a "shift toward pragmatism," Quine, as a semantic and epistemological holist, conceived of our scientific world-conception as a "web of belief" tested as a totality. Scientific experimentation is a matter of pragmatic adjustment between our theories and "recalcitrant experience." Any statements or beliefs we entertain about the existence of certain (kinds of) entities are pragmatic postulations ultimately to be evaluated in terms of their usefulness in the prediction of future experience. Quine never studied the classical pragmatists in any great detail—though his naturalized epistemology (see especially Quine, 1969, 1995) was to some extent indebted to **Dewey**'s naturalism—but his pragmatic and holistic empiricism was one of the background influences of **Rorty**'s and **Putnam**'s neo-pragmatisms in the 1970s and 1980s. (The problem of placing Quine in the pragmatist tradition is considered more closely in the "Introduction" in this volume.)

Richard Rorty (1931–2007) was one of the leading neo-pragmatists; moreover, he was the philosopher who was probably more directly responsible than anyone else for the new rise of interest in pragmatism scholarship toward the end of the twentieth century. His groundbreaking *Philosophy and the Mirror of Nature*

(1979) raised **Dewey** along with Ludwig Wittgenstein and Martin Heidegger to the status of one of the most important philosophers of the century. In later works, Rorty famously—or notoriously—characterized pragmatism as **anti-representationalism**, arguing that the pragmatist should go beyond the traditional philosophical issues of realism versus antirealism, or objectivism versus relativism, by giving up the very idea of there being representational (instead of merely causal) relations between language and reality, and thereby giving up also the traditional conception of knowledge as accurate representation of the world that goes back to antiquity. We should rather, Rorty argued, understand language and **inquiry** as tools that help us to cope with the world we live in. They are not to be understood as serving the task of "getting things right." Rorty's radical neo-pragmatism has been criticized by philosophers representing quite different orientations—including other pragmatists. Fellow neo-pragmatists like Hilary **Putnam** have attacked his view because it seems to give up all normative philosophical concepts, including eventually the one of **truth**, while scholars working on the history of pragmatism have often pointed out that Rorty's readings of the pragmatist classics, especially **James** and **Dewey**, are idiosyncratic and misleading. Rorty's response to such worries is that he is actually inventing hypothetical classics of pragmatism that are deliberately intended to serve his own neo-pragmatist purposes: the versions of James and Dewey he is describing are not really the historical figures themselves—the ideal of accurate representation is given up here, too—but pragmatic constructions of what these classical pragmatists ought to have been like, from the Rortyan perspective. Their views are put to work in Rorty's own project.

In his late work, Rorty increasingly turned to social and political issues, including liberalism and democracy, arguing for the priority of freedom to truth and of democracy to philosophy. While his ideas remain extremely controversial, he was clearly a pragmatist in believing that philosophizing—even in what he called the "post-Philosophical culture"—should attempt to ameliorate the human condition in the contingent historical circumstances human beings find themselves living in.

Josiah Royce (1855–1916) was one of **James**'s most important colleagues at Harvard University and developed his own distinctive version of pragmatism, titled "absolute pragmatism," integrating pragmatist and Hegelian absolute idealist views. The key idea of such idealism is that everything real is ultimately contained in a single all-encompassing mind or consciousness, "the Absolute." Thus, it is perhaps only somewhat problematically that Royce can actually be included among the classical pragmatists; his work stands in a critical relation to James's and Dewey's less idealistic pragmatisms, in particular. In many ways, Royce's philosophical ideas were diametrically opposed to those of James, who favored **pluralism** in contrast to idealistic monism, and the two thinkers engaged in critical (but mostly friendly) dialogue. James rejected "the Absolute" that the Hegelians of his days—in addition to Royce, most prominently the British idealist Bradley—postulated. Royce countered such criticisms by developing a synthesis of pragmatism and absolute idealism, partly based on the more Peircean than Jamesian notion of community. Royce's most important works include *The Religious Aspect of Philosophy* (1885), *The World and the Individual* (1899–1901), *The Philosophy of Loyalty* (1908), and *The Problem of Christianity* (1913); accordingly, he also significantly contributed to the philosophy of religion from a pragmatist and idealist perspective.

Truth. The so-called pragmatic theory of truth (or pragmatic conception of truth) is undoubtedly one of the most controversial aspects of pragmatism. In textbooks and other general presentations, this "theory" is usually presented as the naïve view that whatever is useful, or whatever "works," is true. This theory, associated primarily with William **James** (see especially James's *Pragmatism*, 1907, ch. 6), is not an accurate account of any of the classical pragmatists' views on truth. James did argue that truth should be pragmatically characterized in terms of the satisfactoriness of beliefs, and that we should take seriously the fact that beliefs are always satisfactory or unsatisfactory *for* someone, the subject of the belief, but he never simply reduced truth to satisfactoriness, let alone personal or subjective utility. His main idea that truth is what "works," or what is good for us to believe can be understood as the more general suggestion that true beliefs habitually tend to produce satisfactory results in experience. Thus, his views may not have been as far from **Peirce**'s in this regard as has sometimes been supposed (see, e.g., Cormier, 2001).

The background of James's theory lies in Peirce's **pragmatic maxim**, which James applied to the notion of truth, finding the conceivable practical effects of truth in the satisfactoriness of true beliefs. Peirce himself applied the maxim to the notion of reality, rather than truth, suggesting that the conceivable practical effect of the object of that notion is to produce beliefs and that truth can be defined as the long-run agreement of the scientific community of ideally rational inquirers. This is the key idea of Peirce's well-known account of truth as the "final opinion" of scientific belief-fixation. Peirce has also been interpreted as advancing a fundamentally realistic position: the final opinion the scientific community would arrive at stands in a relation of correspondence to the way the world really is, independently of beliefs, theories, and **inquiry**. However, James also accepted the basic—almost trivial—idea of the so-called correspondence theory of truth: it is undeniable that truth is "agreement" between beliefs and reality. The pragmatic conception of truth is a further characterization of the nature of this agreement.

In twentieth century pragmatism, truth was again an important topic, as neo-pragmatists like Hilary **Putnam** engaged in critical controversies over, for example, scientific realism and related topics. Pragmatist accounts of scientific progress reject the idea that the progress of science could simply be understood as progress toward truth, understood as *non-epistemic* correspondence between theories and the world; on the other hand, Putnam himself in his late writings came to resist his earlier tendency to characterize truth in *epistemic* terms as *idealized rational acceptability* or *idealized warranted assertibility* (the latter notion refers back to **Dewey**'s conception of truth as warranted assertibility). Some neo-pragmatists, especially **Rorty**, have also leaned toward more minimalistic or deflationary views on truth, according to which truth is not a substantial property of beliefs, theories, or anything else, but simply a matter of "disquotation": to say that "snow is white" is true is just to say that snow is white.

James Hayden Tufts (1862–1942) is an almost forgotten early pragmatist. A colleague of **Dewey**'s at both the University of Michigan and the University of Chicago, as well as a collaborator with Dewey in both editions of the *Ethics* (MW 5, 1908 and LW 7, 1932), he was a longtime professor at Chicago as well as dean and, for a time, president. He published several books, edited the *International Journal of Ethics* for 18 years, and served as president of what were to become the three divisions of the American Philosophical Association prior to unification in the late 1920s, playing a leading role in this unification. Yet there is no separate entry devoted to him in the 2008 *American Philosophy: An Encyclopedia* (editors Lachs and Talisse); he does appear in two paragraphs or so in the entry on the Chicago pragmatists, but even then he shares the spotlight with George Herbert **Mead**, his longtime colleague at Chicago, and Dewey. This is regrettable for, as James Campbell observes, Tufts sought "to advance the common good through intelligent social reconstruction," and thus deserves study as one who attempted as a pragmatist to do public philosophy (Campbell, 1992, p. x). In this volume, in his history of pragmatism, Campbell notes of Tufts, "Throughout his extensive writings, there is an emphasis upon the fundamental importance of institutions in human life and the ongoing need to modify and adapt them to new situations." Moreover this writing was informed by his considerable involvement in social reform efforts in the city of Chicago. He is, then, a possible model for pragmatists. On the other hand, Feffer (1993) argues that Tufts, along with Mead and Dewey, was unintentionally elitist and their efforts at promoting social intelligence naïve. Nevertheless, any adequate assessment of pragmatism's promise needs to take into account the actual efforts, imperfect though they may be, of those pragmatists who engaged in public philosophy (see also the chapter "New Directions").

Morton White (1917–) was educated at City College of the City of New York and Columbia University. His teachers included Morris Raphael Cohen (1880–1947) and Ernest Nagel (1901–1985), both of whom were naturalists. Cohen, although educated at Harvard (Ph.D. 1906), was a realist, and White reports that he was antagonistic toward pragmatism (White, 1999, p. 22). Nagel, according to Angelo Juffras, "avoided calling himself a pragmatist," but he did accept **Peirce** and **Dewey**'s "pragmatist views of inquiry" (Lachs and Talisse, 2008, entry on Nagel, p. 523). Morton White regarded him as much a logical positivist as a pragmatist (White, 1999, p. 28). Cohen and Nagel wrote the widely used *Logic and Scientific Method*, and White was a very good student of logic. In 1938 he attended a summer course at Harvard with W. V. O. **Quine**, making a good impression that would serve him well later, first, upon Quine's recommendation, becoming Alfred Tarski's assistant, then later Quine's colleague.

White wrote his dissertation on Dewey's instrumentalism but was attracted to analytic philosophy. There was no future for him at Columbia, where he had been teaching since 1942, so after 4 years he went to the University of Pennsylvania. Then, after only 2 years there, thanks to the advocacy of Henry Aiken (1912–1982) and with the support of Quine, he joined the Department of Philosophy at Harvard. While still at Penn, he began a three-way correspondence with Quine and Nelson Goodman (1906–1999), his Penn colleague, that eventually resulted in White's "The Analytic and the Synthetic: An Untenable Dualism" (1950) and Quine's "Two Dogmas of Empiricism" (1951). In 1951, he became chair of the department. Adept in logic and having taught physics during World War II, he nevertheless distinguished himself as an intellectual historian, publishing *Social Thought in America: The Revolt Against Formalism* in 1949. In 1956 his *Toward Reunion in Philosophy* advocated a rapprochement between pragmatism and analytic philosophy. During the 1950s he encouraged a strong relationship between Harvard and Oxford. In the 1950s–1960s, he moved back and forth between Harvard and the Institute for Advanced Study at Princeton, NJ, ending up as a permanent fellow of the latter. In 2002 he published *A Philosophy of Culture: The Scope of Holistic Pragmatism*, in which he distances himself from Quine's scientism and even finds that **James** and Dewey "never fully developed" "a holistic pragmatism" that escaped rationalism (White, 2002, p. 43).

18

Research Resources

Sami Pihlström

The potential scholar of pragmatism, or anyone interested in learning more about classical and contemporary pragmatism than this book has been able to teach, is encouraged to utilize the ample resources available online at the "Pragmatism Cybrary," www.pragmatism.org, a comprehensive website founded in the late 1990s by John R. Shook and currently primarily maintained by David Hildebrand—two leading pragmatism scholars. The Cybrary includes links to a number of different types of resource: publications; conferences and other events, including calls for papers; philosophy departments and doctoral programs worldwide with a focus on pragmatism; organizations, associations, networks, and societies; websites of classical and contemporary pragmatists, and so on.

Regarding the accuracy and possible updates of the contact information of the various pragmatism-related organizations, the reader is invited to explore the relevant websites, which can be found either through the Pragmatism Cybrary links or through Google. Another continuously updated website that might be useful is the site of the relatively recently established international research network, The Nordic Pragmatism Network (www.nordprag.org).

The Pragmatism Cybrary also contains information about the various web resources available on pragmatism scholarship. The most important publication channels for pragmatism specialists include at least the following journals (to be easily found by googling, or through the Pragmatism Cybrary website):

- *Transactions of the Charles S. Peirce Society*
- *Contemporary Pragmatism*
- *Journal of Speculative Philosophy*
- *Cognitio*
- *William James Studies* (online journal)

- *Pragmatism Today* (online journal)
- *European Journal of Pragmatism and American Philosophy* (online journal)

In addition, most leading academic publishers also publish monographs and collections of articles, as well as book series, on pragmatism and related topics.

The following list of pragmatism-related organizations, centers, networks, associations, and societies has been adopted from the Pragmatism Cybrary.

Centers

The Pragmatism Archive at Center for Inquiry, Buffalo, New York.

The Center for Dewey Studies at Southern Illinois University. The Manuscript Collections at the Morris Library, Southern Illinois University. The archive for the John Dewey Papers, along with the papers of many other pragmatists and progressive educators.

The Bentley Historical Library, at the University of Michigan, has collections of papers of several of Dewey's colleagues and students at Michigan.

John Dewey & Pragmatism Collection, at the Doshisha University Library, Japan.

The Institute for Studies in Pragmaticism at Texas Tech University.

The Peirce Edition Project at Indiana University in Indianapolis.

The Institute for American Thought at Indiana University in Indianapolis.

The Grupo de Estudios Peirceanos is directed by Jaime Nubiola at the Philosophy Department of the University of Navarra, Spain.

The Centro de Estudos Peirceanos (CEPE) in Brazil.

The Peirce Arisbe website lists many more centers and institutes devoted to Peirce.

The Semiotics Research Centre, of the Semiotics and Communication Theory Program at Victoria College, University of Toronto.

The Centro de Estudos em Filosofia Americana e Pragmatismo in Brazil.

The Centro de Estudos do Pragmatismo operates at the Pontificia Universidade Catolica de Sao Paulo in Brazil. This center holds international conferences and publishes papers in a journal, *Cognitio: Revista de Filosofia*.

Societies and networks

- Society for the Advancement of American Philosophy
- Charles S. Peirce Society
- Groupe d'Études sur le Pragmatisme et la Philosophie Américaine
- Centro de Estudos em Filosofia Americana e Pragmatismo
- Groupe de Recherches Associées sur le Pragmatisme et la Philosophie Contemporaine
- Dutch Pragmatism Foundation
- The Central European Pragmatism Forum
- Midwest Study Group of Classical and Contemporary Pragmatism
- Highlands Institute for American Religious and Philosophical Thought
- International Association for Semiotic Studies
- Semiotic Society of America
- The Helsinki Metaphysical Club and Helsinki Peirce Center, placed at the University of Helsinki, Finland
- The Nordic Pragmatism Network, also primarily and administratively based in Helsinki but spread out in all the Nordic countries (Sweden, Norway, Denmark, Iceland, and Finland)
- International Research Group on Abductive Inference, at Johann Wolfgang Goethe-Universität, Germany
- Society for the Study of Symbolic Interaction
- William James Society
- European William James Project
- Alain Leroy Locke Society
- John Dewey Society
- Philosophy of Education Society
- Midwest Philosophy of Education Society
- European John Dewey Society
- John Dewey Society of Japan
- European Pragmatism Association

19

Pragmatism: A Select Bibliography, 1940–2010

John R. Shook

This bibliography has seven sections: introductory and general works; history of pragmatism; analytic philosophy themes; continental and postmodernist themes; ethics and politics; and society and culture. The final section, compiled by the volume editor, includes the works cited in the editorial chapters of this volume (i.e., Chapters 1, 2, 15-18: *Introduction, Research Methods and Problems, New Directions, Chronology, Glossary*), insofar as those works are *not* listed in the thematic sections of the bibliography.

For tables of contents to many books, specialized bibliographies of the writings of individual pragmatists, books published before 1940, dissertations, and other research resources, visit www.pragmatism.org/research.

Introductory and general works

Includes anthologies and books collecting a pragmatist's writings.

Abel, R. (ed.), (1966), *Humanistic Pragmatism: The Philosophy of F. C. S. Schiller*. New York: The Free Press; London: Collier-Macmillan.
Addams, J. (1906), *Newer ideals of peace*. New York: Macmillan.
—(2003), *The Selected Papers of Jane Addams, vol. 1: Preparing to Lead, 1860–81*. Eds Mary Lynn McCree Bryan, Barbara Bair, and Maree de Angury. Urbana: University of Illinois Press.
—(2008), *The Selected Papers of Jane Addams, vol. 2: Venturing into Usefulness*. Eds Mary Lynn McCree Bryan, Barbara Bair, and Maree de Angury. Urbana: University of Illinois Press.

Anderson, D. (2006), *Philosophy Americana: Making Philosophy at Home in American Culture*. New York: Fordham University Press.
Aune, B. (1970), *Rationalism, Empiricism, and Pragmatism: An Introduction*. New York: Random House. Reprinted, New York: McGraw-Hill, 1995.
Ben-Menahem, Y. (2005), *Hilary Putnam*. Cambridge, UK: Cambridge University Press.
Beraldi, P. (2002), *Il pragmatismo americano, intelligenza filosofica e ragione strumentale*. Bari, Italy: Levante.
Bernstein, R. J. (2010), *The Pragmatic Turn*. Cambridge, UK: Polity.
Calcaterra, R. M. (1997), *Introduzione a il pragmatismo americano*. Rome: Laterza.
Callaway, H. G. and Stroh, G. (2000), *American Ethics: A Source Book from Edwards to Dewey*. Lanham, MD: University Press of America.
Capps, J. M. and Capps, D. (eds), (2005), *James and Dewey on Belief and Experience*. Urbana: University of Illinois Press.
Carreira Da Silva, F. (2007), *G. H. Mead: A Critical Introduction*. Cambridge, UK: Polity.
Corrington, R. S. (1993), *An Introduction to C. S. Peirce: Philosopher, Semiotician, and Ecstatic Naturalist*. Lanham, MD: Rowman & Littlefield.
Depew, D. J. and Hollinger, R. (eds), (1995), *Pragmatism: From Progressivism to Postmodernism*. Westport, CT: Praeger.
De Waal, C. (2001), *On Peirce*. Belmont, CA: Wadsworth/Thomson Learning.
—(2002), *On Mead*. Belmont, CA: Wadsworth/Thomson Learning.
—(2004), *On Pragmatism*. Belmont, CA: Wadsworth/Thomson Learning.
Dewey, J. (1967–1987), *The Collected Works of John Dewey, 1882–1953*, 37 vols. Ed. Jo Ann Boydston. Carbondale: Southern Illinois University Press. (Cited as: EW = Early Works; MW = Middle Works; LW = Late Works.) Contains, for example, *Democracy and Education* (MW 16, 1916), *Reconstruction in Philosophy* (MW 12, 1920), *Human Nature and Conduct* (MW 14, 1922), *Experience and Nature* (LW 1, 1925), *The Public and Its Problems* (LW 2, 1927), *The Quest for Certainty* (LW 4, 1929), *Ethics* (with James Tufts, LW 7, 1932), *A Common Faith* (LW 9, 1934), *Art as Experience* (LW 10, 1934), and *Logic: The Theory of Inquiry* (LW 12, 1938).
—(1989), *The Philosophy of John Dewey*. Two volumes in one. Ed. John J. McDermott. Chicago: University of Chicago Press.
—(1998), *The Essential Dewey*, 2 vols. Eds Larry A. Hickman and Thomas M. Alexander. *Pragmatism, Education, Democracy*, vol. 1; *Ethics, Logic, Psychology*, vol. 2. Bloomington: Indiana University Press.
Du Bois, W. E. B. (1996), *The Oxford W. E. B. Du Bois Reader*. Ed. Eric J. Sundquist. New York: Oxford University Press.
Eames, S. M. (1977), *Pragmatic Naturalism: An Introduction*. Carbondale: Southern Illinois University Press.
Feibleman, J. (1970), *An Introduction to the Philosophy of Charles S. Peirce*. Cambridge, MA: MIT Press.
Fisch, M. H. (ed.), (1996), *Classic American Philosophers: Peirce, James, Royce, Santayana, Dewey, Whitehead*, 2nd edn. New York: Fordham University Press.

Flower, E. and Murphey, M. (1977), *A History of Philosophy in America*, 2 vols. New York: G. P. Putnam's Sons.
Føllesdal, D. (ed.), (2001), *Philosophy of Quine*, 5 vols. New York: Garland.
Frankel, C. (ed.), (1960), *The Golden Age of American Philosophy*. New York: George Braziller.
Goetzmann, W. H. (2009), *Beyond the Revolution: A History of American Thought from Paine to Pragmatism*. New York: Basic Books.
Goodman, R. B. (1990), *American Philosophy and the Romantic Tradition*. Cambridge, UK: Cambridge University Press.
Goodman, R. (ed.), (1995), *Pragmatism: A Contemporary Reader*. London and New York: Routledge.
—(ed.), (2005), *Pragmatism: Critical Concepts in Philosophy*. 4 vols. London and New York: Routledge.
Gunn, G. (1992), *Thinking Across the American Grain: Ideology, Intellect, and the New Pragmatism*. Chicago: University of Chicago Press.
Haack, S. (ed.), (2006), *Pragmatism, Old And New: Selected Writings*. Amherst, NY: Prometheus Books.
Hamilton, P. (ed.), (1992), *George Herbert Mead: Critical Assessments*. 4 vols. London and New York: Routledge.
Hampe, M. (2008), *Erkenntnis und Praxis: zur Philosophie des Pragmatismus*. Frankfurt am Main: Suhrkamp.
Harris, L., Pratt, S. L., and Waters, A. (eds), (2001), *American Philosophies: An Anthology*. Oxford: Blackwell.
Hartshorne, C. (1984), *Creativity in American Philosophy*. Albany, NY: State University of New York Press.
Haydon, A. E. (2006), *Pragmatism And the Rise of Religious Humanism: the Writings of Albert Eustace Haydon*, 3 vols. Eds Creighton Peden and John N. Gaston. Lewiston, NY: Edwin Mellon Press.
Hester, D. M., and Talisse, R. B. (2004), *On James*. Belmont, CA: Wadsworth-Thompson Learning.
Hickman, L. (2001), *Philosophical Tools for Technological Culture: Putting Pragmatism to Work*. Bloomington: Indiana University Press.
Hildebrand, D. (2008), *Dewey: A Beginner's Guide*. Oxford, Oneworld.
Hook, S. (1974), *Pragmatism and the Tragic Sense of Life*. New York: Basic Books.
—(2002), *Sidney Hook on Pragmatism, Democracy, and Freedom: The Essential Essays*. Eds Robert Talisse and Robert Tempio. Buffalo, NY: Prometheus Books.
James, W. (1967), *The Writings of William James*. Ed. John J. McDermott. New York: Random House. Reprinted, Chicago: University of Chicago Press, 1978. Includes "Annotated Bibliography of the Writings of William James".
—(1975–1988), *The Works of William James*. Eds Frederick H. Burkhardt, Fredson Bowers, and Ignas K. Skrupskelis. Cambridge, MA and London: Harvard University Press. Contains, for example, *The Principles of Psychology* (1890), *The Will to*

Believe and Other Essays in Popular Philosophy (1897), *The Varieties of Religious Experience* (1902), *Pragmatism: A New Name for Some Old Ways of Thinking* (1907), *The Meaning of Truth* (1909a), *A Pluralistic Universe* (1909b), *Some Problems of Philosophy* (1911), and *Essays on Radical Empiricism* (1912).

Joas, H. (1993), *Pragmatism and Social Theory*. A translation of *Pragmatismus und Gesellschaftstheorie* (1992). Chicago: University of Chicago Press.

Johnson, E. C. (ed.), (1960), *Jane Addams, A Centennial Reader*. New York: Macmillan.

Kemp, G. (2006), *Quine: A Guide for the Perplexed*. London and New York: Continuum.

Kennedy, G. and Konvitz, M. R. (ed.), (1960), *American Pragmatists: Selected Writings*. New York: Meridian Books.

Kuklick, B. (1985), *Churchmen and Philosophers: From Jonathan Edwards to John Dewey*. New Haven: Yale University Press.

Kuklick, B. (2001), *A History of Philosophy in America, 1720–2000*. Oxford: Oxford University Press.

Kurtz, P. (ed.), (1968), *American Philosophy in the Twentieth Century: A Sourcebook from Pragmatism to Philosophical Analysis*. New York: Macmillan.

—(1990), *Philosophical Essays in Pragmatic Naturalism*. Buffalo, NY: Prometheus Books.

Levine, B. (1996), *Works About John Dewey, 1886–1995*. Carbondale, IL: Southern Illinois University Press.

Lewis, C. I. (1970), *Collected Papers of Clarence Irving Lewis*. Eds John Goheen and John Mothershead, Jr. Stanford, CA: Stanford University Press.

Locke, A. (1989), *The Philosophy of Alain Locke: Harlem Renaissance and Beyond*. Ed. Leonard Harris. Philadelphia: Temple University Press.

Lovejoy, A. O. (1968), *The Thirteen Pragmatisms and Other Essays* (first published in 1963). Baltimore: Johns Hopkins University Press.

MacKinnon, B. (ed.), (1985), *American Philosophy: A Historical Anthology*. Albany: State University of New York Press.

Malachowski, A. (ed.), (2004), *Pragmatism*, 3 vols. Thousand Oaks, CA: Sage Publications.

Malachowski, A. R. (2010), *The New Pragmatism*. Montreal: McGill-Queen's University Press.

Margolis, J. (2007), *Pragmatism Without Foundations: Reconciling Realism and Relativism*, 2nd edn (first published in 1986). London and New York: Continuum.

McDermid, D. (2006), *The Varieties of Pragmatism: Truth, Realism, And Knowledge from James to Rorty*. London and New York: Continuum.

McDermott, J. J. (1976), *The Culture of Experience: Philosophical Essays in the American Grain*. New York: New York University Press.

—(1986), *Streams of Experience: Reflections on the History and Philosophy of American Culture*. Amherst: University of Massachusetts Press.

—(2007), *The Drama of Possibility: Experience as a Philosophy of Culture*. Ed. Douglas Anderson. New York: Fordham University Press.

Mead, G. H. (1956), *The Social Psychology of George Herbert Mead*. Ed. Anselm L. Strauss. Chicago: University of Chicago Press. Revised edn published as *George Herbert Mead on Social Psychology*. Chicago: University of Chicago Press, 1964.
—(1964), *Selected Writings: George Herbert Mead*. Ed. Andrew Reck. Indianapolis: Bobbs-Merrill. Reprinted, Chicago: University of Chicago Press, 1981.
—(1982), *The Individual and the Social Self: Unpublished Work of George Herbert Mead*. Ed. David L. Miller. Chicago: University of Chicago Press.
Menand, L. (ed.), (1997), *Pragmatism: A Reader*. New York: Random House.
—(2001), *The Metaphysical Club: A Story of Ideas in America*. New York: Farrar, Straus and Giroux.
Mills, C. W. (1964), *Sociology and Pragmatism: The Higher Learning in America*. New York: Paine-Whitman Publishers.
Misak, C. J. (ed.), (2008), *The Oxford Handbook of American philosophy*. Oxford: Oxford University Press.
Moore, E. C. (1961), *American Pragmatism: Peirce, James and Dewey*. New York: Columbia University Press.
Morris, C. W. (1970), *The Pragmatic Movement in American Philosophy*. New York: George Braziller.
Mounce, H. O. (1997), *The Two Pragmatisms: From Peirce to Rorty*. London and New York: Routledge.
Murphy, J. P. (1990), *Pragmatism From Peirce to Davidson*. Boulder, CO: Westview Press.
Nagl, L. (1998), *Pragmatismus*. Frankfurt am Main: Campus Verlag.
Nelson, L. H. and Nelson, J. (2000), *On Quine*. Belmont, CA: Wadsworth/Thomson Learning.
Oehler, K. (1995), *Sachen und Zeichen: Zur Philosophie des Pragmatismus*. Frankfort am Main: V. Klostemann.
Oller, J. W. (ed.), (1989), *Language and Experience: Classic Pragmatism*. Lanham, MD: University Press of America.
Peirce, C. S. (1931–1958), *The Collected Papers of Charles Sanders Peirce*, 8 vols. Eds Charles Hartshorne and Paul Weiss (vols 1–6) and Arthur Burks (vols 7–8). Cambridge, MA: Harvard University Press. (Cited as CP volume.paragraph.)
—(1980–), *Writings of Charles S. Peirce: A Chronological Edition*, 7 vols to date. Ed. The Peirce Edition Project. Bloomington, ID: Indiana University Press. (Cited as W volume: page.)
—(1992), *The Essential Peirce*, vol. 1, 1867–1893. Ed. The Peirce Edition Project. Bloomington, ID: Indiana University Press. (Cited as EP volume:page.)
—(1998), *The Essential Peirce*, vol. 2, 1893–1913. Ed. The Peirce Edition Project. Bloomington, ID: Indiana University Press.
Perez de Tudela, J. (1988), *El pragmatismo americano: acción racional y reconstrucción del sentido*. Madrid: Cincel. Reprinted, Madrid: Síntesis, 2007.
Poirier, R. (1992), *Poetry and Pragmatism*. Cambridge, MA: Harvard University Press.

Prado, C. G. (1987), *The Limits of Pragmatism*. Atlantic Highlands, NJ: Humanities Press.
Pratt, S. L. (2002), *Native Pragmatism*. Bloomington, ID: Indiana University Press.
Putnam, H. (1995), *Pragmatism: An Open Question*. Oxford: Blackwell.
Quine, W. V. (2004), *Quintessence: Basic Readings from the Philosophy of W. V. Quine*. Ed. Roger Gibson. Cambridge, MA: Harvard University.
Reck, A., Harvath, T., and Krettek, T. (eds), (1994), *American Philosophers' Ideas of Ultimate Reality and Meaning*. Toronto: University of Toronto Press.
Rescher, N. (1977), *Methodological Pragmatism*. Oxford: Basil Blackwell; New York University Press.
—(2000), *Realistic Pragmatism: An Introduction to Pragmatic Philosophy*. Albany: State University of New York Press.
Richardson, J. (2007), *A Natural History of Pragmatism: The Fact of Feeling from Jonathan Edwards to Gertrude Stein*. Cambridge, UK: Cambridge University Press.
Rorty, A. (ed.), (1966), *Pragmatic Philosophy: An Anthology*. Garden City, NY: Anchor Books.
Rosenbaum, S. E. (2009), *Pragmatism and the Reflective Life*. Lanham, MD: Lexington Books.
Roth, R. J. (1998), *Radical Pragmatism: An Alternative*. New York: Fordham University Press.
Royce, J. (1951), *Logical Essays*. Ed. D. S. Robinson. Dubuque, IA: William C. Brown.
—(1969), *The Basic Writings of Josiah Royce*. Ed. John J. McDermott. Chicago: University of Chicago Press. Reprinted, Fordham University Press, 2005.
Rumana, R. (2000), *On Rorty*. Belmont, CA: Wadsworth/Thomson Learning.
—(2002), *Richard Rorty: An Annotated Bibliography of Secondary Literature*. Amsterdam and New York: Rodopi.
Sandbothe, M. and Egginton, W. (eds), (2004), *The Pragmatic Turn in Philosophy: Contemporary Engagements Between Analytic and Continental Thought*. Albany: State University of New York Press.
Scheffler, I. (1974), *Four Pragmatists: A Critical Introduction to Peirce, James, Mead, and Dewey*. New York: Humanities Press; London: Routledge and Kegan Paul.
Schiller, F. C. S. (2008), *F. C. S. Schiller on Pragmatism and Humanism: Selected Writings, 1891–1939*. Eds John R. Shook and Hugh P. McDonald. Amherst, NY: Prometheus Books.
Schillp, P. A. (ed.), (1998), *The Philosophy of W. V. Quine*, 2nd edn. La Salle, IL: Open Court.
Schneider, H. W. (1963), *A History of American Philosophy*, 2nd edn. New York: Columbia University Press.
—(1964), *Sources of Contemporary Philosophical Realism in America*. Indianapolis: Bobbs-Merrill.
Searles, H. L. and Shields, A. (1969), *A Bibliography of the Works of F. C. S. Schiller*. San Diego, CA: San Diego State College Press.

Shook, J. R. (1998), *Pragmatism: An Annotated Bibliography, 1898–1940*. Amsterdam: Editions Rodopi.
—(ed.), (2000), *The Chicago School of Pragmatism*. 4 vols. Bristol, England: Thoemmes.
—(ed.), (2001), *Early Critics of Pragmatism*. 5 vols. Bristol, England: Thoemmes.
—(ed.), (2001), *Early Defenders of Pragmatism*. 5 vols. Bristol, England: Thoemmes.
—(ed.), (2001), *The Chicago School of Functionalism*. 3 vols. Bristol, England: Thoemmes.
—(ed.), (2003), *The Collected Writings of Addison W. Moore*. 3 vols. Bristol, UK: Thoemmes.
Shook, J. R. and De Tienne, A. (eds), (2006), *The Cambridge School of Pragmatism*, 4 vols. Bristol, UK: Thoemmes Continuum.
Shook, J. R. and Margolis, J. (eds), (2006), *A Companion to Pragmatism*. Malden, MA: Blackwell.
Shusterman, R. (1997), *Practicing Philosophy: Pragmatism and the Philosophical Life*. London and New York: Routledge.
—(ed.), (2004), *The Range of Pragmatism and the Limits of Philosophy*. Metaphilosophy special issue. Oxford: Blackwell.
Sini, C., Rendueles, C., and del Olmo, C. (1999), *El pragmatismo*. Madrid: Akal.
Skrupskelis, I. K. (1977), *William James: A Reference Guide*. Boston: G. K. Hall.
Smith, J. E. (1963), *The Spirit of American Philosophy*. New York: Oxford University Press.
—(1970), *Themes in American Philosophy: Purpose, Experience, and Community*. New York: Harper and Row.
—(1978), *Purpose and Thought: The Meaning of Pragmatism*. New Haven, CT: Yale University Press.
—(1992), *America's Philosophical Vision*. Chicago: University of Chicago Press.
Spencer, M. (ed.), (2002), *John Dewey and American Education*, 3 vols. Bristol, UK: Thoemmes.
Stuhr, J. J. (1997), *Genealogical Pragmatism: Philosophy, Experience, and Community*. Albany: State University of New York Press.
—(ed.), (1999), *Pragmatism and Classical American Philosophy: Essential Readings and Interpretive Essays*, 2nd ed. Oxford: Oxford University Press.
—(2003), Pragmatism, Postmodernism, and the Future of Philosophy. New York: Routledge.
Talisse, R. B. (2000), *On Dewey: The Reconstruction of Philosophy*. Belmont, CA: Wadsworth/Thomson Learning.
Talisse, R. B. and Aikin, S. F. (2008), *Pragmatism: A guide for the perplexed*. London and New York: Continuum.
Thayer, H. S. (1981), *Meaning and Action: A Critical History of Pragmatism*. 2nd edn. Indianapolis: Hackett (1st ed. 1968).
—(ed.), (1997), *Pragmatism: The Classic Writings*. First published in 1970. Indianapolis: Hackett.

Tiles, J. E. (ed.), (1992), *John Dewey: Critical Assessments*. 4 vols. London and New York: Routledge.
Tufts, J. H. (1992), *Selected Writings of James Hayden Tufts*, ed. James Campbell. Carbondale: Southern Illinois University Press.
Unger, R. M. (2007), *The Self Awakened: Pragmatism Unbound*. Cambridge, MA: Harvard University Press.
Vailati, G. (2009), *Logic and Pragmatism: Selected Essays by Giovanni Vailati*. Eds Claudia Arrighi, et al. Stanford, CA: CSLI Publications.
West, C. (1999), *The Cornel West Reader*. New York: Basic *Civitas* Books.
White, M. G. (1972), *Science and Sentiment in America: Philosophical Thought from Jonathan Edwards to John Dewey*. New York: Oxford University Press.
—(1973), *Pragmatism and the American Mind: Essays and Reviews in Philosophy and Intellectual History*. Oxford: Oxford University Press.
—(2002), *A Philosophy of Culture: The Scope of Holistic Pragmatism*. Princeton, NJ: Princeton University Press.
Wilson, D. J. (1990), *Science, Community, and the Transformation of American Philosophy, 1860–1930*. Chicago: University of Chicago Press.
Winn, R. B. (1955), *American Philosophy*. New York: Philosophical Library.

History of pragmatism

Includes advanced books about historical pragmatists.

Aasen, J. (2008), *Dewey: John Deweys pedagogiske filosofi*. Vallset, Norway: Oplandske bokforl.
Abel, R. (1955), *The Pragmatic Humanism of F. C. S. Schiller*. New York: King's Crown Press.
Aboulafia, M. (ed.), (1991), *Philosophy, Social Theory and the Thought of George Herbert Mead*. Albany: State University of New York Press.
—(2001), *The Cosmopolitan Self: George Herbert Mead and Continental Philosophy*. Chicago: University of Illinois Press.
Alexander, T. M. (1987), *John Dewey's Theory of Art, Experience, and Nature: The Horizons of Feeling*. Albany: State University of New York Press.
Allen, G. W. (1967), *William James, a Biography*. New York: Viking Press.
Almeder, R. F. (1980), *The Philosophy of Charles S. Peirce: A Critical Introduction*. Totowa, NJ: Rowman & Littlefield.
Alridge, D. P. (2008), *The Educational Thought of W. E. B. Du Bois: an intellectual history*. New York: Teachers College Press.
Ames, E. S. (1959), *Beyond Theology: The Autobiography of Edward Scribner Ames*. Ed. Van Meter Ames. Chicago: University of Chicago Press.
Anderson, D. (1987), *Creativity and the Philosophy of C. S. Peirce*. Dordrecht: Martinus Nijhoff.

Anderson, D. R. (1995), *Strands of System: The Philosophy of Charles Peirce*. West Lafayette, IN: Purdue University Press.
Apel, K.-O. (1981), *Charles S. Peirce: From Pragmatism to Pragmaticism*. Amherst: University of Massachusetts Press.
Arens, E. (1994), *The Logic of Pragmatic Thinking: From Peirce to Habermas*. Atlantic Highlands, NJ: Humanities Press.
Ayer, A. J. (1968), *The Origins of Pragmatism: Studies in the Philosophies of Charles Sanders Peirce and William James*. San Francisco, CA: Freeman, Cooper.
Baldwin, J. D. (1986), *George Herbert Mead: A Unifying Theory for Sociology*. Newbury Park, CA: Sage Publications.
Barzun, J. (1983), *A Stroll with William James*. New York: Harper and Row.
Battistella, E. H. (1983), *Pragmatismo y semiótica en Charles S. Peirce*. Caracas: Ediciones de la Biblioteca, Universidad Central de Venezuela.
Bergman, M. (2009), *Peirce's Philosophy of Communication*. London and New York: Continuum.
Bernstein, R. (ed.), (1965), *Perspectives on Peirce: Critical Essays on Charles Sanders Peirce*. New Haven, CT: Yale University Press, 1965. Reprinted, Westport, CT: Greenwood, 1980.
Bernstein, R. J. (1966), *John Dewey*. New York: Washington Square Press.
Bertilsson, M. (2009), *Peirce's Theory of Inquiry and Beyond: Towards a Social Reconstruction of Science Theory*. Frankfurt am Main: Peter Lang.
Bird, G. (1986), *William James*. London and New York: Routledge and Kegan Paul.
Bjork, D. W. (1988), *William James: The Center of His Vision*. New York: Columbia University Press. Reprinted, Washington, DC: American Psychological Association, 1997.
Blau, J. (1952), *Men and Movements in American Philosophy*. New York: Prentice-Hall.
Blum, D. (2006), *Ghost Hunters: William James and the Search for Scientific Proof of Life after Death*. New York: Penguin Press.
Boisvert, R. D. (1988), *Dewey's Metaphysics*. New York: Fordham University Press.
—(1998). *John Dewey: Rethinking Our Time*. Albany: State University of New York Press.
Boler, J. (1963), *Charles Peirce and Scholastic Realism: A Study of Peirce's Relation to John Duns Scotus*. Seattle: University of Washington Press.
Bordogna, F. (2008), *William James at the Boundaries: Philosophy, Science, and the Geography of Knowledge*. Chicago: University of Chicago Press.
Boydston, J. A. (ed.), (1970), *Guide to the Works of John Dewey*. Carbondale: Southern Illinois University Press.
Brent, J. (1998), *Charles Sanders Peirce: A Life*, 2nd edn. Bloomington: Indiana University Press.
Brown, H. (2000), *William James on Radical Empiricism and Religion*. Toronto: University of Toronto Press.
Brown, V. B. (2007), *The Education of Jane Addams: Politics and Culture in Modern America*. Philadelphia: University of Pennsylvania Press.

Brunning, J. and Forster, P. (eds), (1997), *The Rule of Reason: The Philosophy of Charles Sanders Peirce.* Toronto: University of Toronto Press.
Bullert, G. (1983), *The Politics of John Dewey.* Buffalo, NY: Prometheus Books.
Burke, T. (1994), *Dewey's New Logic: A Reply to Russell.* Chicago: University of Chicago.
Buswell, J. O., Jr. (1950), *The Philosophies of F. R. Tennant and John Dewey.* New York: Philosophical Library.
Cahn, S. M. (ed.), (1977), *New Studies in the Philosophy of John Dewey.* Hanover, NH: University Press of New England.
Carden, S. D. (2006), *Virtue Ethics: Dewey and Macintyre.* London and New York: Continuum.
Carreira da Silva, F. (2007), *G. H. Mead: A Critical Introduction.* Cambridge, UK: Polity.
Carreira da Silva, F. (2008), *Mead and Modernity: Science, Selfhood, and Democratic Politics.* Lanham, MD: Lexington Books.
Carrette, J. (ed.), (2005), *William James And The Varieties Of Religious Experience: A Centenary Celebration.* London: Routledge.
Caruana, F. (2009), *Peirce et une Introduction à la Semiotique de l'art.* Paris: L'Harmattan.
Caspary, W. R. (2000), *Dewey on Democracy.* Ithaca, NY: Cornell University Press.
Caws, P. (ed.), (1980), *Two Centuries of Philosophy in America.* London: Blackwell; Totowa, NJ: Rowman & Littlefield.
Chambliss, J. J. (1990), *The Influence of Plato and Aristotle on John Dewey's Philosophy.* Lewiston, NY: Edwin Mellen Press.
Cheng, C.-Y. (1969), *Peirce's and Lewis's Theories of Induction.* The Hague: Martinus Nijhoff.
Chiasson, P. (2001), *Peirce's Pragmatism: The Design for Thinking.* Amsterdam and New York: Rodopi.
Clendenning, J. (1999), *The Life and Thought of Josiah Royce*, 2nd edn. Nashville, Tenn.: Vanderbilt University Press.
Cochran, M. (ed.), (2010), *The Cambridge Companion to Dewey.* Cambridge, UK: Cambridge University Press.
Colapietro, V. (1989), *Peirce's Approach to the Self: A Semiotic Perspective on Human Subjectivity.* Albany: State University of New York Press.
Cook, G. A. (1993), *George Herbert Mead: The Making of a Social Pragmatist.* Urbana: University of Illinois Press.
Cooke, E. F. (2007), *Peirce's Pragmatic Theory of Inquiry: Fallibilism and Indeterminacy.* London and New York: Continuum.
Cooper, W. (2002), *The Unity of William James's Thought.* Nashville, TN: Vanderbilt University Press.
Corti, W. R. (ed.), (1973), *The Philosophy of George Herbert Mead.* Amriswil, Switzerland: Amriswiler Bücherei.
—(ed.), (1976), *The Philosophy of William James.* Hamburg: Meiner.
Cotkin, G. (1990), *William James: Public Philosopher.* Baltimore: Johns Hopkins University Press. Reprinted, Urbana: University of Illinois Press, 1994.

Cotter, M. J. (ed.), (2004), *Sidney Hook Reconsidered*. Amherst, NY: Prometheus Books.
Coughlan, N. (1975), *Young John Dewey*. Chicago: University of Chicago Press.
Croce, P. J. (1995), *Science and Religion in the Era of William James, vol.1: The Eclipse of Certainty, 1820–1880*. Chapel Hill: University of North Carolina Press.
Cronk, G. (1987), *The Philosophical Anthropology of George Herbert Mead*. New York: Peter Lang.
Crosser, P. K. (1955), *The Nihilism of John Dewey*. New York: Philosophical Library.
Dalton, T. C. (2002), *Becoming John Dewey: Dilemmas of a Philosopher and Naturalist*. Bloomington: Indiana University Press.
Davis, W. H. (1972), *Peirce's Epistemology*. The Hague: Martinus Nijhoff.
Deledalle, G. (1967), *L'idée d'Experience dans la Philosophie de John Dewey*. Paris: Presses Universitaires de France.
—(1990), *Charles S. Peirce, 1839–1914: An Intellectual Biography*. Translation of *Charles S. Peirce: phénoménologue et sémioticien*, translated and introduced by Susan Petrelli. Amsterdam and Philadelphia: John Benjamins.
—(2000), *Charles S. Peirce's Philosophy of Signs*. Bloomington: Indiana University Press.
Dennis, L. J. (1992), *From Prayer to Pragmatism: A Biography of John L. Childs*. Carbondale: Southern Illinois University Press.
Deuser, H. (1993), *Gott: Geist und Natur, Theologische Konsequenzen aus Charles S. Peirce's Religionsphilosophie*. Berlin: Walter de Gruyter.
Dicker, G. (1976), *Dewey's Theory of Knowing*. Philadelphia: Philosophical Monographs.
Dooley, P. K. (1974), *Pragmatism and Humanism: The Philosophy of William James*. Chicago: Nelson-Hall.
Dykhuizen, G. (1973), *The Life and Mind of John Dewey*. Carbondale, Southern Illinois University Press.
Eames, S. M. (2003), *Experience and Value: Essays on John Dewey and Pragmatic Naturalism*. Eds Elizabeth R. Eames and Richard W. Field. Carbondale: Southern Illinois University Press.
Edel, A. (2002), *Ethical Theory and Social Change: The Evolution of John Dewey's Ethics, 1908–1932*. Somerset, NJ: Transaction Publishers.
Edie, J. (2005), *William James and Phenomenology*. Bloomington: Indiana University Press.
Efron, A. (2005), *Experiencing Tess of the d' Urbervilles: A Deweyan Account*. Amsterdam: Rodopi.
Eisele, C. (1979), *Studies in the Scientific and Mathematical Philosophy of Charles S. Peirce: Essays*. The Hague: Mouton.
Eisendrath, C. R. (1971), *The Unifying Moment: The Psychological Philosophy of William James and Alfred North Whitehead*. Cambridge, MA: Harvard University Press.
Ejsing, A. (2007), *Theology of Anticipation: A Constructive Study of C. S. Peirce*. Eugene, OR: Pickwick Publications.
Eldridge, M. (1998), *Transforming Experience: John Dewey's Cultural Instrumentalism*. Nashville, TN: Vanderbilt University Press.

Engler, U. (1992), *Kritik der Erfahring: Die Bedeutung der asthetischen Erfahrung in der Philosophie John Deweys*. Wurzburg: Konigshausen und Neuman.

Fairfield, P. (ed.), (2010), *John Dewey and Continental Philosophy*. Carbondale: Southern Illinois University Press.

Feffer, A. (1993), *The Chicago Pragmatists and American Progressivism*. Ithaca, NY: Cornell University Press.

Ferguson, K. (2007), *William James: Politics in the Pluriverse*. Lanham, MD: Rowman and Littlefield.

Fesmire, S. (2003), *John Dewey and Moral Imagination: Pragmatism in Ethics*. Bloomington: Indiana University Press.

Fisch, M. (1986), *Peirce, Semiotic, and Pragmatism*. Bloomington: Indiana University Press.

Fischer, M., Nackenoff, C., and Chmielewski, W. (ed.), (2009), *Jane Addams and the practice of democracy*. Urbana: University of Illinois Press.

Fishman, S. M. and Parkinson McCarthy, L. (2007), *John Dewey and the Philosophy and Practice of Hope*. Urbana: University of Illinois Press.

Fontinell, E. (1986), *Self, God, and Immortality: A Jamesian Investigation*. Philadelphia: Temple University Press. Reprinted, New York: Fordham University Press, 2000.

Fott, D. (1998), *John Dewey: America's Philosopher of Democracy*. Lanham, MD: Rowman and Littlefield.

Franzese, S. and Kraemer, F. (ed.), (2007), *Fringes of Religious Experience: Cross-Perspectives on William James's The Varieties of Religious Experience*. Frankfurt: Ontos.

Freadman, A. (2004), *The Machinery of Talk: Charles Peirce and the Sign Hypothesis*. Stanford, CA: Stanford University Press.

Freeman, E. (ed.), (1983), *The Relevance of Charles Peirce*. La Salle, IL: Hegeler Institute.

Gale, R. (1999), *The Divided Self of William James*. Cambridge: Cambridge University Press. Abridged version titled *The Philosophy of William James: An Introduction*. Cambridge, UK: Cambridge University Press, 2005.

Gale, R. M. (2009), *John Dewey's Quest for Unity: The Journey of a Promethean Mystic*. Amherst, NY: Prometheus Books.

Gallie, W. B. (1952), *Peirce and Pragmatism*. Harmondsworth, UK: Penguin. Reprinted, New York: Dover, 1966.

Garrison, J. (1997), *Dewey and Eros: Wisdom and Desire in the Art of Thinking*. New York: Teachers College Press.

Gavin, W. J. (1992), *William James and the Reinstatement of the Vague*. Philadelphia: Temple University Press.

Gavin, W. (ed.), (2003), *In Dewey's Wake: Unfinished Work of Pragmatic Reconstruction*. Albany, NY: State University of New York Press.

Geiger, G. R. (1958), *John Dewey in Perspective*. New York: Oxford University Press.

Gelpi, D. L. (2001), *Peirce and Theology: Essays in the Authentication of Doctrine*. Lanham, MD: University Press of America.

Gibson, R. F. (ed.), (2004), *The Cambridge Companion to Quine*. Cambridge: Cambridge University Press.
Good, J. A. (2006), *A Search for Unity in Diversity: The "Permanent Hegelian Deposit" in the Philosophy of John Dewey*. Lanham, MD: Rowman & Littlefield.
Gouinlock, J. (1972), *John Dewey's Philosophy of Value*. New York: Humanities Press.
Grange, J. (2004), *John Dewey, Confucius, and Global Philosophy*. Albany: State University of New York Press.
Granger, D. A. (2006), *John Dewey, Robert Pirsig, and the Art of Living: Revisioning Aesthetic Education*. New York: Palgrave Macmillan.
Grossman, J. D. and Rischin, R. (eds), (2002), *William James in Russian Culture*. Lanham, MD: Lexington Books.
Gunter, P. A. Y. (ed.), (1990), *Creativity in George Herbert Mead*. Lanham, MD: University Press of America.
Hamington, M. (2004), *Embodied Care: Jane Addams, Maurice Merleau-Ponty, and Feminist Ethics*. Urbana: University of Illinois Press.
—(2009), *The Social Philosophy of Jane Addams*. Urbana: University of Illinois Press.
Hardwick, C. S. (1977), *Semiotic and Significs: The Correspondence between Charles S. Peirce and Victoria Lady Welby*. Bloomington: Indiana University Press.
Harris, L. (ed.), (1999), *The Critical Pragmatism of Alain Locke: A Reader on Value Theory, Aesthetics, Community, Culture, Race, and Education*. Lanham, MD: Rowman & Littlefield.
Harris, L. and Molesworth, C. (2008), *Alain L. Locke: The Biography of a Philosopher*. Chicago: University of Chicago Press.
Hausman, C. R. (1993), *Charles S. Peirce's Evolutionary Philosophy*. Cambridge: Cambridge University Press.
Heft, H. (2001), *Ecological Psychology in Context: James Gibson, Roger Barker, and the Legacy of William James's Radical Empiricism*. Mahwah, NJ: Lawrence Erlbaum Associates.
Helm, B. P. (1985), *Time and Reality in American Philosophy*. Amherst: University of Massachusetts Press.
Hickman, L. A. (1990), *John Dewey's Pragmatic Technology*. Bloomington: Indiana University Press.
—(ed.), (1998), *Reading Dewey: Interpretations for a Postmodern Generation*. Bloomington: Indiana University Press.
—(2007), *Pragmatism as Post-postmodernism: Lessons from John Dewey*. New York: Fordham University Press.
Hickman, L. A. and Neubert, S. (ed.), (2009), *John Dewey between Pragmatism and Constructivism*. New York: Fordham University Press.
Hickman, L. A. and Spadafora, G. (2009), *John Dewey's Educational Philosophy in International Perspective: A New Democracy for the Twenty-First Century*. Carbondale: Southern Illinois University Press.

Hildebrand, D. (2003), *Beyond Realism and Antirealism: John Dewey and the Neopragmatists*. Nashville, TN: Vanderbilt University Press.
Hingst, K.-M. (1997), *Perspektivismus und Pragmatismus: Ein Vergleich auf der Grundlage der Wahrheitsbegriffe und der Religionsphilosophie von Neitzsche und James*. Wurzburg: Konigshausen und Neumann.
Hook, S. (ed.), (1950), *John Dewey: Philosopher of Science and Freedom*. New York: Dial Press.
—(1996), *The Metaphysics of Pragmatism* (first published in 1927). Amherst, NY: Prometheus Books.
Hookway, C. (1985), *Peirce*. London: Routledge and Kegan Paul.
—(2000), *Truth, Rationality, and Pragmatism: Themes from Peirce*. Oxford: Oxford University Press.
Houser, N., Roberts, D. D., and Van Evra, J. (eds), (1997), *Studies in the Logic of Charles Sanders Peirce*. Bloomington: Indiana University Press.
Hoy, T. (1998), *The Political Philosophy of John Dewey: Towards a Constructive Renewal*. Westport, CT: Praeger.
Hylton, P. (2007), *Quine*. London and New York: Routledge.
Jackson, P. W. (1998), *John Dewey and the Lessons of Art*. New Haven: Yale University Press.
—(2002), *John Dewey and the Philosopher's Task*. New York: Teachers College Press.
Jaffe, R. (1960), *The Pragmatic Conception of Justice*. Berkeley: University of California Press.
James, E. (2009), *Routledge Philosophy Guidebook to William James on Psychology and Metaphysics*. London and New York: Routledge.
Jenlink, P. M. (ed.), (2009), *Dewey's Democracy and Education Revisited: Contemporary Discourses for Democratic Education and Leadership*. Lanham, MD: Rowman & Littlefield.
Joas, H. (1985), *G. H. Mead: A Contemporary Re-examination of his Thought*. Cambridge, MA: MIT Press.
Johnston, J. S. (2006), *Inquiry And Education: John Dewey And the Quest for Democracy*. Albany: State University of New York Press.
Joslin, K. (2009), *Jane Addams: A Writer's Life*. Urbana: University of Illinois Press.
Kadlec, A. (2007), *Dewey's Critical Pragmatism*. Lanham, MD: Lexington Books.
Kahn, J. S. (2009), *Divine Discontent: The religious imagination of W. E. B. Du Bois*. Oxford: Oxford University Press.
Kegley, J. A. K. (2008), *Josiah Royce in Focus*. Bloomington: Indiana University Press.
Kellogg, F. R. (2007), *Oliver Wendell Holmes, Jr., Legal Theory, and Judicial Restraint*. Cambridge, UK: Cambridge University Press.
Kemp, G. (2006), *Quine: A Guide for the Perplexed*. London and New York: Continuum.
Kent, B. E. (1987), *Charles S. Peirce: Logic and the Classification of the Sciences*. Kingston, Ontario: McGill-Queen's University Press.

Kestenbaum, V. (1977), *The Phenomenological Sense of John Dewey: Habit and Meaning.* Atlantic Highlands, NJ: Humanities Press.
—(2002), *The Grace and Severity of the Ideal: John Dewey and the Transcendent.* Chicago: University of Chicago Press.
Ketner, K. L. (ed.), (1981), *Proceedings of the C. S. Peirce Bicentennial International Congress.* Lubbock, TX: Texas Tech Press.
—(ed.), (1995), *Peirce and Contemporary Thought: Philosophical Inquiries.* New York: Fordham University Press.
—(1998), *His Glassy Essence: An Autobiography of Charles Sanders Peirce.* Nashville, TN: Vanderbilt University Press.
Kevelson, R. (1987), *Charles S. Peirce's Method of Methods.* Philadelphia: J. Benjamins.
—(1993), *Peirce's Esthetics of Freedom: Possibility, Complexity, and Emergent Value.* New York: Peter Lang.
—(1996), *Peirce, Science, Signs.* New York: Peter Lang.
—(1999), *Peirce and the Mark of the Gryphon.* New York: St. Martin's Press; Basingstoke, UK: Macmillan.
Khalil, E. (ed.), (2004), *Dewey, Pragmatism and Economic Methodology.* London and New York: Routledge.
Kloppenberg, J. T. (1986), *Uncertain Victory: Social Democracy and Progressivism in European and American Social Thought, 1870–1920.* New York: Oxford University Press.
Knight, L. W. (2005), *Citizen: Jane Addams and the Struggle for Democracy.* Chicago: University of Chicago Press.
Knight, T. S. (1958), *Charles Peirce.* New York: Washington Square Press.
Konvitz, M. R. (ed.), (1987), *The Legacy of Horace M. Kallen.* Cranbury, NJ: Associated University Presses.
Krikorian, Y. H. (ed.), (1944), *Naturalism and the Human Spirit.* New York: Columbia University Press.
Kurtz, P. (ed.), (1983), *Sidney Hook: Philosopher of Democracy and Humanism.* Buffalo, NY: Prometheus Books.
Lamberth, D. C. (1999), *William James and the Metaphysics of Experience.* Cambridge, UK: Cambridge University Press.
—(ed.), (2010), *James and Royce Reconsidered: Reflections on the Centenary of Pragmatism.* Cambridge, MA: Harvard University Press.
Lapoujade, D. (2007), *William James, empirisme et pragmatisme.* Paris: Empêcheurs de penser en rond; Paris: Seuil.
—(2008), *Fictions du Pragmatisme: William et Henry James.* Paris: Minuit.
Lawson, D. E. and Lean, A. E. (ed.), (1964), *John Dewey and the World View.* Carbondale: Southern Illinois University Press.
Levinson, H. S. (1981), *The Religious Investigations of William James.* Chapel Hill: University of North Carolina Press.

—(1992), *Santayana, Pragmatism, and the Spiritual Life*. Chapel Hill: University of North Carolina Press.

Levitt, M. (1960), *Freud and Dewey on the Nature of Man*. New York: Philosophical Library.

Lewis, J. D. and Smith, R. L. (1980), *American Sociology and Pragmatism: Mead, Chicago Sociology, and Symbolic Interaction*. Chicago: University of Chicago Press.

Liszka, J. J. (1996), *A General Introduction to the Semeiotic of Charles Sanders Peirce*. Bloomington: Indiana University Press.

Madden, E. H. (1958), *The Philosophical Writings of Chauncey Wright: Representative Selections*. New York, Liberal Arts Press.

—(1963), *Chauncey Wright and the Foundations of Pragmatism*. Seattle: University of Washington Press.

Mahowald, M. (1972), *An Idealistic Pragmatism: The Development of the Pragmatic Element in the Philosophy of Josiah Royce*. The Hague: Nijhoff.

Manicas, P. T. (2008), *Rescuing Dewey: essays in pragmatic naturalism*. Lanham, MD: Lexington Books.

Marcell, D. W. (1974), *Progress and Pragmatism: James, Dewey, Beard, and the American Idea of Progress*. Westport, CT: Greenwood Press.

Martin, J. (2003), *The Education of John Dewey: A Biography*. New York: Columbia University Press.

Martland, T. R. (1963), *The Metaphysics of William James and John Dewey: Process and Structure in Philosophy and Religion*. New York: Philosophical Library.

Mathur, D. C. (1971), *Naturalistic Philosophies of Experience: Studies in James, Dewey, and Farber against the Background of Husserl's Phenomenology*. St. Louis: Warren H. Green.

Mayorga, R. (2007), *From Realism to 'Realicism': The Metaphysics of Charles Sanders Peirce*. Lanham, MD: Rowman & Littlefield.

Melvil, Y. K. (1957), *Amerikanskii Pragmatizm: Lektsii, Prochitannye na Filosofskom Fakultete Moskovskogo Gosudarstvennogo Universiteta*. Moscow: Izd-vo Moskovskogo universiteta.

—(1968), *Charlz Pirs i Pragmatizm: U Istokov Amerikanskoi Burzhuaznoi Filosofii XX Veka*. Moscow: Izd-vo Moskovskogo universiteta.

Merrell, F. (1997), *Peirce, Signs, and Meaning*. Toronto: University of Toronto Press.

Meyer, S. (ed.), (1985), *Dewey and Russell: An Exchange*. New York: Philosophical Library.

Miller, D. L. (1973), *George Herbert Mead: Self, Language, and the World*. Austin: University of Texas Press. Reprinted, Chicago: University of Chicago Press, 1980. Misak, C. (ed.), (2004), *The Cambridge Companion to Peirce*. Cambridge: Cambridge University Press.

Mladenov, I. (2005), *Conceptualizing Metaphors: On Charles Peirce's Marginalia*. London: Routledge.

Moore, E. C. (1961), *American Pragmatism: Peirce, James and Dewey*. New York: Columbia University Press.
—(1965), *William James*. New York: Washington Square Press.
Moore, E. C., Robin, R., and Wiener, P. P. (ed.), (1964), *Studies in the Philosophy of Charles Sanders Peirce, Second Series*. Amherst: University of Massachusetts Press.
Moore, E. C. (ed.), (1993), *Charles S. Peirce and the Philosophy of Science Papers from the Harvard Sesquicentennial Congress*. Tuscaloosa: University of Alabama Press.
Morganbesser, S. (ed.), (1977), *Dewey and His Critics: Essays from the Journal of Philosophy*. New York: Journal of Philosophy.
Mullin, R. P. (2007), *The Soul of Classical American Philosophy: The Ethical and Spiritual Insights of William James, Josiah Royce, and Charles Sanders Pierce*. Albany: SUNY Press.
Murphey, M. G. (1961), *The Development of Peirce's Philosophy*. Cambridge, MA: Harvard University Press. Reprinted, Indianapolis: Hackett, 1993.
—(2005), *C. I. Lewis: The Last Great Pragmatist*. Albany: State University of New York Press.
Myers, G. E. (1986), *William James: His Life and Thought*. New Haven, CT: Yale University Press.
Nathanson, J. (1951), *John Dewey: The Reconstruction of the Democratic Life*. New York: Charles Scribner's Sons.
Nelson, C. H. (1987), *John Elof Boodin: Philosopher-Poet*. New York: Philosophical Library.
Nissen, L. (1966), *John Dewey's Theory of Inquiry and Truth*. The Hague: Mouton.
Novack, G. E. (1975), *Pragmatism versus Marxism: An Appraisal of John Dewey's Philosophy*. New York: Pathfinder Press.
Novack, M. (ed.), (1968), *American Philosophy and the Future: Essays for a New Generation*. New York: Scribner's.
Nubiola, J. and Zalamea, F. (2006), *Peirce y el Mundo Hispánico: Lo que C. S. Peirce dijo sobre España y lo que el Mundo Hispánico ha dicho sobre Peirce*. Barañain, Spain: Ediciones Universidad de Navarra.
O'Connell, R. J. (1984), *William James on the Courage to Believe*. New York: Fordham University Press. 2nd edn, 1997.
Oelkers, J. (2009), *John Dewey und die Padagogik*. Weinheim, Germany: Beltz.
Olin, D. (ed.), (1992), *William James: Pragmatism in Focus*. London and New York: Routledge.
Oppenheim, F. M. (2005), *Reverence For The Relations Of Life: Re-imagining Pragmatism Via Josiah Royce's Interactions With Peirce, James, And Dewey*. Notre Dame, IN: University of Notre Dame Press.
Orange, D. M. (1984), *Peirce's Conception of God: A Developmental Study*. Lubbock: Texas Tech University Institute for Studies in Pragmaticism.
Pape, H. (1989), *Erfahrung und Wirklichkeit als Zeichenprozess: Charles S. Peirces Entwurf einer Spekulativen Grammatik des Seins*. Frankfurt am Main: Suhrkamp.

—(2004), *Charles S. Peirce zur Einführung*. Hamburg: Junius.
Pappas, G. F. (2008), *John Dewey's Ethics: Democracy as Experience*. Bloomington: Indiana University Press.
Parker, K. A. (1998), *The Continuity of Peirce's Thought*. Nashville, TN: Vanderbilt University Press.
Pawelski, J. O. (2007), *The Dynamic Individualism of William James*. Albany: State University of New York Press.
Perry, R. B. (1996), *The Thought and Character of William James, Briefer Version* (first published in 1948). Nashville, TN: Vanderbilt University Press.
Peters, R. S. (ed.), (1977), *John Dewey Reconsidered*. London: Routledge and Kegan Paul.
Peterson, F. H. (1987), *John Dewey's Reconstruction in Philosophy*. New York: Philosophical Library.
Phelps, C. (1997), *Young Sidney Hook: Marxist and Pragmatist*. Ithaca, NY: Cornell University Press.
Popkewitz, T. S. (2008), *Inventing the Modern Self and John Dewey: Modernities and the Traveling of Pragmatism in Education*. Basingstoke, UK: Palgrave Macmillan.
Popp, J. A. (2007), *Evolution's First Philosopher: John Dewey and the Continuity of Nature*. Albany: State University of New York Press.
Potter, V. J. (1967), *Charles S. Peirce on Norms and Ideals*. Amherst: University of Massachusetts Press.
—(ed.), (1988), *Doctrine and Experience: Essays in American Philosophy*. New York: Fordham University Press.
—(1996), *Peirce's Philosophical Perspectives*. Ed. Vincent M. Colapietro. New York: Fordham University Press.
Proudfoot, W. (ed.), (2004), *William James and a Science of Religions: Reexperiencing the Varieties of Religious Experience*. New York: Columbia University Press.
Putnam, R. A. (ed.), (1997), *The Cambridge Companion to William James*. Cambridge, UK: Cambridge University Press.
Ratner, S. (ed.), *et al.* (1940), *The Philosopher of the Common Man: Essays in Honor of John Dewey to celebrate his Eightieth Birthday*. New York: Putnam. Reprinted, New York: Greenwood, 1968.
Ratner, S. (ed.), (1953), *Vision & Action: Essays in honor of Horace M. Kallen on his 70th birthday*. New Brunswick, NJ: Rutgers University Press.
Reck, A. J. (ed.), (1972), *Knowledge and Value: Essays in honor of Harold N. Lee*. New Orleans: Tulane University.
Reed, E. S. (1977), *From Soul to Mind: The Emergence of Psychology, from Erasmus Darwin to William James*. New Haven, CT: Yale University Press.
Reilly, F. E. (1970), *Charles Peirce's Theory of Scientific Method*. New York: Fordham University Press.
Rellstab, D. H. (2007), *Charles S. Peirce Theorie natürlicher Sprache und ihre Relevanz für die Linguistik: Logik, Semantik, Pragmatik*. Tübingen, Germany: Narr.

Rescher, N. (1978), *Peirce's Philosophy of Science*. Notre Dame, IN: University of Notre Dame Press.

Reynolds, A. (2002), *Peirce's Scientific Metaphysics: The Philosophy of Chance, Law, and Evolution*. Nashville, TN: Vanderbilt University Press.

Rice, D. F. (1993), *Reinhold Niebuhr and John Dewey: An American Odyssey*. Albany: State University of New York, 1993.

Richardson, R. D. (2006), *William James: In the Maelstrom of American Modernism, a Biography*. Boston: Houghton Mifflin.

Roberts, D. D. (1973), *The Existential Graphs of Charles S. Peirce*. The Hague: Mouton.

Robinson, D. M. (2009), *Emerson and the Conduct of Life: Pragmatism and Ethical Purpose in the Later Work*. Cambridge, UK: Cambridge University Press.

Rockefeller, S. C. (1991), *John Dewey: Religious Faith and Democratic Humanism*. New York: Columbia University Press.

Rogers, M. L. (2009), *The Undiscovered Dewey: Religion, Morality, and the Ethos of Democracy*. New York: Columbia University Press.

Rosenstock, G. G. (1964), *F. A. Trendelenburg, forerunner to John Dewey*. Carbondale: Southern Illinois University Press.

Rosenthal, S. B. (1976), *The Pragmatic A Priori: A Study in the Epistemology of C. I. Lewis*. St. Louis: Warren H. Green.

Rosenthal, S. B. and Bourgeois, P. L. (1991), *Mead and Merleau-Ponty: Toward a Common Vision*. Albany: State University of New York Press.

Rosenthal, S. B. (1994), *Charles Peirce's Pragmatic Pluralism*. Albany: State University of New York Press.

—(2007), *C. I. Lewis in Focus: The Pulse of Pragmatism*. Bloomington: Indiana University Press.

Roth, R. J. (1962), *John Dewey and Self-realization*. Englewood Cliffs, NJ: Prentice-Hall.

—(1993), *British Empiricism and American Pragmatism: New Directions and Neglected Arguments*. New York: Fordham University Press.

Rucker, D. (1969), *The Chicago Pragmatists*. Minneapolis: University of Minnesota Press.

Rud, A. G., Garrison, J., and Stone, L. (ed.), (2010), *John Dewey at 150: Reflections for a New Century*. West Lafayette, IN: Purdue University Press.

Ryan, A. (1995), *John Dewey and the High Tide of American Liberalism*. New York: W.W. Norton.

Saito, N. (2005), *The Gleam Of Light: Dewey, Emerson, And The Pursuit Of Perfection*. New York: Fordham University Press.

Savan, D. (1989), *An Introduction to C. S. Peirce's Full System of Semiotic*. Toronto: Toronto Semiotic Circle.

Schilpp, P. A. (ed.), (1968), *The Philosophy of C. I. Lewis*. La Salle, Ill.: Open Court.

Schilpp, P. A. and Hahn, L. E. (ed.), (1982), *The Philosophy of W. V. Quine*. La Salle, IL: Open Court.

Schilpp, P. A. and Hahn, L. E. (ed.), (1989), *The Philosophy of John Dewey*. 3rd revised edn. La Salle, IL: Open Court.

Schneider, H. W. and Blanshard, B. (eds), (1942), *In Commemoration of William James, 1842–1942*. New York: Columbia University Press.

Schultenover, D. G. (ed.), (2009), *The Reception of Pragmatism in France and the Rise of Roman Catholic Modernism, 1890–1914*. Washington, DC: Catholic University of America Press.

Seibert, C. (2009), *Religion im Denken von William James: eine Interpretation seiner Philosophie*. Tubingen, Germany: Mohr Siebeck.

Seigfried, C. H. (1990), *William James' Radical Reconstruction of Philosophy*. Albany: State University of New York Press.

Shin, S.-J. (2002), *The Iconic Logic of Peirce's Graphs*. Cambridge, MA: MIT Press.

Shook, J. R. (2000), *Dewey's Empirical Theory of Knowledge and Reality*. Nashville, TN: Vanderbilt University Press.

Shook, J. R. and Good, J. A. (2010), *John Dewey's Philosophy of Spirit*. New York: Fordham University Press.

Short, T. L. (2007), *Peirce's Theory of Signs*. Cambridge, UK: Cambridge University Press.

Shuford, A. L. (2010), *Feminist Epistemology and American Pragmatism: Dewey and Quine*. London and New York: Continuum.

Simon, L. (ed.), (1996), *William James Remembered*. Lincoln: University of Nebraska Press.

—(1998), *Genuine Reality: A Life of William James*. New York: Harcourt Brace.

Simpson, D. J. (2006), *John Dewey*. New York: Peter Lang.

Singer, M. G. (ed.), (1985), *American Philosophy*. Cambridge, UK: Cambridge University Press.

Skagestad, P. (1981), *The Road of Inquiry: Charles Peirce's Pragmatic Realism*. New York: Columbia University Press.

Skowronski, K. (ed.), (2009), *Values and Powers: Re-reading the Philosophical Tradition of American Pragmatism*. Amsterdam and New York: Rodopi.

Slater, M. R. (2009), *William James on Ethics and Faith*. Cambridge, UK: Cambridge University Press.

Sleeper, R. W. (1986), *The Necessity of Pragmatism: John Dewey's Conception of Philosophy*. New Haven, CT: Yale University Press. Reprinted, Bloomington: Indiana University Press, 2001.

Smith, J. E. (1950), *Royce's Social Infinite*. New York: Liberal Arts Press.

Smith, J. K. (1979), *Ella Flagg Young: Portrait of a Leader*. Ames: Educational Studies Press and the Iowa State University Research Foundation.

Soneson, J. P. (1993), *Pragmatism and Pluralism: John Dewey's Significance for Theology*. Minneapolis: Fortress Press.

Sorrell, K. (2004), *Representative Practices: Peirce, Pragmatism, and Feminist Epistemology*. New York: Fordham University Press.

Sorzio, P. (2009), *Dewey e l'Educazione Progressiva*. Rome: Carocci.

Sprigge, T. L. S. (1974), *Santayana: An Examination of His Philosophy*. London: Rout-ledge and Kegan Paul.

—(1993), *James and Bradley: American Truth and British Reality.* Chicago: Open Court.
Stuhr, J. J. (ed.), (1993), *Philosophy and the Reconstruction of Culture: Pragmatic Essays after Dewey.* Albany: State University of New York Press.
—(ed.), (2010), *100 Years of Pragmatism: William James's Revolutionary Philosophy.* Bloomington, IN: Indiana University Press.
Suckiel, E. K. (1982), *The Pragmatic Philosophy of William James.* Notre Dame, IN: University of Notre Dame Press.
—(1996), *Heaven's Champion: William James's Philosophy of Religion.* Notre Dame, IN: University of Notre Dame Press.
Sumner, L.W, Slater, J. G., and Wilson, F. (ed.), *Pragmatism and Purpose: Essays presented to Thomas A. Goudge.* Toronto: University of Toronto Press.
Tan, S.-H. (2003), *Confucian Democracy: A Deweyan Reconstruction.* Albany: State University of New York Press.
Tan, S.-H. and Whalen-Bridge, J. (ed.), (2008), *Democracy as Culture: Deweyan Pragmatism in a Globalizing World.* Albany, NY: State University of New York Press.
Taylor, C. (2002), *Varieties of Religion Today: William James Revisited.* Cambridge, MA: Harvard University Press.
Taylor, E. (1996), *William James on Consciousness Beyond the Margin.* Princeton, NJ: Princeton University Press.
Taylor, E. and Wozniak, R. H. (eds), (1996), *Pure Experience: The Response to William James.* Bristol, UK: Thoemmes Press.
Taylor, R. W. (ed.), (1957), *Life, Language, Law: Essays in honor of Arthur F. Bentley.* Yellow Springs, OH: Antioch Press.
Tejera, V. (1984), *History as a Human Science: The Conception of History in some Classic American Philosophers.* Lanham, MD: University Press of America.
—(1996), *American Modern, The Path Not Taken: Aesthetics, Metaphysics, and Intellectual History in Classic American Philosophy.* Lanham, MD: Rowman and Littlefield.
Thayer, H. S. (1952), *The Logic of Pragmatism: An Examination of John Dewey's Logic.* New York: Humanities Press.
Thies, C. (ed.), (2009), *Religiose Erfahrung in der Moderne: William James und die Folgen.* Wiesbaden, Germany: Harrassowitz.
Thompson, M. H. (1953), *The Pragmatic Philosophy of C. S. Peirce.* Chicago: University of Chicago Press.
Tiercelin, C. (1993), *C. S. Peirce et le Pragmatisme.* Paris: Presses Universitaires de France.
—(1993), *La Pensee-signe: Etudes sur C. S. Peirce.* Mimes, France: Editions Jacqueline Chambon.
Tiles, J. E. (1988), *Dewey.* London and New York: Routledge.
Tilman, R. (2004), *Thorstein Veblen, John Dewey, C. Wright Mills and the Generic Ends of Life.* Lanham, MD: Rowman & Littlefield.
Tunstall, D. A. (2009), *Yes, but not Quite: Encountering Josiah Royce's Ethico-Religious Insight.* New York: Fordham University Press.

Turley, P. T. (1977), *Peirce's Cosmology*. New York: Philosophical Library.
Tursman, R. A. (1987), *Peirce's Theory of Scientific Discovery: A System of Logic Conceived as Semiotic*. Bloomington: Indiana University Press.
Vetter, M. (1999), *Zeichen deuten auf Gott: Die zeichentheoretische Beitrag von Charles S. Peirce zur Theologie der Sakramente*. Marburg: N.G. Elwert.
Viegas, J. (2006), *William James: American Philosopher, Psychologist, and Theologian*. New York: Rosen Publishing Group.
Wang, J. C.-S. (2007), *John Dewey in China: To Teach and to Learn*. Albany: State University of New York Press.
Welchman, J. (1995), *Dewey's Ethical Thought*. Ithaca, NY: Cornell University Press.
West, C. (1989), *The American Evasion of Philosophy: A Genealogy of Pragmatism*. Madison: University of Wisconsin Press.
Westbrook, R. B. (1991), *John Dewey and American Democracy*. Ithaca, NY: Cornell University Press.
White, S. S. (1940), *A Comparison of the Philosophies of F. C. S. Schiller and John Dewey*. Chicago: University of Chicago Libraries. Reprinted, New York: AMS Press, 1979.
Wiener, P. P. (1949), *Evolution and the Founders of Pragmatism*. Cambridge, MA: Harvard University Press.
Wiener, P. P. and Young, F. H. (ed.), (1952), *Studies in the Philosophy of Charles Sanders Peirce*. Cambridge, MA: Harvard University Press.
Wild, J. (1969), *The Radical Empiricism of William James*. Garden City, NY: Doubleday and Co.
Wilshire, B. (1968), *William James and Phenomenology: A Study of the Principles of Psychology*. Bloomington: Indiana University Press.
Winetrout, K. (1967), *F. C. S. Schiller and the Dimensions of Pragmatism*. Columbus: Ohio State University Press.
Wirth, A. G. (1966), *John Dewey as Educator: His Design for Work in Education (1894–1904)*. New York: John Wiley and Sons.
Xu, D. (1992), *A Comparison of the Educational Ideas and Practices of John Dewey and Mao Zedong in China*. San Francisco: Mellen Research University Press.
Yu, W. (2007), *Duwei, shi yong zhu yi yu xian dai zhe xue*. Beijing: Ren min chu ban she.
Zeltner, P. M. (1975), *John Dewey's Aesthetic Philosophy*. Amsterdam: B. R. Gruner.

Analytic philosophy themes

Includes cognitive science, mind, language and semiotics, epistemology and logic, ontology and metaphysics, process philosophies, and philosophy of science.

Allen, B. (1993), *Truth in Philosophy*. Cambridge, MA: Harvard University Press.
Apel, K.-O. (1973), *Transformation der Philosophie*. Frankfurt: Suhrkamp. Translated as *Towards a Transformation of Philosophy*. London: Routledge and Kegan Paul, 1980.

—(1998), *From a Transcendental-Semiotic Point of View*. Manchester, UK: Manchester University Press.
Baest, A. V. and Van Driel, H. (1995), *The Semiotics of C. S. Peirce Applied to Music: A Matter of Belief*. Tilburg, The Netherlands: Tilburg University Press.
Balat, M. (2000), *Des Fondements Sémiotiques de la Psychanalyse: Peirce après Freud et Lacan. Suivi de la Traduction de Logique des Mathématiques de C. S. Peirce*. Paris: L'Harmattan.
Barbieri, M. (ed.), (2008), *Introduction to Biosemiotics: The New Biological Synthesis*. Dordrecht: Springer.
Ben-Menahem, Y. (2005), *Hilary Putnam*. Cambridge: Cambridge University Press.
Bertilsson, M. (2009), *Peirce's Theory of Inquiry and Beyond: Towards a Social Reconstruction of Science Theory*. Frankfurt am Main: Peter Lang.
Boersema, D. (2009), *Pragmatism and Reference*. Cambridge, MA: MIT Press.
Bogdan, R. (1994), *Grounds for Cognition: How Goal-Guided Behavior Shapes the Mind*. Hillsdale, NJ: Lawrence Erlbaum, 1994.
Bogdan, R. (2003), *Interpreting Minds*. Cambridge, MA: MIT Press.
—(2010), *Our Own Minds: Sociocultural Grounds for Self-Consciousness*. Cambridge, MA: MIT Press.
Brandom, R. (1998), *Making it Explicit: Reasoning, Representing, and Discursive Commitment*. Cambridge, MA: Harvard University Press.
—(2008), *Between Saying and Doing: Towards an Analytic Pragmatism*. Oxford: Oxford University Press.
Brady, G. (2000), *From Peirce to Skolem: A Neglected Chapter in the History of Logic*. Amsterdam: Elsevier Science.
Buechner, J. (2007), *Godel, Putnam, and Functionalism: A New Reading of Representation and Reality*. Cambridge, MA: MIT Press.
Calcaterra, R. M. (2005), *Semiotica e fenomenologia del sé*. Turin, Italy: Nino Aragno Editore.
Calvo, P. and Gomila, A. (eds), (2008), *Handbook of Cognitive Science: An Embodied Approach*. Amsterdam: Elsevier.
Caruana, F. (2009), *Peirce et une Introduction a la Semiotique de l'Art*. Paris: L'Harmattan.
Chemero, A. (2009), *Radical Embodied Cognitive Science*. Cambridge, MA: MIT Press.
Clark, A. (1998), *Being There: Putting Brain, Body, and World Together Again*. Cambridge, MA: MIT Press.
—(2008), *Supersizing the Mind: Embodiment, Action, and Cognitive Extension*. Oxford: Oxford University Press.
Clark, P. and Hale, B. (eds), (1994), *Reading Putnam*. Oxford: Blackwell.
Clarke, D. S. (1989), *Rational Acceptance and Purpose: An Outline of a Pragmatist Epistemology*. Totowa, NJ: Rowman & Littlefield.
—(2007), *Some Pragmatist Themes*. Lanham, MD: Lexington Books.

Clough, S. (2003), *Beyond Epistemology: A Pragmatist Approach to Feminist Science Studies*. Lanham, MD: Rowman & Littlefield.

Cobley, P. (ed.), (2009), *The Routledge companion to semiotics*. London and New York: Routledge.

Conant, J. and Zeglen, U. (eds), (2002), *Hilary Putnam: Pragmatism and Realism*. London and New York: Routledge.

Cursiefen, S. (2008), *Putnam vs. Putnam fur und wider den Funktionalismus in der Philosophie des Geistes*. Hamburg, Germany: Diplomica-Verlag.

Danesi, M. (2007), *The Quest for Meaning: A Guide to Semiotic Theory and Practice*. Toronto: Toronto University Press.

Debrock, G. (ed.), (2003), *Process Pragmatism: Essays on a Quiet Philosophical Revolution*. Amsterdam and New York: Rodopi.

Deely, J. (1982), *Introducing Semiotic: Its History and Doctrine*. Bloomington: Indiana University Press.

—(1994), *The Human Use of Signs*. Lanham, MD: Rowman & Littlefield. Deely, J. N. (2009), *Purely Objective Reality*. Berlin: Mouton de Gruyter.

—(2009), *Realism for the Twenty-First Century: A John Deely Reader*. Ed. Paul Cobley. Scranton, PA: University of Scranton Press.

—(2010), *Semiotic Animal: A Postmodern Definition of "Human Being" Transcending Patriarchy and Feminism*. South Bend, IN: St. Augustine's Press.

De Gaynesford, M. (2006), *Hilary Putnam*. Chesham, UK: Acumen; Montreal: McGill-Queen's University Press.

Elizondo Martínez, J. O. (2003), *Signo en acción: el origen común de la semiótica y el pragmatismo*. México, D. F.: Universidad Iberoamericana, Fundación Información y Democracia.

Flanagan, O. (1992), *Consciousness Reconsidered*. Cambridge, MA: MIT Press.

—(2007), *The Really Hard Problem: Meaning in a Material World*. Cambridge, MA: MIT Press.

Franks, D. D. (2010), *Neurosociology: the nexus between neuroscience and social psychology*. New York: Springer.

Freeman, W. J. (2001), *How Brains Make Up Their Minds*. New York: Columbia University Press.

Frisina, W. G. (2002), *The Unity of Knowledge and Action: Toward a Nonrepresentational Theory of Knowledge*. Albany: State University of New York Press.

Gibson, J. J. (1979), *The Ecological Approach to Visual Perception*. Boston: Houghton Mifflin. Reprinted, Hillsdale, NJ: Lawrence Erlbaum Associates, 1986.

Glock, H.-J. (2009), *Quine and Davidson on Language, Thought and Reality*. Cambridge, UK: Cambridge University Press.

Godfrey-Smith, P. (1998), *Complexity and the Function of Mind in Nature*. Cambridge, UK: Cambridge University Press.

—(2003), *Theory and Reality: An Introduction to the Philosophy of Science*. Chicago: University of Chicago Press.

Goodman, R. B. (2002), *Wittgenstein and William James*. Cambridge, UK: Cambridge University Press.
Gregory, P. A. (2008), *Quine's Naturalism: Language, Theory, and the Knowing Subject*. London and New York: Continuum.
Haack, S. (2009), *Evidence and Inquiry: A pragmatist reconstruction of epistemology*, 2nd edn (1st edn 1993). Amherst, NY: Prometheus Books.
Hacking, I. (1983), *Representing and Intervening*. Cambridge, UK: Cambridge University Press.
—(1999), *The Social Construction of What?* Cambridge, MA: Harvard University Press.
Heft, H. (2001), *Ecological Psychology in Context: James Gibson, Roger Barker, and the Legacy of William James's Radical Empiricism*. Mahwah, NJ: Lawrence Erlbaum Associates.
Hickey, L. P. (2009), *Hilary Putnam*. London and New York: Continuum.
Hoffmeyer, J. (1996), *Signs of Meaning in the Universe*. Bloomington: Indiana University Press.
—(2008), *Biosemiotics: An Examination into the Signs of Life and the Life of Signs*. Scranton: University of Scranton Press.
Hookway, C. (2000), *Truth, Rationality, and Pragmatism: Themes from Peirce*. Oxford: Oxford University Press.
Hoopes, J. (1989), *Consciousness in New England: From Puritanism and Ideas to Psychoanalysis and Semiotic*. Baltimore, MD: Johns Hopkins University Press.
Hulswit, M. (2002), *From Cause to Causation: A Peircean Perspective*. Dordrecht: Kluwer.
Hurley, S. L. (1998), *Consciousness in Action*. Cambridge, MA: Harvard University Press.
Hylton, P. (2007), *Quine*. London and New York: Routledge.
Innis, R. (2002), *Pragmatism and the Forms of Sense: Language, Perception, Technics*. University Park: Penn State University Press.
Johnson, M. (1987), *The Body in the Mind: The Bodily Basis of Meaning, Imagination, and Reason*. Chicago: University of Chicago Press.
Johnson, M. and Lakoff, G. (1999), *Philosophy in the Flesh: The Embodied Mind and Its Challenge to Western Thought*. New York: Basic Books.
—(2003), *Metaphors We Live By*, 2nd edn. Chicago: University of Chicago Press.
Johnson, M. (2007), *The Meaning of the Body: Aesthetics of Human Understanding*. Chicago: University of Chicago Press.
Koons, J. R. (2009), *Pragmatic reasons: a defense of morality and epistemology*. Basingstoke, UK: Palgrave Macmillan.
Kulp, C. B. (1992), *The End of Epistemology: Dewey and His Current Allies on the Spectator Theory of Knowledge*. Westport, CT: Greenwood Press.
Lafferty, T. T. (1976), *Nature and Values: Pragmatic Essays in Metaphysics*. Columbia: University of South Carolina Press.
Laudan, L. (1977), *Progress and Its Problems: Toward a Theory of Scientific Growth*. Berkeley: University of California Press.

—(1984), *Science and Values: The Aims of Science and their Role in Scientific Debate.* Berkeley: University of California Press.
—(1990), *Science and Relativism: Some Key Controversies in the Philosophy of Science.* Chicago: University of Chicago Press.
Lee, H. N. (1973), *Percepts, Concepts, and Theoretic Knowledge. A Study in Epistemology.* Memphis, TN: Memphis State University Press.
Levi, I. (1991), *The Fixation of Belief and Its Undoing: Changing Belief through Inquiry.* Cambridge, UK: Cambridge University Press.
Lewis, C. I. (1946), *An Analysis of Knowledge and Valuation.* La Salle, IL: Open Court.
Lieb, I. (1971), *The Four Faces of Man: A Philosophical Study of Practice, Reason, Art and Religion.* Philadelphia: University of Pennsylvania Press.
Maitra, K. (2003), *On Putnam.* Belmont, CA: Wadsworth/Thomson Learning.
Manicas, P. T. (2008), *Rescuing Dewey: Essays in Pragmatic Naturalism.* Lanham, MD: Lexington Books.
Marchetti, G. (2008), *Verità e Valori. Tra Pragmatismo e Filosofia Analitica.* Milan: Mimesis.
Margolis, J. (2002), *Reinventing Pragmatism: American Philosophy at the End of the Twentieth Century.* Ithaca, NY: Cornell University Press.
—(2010), *Pragmatism's Advantage: American and European Philosophy at the End of the Twentieth Century.* Stanford, CA: Stanford University Press.
Marty, R. (1990), *L'Algèbre des Signes: Essai de Sémiotique d'après Charles Sanders Peirce.* Amsterdam: John Benjamins.
McDermid, D. (2006), *The Varieties of Pragmatism: Truth, Realism, and Knowledge from James to Rorty.* London and New York: Continuum.
Mellor, D. H. (ed.), (1980), *Prospects for Pragmatism: Essays in Memory of F. P. Ramsey.* Cambridge, UK: Cambridge University Press.
Menary, R. (ed.), (2010), *The Extended Mind.* Cambridge, MA: MIT Press.
Merrell, F. (1991), *Signs Becoming Signs: Our Perfusive, Pervasive Universe.* Bloomington: Indiana University Press.
—(1992), *Sign, Textuality, World.* Bloomington: Indianapolis University Press.
—(1995), *Semiosis in the Postmodern Age.* West Lafayette, IN: Purdue University Press.
Misak, C. J. (1991), *Truth and the End of Inquiry: A Peircean Account of Truth.* Oxford: Clarendon Press.
—(ed.), (2007), *New Pragmatists.* Oxford: Clarendon Press; New York: Oxford University Press.
Morris, C. W. (1946), *Signs, Language and Behavior.* New York: Prentice-Hall. Reprinted, New York: George Braziller, 1955.
—(1964), *Signification and Significance: A Study of the Relations of Signs and Values.* Cambridge, MA: MIT Press.
—(1971), *Writings on the General Theory of Signs.* The Hague: Mouton.
Mosteller, T. M. (2006), *Relativism in Contemporary American Philosophy: Macintyre, Putnam, and Rorty.* London and New York: Continuum.

Murphey, M. G. (1994), *Philosophical Foundations of Historical Knowledge*. Albany: State University of New York Press.
Nagel, E. (1954), *Sovereign Reason, and other studies in the Philosophy of Science*. Glencoe, IL: Free Press.
Noë, A. (2006), *Action in Perception*. Cambridge, MA: MIT Press.
—(2009), *Out of Our Heads: Why You are not Your Brain, and Other Lessons from the Biology of Consciousness*. New York: Hill and Wang.
Norris, C. (2002), *Hilary Putnam: Realism, Reason, and the Uses of Uncertainty*. Manchester, England: Manchester University Press.
Okrent, M. (2007), *Rational Animals: The Teleological Roots of Intentionality*. Athens: Ohio University Press.
Olsson, E. J. (ed.), (2006), *Knowledge and Inquiry: Essays on the Pragmatism of Isaac Levi*. Cambridge, UK: Cambridge University Press.
Otto, M. C. (1949), *Science and the Moral Life: Selected Writings*. New York: New American Library.
Orenstein, A. (2002), *W. V. Quine*. Princeton, NJ: Princeton University Press.
Peirce, C. S. (1991), *Peirce on Signs: Writings on Semiotic*. Ed. James Hoopes. Chapel Hill: University of North Carolina Press.
Pihlström, S. (2003), *Naturalizing the Transcendental: A Pragmatic View*. Amherst, NY: Prometheus Books.
—(2008), *"The Trail of the Human Serpent is over Everything": Jamesian Perspectives on Mind, World, and Religion*. Lanham, MD: University Press of America.
—(2009), *Pragmatist Metaphysics: An Essay on the Ethical Grounds of Ontology*. London and New York: Continuum.
Pred, R. (2005), *Onflow: Dynamics of Consciousness and Experience*. Cambridge, MA: MIT Press.
Prien, B. and Schweikard, D. P. (eds), (2008), *Robert Brandom: Analytic Pragmatist*. Frankfurt: Ontos.
Pruisken, T. (2007), *Medialität und Zeichen: Konzeption einer pragmatisch-sinnkritischen Theorie medialer Erfahrung*. Würzburg, Germany: Königshausen & Neumann.
Putnam, H. (1990), *Realism with a Human Face*. Edited by James Conant. Cambridge, MA: Harvard University Press.
—(1992), *Renewing Philosophy*. Cambridge, MA: Harvard University Press.
—(1994), *Words and Life*. Edited by James Conant. Cambridge, MA: Harvard University Press.
—(1995), *Pragmatism: An Open Question*. Oxford: Blackwell.
—(1999), *The Threefold Cord: Mind, Body, and World*. New York: Columbia University Press.
Quine, W. V. (1969), *Ontological Relativity and Other Essays*. New York: Columbia University Press.
Quine, W. V. and Ullian, J. S. (1970), *The Web of Belief*. New York: Random House. 2nd edn, 1978.
Quine, W. V. (1974), *The Roots of Reference*. La Salle, IL: Open Court.

—(1981), *Theories and Things*. Cambridge, MA: Harvard.
Racine, E. (2009), *Pragmatic Neuroethics: Improving Treatment and Understanding of the Mind-Brain*. Cambridge, MA: MIT Press.
Randall, J. H., Jr. (1958), *Nature and Historical Experience: Essays in Naturalism and in the Theory of History*. New York: Columbia University Press.
Rescher, N. (1977), *Methodological Pragmatism*. Oxford: Basil Blackwell; New York University Press.
—(1991), *A System of Pragmatic Idealism, vol. 1: Human Knowledge in Idealistic Perspective*. Princeton, NJ: Princeton University Press.
Rescher, N. (2001), *Cognitive Pragmatism: The Theory of Knowledge in Pragmatic Perspective*. Pittsburgh: University of Pittsburgh Press.
—(2008), *Epistemic Pragmatism and other Studies in the Theory of Knowledge*. Frankfurt, Germany: Ontos Verlag.
Rivas Monroy, M. U., Cancela Silva, C. and Martinez Vidal, C. (ed.), (2008), *Following Putnam's Trail: On Realism and Other Issues*. Amsterdam and New York: Rodopi.
Rockwell, W. T. (2005), *Neither Brain nor Ghost: A Nondualist Alternative to the Mind-Brain Identity Theory*. Cambridge, MA: MIT Press.
Rosenthal, S. (1986), *Speculative Pragmatism*. Amherst: University of Massachusetts Press.
Rosenthal, S. B. (2000), *Time, Continuity, and Indeterminacy: A Pragmatic Engagement with Contemporary Perspectives*. Albany: State University of New York Press.
Sahlin, N.-E. (1990), *The Philosophy of F. P. Ramsey*. Cambridge, England: Cambridge University Press.
Scheffler, I. (1963), *The Anatomy of Inquiry: Philosophical Studies in the Theory of Science*. New York: Alfred A. Knopf. Reprinted, London: Routledge and Kegan Paul, 1964.
Schneider, H. W. (1962), *Ways of Being: Elements of Analytic Ontology*. New York: Columbia University Press. Reprinted, New York: Greenwood Press, 1974.
Schulkin, J. (1992), *The Pursuit of Inquiry*. Albany: State University of New York Press.
—(2000), *Roots of Social Sensibility and Neural Function*. Cambridge, MA: MIT Press.
—(2004), *Bodily Sensibility: Intelligent Action*. Oxford: Oxford University Press.
—(2007), *Effort: a behavioral neuroscience perspective on the will*. Mahwah, NJ: Lawrence Erlbaum Associates.
—(2009), *Cognitive Adaptation: A Pragmatist Perspective*. Cambridge, UK: Cambridge University Press.
Schwartz, R. (2006), *Visual Versions*. Cambridge, MA: MIT Press.
Sebiok, T. A. (1972), *Perspectives in Zoosemiotics*. The Hague: Mouton.
Sebeok, T. A. and Eco, U. (1983), *The Sign of Three: Dupin, Holmes, Peirce*. Bloomington: Indiana University Press.
Sebeok, T. A. and Umiker-Sebeok, D. J. (1986), *The Semiotic Sphere*. New York: Plenum Press.
Sebeok, T. A. (1991), *Semiotics in the United States*. Bloomington: Indiana University Press.
—(1994), *Signs: An Introduction to Semiotics*. Toronto: University of Toronto Press. 2nd edn, 2001.

Shapiro, M. (1983), *The Sense of Grammar: Language as Semeiotic*. Bloomington: Indiana University Press.

Shook, J. R. (ed.), (2003), *Pragmatic Naturalism and Realism*. Amherst, NY: Prometheus Books. Shook, J. R. and Kurtz, P. (2009), *The Future of Naturalism*. Amherst, NY: Prometheus Books.

Shuford, A. L. (2010), *Feminist Epistemology and American Pragmatism: Dewey and Quine*. London and New York: Continuum.

Sorrell, K. (2004), *Representative Practices: Peirce, Pragmatism, and Feminist Epistemology*. New York: Fordham University Press.

Stapp, H. P. (2007), *Mindful Universe: Quantum Mechanics and the Participating Observer*. Berlin and New York: Springer.

Stewart, A. F. (1997), *Elements of Knowledge: Pragmatism, Logic, and Inquiry*. Nashville, Tenn.: Vanderbilt University Press.

Tartaglia, J. (2007), *Routledge Philosophy Guidebook to Rorty and the Mirror of Nature*. London and New York: Routledge.

Taylor, R. W. (ed.), (1957), *Life, Language, Law: Essays in Honor of Arthur F. Bentley*. Yellow Springs, OH: Antioch Press.

Thompson, E. (2007), *Mind in Life: Phenomenology and the Sciences of the Mind*. Cambridge, MA: Harvard University Press.

Tomida, Y. (2007), *Quine, Rorty, Locke: Essays and Discussions on Naturalism*. Hildesheim, Germany: Olms.

Toulmin, S. (2001), *Return to Reason*. Cambridge, MA: Harvard University Press.

—(2003), *The Uses of Argument*, revised edn. Cambridge, UK: Cambridge University Press.

Valsiner, J. and van der Veer, R. (2000), *The Social Mind: Construction of the Idea*. Cambridge, UK: Cambridge University Press.

Varela, F. J., Thompson, E., and Rosch, E. (1992), *The Embodied Mind: Cognitive Science and Human Experience*. Cambridge, MA: MIT Press.

Walton, D. (2003), *A Pragmatic Theory of Fallacy*. Tuscaloosa: University of Alabama Press.

Walton, D. N. (2008). *Informal logic: a pragmatic approach*, 2nd edn. Cambridge, UK: Cambridge University Press.

Westphal, K. R. (ed.), (1998), *Pragmatism, Reason, & Norms: A Realistic Assessment*. New York: Fordham University Press.

White, M. (2002), *A Philosophy of Culture: The Scope of Holistic Pragmatism*. Princeton, NJ: Princeton University Press.

White, M. G. (1956), *Toward Reunion in Philosophy*. Cambridge, MA: Harvard University Press.

—(1965), *Foundations of Historical Knowledge*. New York: Harper and Row.

Wiley, N. (1994), *The Semiotic Self*. Chicago: University of Chicago Press.

Will, F. L. (1997), *Pragmatism and Realism*. Ed. Kenneth R. Westphal. Lanham, MD: Rowman & Littlefield.

Zanet, G. (2007), *Le Radici del Naturalismo: W. V. Quine tra Eredità Empirista e Pragmatismo.* Macerata, Italy: Quodlibet.

Continental and postmodernism themes

Includes phenomenology, psychoanalytics, existentialism, critical theory, hermeneutics, deconstruction, neo-pragmatism, and other postmodernism movements.

Aboulafia, M., Bookman, M., and Kemp, C. (eds), (2002), *Habermas and Pragmatism.* London and New York: Routledge.

Agwuele, A. O. (2009), *Rorty's Deconstruction of Philosophy and the Challenge of African Philosophy.* Berlin: Peter Lang.

Alexandrescu, S. (ed.), (1995), *Richard Rorty.* Kampen, The Netherlands: Kok Agora.

Arcilla, R. V. (1995), *For the Love of Perfection: Richard Rorty and Liberal Education.* London and New York: Routledge.

Auxier, R. E. and Hahn, L. E. (ed.), (2009), *The Philosophy of Richard Rorty.* Chicago: Open Court.

Baert, P. and Turner, B. S. (ed.), (2007), *Pragmatism and European Social Theory.* Oxford: Bardwell Press.

Balat, M. (2000), *Des Fondements Sémiotiques de la Psychanalyse: Peirce après Freud et Lacan. Suivi de la Traduction de Logique des Mathématiques de C. S. Peirce.* Paris: L'Harmattan.

Baynes, K., Bohman, J., and McCarthy, T. (ed.), (1987), *After Philosophy: End or Transformation?* Cambridge, MA: MIT Press.

Benhabib, S. and Fraser, N. (eds), (2004), *Pragmatism, Critique, Judgment: Essays for Richard J. Bernstein.* Cambridge, MA: MIT Press.

Bernstein, R. J. (1971), *Praxis and Action: Contemporary Philosophies of Human Activity.* Philadelphia: University of Pennsylvania Press.

—(1983), *Beyond Objectivism and Relativism: Science, Hermeneutics, and Praxis.* Philadelphia: University of Pennsylvania Press.

—(2010), *The Pragmatic Turn.* Cambridge, UK: Polity.

Bohman, J. and Rehg, W. (eds), (2001), *Pluralism and the Pragmatic Turn: The Transformation of Critical Theory, Essays in Honor of Thomas McCarthy.* Cambridge: MIT Press.

Brandom, R. B. (ed.), (2000), *Rorty and His Critics.* Oxford: Blackwell.

Cahoone, L. E. (2002), *The Ends of Philosophy: Pragmatism, Foundationalism and Postmodernism.* Oxford: Blackwell.

Calder, G. (2007), *Rorty's Politics of Redescription.* Cardiff, UK: University of Wales Press.

Corrington, R. S., Hausman, C., and Seebohm, T. (ed.), (1987), *Pragmatism Considers Phenomenology*. Lanham, MD: Center for Advanced Research in Phenomenology.
Crosby, D. A. and Hardwick, C. D. (eds), (1998), *Pragmatism, Neo-Pragmatism, and Religion: Conversations with Richard Rorty*. New York: Peter Lang.
Cruz, O. (2009), *Neo-pragmatisms and New Romanticisms*. London and New York: Routledge.
Dann, G. E. (2006), *After Rorty: The Possibilities for Ethics and Religious Belief*. London and New York: Continuum.
Davaney, S. G. and Frisina, W. G. (eds), (2006), *The Pragmatic Century: Conversations with Richard J. Bernstein*. Albany: State University of New York Press.
Deely, J. N. (2009), *Postmodernity in Philosophy, a Poinsot Trilogy: Determining the Standpoint for a Doctrine of Signs*. Scranton, PA: University of Scranton Press.
Fabbri, L. (2008), *The Domestication of Derrida: Rorty, Pragmatism, and Deconstruction*. London and New York: Continuum.
Fairfield, P. (ed.), (2010), *John Dewey and Continental Philosophy*. Carbondale: Southern Illinois University Press.
Festenstein, M. and Thompson, S. (eds), (2001), *Richard Rorty: Critical Dialogues*. Malden, MA: Polity Press.
Gascoigne, N. (2008), *Richard Rorty: Liberalism, Irony, and the Ends of Philosophy*. Oxford: Polity.
Gasparski, W., Ryan, L. V., and Nahser, F. B. (eds), (2002), *Praxiology and Pragmatism*. New Brunswick, NJ: Transaction Publishers.
Gavin, W. J. (ed.), (1988), *Context over Foundation: Dewey and Marx*. Dordrecht: D. Reidel.
Ghiraldelli, P., Jr. (1999), *Richard Rorty: A Filosofia do Novo Mundo em Busca de Novos Mundos*. Petropolis, Brazil: Editora Vozes.
Gross, N. (2008), *Richard Rorty: The Making of an American Philosopher*. Chicago: University of Chicago Press.
Guignon, C. and Hiley, D. R. (eds), (2003), *Richard Rorty*. Cambridge: Cambridge University Press.
Gunn, G. (1992), *Thinking Across the American Grain: Ideology, Intellect, and the New Pragmatism*. Chicago: University of Chicago Press.
Haber, H. F. (1994), *Beyond Postmodern Politics: Lyotard, Rorty, Foucault*. New York: Routledge.
Habermas, J. (1972), *Knowledge and Human Interests*. Boston: Beacon Press.
—(1988), *Theory and Practice*. Boston: Beacon Press.
—(1989), *The Structural Transformation of the Public Sphere*. Cambridge, MA: MIT Press.
—(1990), *Moral Consciousness and Communicative Action*. Cambridge, MA: MIT Press.
—(1998), *Between Facts and Norms*. Cambridge, MA: MIT Press.
Hall, D. L. (1994), *Richard Rorty: Prophet and Poet of the New Pragmatism*. Albany: State University of New York Press.

Hamington, M. (2004), *Embodied Care: Jane Addams, Maurice Merleau-Ponty, and Feminist Ethics*. Urbana: University of Illinois Press.
Hildebrand, D. (2003), *Beyond Realism and Antirealism: John Dewey and the Neopragmatists*. Nashville, TN: Vanderbilt University Press.
Hollinger, R. (1985), *Hermeneutics and Praxis*. Notre Dame, IN: University of Notre Dame Press.
Horkheimer, M. (1947), *Eclipse of Reason*. New York: Oxford University Press.
Huang, Y. (ed.), (2009), *Rorty, Pragmatism, and Confucianism: With Responses by Richard Rorty*. Albany: State University of New York Press.
Joas, H. (1997), *The Creativity of Action*. Chicago: University of Chicago Press.
Kimura, G. W. (2007), *Neopragmatism and Theological Reason*. Aldershot, UK and Burlington, VT: Ashgate.
Kolenda, K. (1990), *Rorty's Humanistic Pragmatism: Philosophy Democratized*. Tampa: University of South Florida Press.
Kolesnikov, A. C. (1997), *Filosofia Richarda Rorty i Postmodernizm Konza XX veka*. Saint Petersburg: Gosudarstvennii Universitat.
Langsdorf, L. and Smith, A. R. (eds), (1995), *Recovering Pragmatism's Voice: The Classical Tradition, Rorty, and the Philosophy of Communication*. Albany: State University of New York Press.
Levitt, M. (1960), *Freud and Dewey on the Nature of Man*. New York: Philosophical Library.
Malachowski, A. (ed.), (1990) *Reading Rorty: Critical Responses to Philosophy and the Mirror of Nature (and Beyond)*. Oxford: Basil Blackwell.
—(2002), *Richard Rorty*. Princeton, NJ: Princeton University Press.
—(ed.), (2002), *Richard Rorty*. 4 vols. Thousand Oaks, CA: Sage Publications.
Margolis, J. (2010), *Pragmatism's Advantage: American and European Philosophy at the End of the Twentieth Century*. Stanford, CA: Stanford University Press.
Mathur, D. C. (1971), *Naturalistic Philosophies of Experience: Studies in James, Dewey, and Farber against the Background of Husserl's Phenomenology*. St. Louis: Warren H. Green.
Mba, J.-R.-E. and Medoux, I. (2007), *Richard Rorty: La Fin de la Metaphysique et la Pragmatique de la Science*. Paris: L'Harmattan.
McDermid, D. (2006), *The Varieties of Pragmatism: Truth, Realism, And Knowledge from James to Rorty*. London and New York: Continuum.
Medoux, I. (2009), *Richard Rorty: Un Philosophe Consequent*. Paris: Harmattan. Mitchell, W. J. T. (1985), *Against Theory: Literary Theory and the New Pragmatism*. Chicago: University of Chicago Press.
Mosteller, T. M. (2006), *Relativism in Contemporary American Philosophy: Macintyre, Putnam, and Rorty*. London and New York: Continuum.
Mouffe, C. (ed.), (1996), *Deconstruction and Pragmatism*. London and New York: Routledge.
Mouffe, C. and Nagl, L. (eds), (2001), *The Legacy of Wittgenstein: Pragmatism or Deconstruction*. New York: Peter Lang.

Navia, R. (2008), *Richard Rorty: Emplazamiento a la Tradicion Filosofica*. Montevideo, Uruguay: Departamento de Publicaciones de la Facultad de Humanidades y Ciencias de la Educacion, Universidad de la Republica.

Nielsen, K. (1991), *After the Demise of the Tradition: Rorty, Critical Theory, and the Fate of Philosophy*. Boulder, CO: Westview Press.

Okrent, M. (1988), *Heidegger's Pragmatism: Understanding, Being, and the Critique of Metaphysics*. Ithaca, NY: Cornell University Press.

Pettegrew, J. (ed.). (2000), *A Pragmatist's Progress?: Richard Rorty and American Intellectual History*. Lanham, MD: Rowman & Littlefield.

Piercey, R. (2009), *The Uses of the Past from Heidegger to Rorty: Doing Philosophy Historically*. Cambridge, UK: Cambridge University Press.

Prado, C. G. (1987), *The Limits of Pragmatism*. Atlantic Highlands, NJ: Humanities Press.

Puke, O. (2008), *Zur Kritik Philosophischer Unbedingtheitsanspruche: Jurgen Habermas' Transformation der Kritischen Gesellschaftstheorie und die Herausforderung des Amerikanischen Pragmatismus*. Munster, Germany: Waxmann.

Rockmore, T. (1981), *Marxism and Alternatives: Towards the Conceptual Interaction among Soviet Philosophy, Neo-Thomism, Pragmatism, and Phenomenology*. Dordrecht: D. Reidel; Boston: Kluwer.

Rodriguez, J. S. A. (ed.), (2007), *Redescripcion y Moralidad: Una Entrevista con Richard Rorty y Cuatro Ensayos sobre Su Filosofia*. Queretaro, Mexico: Universidad Autonoma de Queretaro.

Rorty, R. (1979), *Philosophy and the Mirror of Nature*. Princeton, NJ: Princeton University Press. Thirtieth Anniversary Edition, Princeton, NJ: Princeton University Press, 2009.

—(1982), *Consequences of Pragmatism: Essays, 1972–1980*. Minneapolis: University of Minnesota Press.

—(1989), *Contingency, Irony, and Solidarity*. Cambridge, UK: Cambridge University Press.

—(1991), *Essays on Heidegger and Others: Philosophical Papers II*. Cambridge, UK: Cambridge University Press.

—(1991), *Objectivity, Relativism, and Truth: Philosophical Papers I*. Cambridge, UK: Cambridge University Press.

—(1998), *Truth and Progress: Philosophical Papers III*. Cambridge, UK: Cambridge University Press.

—(2007), *Philosophy as Cultural Politics: Philosophical Papers IV*. Cambridge, UK: Cambridge University Press.

Rorty, R. and Engel, P. (2007), *What's the Use of Truth?* Ed. Patrick Savidan. New York: Columbia University Press.

Rosenthal, S. B. and Bourgeois, P. L. (1980), *Pragmatism and Phenomenology: A Philosophic Encounter*. Amsterdam: Gruner.

—(1991), *Mead and Merleau-Ponty: Toward a Common Vision*. Albany: State University of New York Press.

Saatkamp, H. J., Jr. (ed.), (1995), *Rorty and Pragmatism: The Philosopher Responds to His Critics*. Nashville: Vanderbilt University Press.
Scheler, M. (1980), *Problems of a Sociology of Knowledge*. Translated by Kenneth W. Stikkers. London: Routledge & Kegan Paul.
Sieverding, J. (2007), *Sensibilitat und Solidaritat: Skizze einer Dialogischen Ethik im Anschluss an Ludwig Feuerbach und Richard Rorty*. Munster, Germany: Waxmann.
Sip, R. (2008), *Richard Rorty: Pragmatismus Mezi Jazykem a Zkus Enosti*. Brno, Czech Republic: Paido.
Smith, J. H. and Kerrigan, W. (ed.), (1986), *Pragmatism's Freud: The Moral Disposition of Psychoanalysis*. Baltimore: Johns Hopkins University Press.
Snell, R. J. (2006), *Through a Glass Darkly: Bernard Lonergan & Richard Rorty on Knowing Without a God's-eye View*. Milwaukee, WI: Marquette University Press.
Stuhr, J. J. (2003), *Pragmatism, Postmodernism, and the Future of Philosophy*. New York: Routledge.
Swartz, O. (1997), *Conducting Socially Responsible Research: Critical Theory, Neo-Pragmatism, and Rhetorical Inquiry*. Thousand Oaks, CA: Sage Publications. Swartz, O., Campbell, K., and Pestana, C. (2009), *Neo-Pragmatism, Communication, and the Culture of Creative Democracy*. New York: Peter Lang.
Tartaglia, J. (2007), *Routledge Philosophy Guidebook to Rorty and the Mirror of Nature*. London and New York: Routledge.
—(ed.), (2009), *Richard Rorty. Critical Assessments of Leading Philosophers*, 4 vols. London and New York: Routledge.
Tomida, Y. (2007), *Quine, Rorty, Locke: Essays and Discussions on Naturalism*. Hildesheim, Germany: Olms.
Valdman, E. (2009), *Idealisme Français, Pragmatisme Americain: Une Necessaire Union*. Paris: Harmattan.
Van den Bossche, M. (2005), *Ironie et Solidarité: Une Introduction au Pragmatisme de Richard Rorty*. Paris: L'Harmattan.
Vidu, A. (2008), *Theology after Neo-pragmatism*. Milton Keys, UK; Colorado Springs, CO: Paternoster.
Vieth, A. (ed.), (2005), *Richard Rorty: His Philosophy under Discussion*. Heusenstamm, Germany: Ontos.
Webb, R. B. (1976), *The Presence of the Past: John Dewey and Alfred Schutz on the Genesis and Organization of Experience*. Gainesville: University of Presses of Florida.
Wihl, G. (1994), *The Contingency of Theory: Pragmatism, Expressivism, and Deconstruction*. New Haven, CT: Yale University Press.
Wilshire, B. (2000), *The Primal Roots of American Philosophy: Pragmatism, Phenomenology, and Native American Thought*. University Park: Pennsylvania State University Press.
Zhang, W. (2006), *Heidegger, Rorty, and the Eastern Thinkers: A Hermeneutics of Cross-cultural Understanding*. Albany: State University of New York Press.

Ethics and politics

Includes value theory, applied ethics, aesthetics, social and political philosophy, economics, public policy, law, and international relations.

Addams, J. (2002), *Democracy and Social Ethics*, (first published in 1902). Urbana, IL: University of Illinois Press.
Anderson, C. W. (1990), *Pragmatic Liberalism*. Chicago: University of Chicago Press.
Bacon, M. (2007), *Richard Rorty: Pragmatism and Political Liberalism*. Lanham, MD: Lexington Books.
Baert, P. (2005), *Philosophy of the Social Sciences: Towards Pragmatism*. Cambridge: Polity Press.
Baert, P. and Turner, B. S. (ed.), (2007), *Pragmatism and European Social Theory*. Oxford: Bardwell Press.
Bantegne, G. (2007), *14 Femmes: Pour un Féminisme Pragmatique*. Paris: Gallimard.
Bauer, H. and Brighi, E. (ed.), *Pragmatism in International Relations*. London and New York: Routledge.
Beardsley, M. C. (1958), *Aesthetics: Problems in the Philosophy of Criticism*. New York: Harcourt, Brace, and World.
—(1982), *The Aesthetic Point of View: Selected Essays*. Eds Michael J. Wreen and Donald M. Callen. Ithaca, NY: Cornell University Press.
Bentley, A. F. (1954), *Inquiry into Inquiries: Essays in Social Theory*. Edited by Sidney Ratner. Boston: Beacon Press.
Blumer, H. (2004), *George Herbert Mead and Human Conduct*. Ed. Thomas J. Morrione. Walnut Creek, CA: AltaMira Press.
Bohman, J. (2007), *Democracy Across Borders: From Demos to Demoi*. Cambridge, MA: MIT Press.
Bridge, G. (2004), *Reason in the City of Difference: Pragmatism, Communicative Action and Contemporary Urbanism*. London and New York: Routledge.
Brint, M. and Weaver, W. (eds), (1991), *Pragmatism in Law and Society*. Boulder, CO: Westview Press.
Brion, D. J. (2003), *Pragmatism and Judicial Choice*. New York: Peter Lang.
Bromley, D. W. (2006), *Sufficient Reason: Volitional Pragmatism and the Meaning of Economic Institutions*. Princeton, NJ: Princeton University Press.
Bulmer, M. (1984), *The Chicago School of Sociology*. Chicago: University of Chicago Press.
Cain, R. A. K. (2004), *Alain Leroy Locke: Race, Culture, and the Education of African American Adults*. Amsterdam: Rodopi.
Campbell, J. (1992), *The Community Reconstructs: The Meaning of Pragmatic Social Thought*. Chicago: University of Illinois Press.
Carden, S. D. (2006), *Virtue Ethics: Dewey and Macintyre*. London and New York: Continuum.

Casil, A. S. (2006), *John Dewey: The Founder of American Liberalism*. New York: Rosen Publishing Group.

Clanton, J. C. (2008), *Religion and Democratic Citizenship: Inquiry and Conviction in the American Public Square*. Lanham, MD: Lexington Books.

Coeckelbergh, M. (2007), *Imagination and Principles: An Essay on the Role of Imagination in Moral Reasoning*. Basingstoke, UK and New York: Palgrave Macmillan. Cowan, R. (2003), *Cornel West: The Politics of Redemption*. Cambridge, UK: Polity.

Curco, F. (2009), *Ironia y Democracia Liberal: Rorty y el Giro Hermeneutico en la Politica*. Mexico: Ediciones CoyoacAn, ITAM.

Danisch, R. (2007), *Pragmatism, Democracy, and the Necessity of Rhetoric*. Columbia: University of South Carolina Press.

Deegan, M. J. (2008), *Self, War, and Society: George Herbert Mead's Macrosociology*. New Brunswick, NJ: Transaction Publishers.

Dewey, J. (1989), *Freedom and Culture* (first published in 1939). Reprinted, Amherst, NY: Prometheus Books.

Dickstein, M. (ed.), (1998), *The Revival of Pragmatism: New Essays on Social Thought, Law, and Culture*. Durham, NC: Duke University Press.

Diggins, J. P. (1994), *The Promise of Pragmatism: Modernism and the Crisis of Knowledge and Authority*. Chicago: University of Chicago Press.

Durkheim, É. (1983), *Pragmatism and Sociology*. Ed. John B. Allcock. Cambridge, UK: Cambridge University Press.

Farber, D. A. (1999), *Eco-Pragmatism: Making Sensible Environmental Decisions in an Uncertain World*. Chicago: University of Chicago Press.

Feldman, J. R. (2009), *Victorian Modernism: Pragmatism and the Varieties of Aesthetic Experience*. Cambridge, UK: Cambridge University Press.

Festenstein, M. (1997), *Pragmatism and Political Theory: From Dewey to Rorty*. Chicago: University of Chicago Press; Cambridge: Polity Press.

Fischer, M., Nackenoff, C., and Chmielewski, W. (ed.), (2009), *Jane Addams and the Practice of Democracy*. Urbana: University of Illinois Press.

Garrison, J. (ed.), (2008), *Reconstructing Democracy, Recontextualizing Dewey: Pragmatism and Interactive Constructivism in the Twenty-First Century*. Albany, NY: State University of New York Press.

Gasparski, W., Ryan, L. V., and Nahser, F. B. (eds), (2002), *Praxiology and Pragmatism*. New Brunswick, NJ: Transaction Publishers.

Glaude, E. S. (2007), *In a Shade of Blue: Pragmatism and the Politics of Black America*. Chicago: University of Chicago Press.

Gouinlock, J. (1986), *Excellence in Public Discourse: John Stuart Mill, John Dewey, and Social Intelligence*. New York: Teachers College Press.

Green, J. M. (1999), *Deep Democracy: Community, Diversity, and Transformation*. Lanham, MD: Rowman & Littlefield.

Green, J. M. (2008), *Pragmatism and Social Hope: Deepening Democracy in Social Contexts*. New York: Columbia University Press.

Grippe, E. (2007), *Richard Rorty's New Pragmatism: Neither Liberal Nor Free*. London and New York: Continuum.

Gunn, G. (2001), *Beyond Solidarity: Pragmatism and Difference in a Globalized World*. Chicago: University of Chicago Press.

Gutting, G. (1999), *Pragmatic Liberalism and the Critique of Modernity*. Cambridge, UK: Cambridge University Press.

Halton, E. (1986), *Meaning and Modernity: Social Theory in the Pragmatic Attitude*. Chicago: University of Chicago Press.

Hester, D. M. (2001), *Community as Healing: Pragmatist Ethics in Medical Encounters*. Lanham, MD: Rowman & Littlefield.

—(2010), *End-of-Life Care and Pragmatic Decision Making: A Bioethical Perspective*. Cambridge, UK: Cambridge University Press.

Hillier, J. and Healy, P. (ed.), (2008), *Political economy, diversity and pragmatism*. Aldershot, UK: Ashgate.

Hook, S. (1940), *Reason, Social Myths, and Democracy*, 1st edn. New York: John Day Co. Reprinted, Buffalo, NY: Prometheus Books, 1991.

—(1962), *The Paradoxes of Freedom*. Berkeley: University of California Press. Reprinted, Buffalo, NY: Prometheus, 1987.

—(1980), *Philosophy and Public Policy*. Carbondale: Southern Illinois University Press.

Hoopes, J. (1998), *Community Denied: The Wrong Turn of Pragmatic Liberalism*. Ithaca, NY: Cornell University Press.

Horowitz, I. L. (ed.), (1963), *Power, Politics, and People: The Collected Essays of C. Wright Mills*. New York: Oxford University Press.

—(1983), *C. Wright Mills: An American Utopian*. New York: Free Press.

Hunter, A. and Milofsky, C. (2007), *Pragmatic Liberalism: Constructing a Civil Society*. New York: Palgrave Macmillan.

Jaffe, R. (1960), *The Pragmatic Conception of Justice*. Berkeley: University of California Press.

Joas, H. (1993), *Pragmatism and Social Theory*. A translation of *Pragmatismus und Gesellschaftstheorie* (1992). Chicago: University of Chicago Press.

—(1997), *The Creativity of Action*. Chicago: University of Chicago Press.

Johnson, C. S. (2003), *Cornel West and Philosophy: The Quest for Social Justice*. New York and London: Routledge.

Johnson, M. (2007), *The Meaning of the Body: Aesthetics of Human Understanding*. Chicago: University of Chicago Press.

Kasiske, P. (2009), *Rechts- und Demokratietheorie im Amerikanischen Pragmatismus*. Baden-Baden, Germany: Nomos.

Katz, E. and Light, A. (ed.), (1996), *Environmental Pragmatism*. London and New York: Routledge.

Kaufman-Osborn, T. V. (1991), *Politics/Sense/Experience: A Pragmatic Inquiry into the Promise of Democracy*. Ithaca, NY: Cornell University Press.

Kautzer, C. and Mendieta, E. (2009), *Pragmatism, Nation, and Race: Community in the Age of Empire*. Bloomington: Indiana University Press.

Keulartz, J., Korthals, M., Schermer, M., and Swierstra, T. (ed.), (2002), *Pragmatist Ethics for a Technological Culture*. Dordrecht: Kluwer.

Khalil, E. (ed.), (2004), *Dewey, Pragmatism and Economic Methodology*. London and New York: Routledge.

Kloppenberg, J. T. (1986), *Uncertain Victory: Social Democracy and Progressivism in European and American Social Thought, 1870–1920*. New York: Oxford University Press.

Koch, D. F. and Lawson, B. K. (eds), (2004), *Pragmatism and the Problem of Race*. Bloomington: Indiana University Press.

Kremer, A. and Ryder, J. (ed.), (2009), *Self and Society: Central European Pragmatist Forum*, vol. 4. Amsterdam and New York: Rodopi.

Kurtz, P. (1983), *In Defense of Secular Humanism*. Amherst, NY: Prometheus Books.

Kurtz, P. (1987), *Forbidden Fruit: The Ethics of Humanism*. Amherst, NY: Prometheus Books. Reprinted, 2008.

—(2010), *Multi-Secularism: A New Agenda*. New Brunswick, NJ: Transaction Books.

Lacey, R. J. (2008), *American Pragmatism and Democratic Faith*. DeKalb, IL: Northern Illinois University Press.

LaFollette, H. (2007), *The Practice of Ethics*. Malden, MA: Blackwell.

Leaf, M. J. (2009), *Human Organizations and Social Theory: Pragmatism, Pluralism, and Adaptation*. Urbana: University of Illinois Press.

Lekan, T. (2003), *Making Morality: Pragmatist Reconstruction in Ethical Theory*. Nashville, TN: Vanderbilt University Press.

Lepley, R. (ed.), (1949), *Value: A Cooperative Inquiry*. New York: Columbia University Press.

Lewis, C. I. (1955), *The Ground and the Nature of the Right*. New York: Columbia University Press.

—(1957), *Our Social Inheritance*. Bloomington: Indiana University Press.

—(1969), *Values and Imperatives: Studies in Ethics*. Ed. John Lange. Stanford: Stanford University Press.

Lewis, J. D. and Smith, R. L. (1980), *American Sociology and Pragmatism: Mead, Chicago Sociology, and Symbolic Interaction*. Chicago: University of Chicago Press.

Light, A. and McKenna, E. (eds), (2004), *Animal Pragmatism: Rethinking Human-Non-human Relationships*. Bloomington: Indiana University Press.

Livingston, J. (1994), *Pragmatism and the Political Economy of Cultural Revolution, 1850–1940*. Chapel Hill: University of North Carolina Press.

Lloyd, B. (1997), *Left Out: Pragmatism, Exceptionalism, and the Poverty of American Marxism, 1890–1922*. Baltimore, MD: Johns Hopkins University Press.

MacGilvray, E. A. (2004), *Reconstructing Public Reason*. Cambridge, MA: Harvard University Press.

Marcell, D. W. (1974), *Progress and Pragmatism: James, Dewey, Beard, and the American Idea of Progress*. Westport, CT: Greenwood Press.
Margolis, J. (1995), *Historied Thought, Constructed World: A Conceptual Primer for the Turn of the Millennium*. Berkeley: University of California Press.
—(1996), *Life without Principles: Reconciling Theory and Practice*. Oxford: Basil Blackwell.
—(2004), *Moral Philosophy after 9/11*. University Park: Pennsylvania State University Press.
—(2009), *Culture and Cultural Entities: Toward a New Unity of Science*, 2nd edn. Dordrecht: Springer.
McDonald, H. P. (2003), *John Dewey and Environmental Philosophy*. Albany: State University of New York Press.
McGee, G. (ed.), (2003), *Pragmatic Bioethics*, 2nd edn. Cambridge, MA: MIT Press.
McKenna, E. (2002), *The Task of Utopia: A Pragmatist and Feminist Perspective*. Lanham, MD: Rowman & Littlefield.
Mead, G. H. (1967), *Mind, Self, and Society from the Standpoint of a Social Behaviorist*. Ed. Charles W. Morris (first published in 1934). Reprinted, Chicago: University of Chicago Press.
Mills, C. W. (1964), *Sociology and Pragmatism: The Higher Learning in America*. New York: Paine-Whitman Publishers.
Minteer, B. A. (2006), *The Landscape of Reform: Civic Pragmatism and Environmental Thought in America*. Cambridge, MA: MIT Press.
Misak, C. J. (2000), *Truth, Politics, Morality: Pragmatism and Deliberation*. London and New York: Routledge.
Morales, A. (ed.), (2003), *Renascent Pragmatism: Studies in Law and Social Science*. Burlington, Vermont: Ashgate.
Morris, C. W. (1956), *Varieties of Human Value*. Chicago: University of Chicago Press.
Muyumba, W. M. (2009), *The Shadow and the Act: Black Intellectual Practice, Jazz Improvisation, and Philosophical Pragmatism*. Chicago: University of Chicago Press.
Paringer, W. A. (1990), *John Dewey and the Paradox of Liberal Reform*. Albany: State University of New York Press.
Pihlstrom, S. (2005), *Pragmatic Moral Realism: A Transcendental Defense*. Amsterdam: Editions Rodopi.
Posner, R. A. (2003), *Law, Pragmatism, and Democracy*. Cambridge: Harvard University Press.
Putnam, H. (2002), *The Collapse of the Fact/Value Dichotomy and Other Essays*. Cambridge, MA: Harvard University Press.
—(2004), *Ethics Without Ontology*. Cambridge, MA: Harvard University Press.
Racine, E. (2009), *Pragmatic Neuroethics: Improving Treatment and Understanding of the Mind-Brain*. Cambridge, MA: MIT Press, 2009.
Rorty, R. (1998), *Achieving Our Country: Leftist Thought in Twentieth-Century America*. Cambridge, MA: Harvard University Press.

—(1999), *Philosophy and Social Hope.* New York: Penguin.
Rosenthal, S. B. and Buchholz, R. A. (1997), *Business Ethics: The Pragmatic Path Beyond Principles to Process.* Upper Saddle River, NJ: Prentice Hall.
—(2000), *Rethinking Business Ethics: A Pragmatic Approach.* New York: Oxford University Press.
Ryder, J. and Visnovsky, E. (eds), (2004), *Pragmatism and Values: The Central European Pragmatist Forum, Volume One.* Amsterdam and New York: Rodopi.
Ryder, J. and Wilkoszewska, K. (eds), (2004), *Deconstruction and Reconstruction: The Central European Pragmatist Forum, Volume Two.* Amsterdam and New York: Rodopi.
Saunders, W. S. (ed.), (2007), *The New Architectural Pragmatism: A Harvard Design Magazine Reader.* Minneapolis: University of Minnesota Press.
Schollmeier, P. (2006), *Human Goodness: Pragmatic Variations on Platonic Themes.* Cambridge, UK: Cambridge University Press.
Seigfried, C. H. (1996), *Pragmatism and Feminism: Reweaving the Social Fabric.* Chicago: University of Chicago Press.
—(ed.), (2009), *Feminist Interpretations of John Dewey.* University Park: Pennsylvania State Press.
Shusterman, R. (2000), *Performing Live: Aesthetic Alternatives for the Ends of Art.* Ithaca, NY: Cornell University Press.
—(2000), *Pragmatist Aesthetics: Living Beauty, Rethinking Art,* 2nd edn. Lanham, MD: Rowman & Littlefield.
—(2002), *Surface and Depth: Dialectics of Criticism and Culture.* Ithaca, NY: Cornell University Press.
—(2008), *Body Consciousness: A Philosophy of Mindfulness and Somaesthetics.* Cambridge, UK: Cambridge University Press.
Singer, B. J. (1998), *Pragmatism, Rights, and Democracy.* New York: Fordham University Press.
Sobrinho, B. J. (2001), *Signs, Solidarities, and Sociology: Charles S. Peirce and the Pragmatics of Globalization.* Lanham, MD: Rowman & Littlefield.
Stout, J. (2004), *Democracy and Tradition.* Princeton, NJ: Princeton University Press.
Sullivan, S. (2001), *Living Across and Through Skins: Transactional Bodies, Pragmatism, and Feminism.* Bloomington: Indiana University Press.
Talisse, R. B. (2005), *Democracy after Liberalism: Pragmatism and Deliberative Politics.* London: Routledge.
—(2007), *A Pragmatist Philosophy of Democracy: Communities of Inquiry.* London and New York: Routledge.
Tan, S.-H. (2003), *Confucian Democracy: A Deweyan Reconstruction.* Albany: State University of New York Press.
Tan, S.-H. and Whalen-Bridge, J. (ed.), (2008), *Democracy as Culture: Deweyan Pragmatism in a Globalizing World.* Albany, NY: State University of New York Press.

Thomas, E. W. (2005), *The Judicial Process: Realisms, Pragmatism, Practical Reasoning and Principles*. Cambridge, UK: Cambridge University Press.
Tilman, R. (2004), *Thorstein Veblen, John Dewey, C. Wright Mills and the Generic Ends of Life*. Lanham, MD: Rowman & Littlefield.
Urbinati, N. (2009), *Individualismo Democratico: Emerson, Dewey e la Cultura Politica Americana*, 2nd edn. Rome: Donzelli.
Wallace, J. D. (1988), *Moral Relevance and Moral Conflict*. Ithaca, NY: Cornell University Press.
—(1996), *Ethical Norms, Particular Cases*. Ithaca, NY: Cornell University Press.
—(2008), *Norms and Practices*. Ithaca, NY: Cornell University Press.
Wells, H. K. (1954), *Pragmatism, Philosophy of Imperialism*. London: Lawrence & Wishart; New York: International Publishers.
West, C. (1993), *Beyond Eurocentism and Multiculturalism*. Vol. 1: *Prophetic Thoughts in Post-Modern Times*. Vol. 2: *Prophetic Reflections: Notes on Race and Power in America*. Monroe, ME: Common Courage Press.
—(1993), *Keeping Faith: Philosophy and Race in America*. New York: Routledge.
—(2004), *Democracy Matters: Winning the Fight against Imperialism*. New York: Penguin.
West, C. and Unger, R. (1998), *The Future of American Progressivism: An Initiative for Political and Economic Reform*. Boston: Beacon.West, C. (2001), *Race Matters*. Boston: Beacon Press. Reissued in hardcover with new introduction, 2001.
Westbrook, R. B. (2005), *Democratic Hope: Pragmatism and the Politics of Truth*. Ithaca, NY: Cornell University Press.
Willett, C. (2008), *Irony in the Age of Empire: Comic Perspectives on Democracy and Freedom*. Bloomington: Indiana University Press.
Wisnewski, J. J. (2008), *The Politics of Agency: Towards a Pragmatic Approach to Philosophical Anthropology*. Aldershot, UK and Burlington, VT: Ashgate.
Wood, M. D. (2000), *Cornel West and the Politics of Prophetic Pragmatism*. Urbana: University of Illinois Press.
Woodward, C. (2008), *Reasons, Patterns, and Cooperation*. London and New York: Routledge.
Yancy, G. (ed.), (2001), *Cornel West: A Critical Reader*. Oxford: Blackwell.

Society and culture

Includes the social sciences, culture studies, religion and world philosophies, education, and literature.

Allan, G. (2004), *Higher Education in the Making: Pragmatism, Whitehead, and the Canon*. Albany: State University of New York Press.

Alridge, D. P. (2008), *The Educational Thought of W. E. B. Du Bois: An Intellectual History.* New York: Teachers College Press.
Ames, R. T. and Hall, D. L. (1998), *The Democracy of the Dead: Dewey, Confucius, and the Hope for Democracy in China.* Chicago: Open Court.
Ames, V. M. (1962), *Zen and American Thought.* Honolulu: University of Hawaii Press.
Anderson, V. (1998), *Pragmatic Theology: Negotiating the Intersections of an American Philosophy of Religion.* Albany: State University of New York Press.
Aycock, J. C., Brierley, M. J., and Simpson, D. J. (2005), *John Dewey and the Art of Teaching: Toward Reflective and Imaginative Practice.* Thousand Oaks, CA: Sage Publications.
Bayles, E. B. (1966), *Pragmatism in Education.* New York: Harper and Row.
Biesta, G. and Burbules, N. C. (2003), *Pragmatism and Educational Research.* Lanham, MD: Rowman & Littlefield.
Blumer, H. (1969), *Symbolic Interactionism: Perspective and Method.* Englewood Cliffs, NJ: Prentice-Hall.
Boulting, N. E. (2006), *On Interpretative Activity: A Peircian Approach to the Interpretation of Science, Technology and the Arts.* Leiden: Brill.
Briggs, T. H. (1940), *Pragmatism and Pedagogy.* New York: Macmillan.
Browne, N. W. (2007), *The World in which We Occur: John Dewey, Pragmatist Ecology, and American Ecological Writing in the Twentieth Century.* Tuscaloosa: University of Alabama Press.
Burke, K. (1945), *A Grammar of Motives.* Berkeley: University of California Press. Reprinted, 1969.
—(1945), *Language as Symbolic Action: Essays on Life, Literature, and Method.* Berkeley: University of California Press.
—(1950), *A Rhetoric of Motives.* New York: Prentice-Hall. Reprinted, Berkeley: University of California Press, 1969.
Childs, J. L. (1931), *Education and the Philosophy of Experimentalism.* New York and London: The Century Co. Reprinted, New York: Arno Press, 1971.
—(1956), *American Pragmatism and Education: An Interpretation and Criticism.* New York: Henry Holt.
Dann, G. E. (2006), *After Rorty: The Possibilities for Ethics and Religious Belief.* London and New York: Continuum.
Davaney, S. G. (2000), *Pragmatic Historicism: A Theology for the Twenty-First Century.* Albany: State University of New York Press.
Dean, W. (1986), *American Religious Empiricism.* Albany: State University of New York Press.
Dewey, J. (1990), *John Dewey on Education.* Ed. Reginald D. Archambault. Chicago: University of Chicago Press.
Dorrien, G. (2003), *The Making of American Liberal Theology: Idealism, Realism, and Modernity 1900–1950.* Louisville, KY: Westminster John Knox Press.

Drong, L. (2007), *Disciplining the New Pragmatism: Theory, Rhetoric, and the Ends of Literary Study*. Frankfurt am Main and New York: Peter Lang.

Dumais, F. (2009), *L'Appropriation d'un Objet Culturel: Une Reactualisation des Theories de C. S. Peirce a Propos de l'Interpretation*. Sainte-Foy: Presses de l'Universite du Quebec.

Eco, U. (1990), *The Limits of Interpretation*. Bloomington: Indiana University Press.

Edwards, A. and Mayhew, K. (2009), *The Dewey School: The Laboratory School of the University of Chicago, 1896–1903*, (first published in 1936). New Brunswick, NJ: Transaction Publisher.

Ehrat, J. (2005), *Cinema And Semiotic: Peirce And Film Aesthetics, Narration, And Representation*. Toronto: University of Toronto Press.

Fairfield, P. (2009), *Education after Dewey*. London and New York: Continuum.

Fishman, S. M. and Parkinson McCarthy, L. (1998), *John Dewey and the Challenge of Classroom Practice*. New York: Teachers College Press.

Fontinell, E. (1970), *Toward a Reconstruction of Religion: A Philosophical Probe*. Garden City, NY: Doubleday.

Fontrodona, J. (2002), *Pragmatism and Management Inquiry: Insights from the Thought of Charles S. Peirce*. Westport, CT: Greenwood.

Frankenberry, N. (1987), *Religion and Radical Empiricism*. Albany: State University of New York Press.

Franks, D. D. and Lyng, S. (2002), *Sociology and the Real World*. Lanham, MD: Rowman & Littlefield.

Garrison, J. (ed.), (2008), *Reconstructing Democracy, Recontextualizing Dewey: Pragmatism and Interactive Constructivism in the Twenty-First Century*. Albany, NY: State University of New York Press.

Gelpi, D. L. (2001), *The Gracing of Human Experience: Rethinking the Relationship between Nature and Grace*. Collegeville, MN: The Liturgical Press.

Gonon, P. (2009), *The Quest for Modern Vocational Education: George Kerschensteiner between Dewey, Weber and Simmel*. Berlin: Peter Lang.

Grange, J. (2004), *John Dewey, Confucius, and Global Philosophy*. Albany: State University of New York Press.

Granger, D. A. (2006), *John Dewey, Robert Pirsig, and the Art of Living: Revisioning Aesthetic Education*. New York: Palgrave Macmillan.

Hammer, M. G. (2003), *American Pragmatism: A Religious Genealogy*. Oxford: Oxford University Press.

Handy, R. (1969), *Value Theory and the Behavioral Sciences*. Springfield, IL: Charles C. Thomas.

Handy, R. and Harwood, E. C. (1973), *A Current Appraisal of the Behavioral Sciences*. Great Barrington, MA: Behavioral Research Council.

—(1973), *Useful Procedures of Inquiry*. Great Barrington, MA: Behavioral Research Council.

Hansen, D. T. (ed.), (2006), *John Dewey and Our Educational Prospect: A Critical Engagement with Dewey's Democracy and Education*. Albany: State University of New York Press.
Johann, R. O. (1966), *The Pragmatic Meaning of God*. Milwaukee, WI: Marquette University Press.
Johansen, J. D. (2002), *Literary Discourse: A Semiotic-Pragmatic Approach to Literature*. Toronto: University of Toronto Press.
Johnston, J. S. (2009), *Deweyan Inquiry: From Education Theory to Practice*. Albany: State University of New York Press.
Jordan, J. (2006), *Pascal's Wager: Pragmatic Arguments and Belief in God*. Oxford: Oxford University Press.
Kahn, J. S. (2009), *Divine Discontent: The Religious Imagination of W. E. B. Du Bois*. Oxford: Oxford University Press.
Kandel, I. L. (1943), *The Cult of Uncertainty*. New York: Macmillan.
Kaplan, A. (1964), *The Conduct of Inquiry: Methodology for Behavioral Science*. Scranton, PA: Chandler Publishing.
Kilpatrick, W. H. (1951), *Philosophy of Education*. New York: Macmillan.
Kimura, G. W. (2007), *Neopragmatism and Theological Reason*. Aldershot, UK and Burlington, VT: Ashgate.
Kurtz, P. (1986), *The Transcendental Temptation: A Critique of Religion and the Paranormal*. Amherst, NY: Prometheus Books.
—(1989), *Eupraxophy: Living Without Religion*. Amherst, NY: Prometheus Books. Reprinted as *Living without Religion*, 1994.
Langsdorf, L. and Smith, A. R. (eds), (1995), *Recovering Pragmatism's Voice: The Classical Tradition, Rorty, and the Philosophy of Communication*. Albany: State University of New York Press.
Levinson, S. C. (1983), *Pragmatics*. Cambridge, UK: Cambridge University Press.
Lipman, M. (1991), *Thinking in Education*. Cambridge, UK: Cambridge University Press.
Magee, M. C., Jr. (2004), *Emancipating Pragmatism: Emerson, Jazz and Experimental Writing*. Tuscaloosa: University of Alabama Press.
Mailloux, S. (ed.), (1995), *Rhetoric, Sophistry, Pragmatism*. Cambridge, UK: Cambridge University Press.
Margolis, J. (2009), *Culture and cultural entities: toward a new unity of science*, 2nd edn (1st edn 1984). Dordrecht: Springer.
Mead, G. H. (1999), *Play, School, and Society*. Ed. Mary Jo Deegan. New York: Peter Lang.
—(2008), *The Philosophy of Education*. Eds Gert Biesta and Daniel Trohler. Boulder, CO: Paradigm Publishers.
Miller, R. C. (1974), *The American Spirit in Theology*. Philadelphia: United Church Press.
Minnich, E. K. (2005), *Transforming Knowledge*, 2nd edn. Philadelphia: Temple University Press.
Mitchell, W. J. T. (ed.), (1985), *Against Theory: Literary Theory and the New Pragmatism*. Chicago: University of Chicago Press.

Mullin, R. P. (2007), *The Soul of Classical American Philosophy: The Ethical and Spiritual Insights of William James, Josiah Royce, and Charles Sanders Pierce.* Albany: SUNY Press.

Neville, R. C. (2009), *Realism in Religion: a pragmatist's perspective.* Albany: State University of New York Press.

Ochs, P. (1998), *Peirce, Pragmatism and the Logic of Scripture.* Cambridge, UK: Cambridge University Press.

Odin, S. (1996), *The Social Self in Zen and American Pragmatism.* Albany: State University of New York Press.

Pecknold, C. C. (2005), *Transforming Postliberal Theology: George Lindbeck, Pragmatism and Scripture.* London and New York: T&T Clark International.

Pfuetze, P. E. (1954), *The Social Self.* New York: Bookman Associates. Reprinted as *Self, Society, and Existence: Human Nature and Dialogue in the thought of George Herbert Mead and Martin Buber.* New York: Harper, 1961.

Poirier, R. (1992), *Poetry and Pragmatism.* Cambridge, MA: Harvard University Press; London: Faber and Faber.

Popkewitz, T. S. (ed.), (2005), *Inventing the Modern Self and John Dewey: Modernities and the Traveling of Pragmatism in Education.* London: Macmillan.

Putnam, H. (2008), *Jewish Philosophy as a Guide to Life: Rosenzweig, Buber, Levinas, Wittgenstein.* Bloomington: Indiana University Press.

Rammert, W. (2007), *Technik—Handeln—Wissen: Zu Einer Pragmatistischen Technikund Sozialtheorie.* Wiesbaden, Germany: VS Verlag für Sozialwissenschaften.

Rao, K. R. (1968), *Gandhi and Pragmatism: An Intercultural Study.* Calcutta and Oxford: IBH Publ. Co.

Rosenbaum, S. (ed.), (2003), *Pragmatism and Religion: Classical Sources and Original Essays.* Urbana: University of Illinois Press.

Roth, R. J. (1967), *American Religious Philosophy.* New York: Harcourt, Brace, and World.

Ryder, J. and Wegmarshaus, G. R. (ed.), (2007), *Education for a Democratic Society: Central European Pragmatist Forum, Volume Three.* Amsterdam and New York: Rodopi.

Sahay, Y. (2009), *A Critical Appraisal of Truth: Buddhism and Pragmatism.* Patna, India: Janaki Prakashan.

Scott, S. J. (1991), *Frontiers of Consciousness: Interdisciplinary Studies in American Philosophy and Poetry.* New York: Fordham University Press.

Silva Jr., J. D. R. (2007), *O Pragmatismo como Fundamento das Reformas Educacionais no Brasil.* Campinas, Brazil: Alínea Editora/ANPED.

Stone, J. A. (1992), *The Minimalist Vision of Transcendence: A Naturalist Philosophy of Religion.* Albany: State University of New York Press.

—(2008), *Religious Naturalism Today: The Rebirth of a Forgotten Alternative.* Albany, NY: State University of New York Press.

Stout, J. (2004), *Democracy and Tradition.* Princeton, NJ: Princeton University Press.

Strout, C. (1958), *The Pragmatic Revolt in American History: Carl Becker and Charles Beard*. New Haven, CT: Yale University Press.
Swartz, O., Campbell, K., and Pestana, C. (2009), *Neo-Pragmatism, Communication, and the Culture of Creative Democracy*. New York: Peter Lang.
Taylor, M., Schreier, H., and Ghiraldelli Jr., P. (ed.), (2008), *Pragmatism, Education, and Children: International Philosophical Perspectives*. Amsterdam and New York: Rodopi.
Tejera, V. (1984), *History as a Human Science: The Conception of History in some Classic American Philosophers*. Lanham, MD: University Press of America.
Vidu, A. (2009), *Theology after Neo-Pragmatism*. Eugene, OR: Wipf and Stock.
Ward, R. (2004), *Conversion in American Philosophy: Exploring the Practice of Transformation*. New York: Fordham University Press.
Wasmaier, M. (2007), *Zwischen Pragmatismus und Realismus: Eine Analyse der Religionsphilosophie von William P. Alston*. Frankfurt: Ontos.
Wen, H. (2009), *Confucian Pragmatism as the Art of Contextualizing Personal Experience and World*. Lanham, MD: Lexington Books.
West, C. (1982), *Prophesy Deliverance! An African American Revolutionary Christianity*. Louisville, KY: Westminster Press. Anniversary reissue, 2002.
—(1988), *Prophetic Fragments: Illuminations of the Crisis in American Religion and Culture*. Grand Rapids, Eerdmans; Trenton, NJ: Africa World Press.
Wood, M. D. (2000), *Cornel West and the Politics of Prophetic Pragmatism*. Urbana: University of Illinois Press.
Zackariasson, U. (2002), *Forces by Which We Live: Religion and Religious Experience from the Perspective of a Pragmatic Philosophical Anthropology*. Uppsala, Sweden: Uppsala University.

Works cited in the editorial chapters (Chapters 1, 2, 15–18)

Allison, H. E. (2004), *Kant's Transcendental Idealism: An Interpretation and Defense—Revised and Enlarged Edition*. New Haven, CT: Yale University Press, (1st edn 1983).
Armstrong, D. M. (2004), *Truth and Truthmakers*. Cambridge: Cambridge University Press.
Bernstein, R. J. (1995), "American Pragmatism", in H. J. Saatkamp (ed.), *Rorty & Pragmatism: The Philosopher Responds to His Critics*. Nashville, TN: Vanderbilt University Press.
—(2005), *The Abuse of Evil*. Cambridge: Polity Press.
Callaway, H. G. (2006), "Introduction", in R. W. Emerson, *The Conduct of Life*, ed. H. G. Callaway. Lanham, MD: University Press of America.
—(2008), "Introduction", in Emerson (1870/2008).

Carnap, R. (1950), "Empiricism, Semantics and Ontology", *Revue International de Philosophie*, 4, pp. 20–40.

Carr, D. (1999), *The Paradox of Subjectivity: The Self in the Transcendental Tradition*. Oxford: Oxford University Press.

Colella, E. P. (2005), "Reflex Action and the Pragmatism of Giovanni Papini", *Journal of Speculative Philosophy*, 19, pp. 187–215.

Conant, J. (1997), "The James/Royce Dispute and the Development of James's 'Solution'", in R. A. Putnam (ed.), *The Cambridge Companion to William James*. Cambridge: Cambridge University Press.

Crary, A. and Read, R. (eds), (2000), *The New Wittgenstein*. London: Routledge.

Creath, R. (ed.), (1990), *Dear Carnap, Dear Van: The Quine-Carnap Correspondence and Related Work*. Berkeley: University of California Press.

Davidson, D. (1984), *Inquiries into Truth and Interpretation*. Oxford: Clarendon Press.

Dawkins, R. (2003), *The God Delusion*. London: Bantam Books.

Dennett, D. C. (2006), *Breaking the Spell: Religion as a Natural Phenomenon*. New York: Viking. Dewey, J. and Bentley, A. (1949), *Knowing and the Known*. Boston: Beacon Press (reprinted in Dewey, LW).

Emerson, R. W. (1870), *Society and Solitude*. Ed. H. G. Callaway. Lewiston: The Edwin Mellen Press, 2008.

Feyerabend, P. (1975), *Against Method: Outline of an Anarchistic Theory of Knowledge*, 3rd edn. London and New York: Verso, 1993.

Franzese, S. (2008), *The Ethics of Energy: William James's Moral Philosophy in Focus*. Frankfurt: Ontos Verlag.

Golino, C. L. (1955), "Giovanni Papini and American Pragmatism", *Italica*, 32, pp. 38–48.

Gullace, G. (1962), "The Pragmatist Movement in Italy", *Journal of the History of Ideas*, 23, pp. 91–105.

Goodman, N. (1978), *Ways of Worldmaking*. Hassocks: Harverster Press, 1992.

—(1984), *Of Mind and Other Matters*. Cambridge, MA: Harvard University Press.

Haack, S. (1998), *Manifesto of a Passionate Moderate: Unfashionable Essays*. Chicago: The University of Chicago Press.

—(2004), "Pragmatism, Old and New", *Contemporary Pragmatism*, 1, pp. 3–41.

—(2005), "Not Cynicism, but Synechism: Lessons from Classical Pragmatism", *Transactions of the Charles S. Peirce Society*, 41, pp. 239–253.

Heinämaa, S. (2003), *The Phenomenology of Sexual Difference*. Lanham, MD: Rowman & Littlefield.

Hingst, K.-M. (2000), "James' Transformation der Pragmatischen Maxime von Peirce", in K. Oehler (ed.), *William James: Pragmatismus*. Berlin: Akademie Verlag.

Hookway, C. (1988), *Quine: Language, Experience and Reality*. Stanford, CA: Stanford University Press.

Husserl, E. (1936), *The Crisis of European Sciences and Transcendental Phenomenology*. Translated by D. Carr. Chicago: Northwestern University Press, 1974.

Isaac, J. (2005), "W.V. Quine and the Origins of Analytic Philosophy in the United States", *Modern Intellectual History*, 2, pp. 205-234.

Jacobsson, M. (1910), *Pragmatismen: särskilt i dess förhållande till kriticismen* [Pragmatism, especially in relation to criticism]. Lund: Berlingska boktryckeriet.

James, W. (1906), "G. Papini and the Pragmatist Movement in Italy", *The Journal of Philosophy, Psychology and Scientific Methods*, 3, pp. 337-341.

Kaila, E. (1912), "William James: Amerikan filosofi" [William James: The Philosopher of America], in E. Kaila, *Valitut teokset* [Selected Works], vol. 1, edn. I. Niiniluoto, Helsinki: Otava, pp. 80-92. Forthcoming as an English translation, by H. A. Kovalainen, in *Transactions of the Charles S. Peirce Society*.

—(1934), *Persoonallisuus* [Personality]. Helsinki, Otava, (3rd edn 1946.)

—(1986), *Syvähenkinen elämä: Keskusteluja viimeisistä kysymyksistä* [Deep-Mental Life: Discussions of Ultimate Questions]. Helsinki, Otava, 3rd edn (1st edn 1943.)

Kant, I. (1781/1787), *Kritik der reinen Vernunft*. Ed. R. Schmidt. Hamburg: Felix Meiner, 1990. (A = 1st edn, 1781; B = 2nd edn, 1787.)

Kilpinen, E. (2000), *The Enormous Fly-Wheel of Society: Pragmatism's Habitual Conception of Rationality and Social Theory*. Helsinki: Research Reports 235, Department of Sociology, University of Helsinki.

Koskinen, H. J. (2004), *From a Metaphilosophical Point of View: A Study of W. V. Quine's Naturalism*. Acta Philosophica Fennica 74. Helsinki: The Philosophical Society of Finland.

Koskinen, H. J. and Pihlström, S. (2006), "Quine and Pragmatism", *Transactions of the Charles S. Peirce Society*, 42, pp. 309-346.

Kovalainen, H. A. (2010), *Self and World: The New Emerson*. Ph.D. Diss., University of Tampere, Finland.

Kuhn, T. S. (1970), *The Structure of Scientific Revolutions*, 2nd edn. Chicago: The University of Chicago Press (1st ed. 1962).

Lagerlund, H. (2003), *Filosofi i Sverige under tusen år*. Lund: Studentlitteratur.

Lowe, E. J. (1998), *The Possibility of Metaphysics: Substance, Identity and Time*. Oxford: Clarendon Press, 2001.

—(2006), *The Four-Category Ontology: A Metaphysical Foundation for Natural Science*. Oxford: Clarendon Press.

Mackie, J. L. (1977), *Ethics: Inventing Right and Wrong*. London: Penguin.

Margolis, J. (2004), "The First Pragmatists", in A. T. Marsoobian and J. Ryder (eds), *The Blackwell Guide to American Philosophy*. Malden MA: Blackwell, pp. 35-51.

McDowell, J. (1996), *Mind and World*, rev. edn. Cambridge, MA: Harvard University Press (1st ed. 1994).

Niiniluoto, I. (1999), *Critical Scientific Realism*. Oxford: Oxford University Press.

Perry, R. B. (1935), *The Thought and Character of William James*, 2 vols. London: Macmillan.

Pihlström, S. (1996), *Structuring the World: The Issue of Realism and the Nature of Ontological Problems in Classical and Contemporary Pragmatism*. Acta Philosophica Fennica 59. Helsinki: The Philosophical Society of Finland.

—(1998), *Pragmatism and Philosophical Anthropology: Understanding Our Human Life in a Human World.* New York: Lang.
—(2004), "Peirce's Place in the Pragmatist Tradition", in C. Misak (ed.), *The Cambridge Companion to Peirce.* Cambridge: Cambridge University Press, pp. 27–57.
—(2007), "Religion and Pseudo-Religion: An Elusive Boundary", *International Journal for Philosophy of Religion*, 62, pp. 3–32.
—(2008b), "How (Not) to Write the History of Pragmatist Philosophy of Science", *Perspectives on Science*, 16, pp. 26–69.
—(2009b), "Nordic Pragmatism", in S. Pihlström and H. Rydenfelt (eds), *Pragmatist Perspectives.* Acta Philosophica Fennica 86. Helsinki: The Philosophical Society of Finland.
—(2009c), "Pragmatism and Naturalized Transcendental Subjectivity", *Contemporary Pragmatism*, 6, pp. 1–13.
—(2010), "Dewey and Pragmatic Religious Naturalism", in M. Cochran (ed.), *The Cambridge Companion to Dewey.* Cambridge: Cambridge University Press, pp. 211–241.
—(2011), "Contingency, Democracy, and the Human Sciences: Challenges for Pragmatic Naturalism", in J. Knowles and H. Rydenfelt (eds), *Pragmatism, Science and Naturalism.* Berlin: Peter Lang.
Popper, K. R. (1994), *The Myth of the Framework: In Defence of Science and Rationality.* Ed. M. A. Notturno. London and New York: Routledge, 1996.
Putnam, H. (1981), *Reason, Truth and History.* Cambridge: Cambridge University Press.
Quine, W. V. (1960), *Word and Object.* Cambridge, MA: The MIT Press.
—(1969), *Ontological Relativity and Other Essays*, Columbia University Press, New York.
—(1980), *From a Logical Point of View.* Cambridge, MA: Harvard University Press, 2nd ed. (1st ed. 1953).
—(1985), *The Time of My Life: An Autobiography*, Cambridge, MA: The MIT Press.
—(1991), "Two Dogmas in Retrospect", *Canadian Journal of Philosophy*, 21, pp. 265–274.
—(1992), *Pursuit of Truth*, rev. edn. Cambridge, MA: Harvard University Press.
Ramberg, B. (2000), "Post-Ontological Philosophy of Mind: Rorty vs. Davidson", in R. B. Brandom (ed.), *Rorty and His Critics.* Malden, MA: Blackwell.
Rescher, N. (2005), "Pragmatism at the Crossroads", *Transactions of the Charles S. Peirce Society*, 41, pp. 355–365.
Rouse, J. (2002), *How Scientific Practices Matter: Reclaiming Philosophical Naturalism*, Chicago and London: The University of Chicago Press.
Sandbothe, M. (2004), "The Pragmatic Twist of the Linguistic Turn". Translated by L. Vizenor, in W. Eggington & M. Sandbothe (eds), *The Pragmatic Turn in Philosophy: Contemporary Engagements between Analytic and Continental Thought.* Albany: SUNY Press, pp. 67–91.
Sellars, W. (1963), *Science, Perception and Reality.* London: Routledge and Kegan Paul.
Skrbina, D. (2005), *Panpsychism in the West.* Cambridge, MA and London: The MIT Press.

Turrisi, P. A. (ed.), (1997), *Pragmatism as a Principle and as a Method of Right Thinking: The 1903 Harvard Lectures on Pragmatism*, by Charles S. Peirce. Albany, NY: SUNY Press. (Contains the editor's introduction and commentary.)

Voparil, C. (2006), *Richard Rorty: Politics and Vision*. Lanham, MD: Rowman & Littlefield.

White, M. (1950), "The Analytic and the Synthetic: An Untenable Dualism", in M. White, *Pragmatism and the American Mind: Essays and Reviews in Philosophy and Intellectual History*. London: Oxford University Press, 1973, chapter 8.

—(1956), *Toward Reunion in Philosophy*. Cambridge, MA: Harvard University Press.

—(1986), "Normative Ethics, Normative Epistemology, and Quine's Holism", in L. E. Hahn & P. A. Schilpp (eds), *The Philosophy of W. V. Quine*. La Salle, IL: Open Court, pp. 649–662.

—(1999), *A Philosopher's Story*. University Park: The Pennsylvania State University Press.

Wittgenstein, L. (1953), *Philosophical Investigations*. Translated by G. E. M. Anscombe. Oxford: Blackwell, 1958.

—(1969), *On Certainty*. Translated by G. E. M. Anscombe and D. Paul. Oxford: Blackwell.

Zanoni, C. P. (1979), "Development of Logical Pragmatism in Italy", *Journal of the History of Ideas*, 40, pp. 603–619.

Index

Aboulafia, M.   145
Absolute, the   275, 279
absolute pragmatism   17, 279
Addams, J.   4, 74, 150, 199, 204, 215, 265, 273
Adorno, T.   117
aesthetics   122–36
   contemporary pragmatist aesthetics   131–6
   Dewey's contribution to   126–31
   Emerson's understanding of artististic creation   122–4
   James's artistic vision   125–6
   Peirce's semeiotic theory   125
Aiken, H.   282
Aikin, S. F.   5
Allison, H. E.   101
American Journal of Political Science   170
American Philosophy: An Encyclopedia   281
American pragmatism   19, 27, 74, 145, 149, 173, 215, 224, 277
American transcendentalism   8
Anderson, E.   150
   antirealism   59–60, 100–1, 241
   anti-representationalism   265–6
Appiah, K. A.   216, 217
Archer, M.   160
Aristotle   66, 101, 112, 155, 199
Armstrong, D. M.   99
Ayres, C. E.   204, 206, 208

Barber, B.   191
Barnes, A. C.   126
Barnes, H. E.   164
Beardsley, M. C.   131
Behavioralist Revolution   180
Bell, C.   130
Bentley, A.   48, 163
Bentley, A. F.   171
Berkeley, G.   268
Berleant, A.   131–3
   The Aesthetic Field   131

Aesthetics of the Environment   133
   Art and Engagement   132–3
   Living in the Landscape   133
Bernstein, R.   76, 235, 244, 246, 248–50
Bessette, J.   174
Biesta, G. J. J.   192, 197
Blumer, H.   272
Bogdan, R.   159
Bohman, J.   171–4
   "Democracy as Inquiry, Inquiry as Democratic"   171
Boland, L.   205
Borgmann, A.   118
Bradley, F. H.   276, 280
Brandom, R. B.   4, 6, 22, 24, 89, 213
Breault, D.   188
Breault, R.   188
British empiricism   8
Bromley, D.   203, 208–13
   Sufficient Reason   209, 211, 212
Buchler, J.   131
Bullert, G.   170
Burch, R.   109
Burke, E.   173
Burke, T.   277

Cahn, S. N.   190
Calderoni, M.   12, 26
Callaway, H. G.   50, 250
Campbell, J.   75, 179, 274, 281
Carnap, R.   4, 6, 20, 21, 29, 31, 42, 103, 278
Carr, D.   51
Cartesian epistemology   16, 83
Caspary, W.   176
Clapp, E. R.   199
Coase, R.   205
Cohen, M. R.   282
Colella, E. P.   26
Commons, J. R.   203, 210
Communist Manifesto (by Marx and Engels)   267
Conant, J.   39, 240

contextualism 87
contractualism 138
Cook, G. 273
Cooke, E. 268
Cooley, C. H. 163
Cormier, H. 280, 84
corridor metaphor 266
Coughlan, N. 270
 Young John Dewey 270
Croce, P. J. 111

Dalton, T. C. 108
Damasio, A. 161
Darwall, S. 141
Darwin, C. 8, 76, 147, 206, 228
 The Origin of Species 228
Davidson, D. 22
Dawkins, R. 58, 60
Dayton, E. 144
Dennett, D. C. 58, 112, 115, 158
DeRose, K. 87
Derrida, J. 98
Descartes, R. 83
Dewey, A. C. 199
Dewey, J. 4, 6, 7, 9, 11, 12, 14–19, 22, 23, 27, 29, 30, 31, 42, 47, 48, 50, 53, 55, 56, 64, 65, 67, 72, 73, 74, 81, 85, 86, 88, 89, 95, 96, 97, 102, 104, 108, 110, 111–19, 122, 124, 126, 127–31, 132, 133, 134, 136, 138, 142, 143, 145, 146, 147, 148, 149, 150, 154, 158, 163, 169, 170, 172, 173, 174, 175, 176, 177, 178, 179, 180, 188, 189, 190–4, 195, 197, 198, 199, 200, 204, 205, 206, 209, 213, 215, 218, 219, 220, 222, 229, 231, 232, 234, 247, 250, 265, 266–7, 268, 269, 270, 271, 272, 275, 278, 280, 281, 282, 283
 "From Absolutism to Experimentalism" 270
 Art as Experience 124, 127, 128, 129, 130, 134, 136, 267
 and the Chicago School 72–4
 "The Child and the Curriculum" 191
 A Common Faith 29, 231
 Democracy and Education 267
 Ethics (with James Tufts) 267
 Experience and Education 147, 198
 Experience and Nature 114, 116, 126, 267
 How We Think 213
 Human Nature and Conduct 143, 174, 267
 Liberalism and Social Action 267
 Logic: The Theory of Inquiry 113, 267
 "The Postulate of Immediate Empiricism" 110, 111
 The Public and Its Problems 171, 173, 175, 176, 267
 The Quest for Certainty 47, 267
 Reconstruction in Philosophy 267
 "The Reflex Arc Concept in Psychology" 112
 The School and Society 191, 192, 197
 "The Pragmatism of Peirce" 14
Dryzek, J. 173
Du Bois, W. E. B 215, 217, 218, 220, 222
 "The Conservation of Races" 217
Durkheim, E. 161, 163, 164, 165
 Suicide 163
Dykhuizen, G. 270
 The Life and Mind of John Dewey 270

economics 203–13
 Bromley and pragmatism 209–13
 Polanyi and pragmatism 206–8
 pragmatism and institutional economics 203–6
economizing 210
education 188–200
 classical pragmatism 195–200
 John Dewey and the Chicago Lab School 190–4
 recent contributions to 199–200
Eldridge, M. 232, 266, 275
Ellul, J. 117
emergence 47
Emerson, R. W. 6, 7, 49, 50, 76, 122–4
 "Art" 122
 Society and Solitude 49
empiricism 18
Engels, F. 267
English Speenhamland Law (1795) 206
epistemology 82–3
The Essential Peirce 274
ethics 138–51, 210
 ameliorating consequentialism, James' ethics as 140

pragmatic ethics   138
evidentialism   58, 59
experience   127–9, 178, 198, 267–8, 271
   primary experience   27, 268
   pure experience   27, 268

fallibilism   67, 109, 115, 171, 189, 195,
   198, 244, 246, 248, 251, 268–70
Farr, J.   171, 180
   "John Dewey and American Political
      Science"   171
Feffer, A.   282
Feibleman, J.   144
feminist ethics   138
Feuerbach, L.   272
fideism   58, 59
Fischer, F.   180
Fischer, M.   177
Fiske, J.   273
Franzese, S.   49
Frege, G.   273, 88
Friedman, M.   204–5, 208
Fry, R.   130

Galison, P.   118
Garrison, J.   193, 196
Gegenstandskonstitution   52
Gellner, E.   19
Gentry, G.   109
Geodesy   108
Giddens, A.   157
Glaude, E. S.   216, 218, 219
God   269–70
Golino, C. L.   26
Good, J. A.   271
   A Search for Unity in Diversity   271
Goodman, N.   6, 42, 81, 277, 282,
Goodman, R. B.   27
Great Depression, the   74, 116
Green, J. M.   191
Greene, M.   192, 193
Gullace, G.   26
Gutmann, A.   173, 192

Haack, S.   21, 23, 25, 100
Habermas, J.   118, 144, 173, 189, 192, 199,
   211, 241, 272
habit   49, 156, 209, 221, 223, 270–1, 272,
   275, 277

Haddock, C.   150
   Pragmatism and Feminism   150
Haraway, D.   118
Hawthorne, J.   88
Hegel, G. W. F.   6, 17, 270, 275, 279, 95,
   101, 134, 142
Hegelian deposit   142, 270
Hegelian idealism   6, 17
Heidegger, M.   8, 22, 100, 116, 117, 118,
   252, 279
   Being and Time   116
Herrmann, E.   233
Hickman, L. A.   116, 150, 177, 204
Hildebrand, D.   53, 268, 275
Hintikka, J.   158, 162
Hodgson, G. M.   206
Hohfeld, W.   210
Holcombe, R.   205
Holmes, O. W.   273
Hook, S.   31, 267
Hookway, C.   12, 20
Horkheimer, M.   117, 252
Horton, M.   190
Hume, D.   66, 95, 156, 268,
Husserl, E.   26, 27, 51
   The Crisis of European Sciences
      and Transcendental
      Phenomenology   27
Hypatia   150

Ihde, D.   118
inquiry   270–4, 275
"Inquiry into Democracy" (by Knight and
   Johnson)   170
instrumentalism   15, 117, 205
interest relative invariantism   87
International Journal of Ethics   281
Italian pragmatism   26, 28

Jackson, P. W.   191, 193
James, W.   4, 6, 7, 8, 9, 10, 11, 12, 13, 14,
   15, 17, 18, 21, 22, 24, 25, 26, 27,
   28, 29, 30, 31, 38, 40, 41, 42, 49,
   50, 51, 54, 55, 64, 66, 68–72, 74,
   75, 81, 83, 85, 95, 97, 100, 102,
   104, 108, 111–12, 113, 122, 126,
   127, 131, 139, 140, 141, 142, 143,
   144, 154, 155, 159, 169, 189, 196,
   198, 199, 204, 215, 228, 230–1,

266, 267, 268, 270, 272, 273, 274, 275–6, 277, 280, 281, 283
"The Function of Cognition" 38
The Meaning of Truth 38, 66, 65
"The Moral Philosopher and the Moral Life" 139, 272
"Philosophical Conceptions and Practical Results" 10, 38, 65, 273
A Pluralistic Universe 12, 196, 249, 269, 276
Pragmatism: A New Name for Some Old Ways of Thinking 83, 271
Principles of Psychology 125, 155, 271
Talks to Teachers 196
The Varieties of Religious Experience 38, 229, 271
The Will to Believe 13, 65, 272
Jerusalem, K. W. 28
Joas, H. 272, 273
Johnson, J. 170, 171
jurisprudence 210

Kaila, E. 28–30
Persoonallisuus 29
Syvähenkinen elämä 29
Kant, I. 4, 8, 9, 10, 17, 18, 24, 25, 26, 27, 28, 30, 42, 51, 52, 53, 58, 66, 73, 95, 99, 101, 102, 104, 110, 122, 138, 140, 144, 147, 148, 155, 240, 245, 247, 248, 253, 268
Critique of Pure Reason 9, 52, 99, 247
Kantianism 28, 138
Khalil, E. 203
Pragmatism and Economic Methodology 203
Kilpinen, E. 155, 156, 158, 162, 270
Kitcher, P. 115
Knight, J. 170, 171
knowledge and justification 86–8
Koopman, C. 177
Koskinen, H. J. 21
Krugman, P. 203
Kuhn, T. 22, 32, 42, 115, 211

Lachs, J. 77, 149, 281
Laclau, E. 193
LaFollette, H. 138, 149, 151

The Practice of Ethics 138, 151
Lagerlund, H. 28
Langer, S. K. 131
Laswell, H. D. 179
Latour, B. 119
Laudan, L. 115
Leibniz, G. 101
Lester, J. 179
Lewis, C. I. 7, 17, 20, 76, 144
Mind and the World-Order 17
Lipman, M. 193
Locke, A. 66, 215
Locke, J. 110, 268
logic 88–9

Macarthur, D. 95
Maccia, G. 195
MacGilvray, E. 172
"Experience as Experiment" 172
Macintyre, A. 155
MacKenzie, D. W. 203
Mackie, J. L. 55
MacMullan, T. 216, 220, 222, 223, 224
Maddy, P. 89
Madge, J. 163
Marcus, H. 119
Margolis, J. 19, 25, 99, 131, 133–4
Pragmatism's Advantage 133
Margonis, F. 193
Marshall, J. 192
Martin, J. R. 192, 200
Marx, K. 205, 267
McAfee, N. 176
McDowell, J. 6
McGraw, M. 108
Mead, G. H. 4, 6, 7, 11, 15, 17, 47, 73, 154, 157, 159, 160, 196, 197, 198–9, 204, 265, 272–3, 281
Menand, L. 273
The Metaphysical Club 273
Menger, C. 205
Merriam, C. E. 171
Metaphysical Club, The 6, 8, 10, 38, 65, 273, 274
metaphysics 95–104
epistemology, ethics and 102–4
Kantian reinterpretation of 101–2
pragmatist contributions to 98–101

pragmatist criticisms of 96–8
    metaphysical realism 96
Mill, J. S. 173, 204, 206
Miller, H. T. 177, 178
    "Why Old Pragmatism Needs an
        Upgrade" 178
Misak, C. 85
Mitcham, C. 118
Mitchell, L. S. 145, 199
Moore, G. E. 141, 142
Morris, D. 170
    "'How Shall We Read What We
        Call Reality?'" 170
Morrison, T. 218
    Beloved 218
Mouffe, C. 193
Murphey, M. G. 17, 144
Myers, G. E. 95

Nagel, E. 282
neo-pragmatism 6, 7, 22–5, 27, 30, 42,
    53, 58, 59, 60, 76, 95, 97, 98, 241,
    265, 278
Neurath, O. 112
Nietzsche, F. 95, 124, 155
Noddings, N. 192
non-reductive naturalism 7, 16, 46, 47,
    51, 247
Norström, V. 28
    "Hvad är sanningen?" (What
        Is Truth?) 28
North, D. 205

Olsen, J. 119
Outlaw, L. T. 216–20, 222

Panpsychism 50, 51
Papini, G. 26, 228, 259, 266
Pappas, G. 149
    *John Dewey's Ethics: Democracy as
        Experience* 149
Peirce, B. 274
Peirce, C. S. 4, 6, 7, 8, 10, 11, 12, 13, 14,
    15, 17, 18, 21, 23, 24, 25, 26, 27,
    30, 37, 38, 39, 40, 41, 49, 50, 64,
    65, 66–8, 69, 70, 71, 72, 81, 82,
    83, 84, 85, 86, 88, 89, 92, 97, 100,
    102, 104, 108–10, 111, 112, 113,
    122, 125–6, 131, 143, 144, 154,
    155, 157, 158, 162, 169, 189, 193,
    195, 196, 198, 206, 215, 229, 244,
    246, 268, 269, 270, 271, 273–4,
    277, 280, 282
    Collected Papers 274
    "The Fixation of Belief" 82, 273, 274
    "How To Make Our Ideas Clear" 38, 83,
        273, 274, 277
    "*Neglected Argument for the Reality of
        God*" 269, 274
    "What Pragmatism Is" 10
Perry, R. B. 12, 39
phaneroscopy 27
Pihlström, S. 6, 17, 21, 24, 25, 32, 39, 42,
    49, 50, 53, 102, 103, 110, 147,
    148, 149, 241, 265
Plato 15, 16, 99, 146, 159
pluralism (the one and the many) 40, 41,
    60, 172, 176, 178, 189, 196, 217,
    246, 249, 250, 275–6, 280
Polanyi, K. 203, 206–8, 213
    The Great Transformation 206, 213
politics 169–80
    democratic theory 173–5
    global political theory 176–7
    political science 169–73
    public administration 177–9
    public policy 179–80
Poor Law Reform (1834) 206
Popper, K. 31, 157, 208, 246
Popular Science Monthly 65, 82
Portis, E. B. 205
positivism 204
Posner, R. 169, 203, 213
Postel, D. 146
post-Philosophical culture 279
practical starting point (PSP) 275
practical syllogism 156
pragmatic contextualization 43–5
pragmatic feminism 149–50
pragmaticism 6, 10, 12, 69, 273
pragmatic maxim 40, 277, 280
pragmatic method 3, 41, 273, 274
    in metaphysics 41–4
    an overview 37–41
    Peirce and James on 10–14
    in the philosophy of mind 45–54

pragmatist approach to
    subjectivity 46–7
  in the philosophy of religion 57–61
  in the philosophy of value 54–7
pragmatism 3–32
  constructive and deconstructive
    approaches 240–1
  description of 3–5
  Geography of 26–30
    European analogies 26–8
    Nordic pragmatism 28–30
  historical and systematic
    approaches 238–40
  interdisciplinarity 242–8
  as a living philosophy 5
  major characteristic of 4
  methods and problems 30–2
  and other philosophical
    traditions 251–4
  as pluralistic anti-
    foundationalism 248–51
  stages in the history of 5–7
    contemporary pragmatism
      scholarship 25–6
    Deweyan reconstruction and other
      developments 14–19
    late pragmatism 74–7
    neo-pragmatism 22–5
    pragmatism and logical
      empiricism 18–22
    prehistory of 7–10
    rise of pragmatism 10–14
  scientific realism vs.
    instrumentalism 31
pragmatists 4
  as public intellectuals 241–2
Putnam, H. 4, 6, 22, 24, 25, 27, 31, 42,
    48, 55, 56, 57, 76, 81, 96, 98, 100,
    101, 104, 110, 115, 133, 148,
    149, 208, 213, 218, 239, 241,
    242, 250, 266, 276, 277, 278,
    279, 281
  *The Collapse of the Fact/Value
    Dichotomy and Other
    Essays* 148

Quine, W. V. 4, 6, 17, 18, 19, 20, 21, 22,
    23, 89, 115, 244, 278, 282, 283
  "Five Milestones of Empiricism" 19
  "On What There Is" 20
  "Two Dogmas of Empiricism" 19,
    115, 278, 282
  Word and Object 20

race 215–24
  racialism vs. racism 216
radical empiricism 268
Ramberg, B. 53
Rawls, J. 140, 149, 172, 275
realism 59
Reichenbach, H. 103
religion 228–36
  in contemporary pragmatism 232–4
  Dewey on 231–2
    religion vs. religious 231
  James on 229–31
  pragmatism and contemporary
    philosophy of 234–6
Rescher, N. 23, 100, 157
Rockefeller, S. C. 232, 270
  John Dewey 34
Rockwell, W. T. 112
Rogers, M. 176
Rorty, R. 4, 6, 7, 8, 22, 23, 24, 25, 27, 30, 42,
    53, 57, 59, 60, 76, 81, 95, 98, 100,
    115, 133, 138, 144, 145, 146, 147,
    148, 149, 151, 155, 163, 169, 178,
    189, 199, 213, 233, 235, 240, 245,
    265, 266, 267, 269, 277, 278, 281
  "Ethics Without Principles" 145
  Kant vs. Dewey: The Current Situation
    of Moral Philosophy 146
  *Philosophy and the Mirror of
    Nature* 23, 265, 278
Rouse, J. 32
Royce, J. 6, 7, 12, 17, 142, 143, 144, 204,
    215, 279
  The Philosophy of Loyalty 280
  The Problem of Christianity 280
  *The Religious Aspect of
    Philosophy* 280
  The World and the Individual 280
Russell, B. 27, 113, 114, 190, 250,
    273, 278
Ryan, A. 271, 155
  *John Dewey and the High Tide of
    American Liberalism* 271

Samuels, W. J. 203
Sandbothe, M. 145

Schiller, F. C. S. 6, 7, 11, 12, 13, 17, 18, 26, 42, 50
science Dewey's contributions to 111–15
  James's contributions to 110–11
  Peirce's contributions to 108–10
  Quine's contributions to 115
scientism 114, 244, 245, 283
Seigfried, C. H. 74, 95, 149, 150, 189, 199
  Pragmatism and Feminism 150
Sellars, W. 4, 6, 22, 23, 43, 81, 112, 233
Sen, A. 160
sensitive moderate invariantism (SNMI) 87
Shalin, D. 144–5
Shapin, S. 115
Shields, P. M. 177–8
  "The Community of Inquiry" 177
Shook, J. R. 271
  Dewey's Empirical Theory of Knowledge and Reality 271
Shusterman, R. 131, 134, 135, 136
  Pragmatist Aesthetics 134, 135
Sidgwick, H. 140, 142, 275
  Methods of Ethics 140
Skrbina, D. 50
Smiley, M. 173
  "Pragmatic Inquiry and Democratic Politics" 173
social hope 155
social intelligence 129, 143, 159, 200, 267, 282
social psychology 164
social theory 154–65
  applied 162–5
  The Polish Peasant in Europe and America (by Thomas and Znaniecki) 163
  empirically responsible philosophy, need for 154–6
  philosophy of action, pragmatism as 156–8
  rational choice and the economic man 161
  self 158
  social action 159
somaesthetics 131, 135, 136
Stanford Encyclopedia of Philosophy 150
Stanley, J. 87
Stevenson, C. 149

Stiglitz, J. 203, 213
Stob, P. 176
Stuart, J. 179
subjectivity 46, 50, 51, 52
Sullivan, S. 216, 220, 221, 223

Talisse, R. B. 5, 149, 169, 281
Tanner, L. 188
Tarski, A. 282
technology
  Dewey's treatment of 116–19
Thayer-Bacon, B. 191, 193, 197
Thomas, W. I. 162, 163, 164, 165
Thompson, D. 173
Thoreau, H. D. 8
Tiles, J. E. 47
Torgerson, D. 180
Tozer, S. 188
Tritter, J. Q. 160
Trotsky, L. 190
Truman, D. B. 171
truth 83–6, 266, 279–80
Tufts, J. H. 272, 281–2

utilitarianism 138

Veblen, T. 163, 203, 204, 206
Verbeek, P. P. 118
virtue ethics 138, 155
Von Hayek, F. 205
Von Mises, L. 205

Wagner, P. 160
Wallace, J. D. 138, 148, 149
  Ethical Norms, Particular Cases 148
  Moral Relevance and Moral Conflict 148
  Norms and Practices 148
  Virtues and Vices 148
Weber, M. 161, 163
Weitz, M. 133
Welchman, J. 138, 140, 142, 144, 149
West, C. 169, 189, 215, 218, 241
  The Evasion of American Philosophy 215
Westbrook, R. 174, 175, 270
  John Dewey and American Democracy 174, 270
Whipps, J. 150
White, M. 6, 20, 21, 282–3

"The Analytic and the Synthetic: An Untenable Dualism" 17, 282
A Philosophy of Culture 283
Social Thought in America: The Revolt Against Formalism 282
Toward Reunion in Philosophy 282
Whitehead, A. N. 131
Will, F. 148
Williamson, O. 205
Wittgenstein, L. 4, 22, 26, 27, 42, 45, 53, 58, 89, 98, 102, 114, 133, 147, 148, 240, 244, 252, 279
On Certainty 27

Wolff, C. 99
Wright, C. 8, 273
Writings of Charles Sanders Peirce 274

Young, E. F. 199
Young, I. R. 193

Zack, N. 216
Zanoni, C. P. 26
Znaniecki, F. 162, 163, 165
Zweckrationalität (straight line instrumentalism) 117